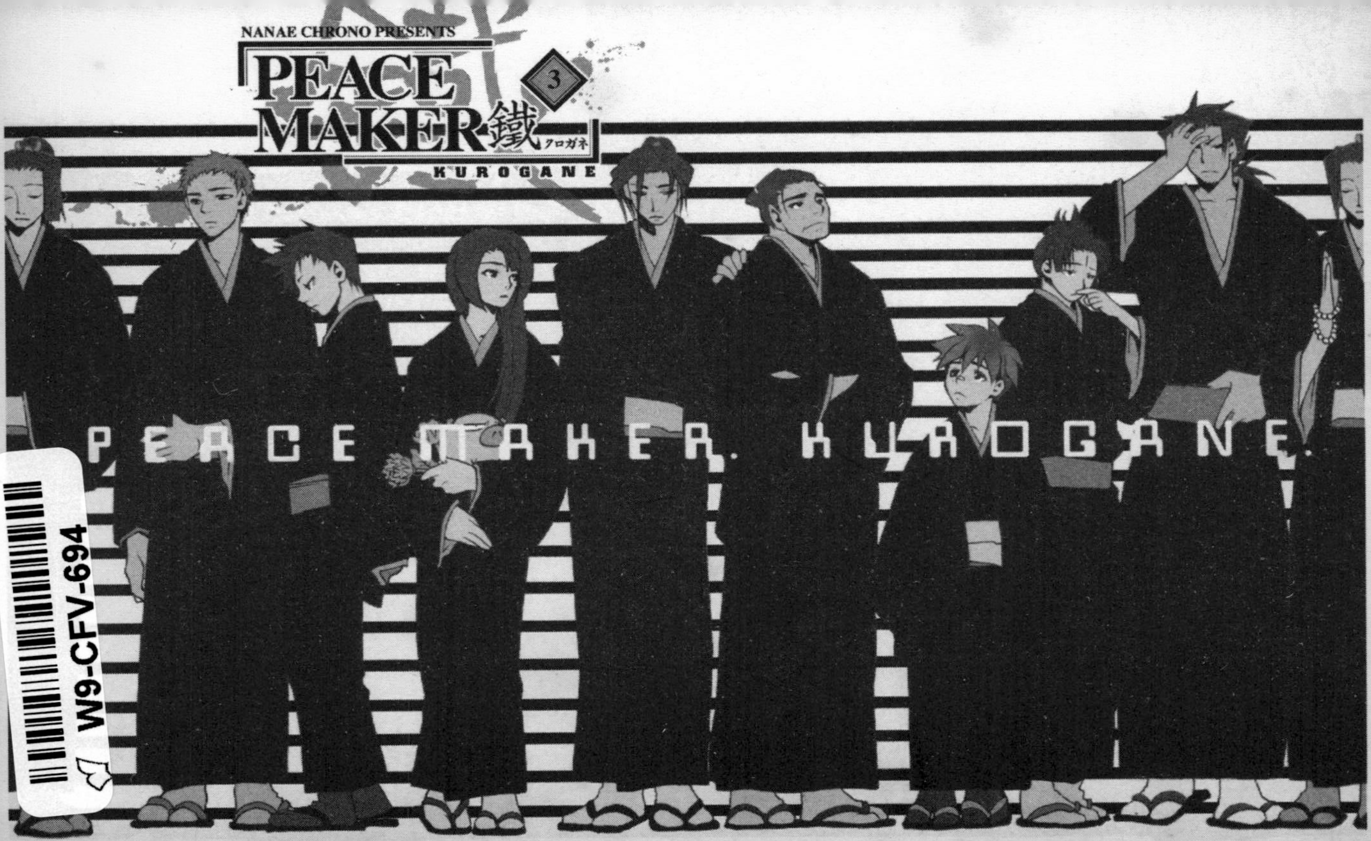
NANAE CHRONO PRESENTS
PEACE MAKER 鐵 クロガネ
3
KUROGANE
PEACE MAKER. KUROGANE.

CONTENTS

TEARS  泪 3

ENCOUNTER 遭 35

ANOTHER 别 69

GUN 銃 103

SICKNESS 病 139

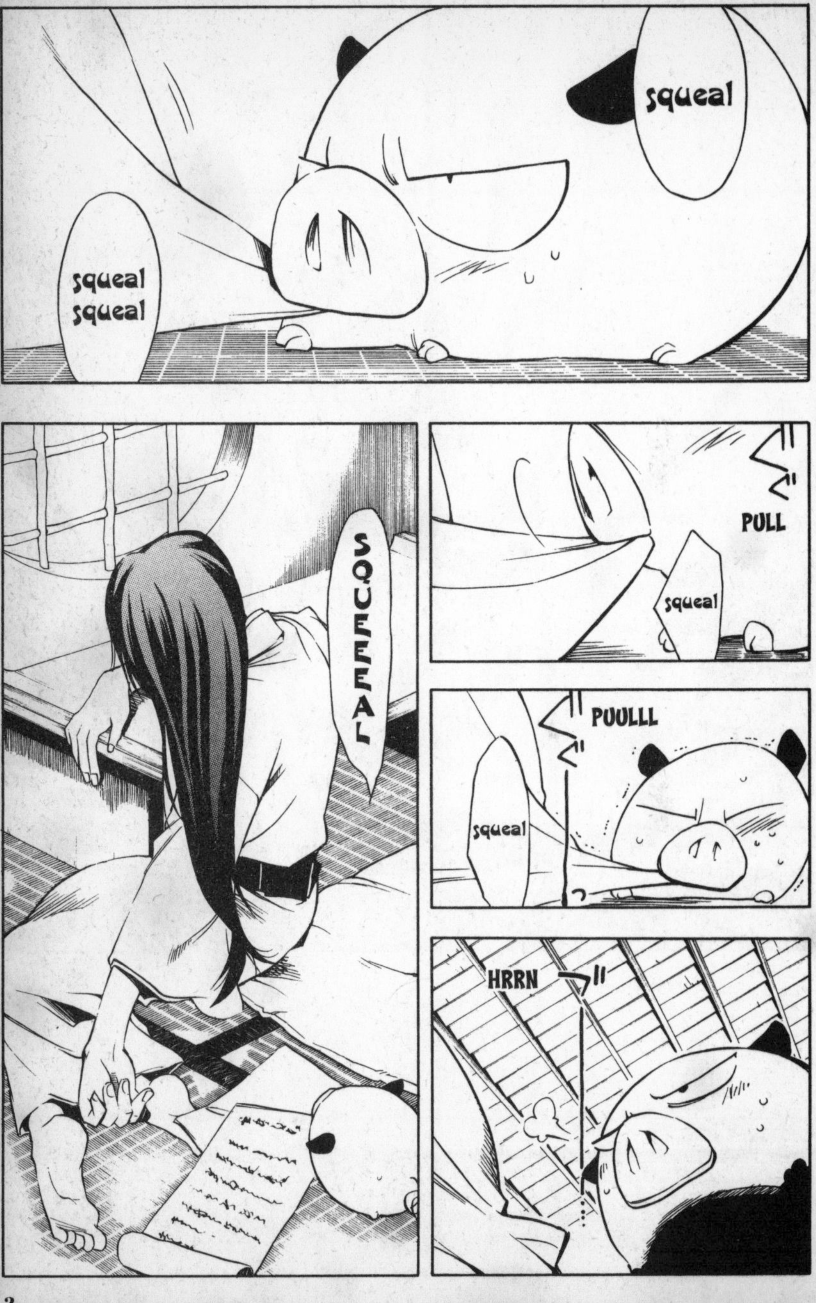
squeal
squeal squeal
PULL
squeal
PUULLL
squeal
HRRN
SQUEEEAL

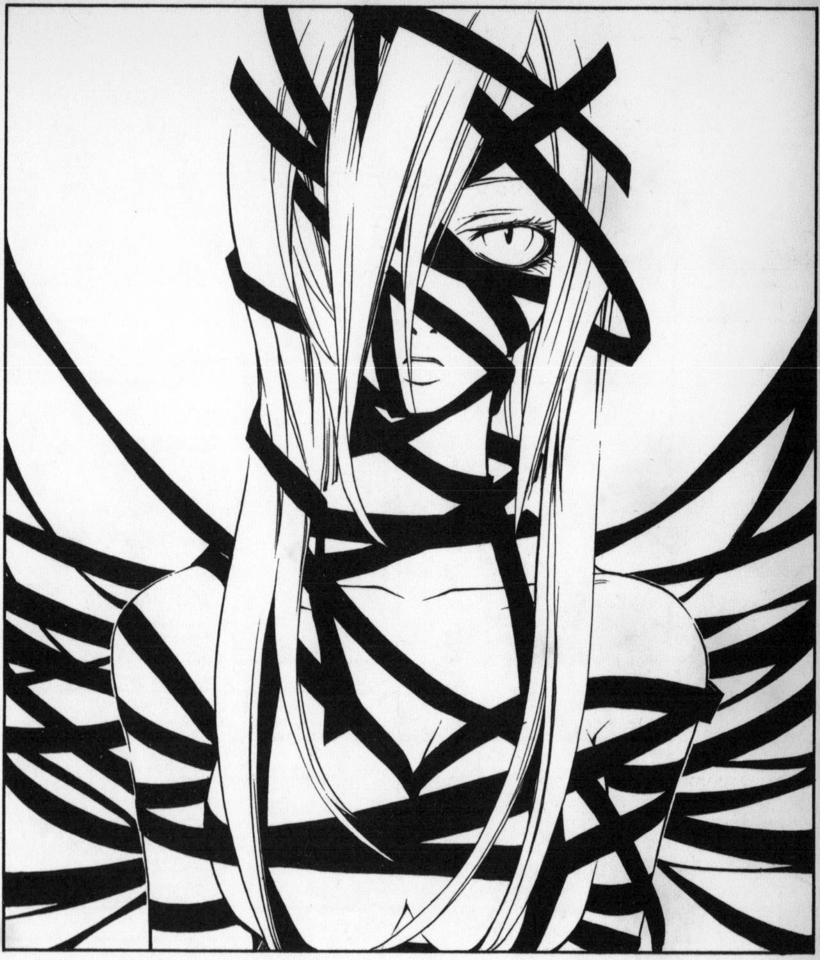

CHAPTER 11

TEARS

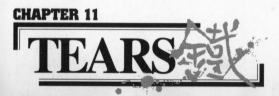

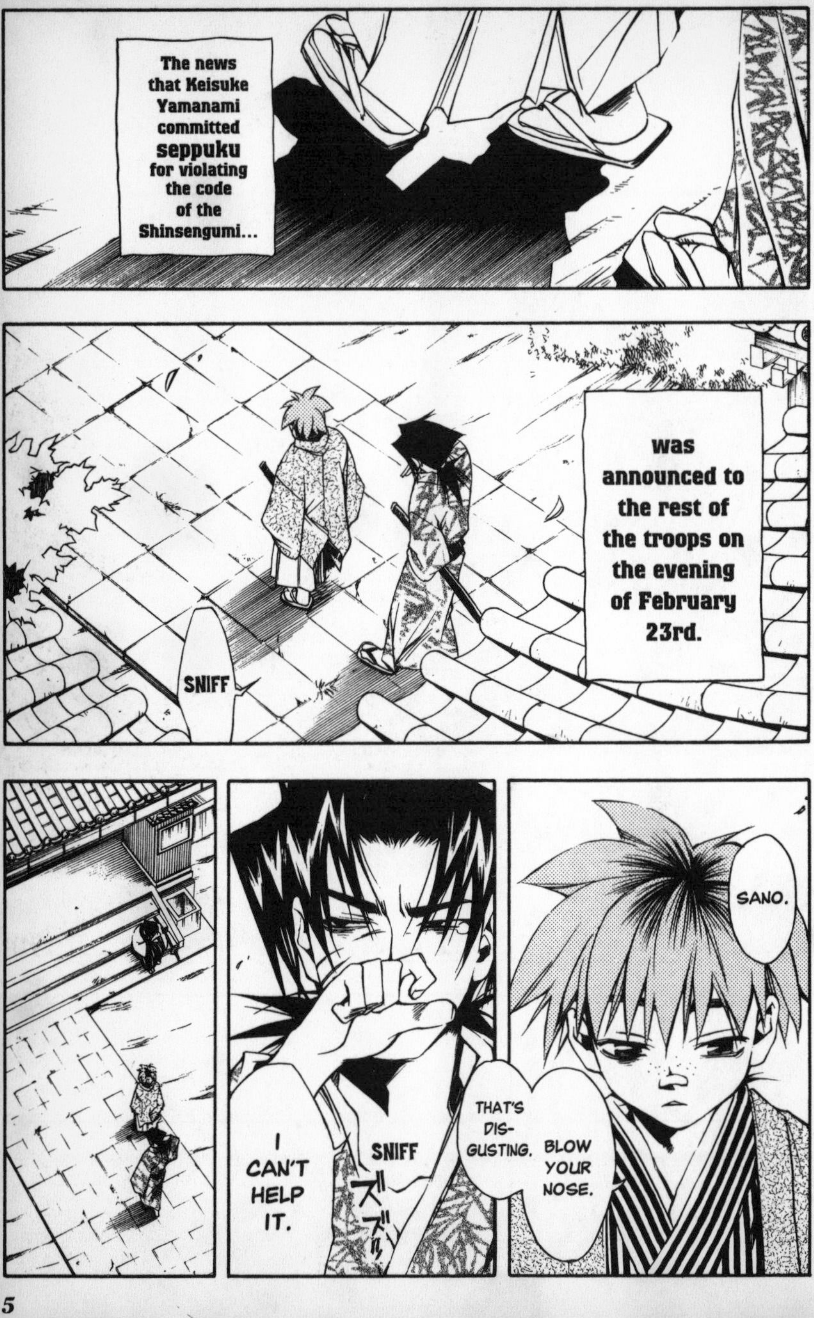
The news that Keisuke Yamanami committed seppuku for violating the code of the Shinsengumi...
was announced to the rest of the troops on the evening of February 23rd.
SNIFF
SANO.
BLOW YOUR NOSE.
THAT'S DIS-GUSTING.
SNIFF
I CAN'T HELP IT.

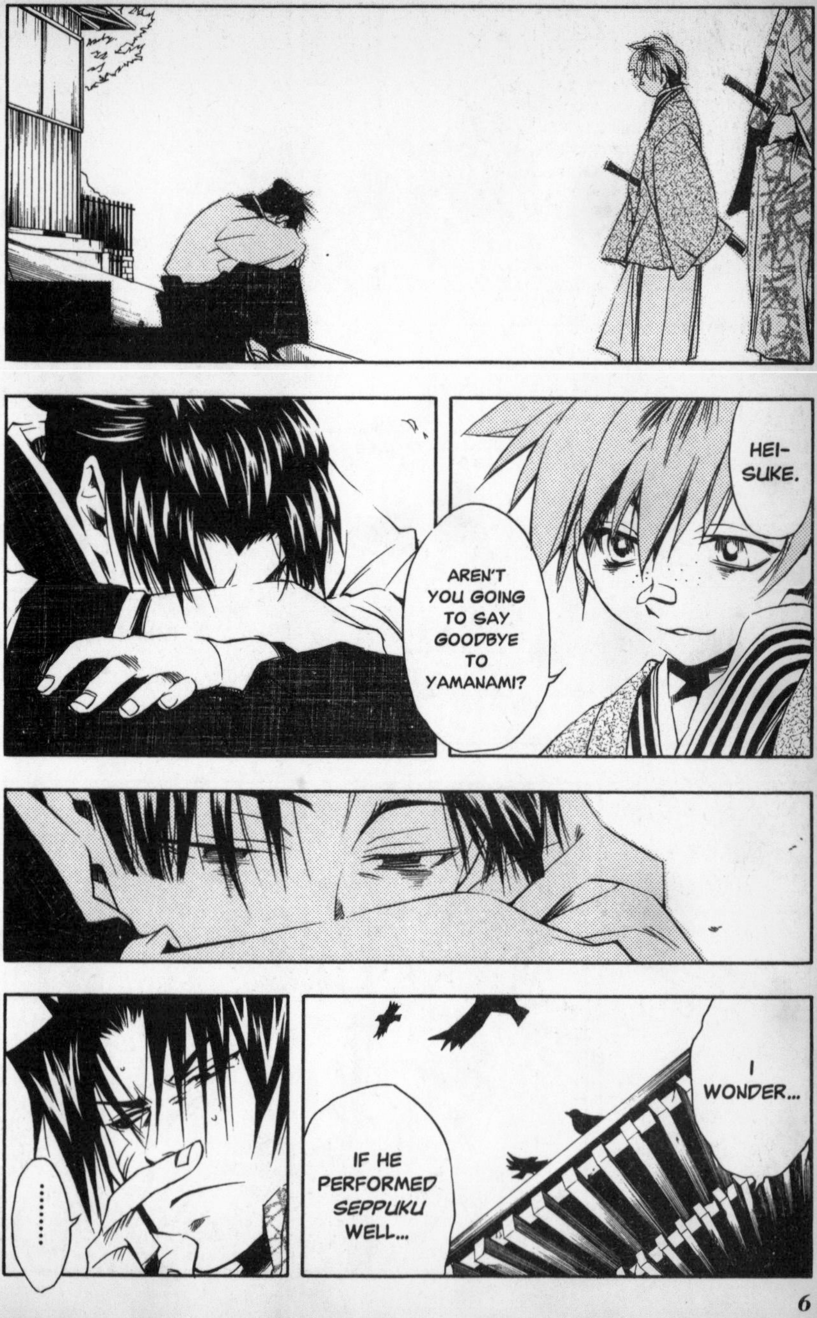
HEI-SUKE.
AREN'T YOU GOING TO SAY GOODBYE TO YAMANAMI?
I WONDER...
IF HE PERFORMED SEPPUKU WELL...
....

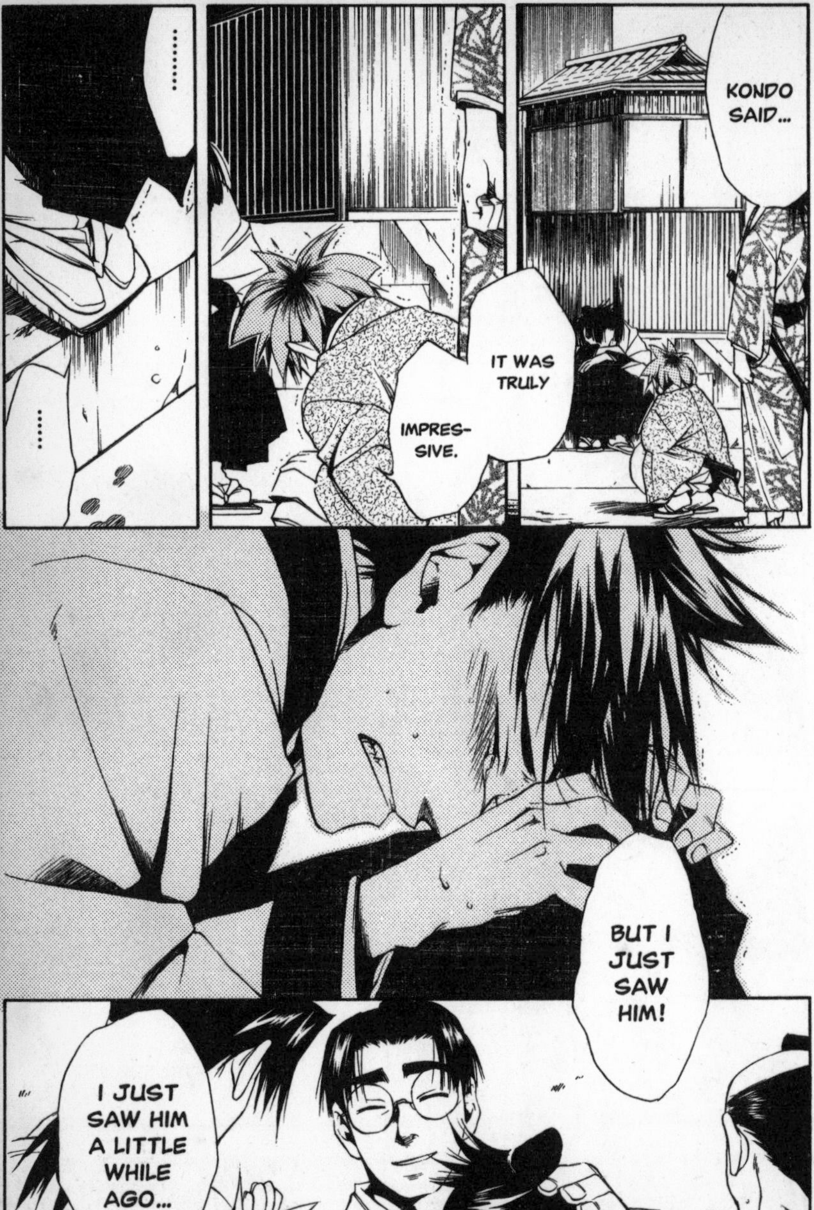
KONDO SAID...
IT WAS TRULY IMPRESSIVE.
......
......
BUT I JUST SAW HIM!
I JUST SAW HIM A LITTLE WHILE AGO...

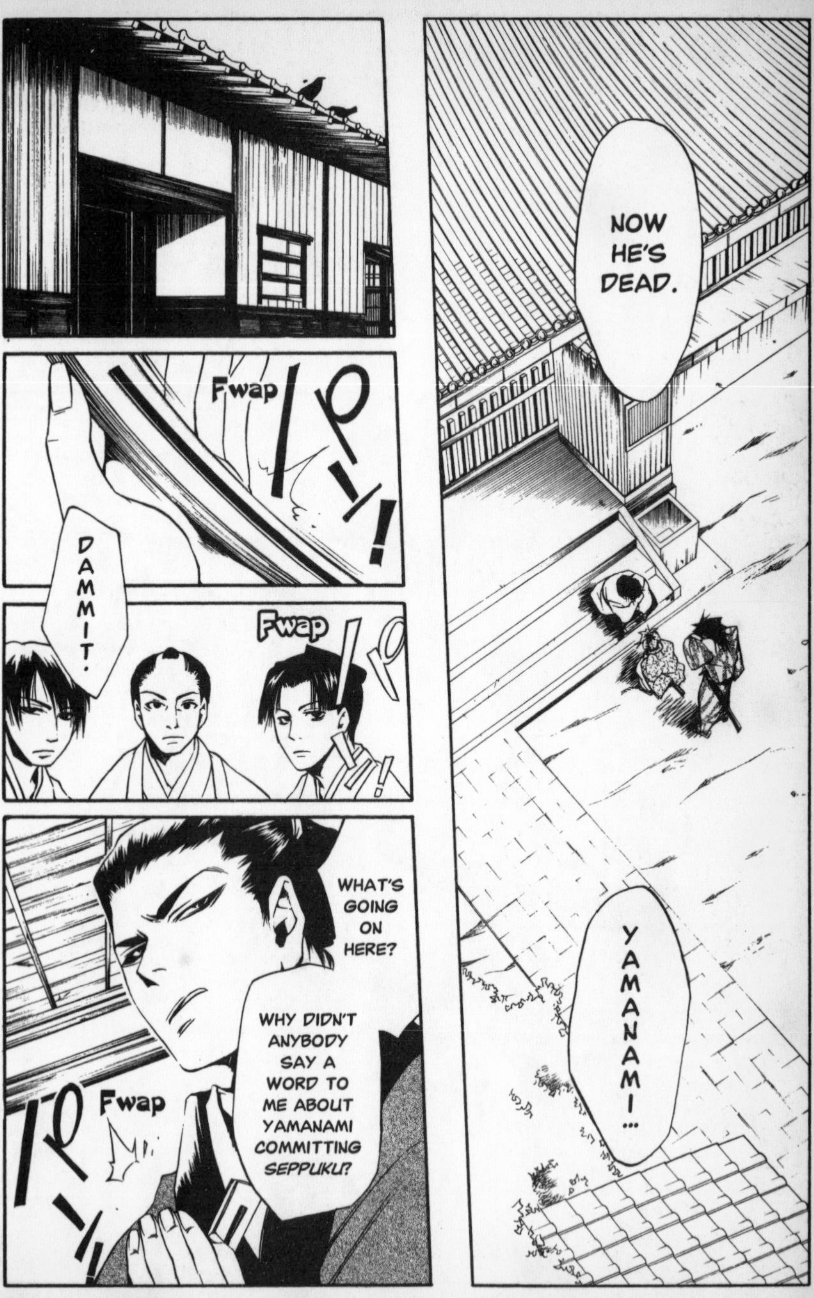
NOW HE'S DEAD.
YAMANAMI...
Fwap
DAMMIT.
Fwap
WHAT'S GOING ON HERE?
WHY DIDN'T ANYBODY SAY A WORD TO ME ABOUT YAMANAMI COMMITTING SEPPUKU?
Fwap

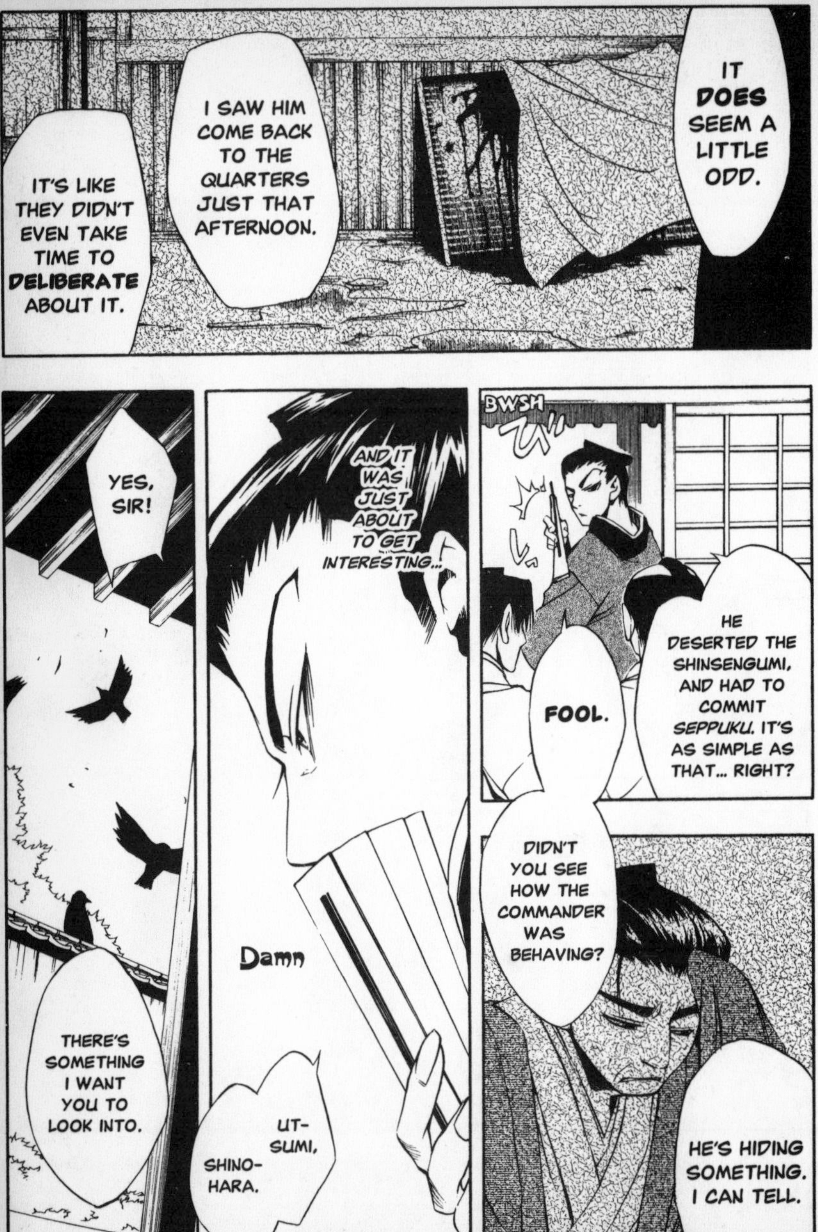
IT DOES SEEM A LITTLE ODD.
I SAW HIM COME BACK TO THE QUARTERS JUST THAT AFTERNOON.
IT'S LIKE THEY DIDN'T EVEN TAKE TIME TO DELIBERATE ABOUT IT.
BWSH
HE DESERTED THE SHINSENGUMI, AND HAD TO COMMIT SEPPUKU. IT'S AS SIMPLE AS THAT... RIGHT?
FOOL.
DIDN'T YOU SEE HOW THE COMMANDER WAS BEHAVING?
HE'S HIDING SOMETHING. I CAN TELL.
AND IT WAS JUST ABOUT TO GET INTERESTING...
Damn
UT-SUMI, SHINO-HARA.
THERE'S SOMETHING I WANT YOU TO LOOK INTO.
YES, SIR!

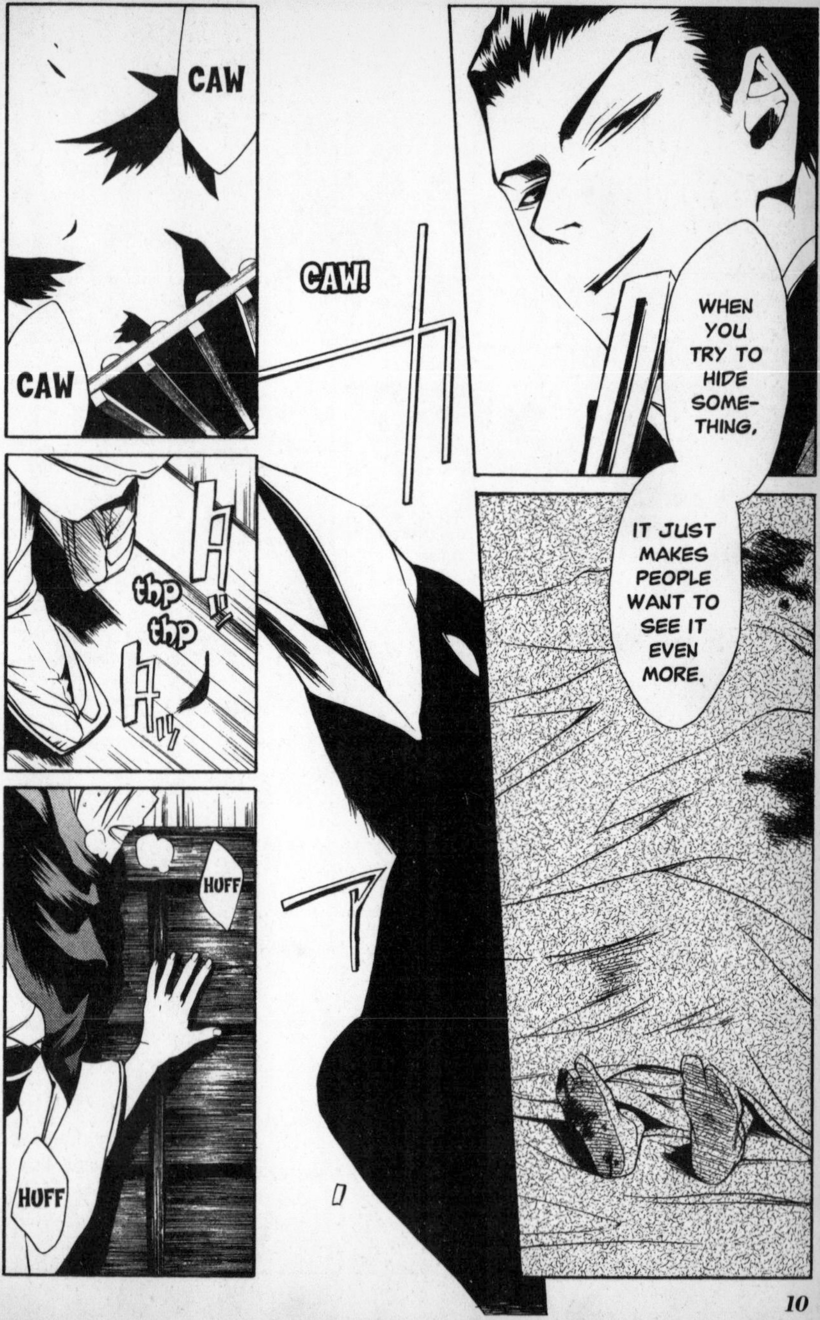
WHEN YOU TRY TO HIDE SOME-THING,
IT JUST MAKES PEOPLE WANT TO SEE IT EVEN MORE.
CAW!
CAW
CAW
thp
thp
HUFF
HUFF

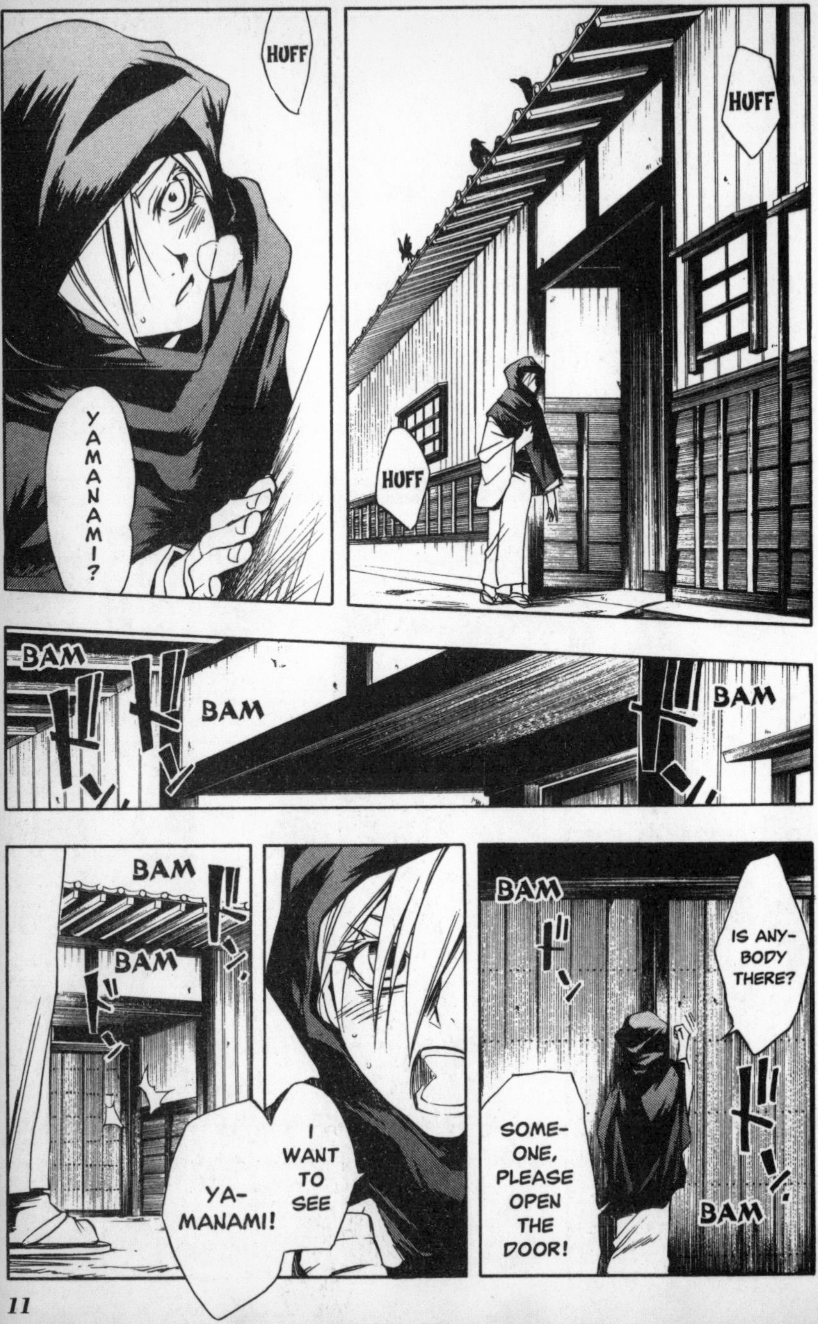
HUFF
HUFF
HUFF
YAMANAMI?
BAM
BAM
BAM
BAM
IS ANYBODY THERE?
SOMEONE, PLEASE OPEN THE DOOR!
BAM
I WANT TO SEE YAMANAMI!
BAM
BAM

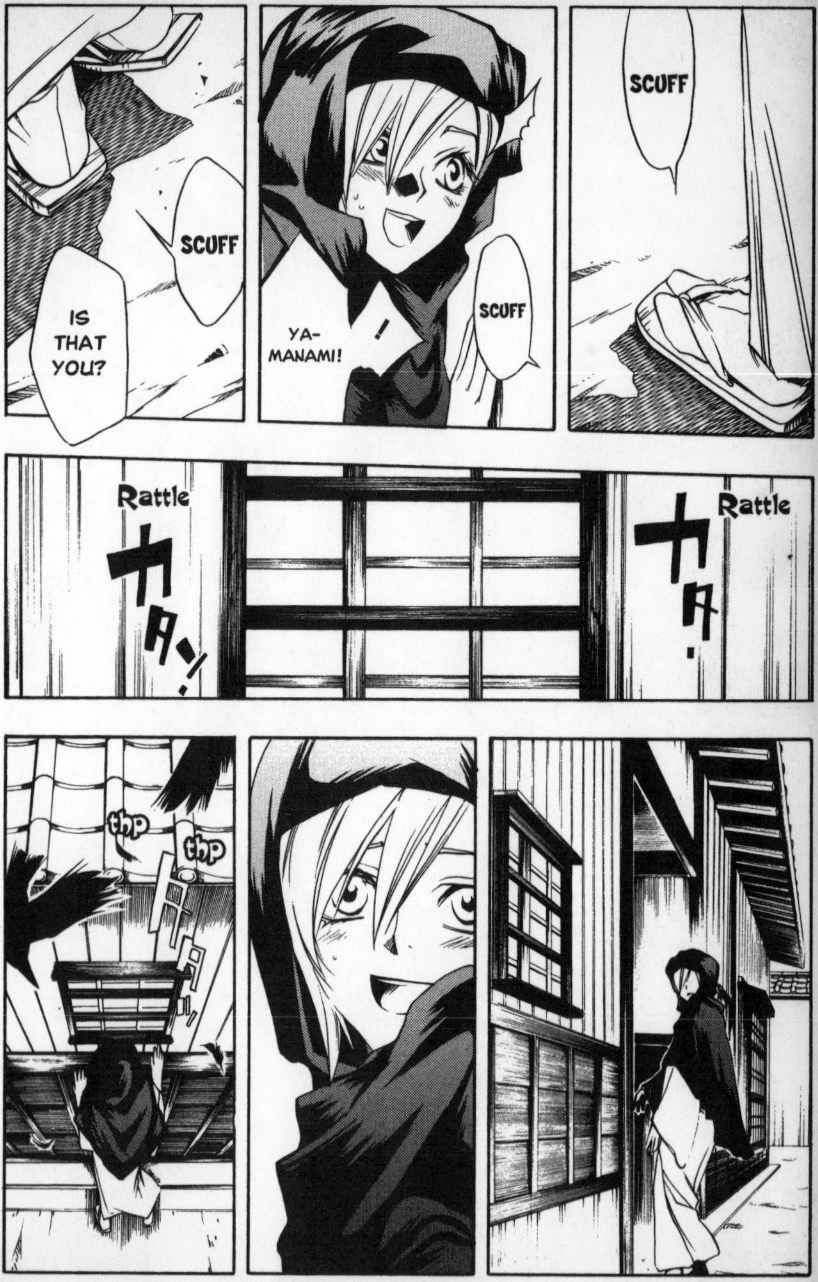
SCUFF
SCUFF
!
YA-MANAMI!
SCUFF
IS THAT YOU?
Rattle
カタ
Rattle
カタン!
thp
thp

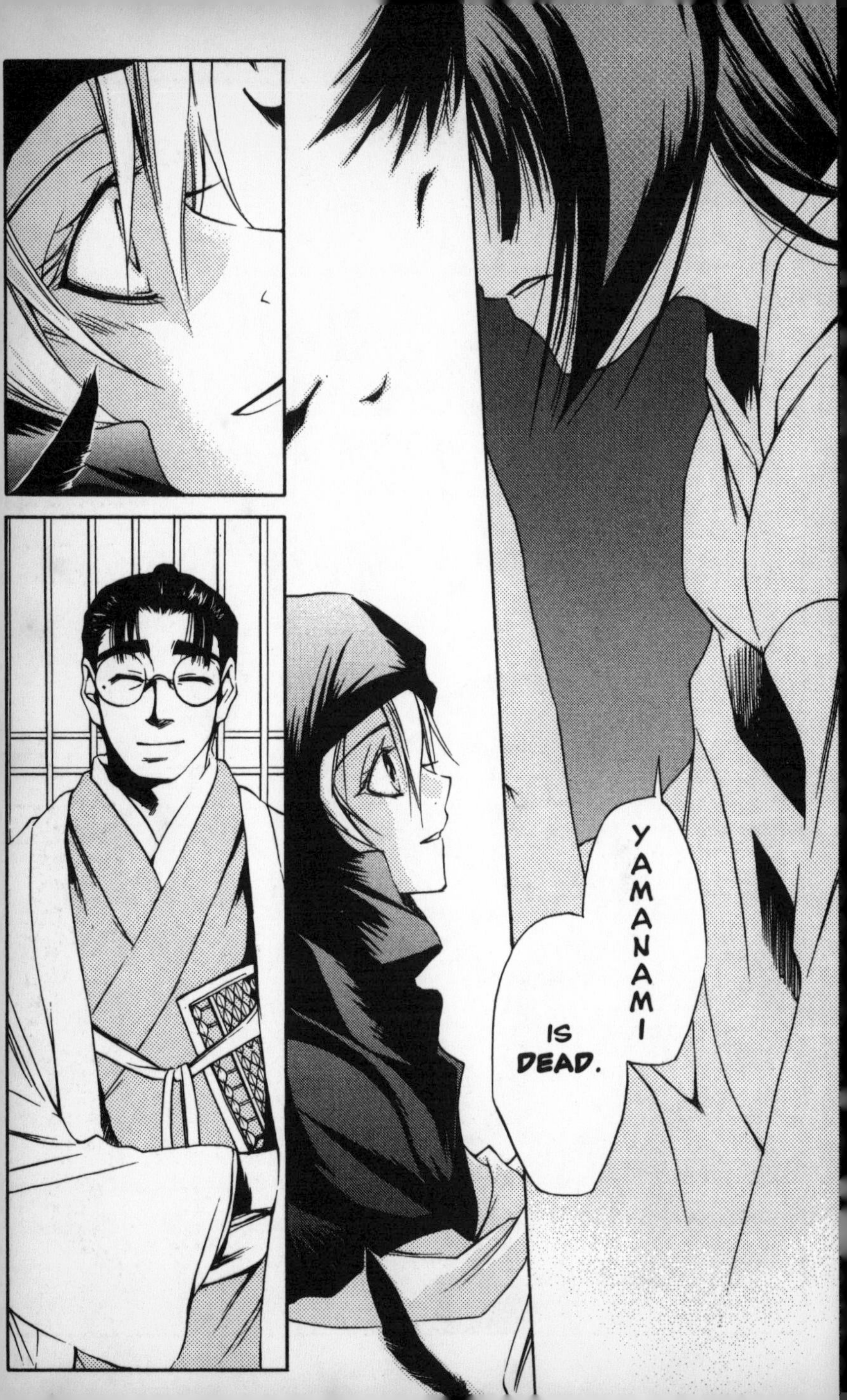
YAMANAMI IS DEAD.

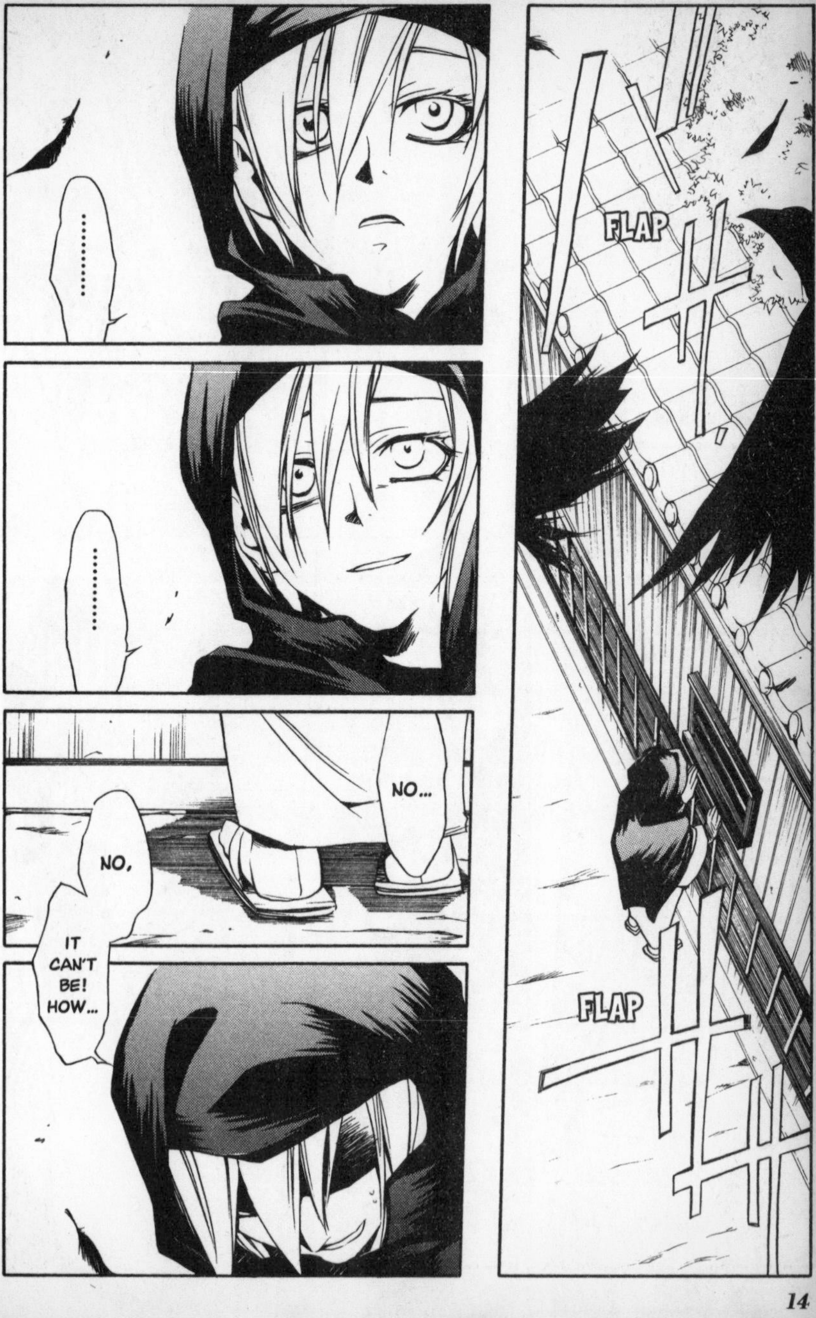
FLAP
FLAP
....
....
NO...
NO,
IT CAN'T BE! HOW...

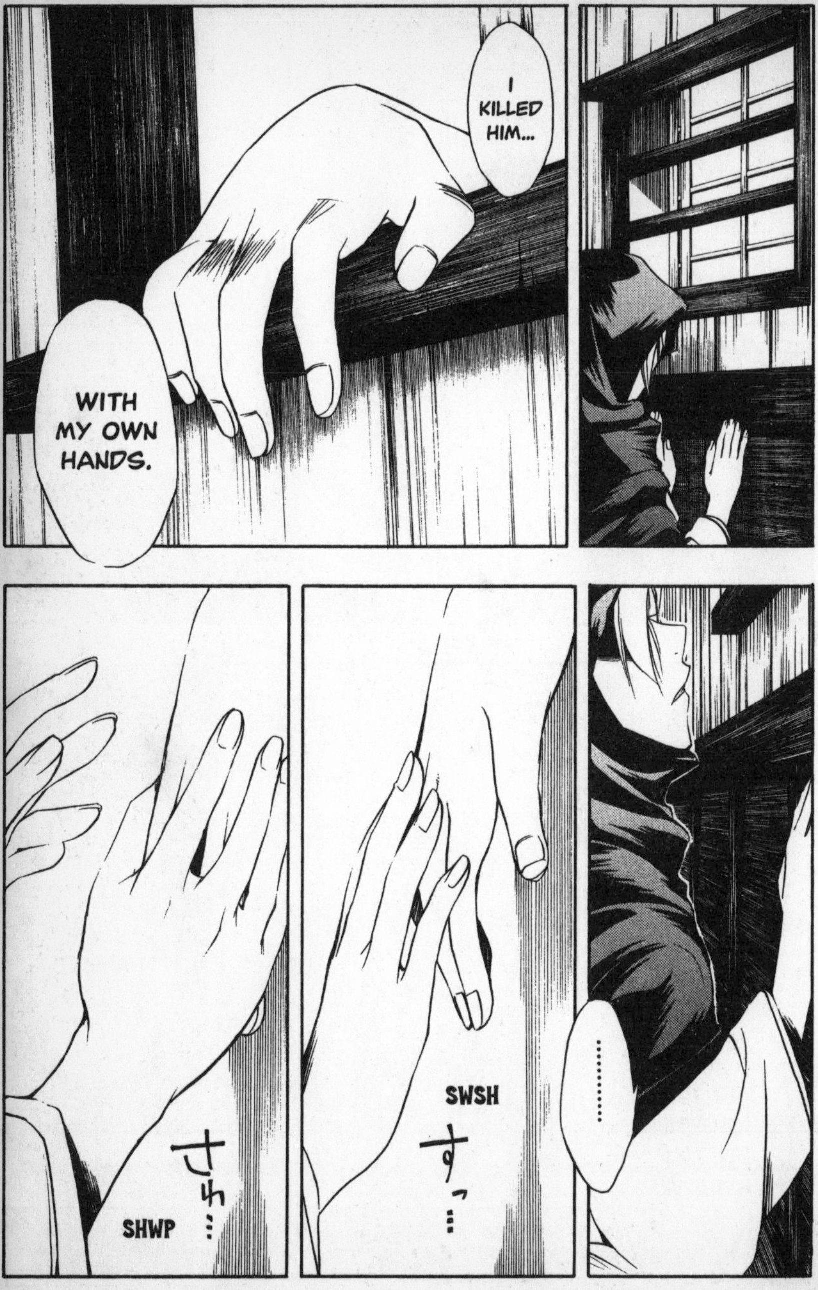
I KILLED HIM...
WITH MY OWN HANDS.
......
SWSH
すっ…
さわ…
SHWP

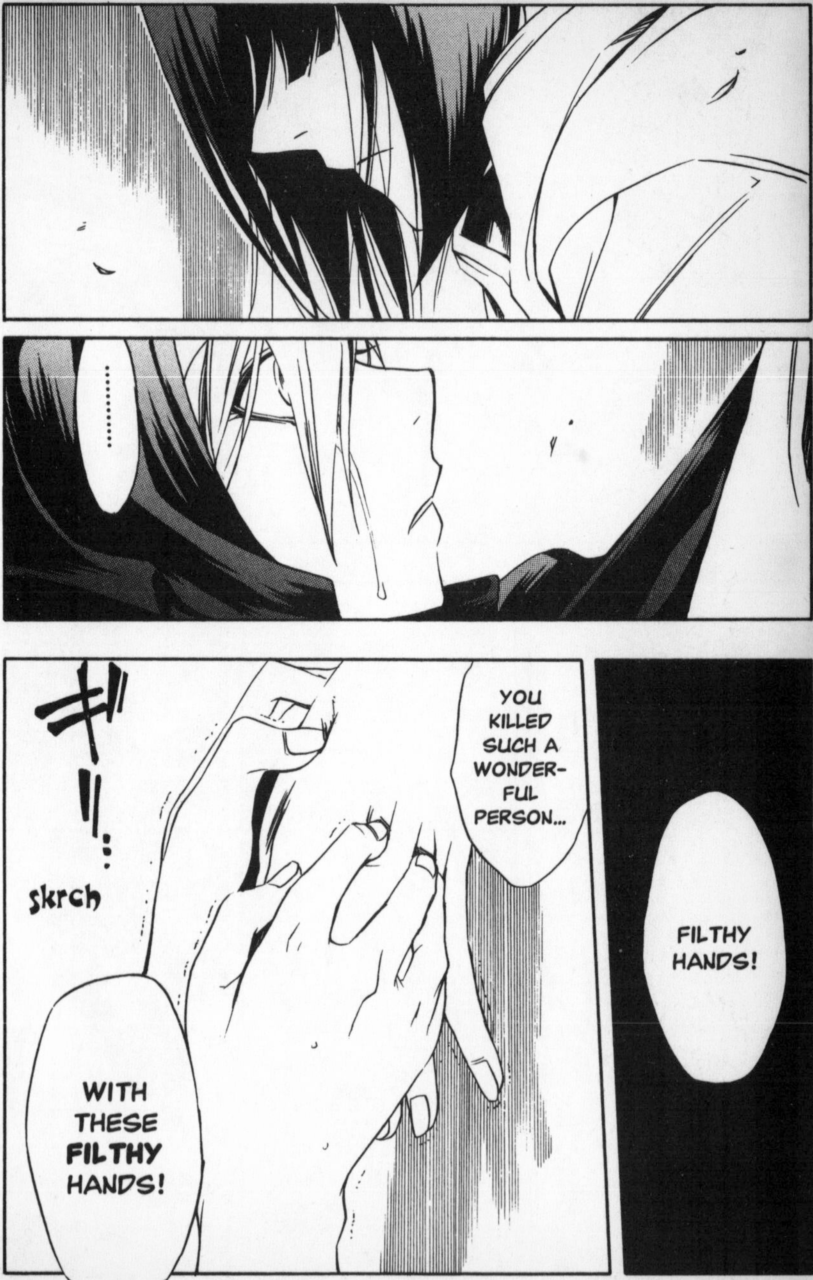

......
YOU KILLED SUCH A WONDER-FUL PERSON...
skrch
WITH THESE FILTHY HANDS!
FILTHY HANDS!

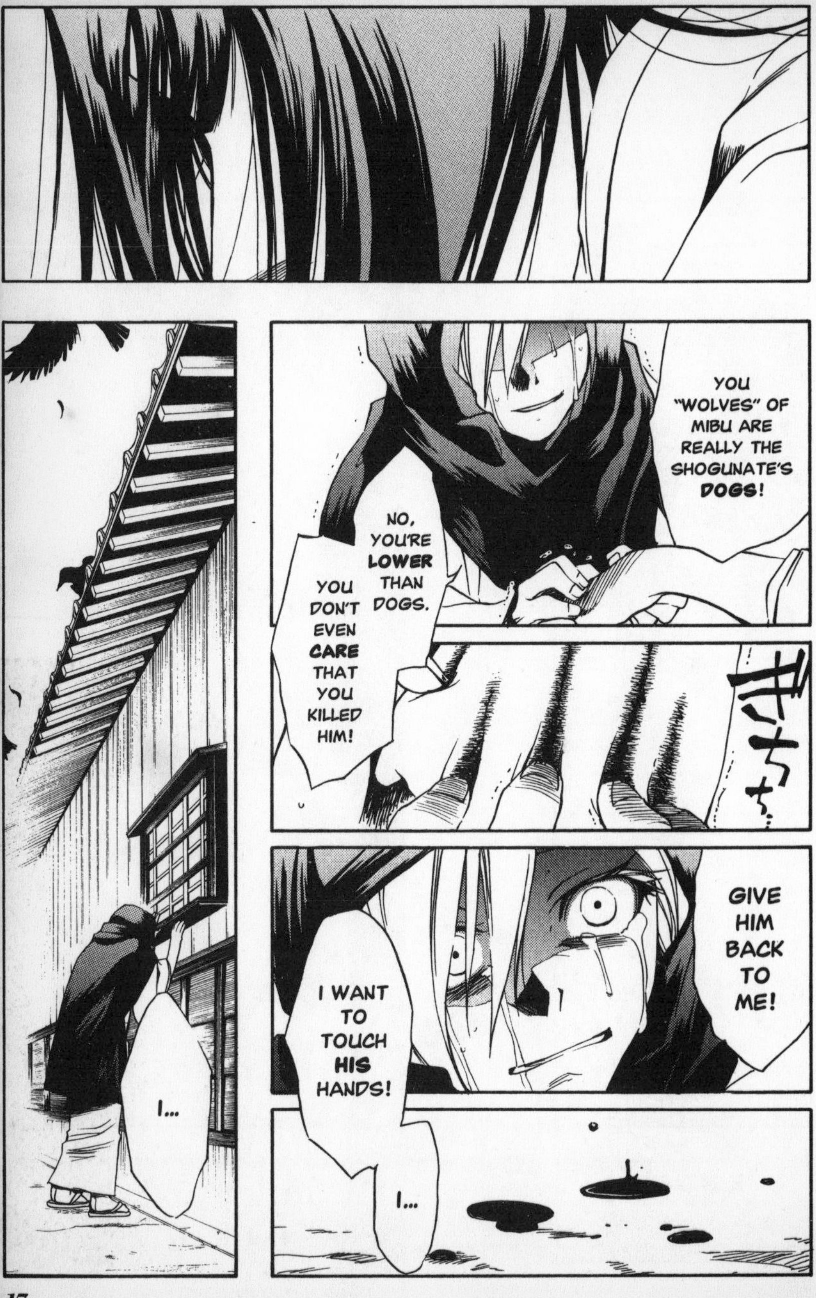
YOU "WOLVES" OF MIBU ARE REALLY THE SHOGUNATE'S **DOGS**!
NO, YOU'RE **LOWER** THAN DOGS.
YOU DON'T EVEN **CARE** THAT YOU KILLED HIM!
ぎちち…
GIVE HIM BACK TO ME!
I WANT TO TOUCH **HIS** HANDS!
I...
I...

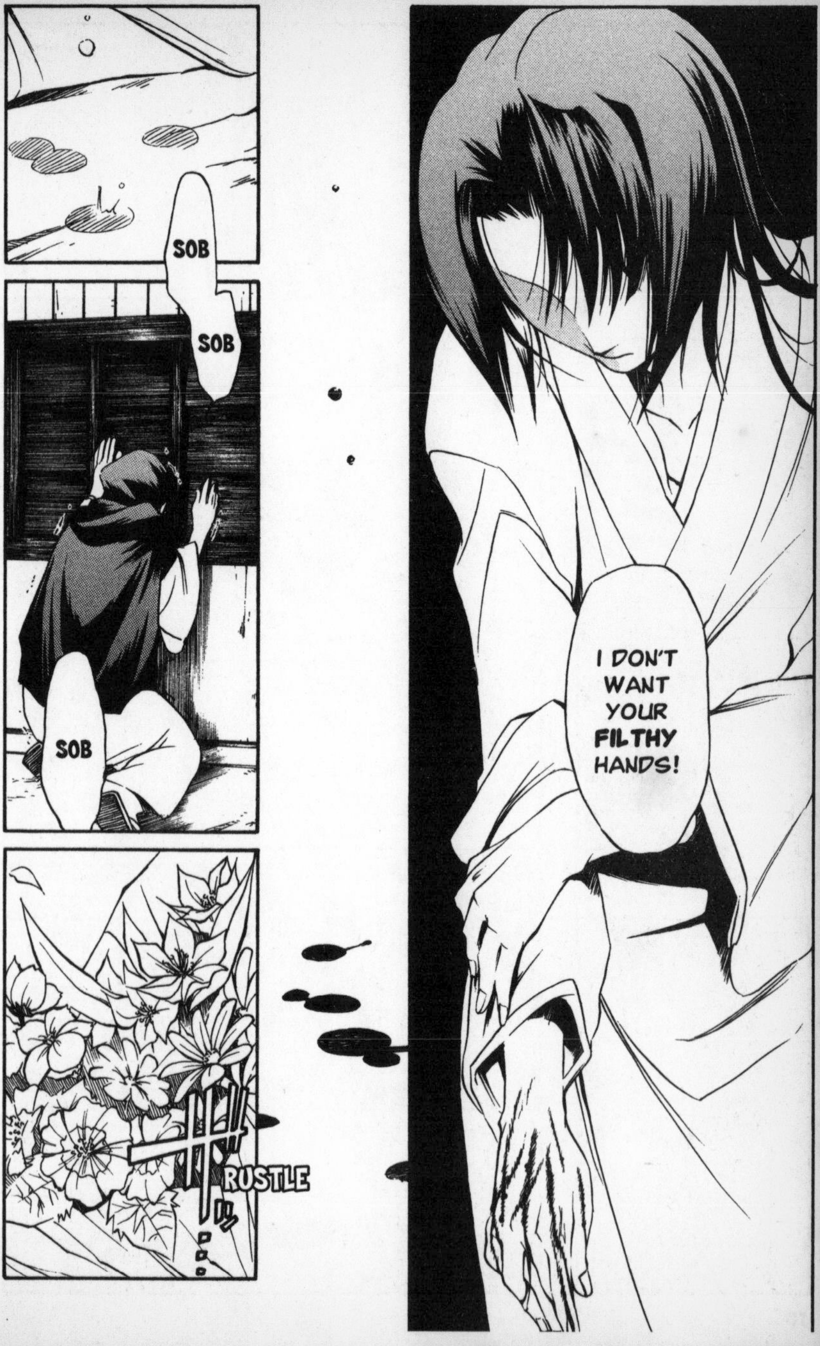
I DON'T WANT YOUR FILTHY HANDS!
SOB
SOB
SOB
RUSTLE

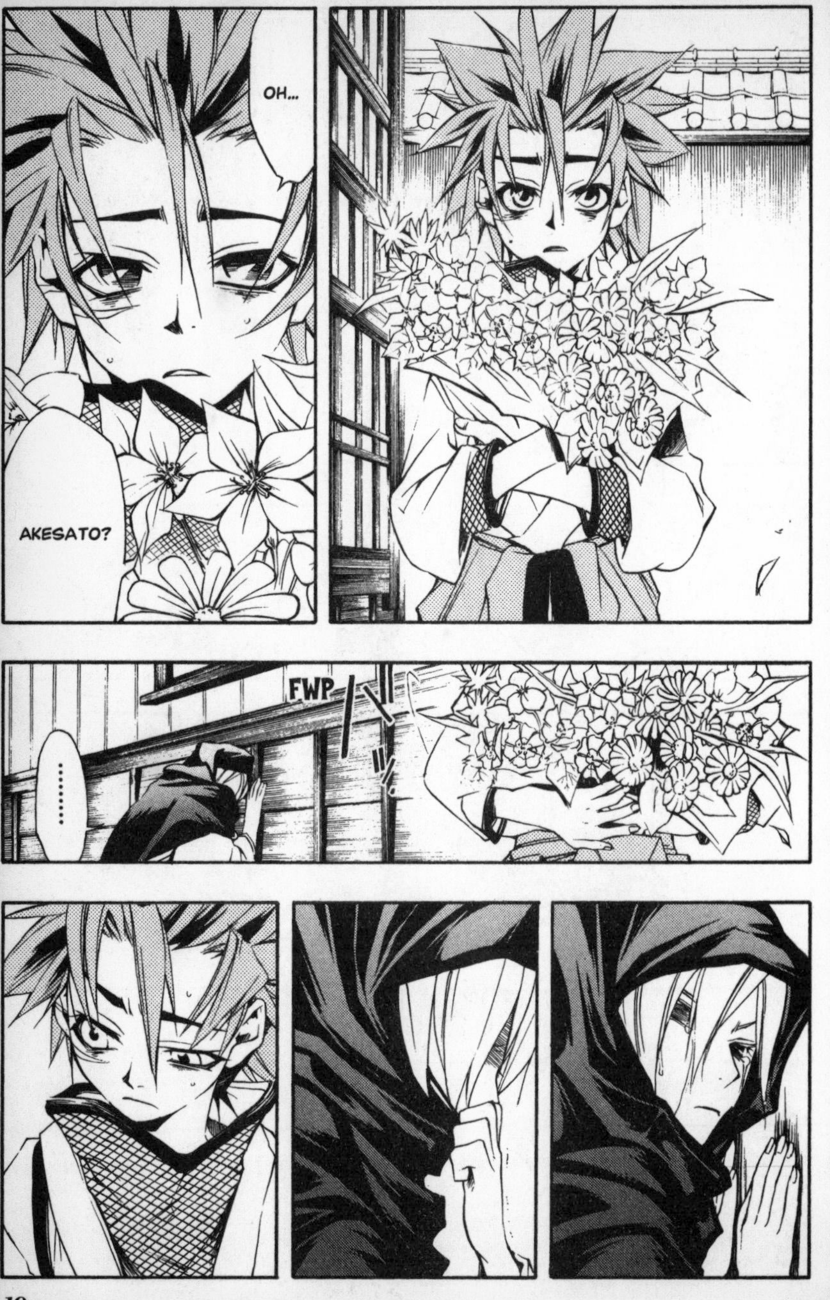
OH...
AKESATO?
FWP
......

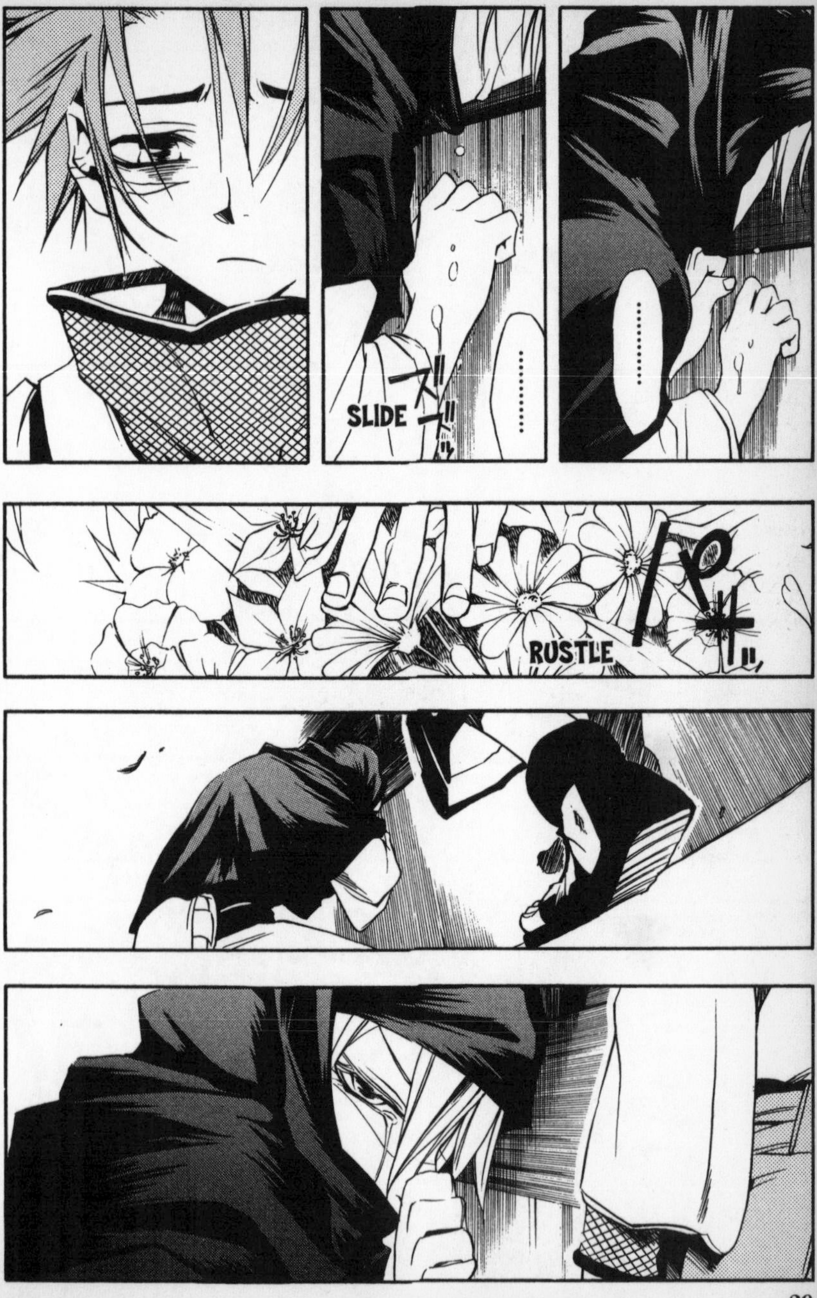

SLIDE
....
....
RUSTLE

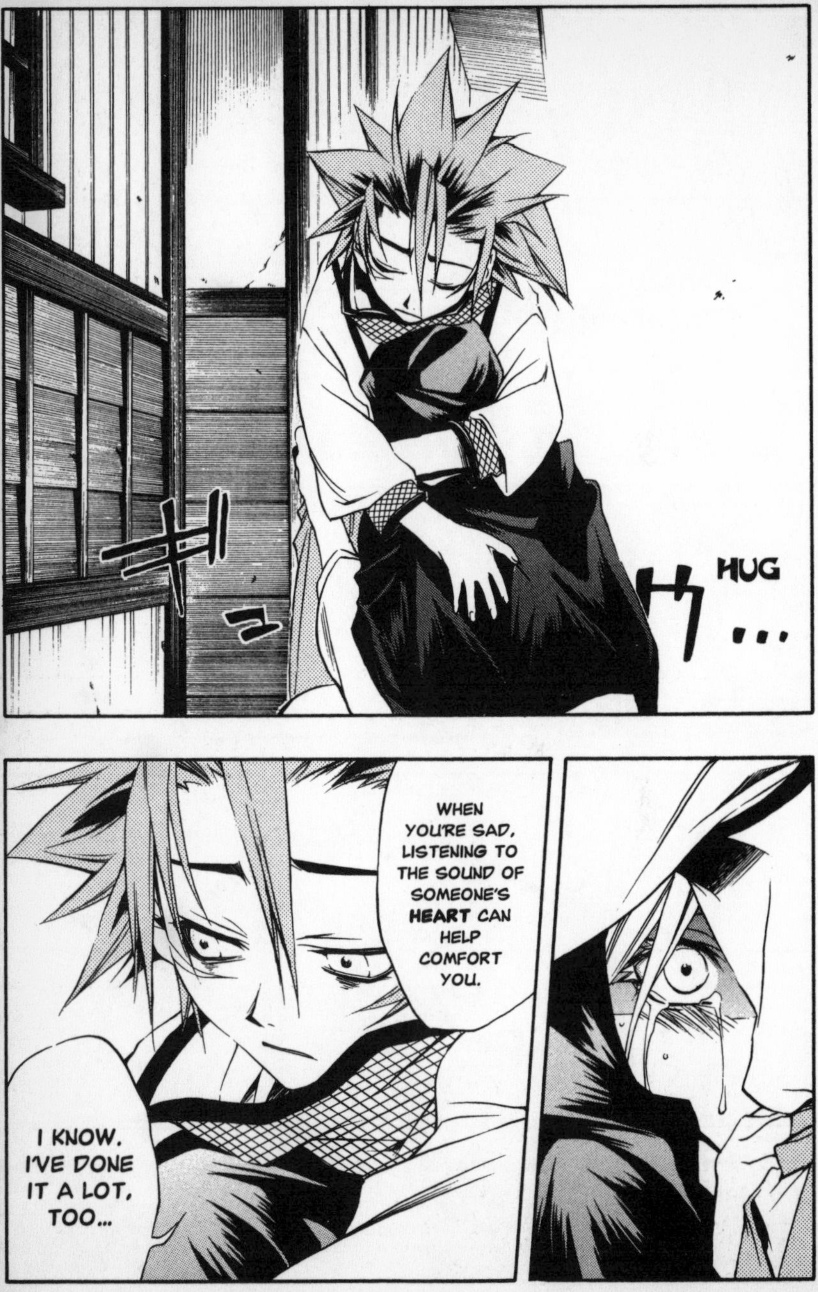
ギュ
ウ...
HUG
WHEN YOU'RE SAD, LISTENING TO THE SOUND OF SOMEONE'S HEART CAN HELP COMFORT YOU.
I KNOW. I'VE DONE IT A LOT, TOO...

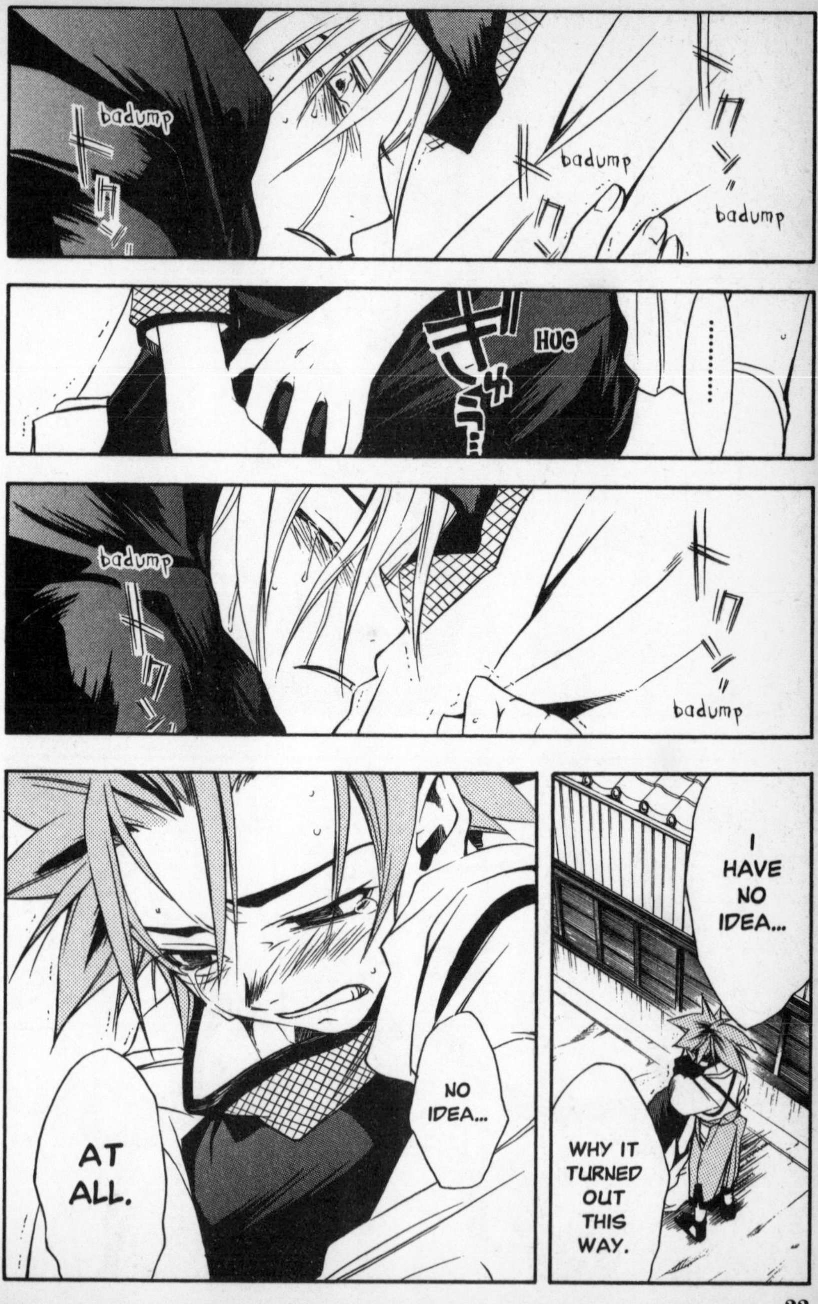
badump
badump
badump
......
HUG
badump
badump
I HAVE NO IDEA...
WHY IT TURNED OUT THIS WAY.
NO IDEA...
AT ALL.

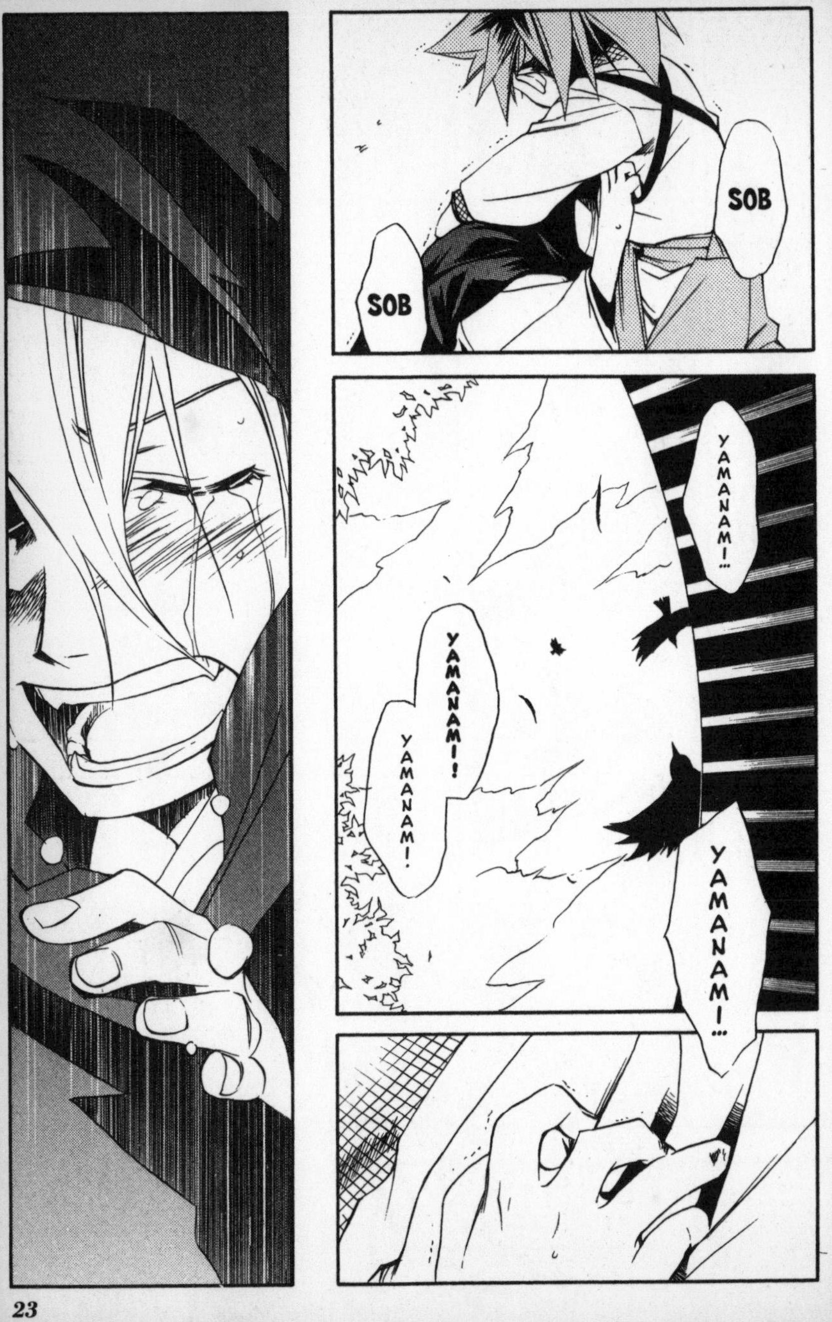
SOB
SOB
YAMANAMI!...
YAMANAMI!
YAMANAMI!
YAMANAMI!...

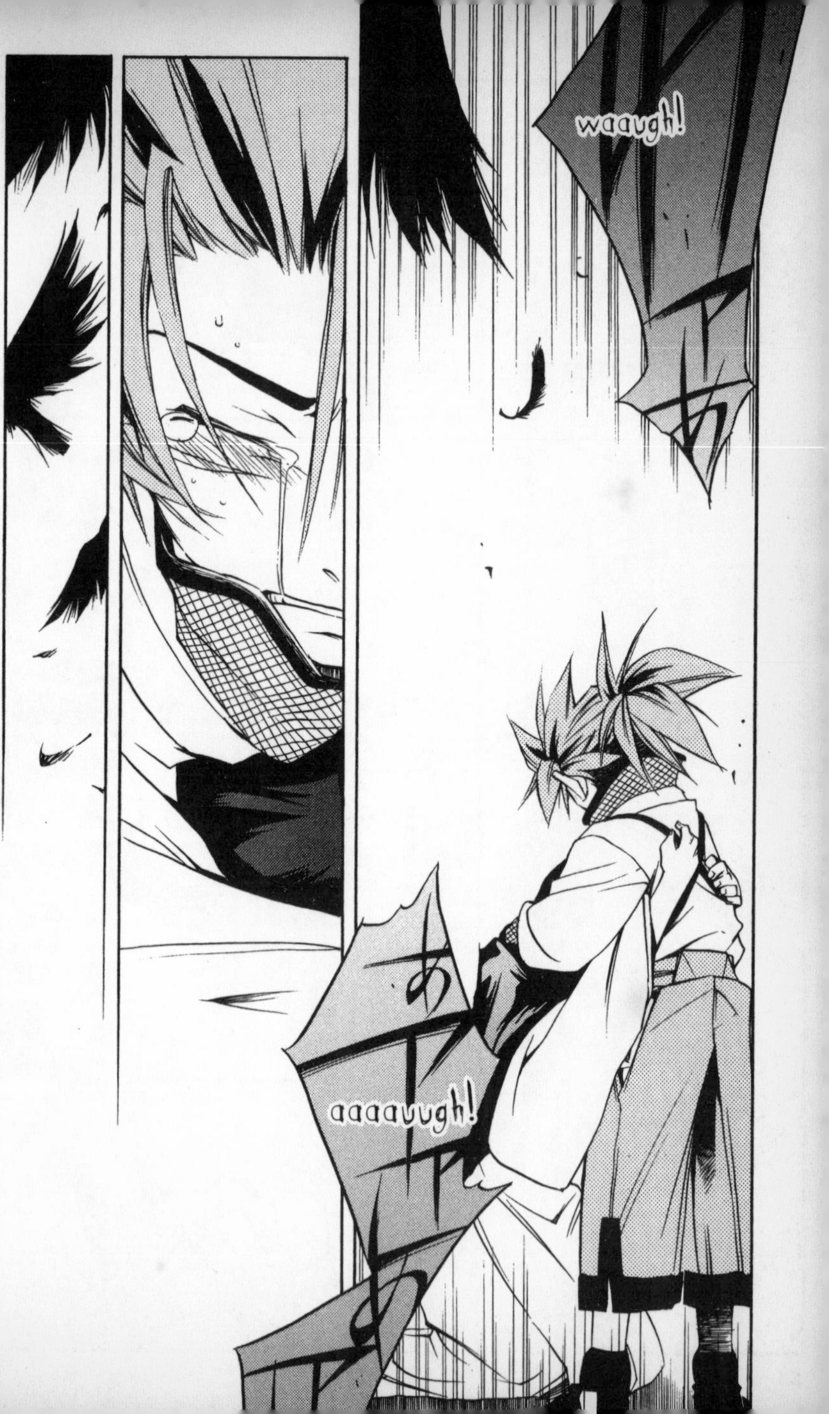
waaugh!
あ
あ
aaaauugh!

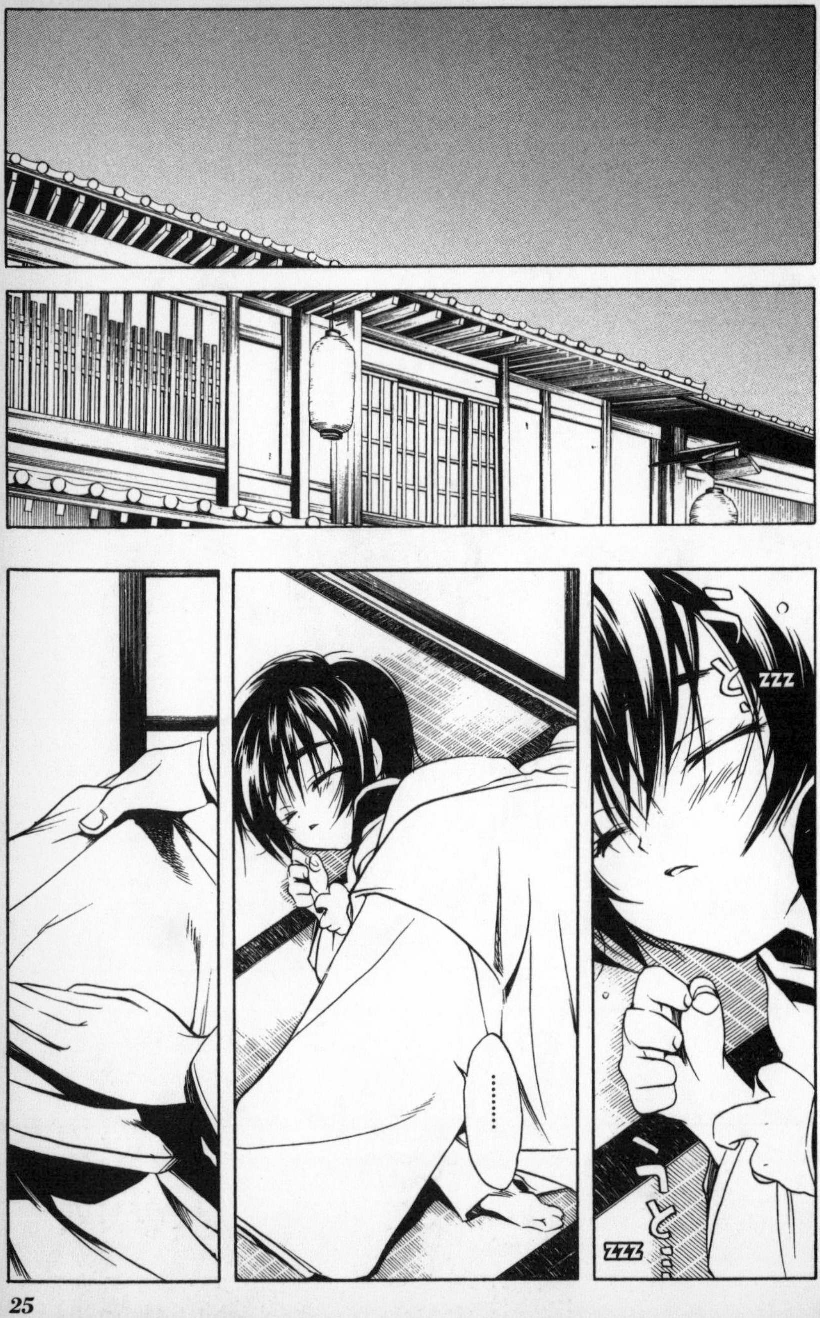

....
ZZZ
ZZZ

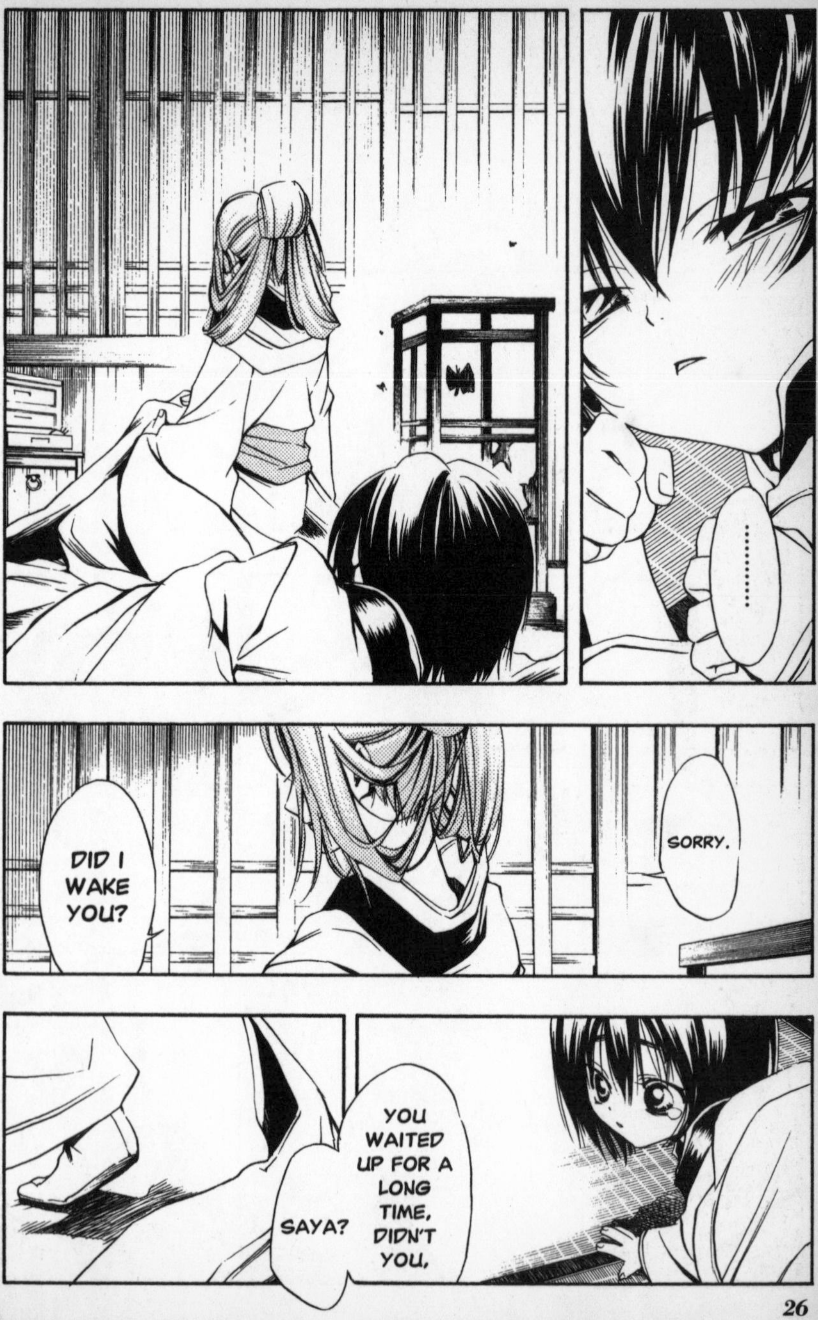
....
SORRY.
DID I WAKE YOU?
YOU WAITED UP FOR A LONG TIME, DIDN'T YOU,
SAYA?

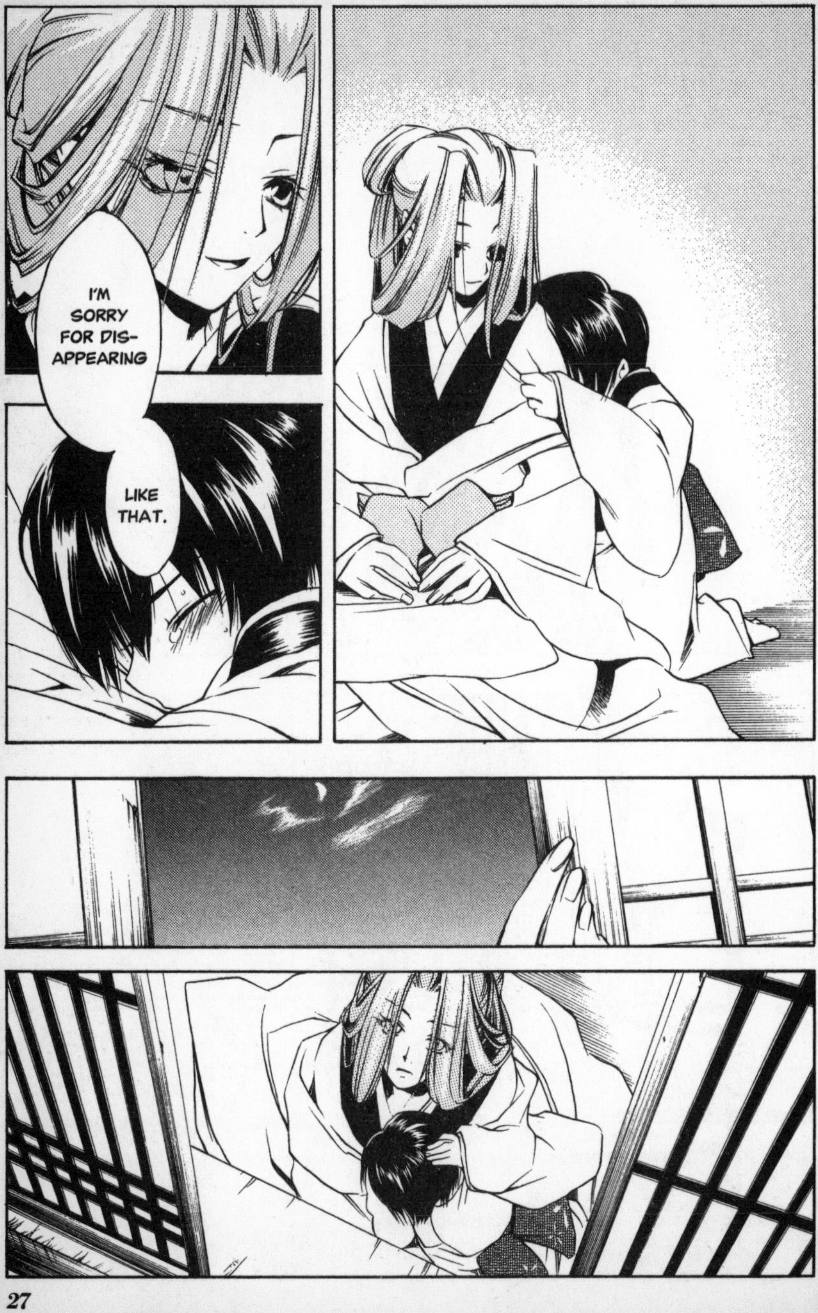
I'M SORRY FOR DIS- APPEARING
LIKE THAT.

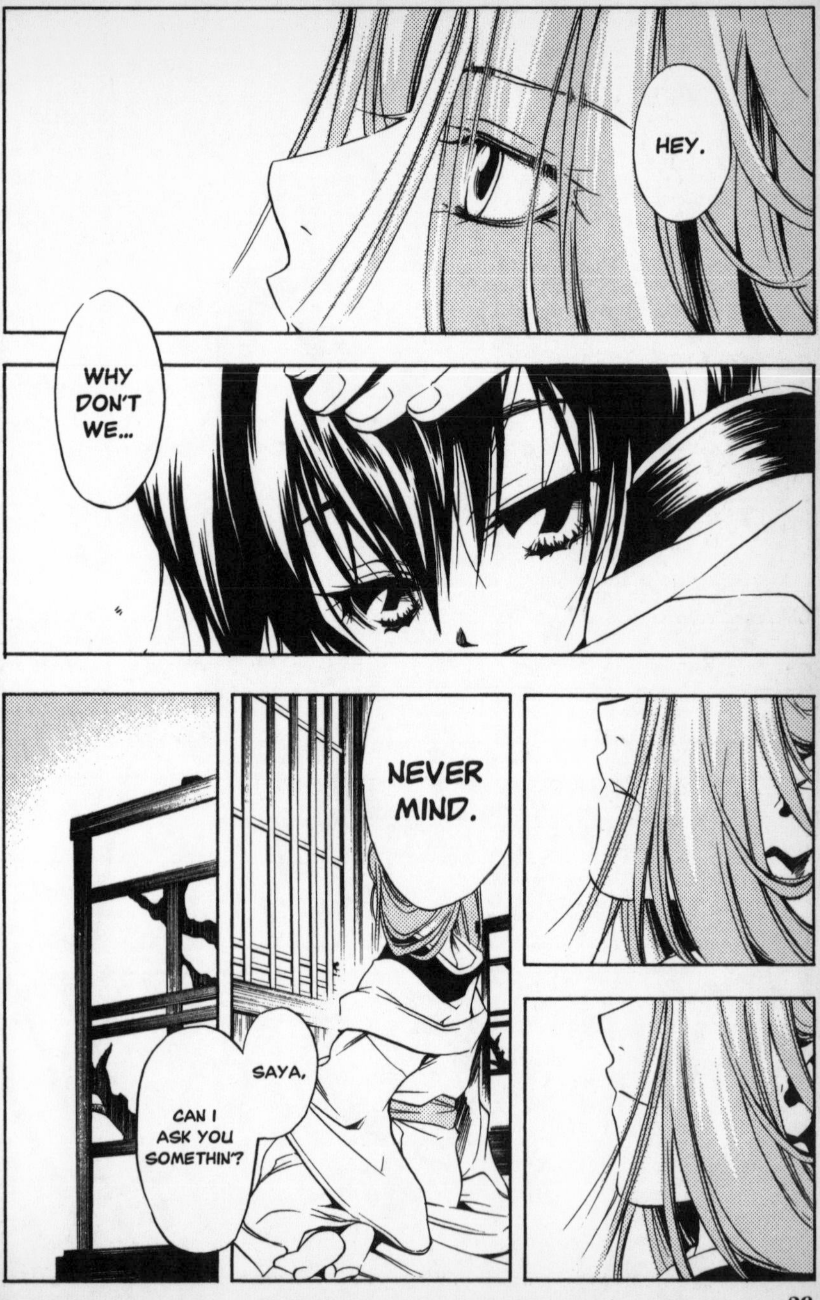
HEY.
WHY DON'T WE...
NEVER MIND.
SAYA,
CAN I ASK YOU SOMETHIN'?

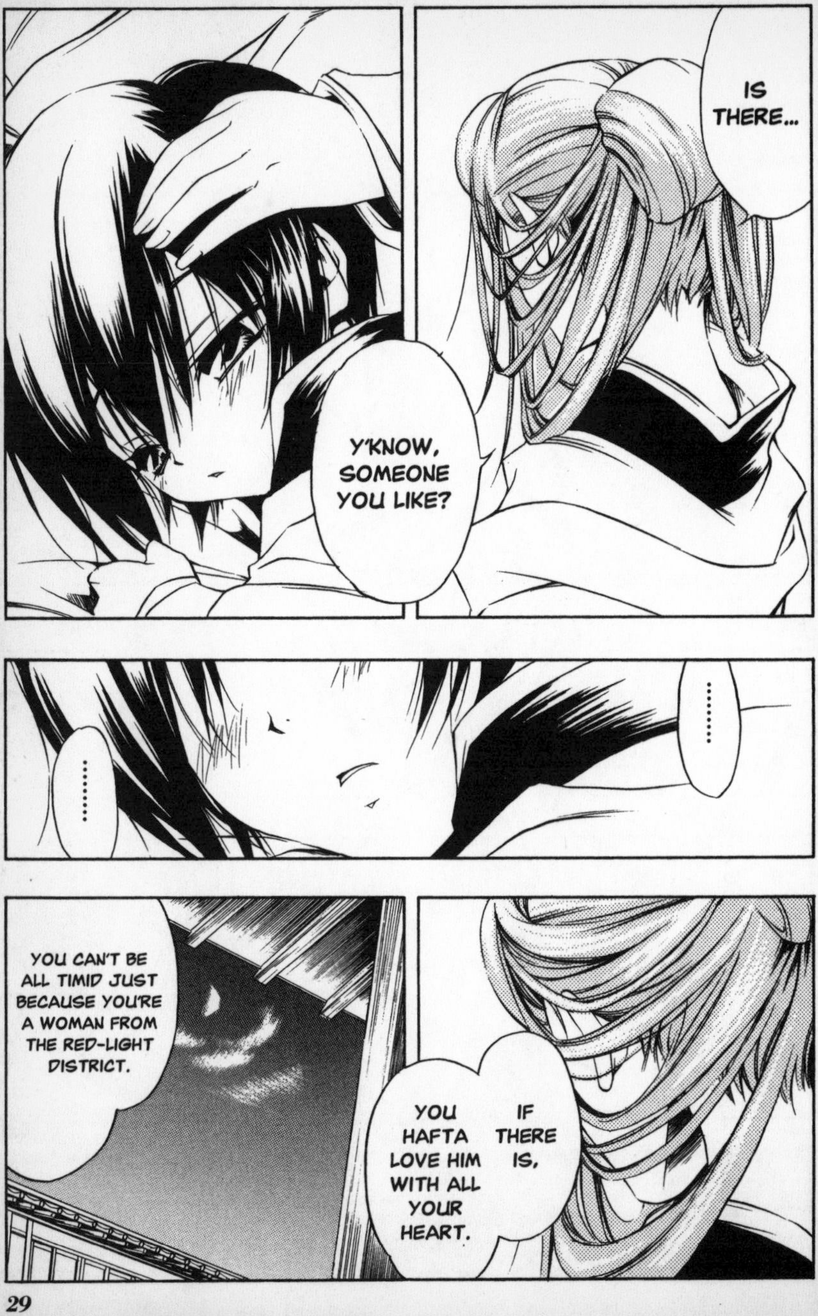
IS THERE...
Y'KNOW, SOMEONE YOU LIKE?
....
....
IF THERE IS,
YOU HAFTA LOVE HIM WITH ALL YOUR HEART.
YOU CAN'T BE ALL TIMID JUST BECAUSE YOU'RE A WOMAN FROM THE RED-LIGHT DISTRICT.

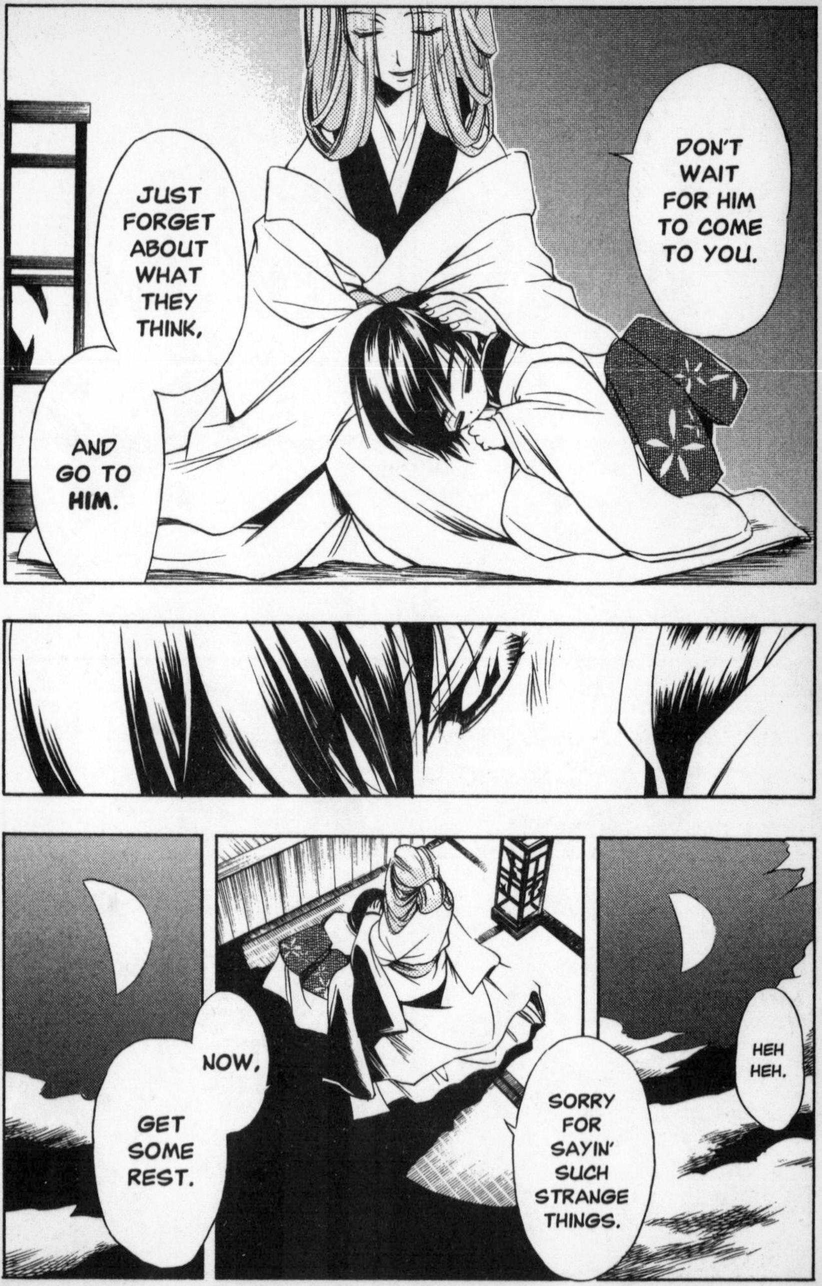
DON'T WAIT FOR HIM TO COME TO YOU.
JUST FORGET ABOUT WHAT THEY THINK,
AND GO TO HIM.
HEH HEH.
SORRY FOR SAYIN' SUCH STRANGE THINGS.
NOW, GET SOME REST.

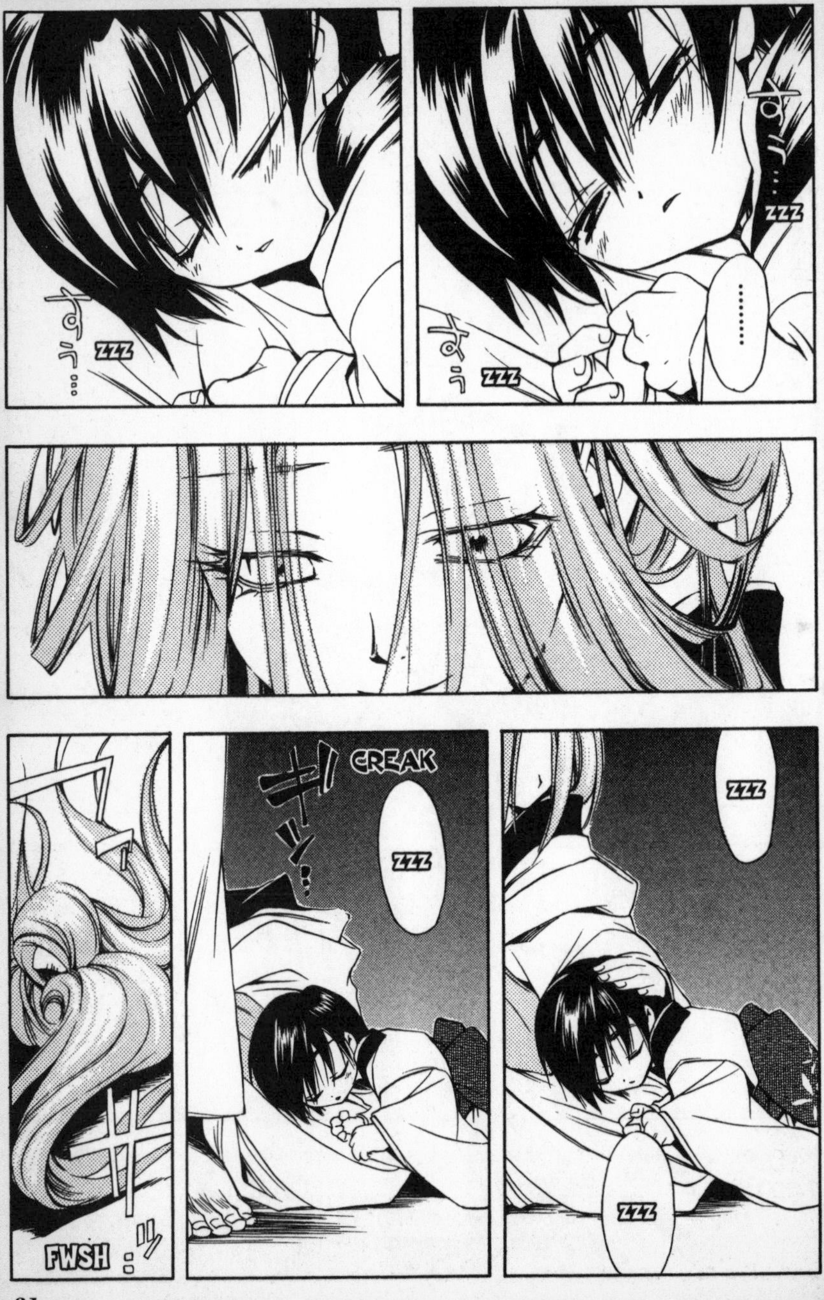
すぅ...
ZZZ
......
すぅ
ZZZ
すぅ...
ZZZ
ZZZ
ZZZ
CREAK
ZZZ
FWSH

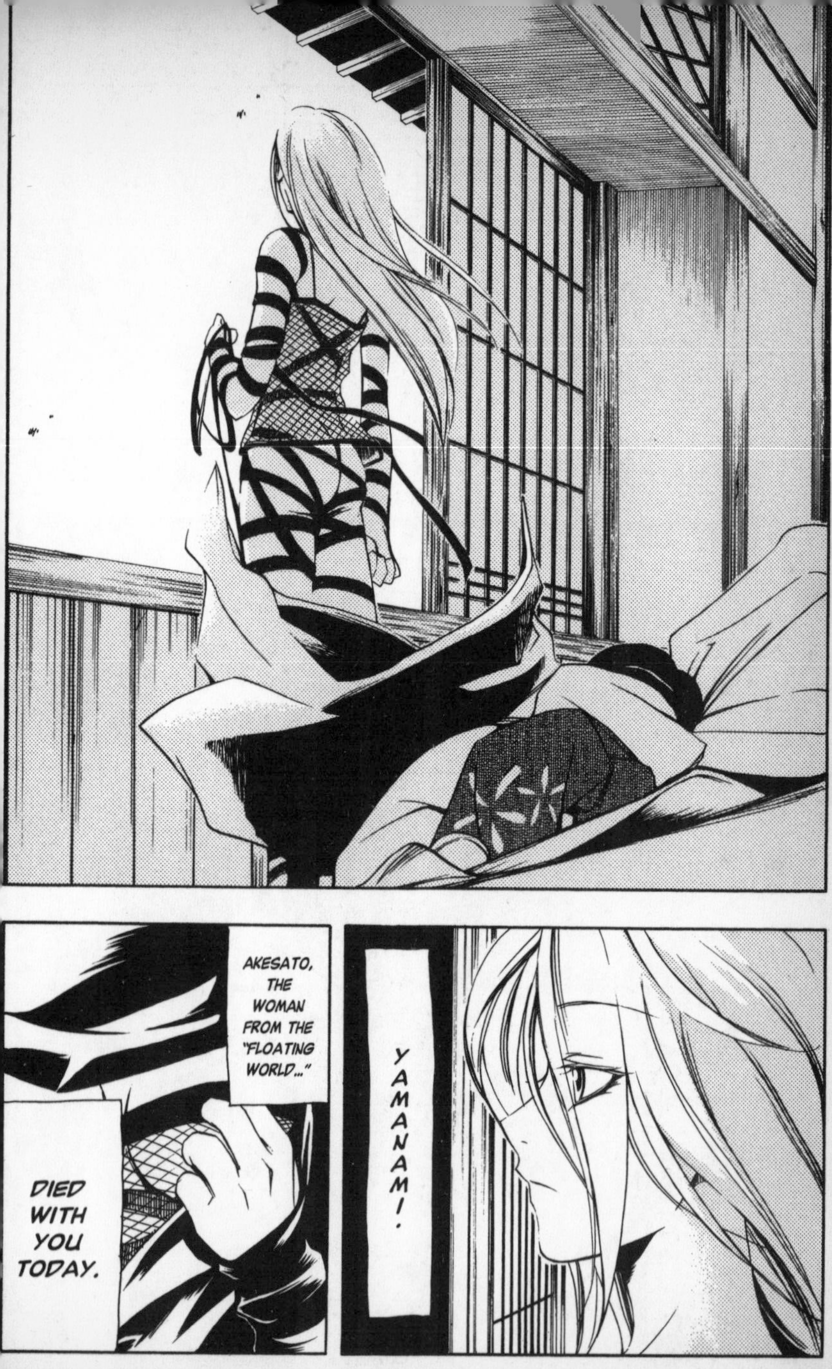
YAMANAMI!
AKESATO, THE WOMAN FROM THE "FLOATING WORLD..."
DIED WITH YOU TODAY.

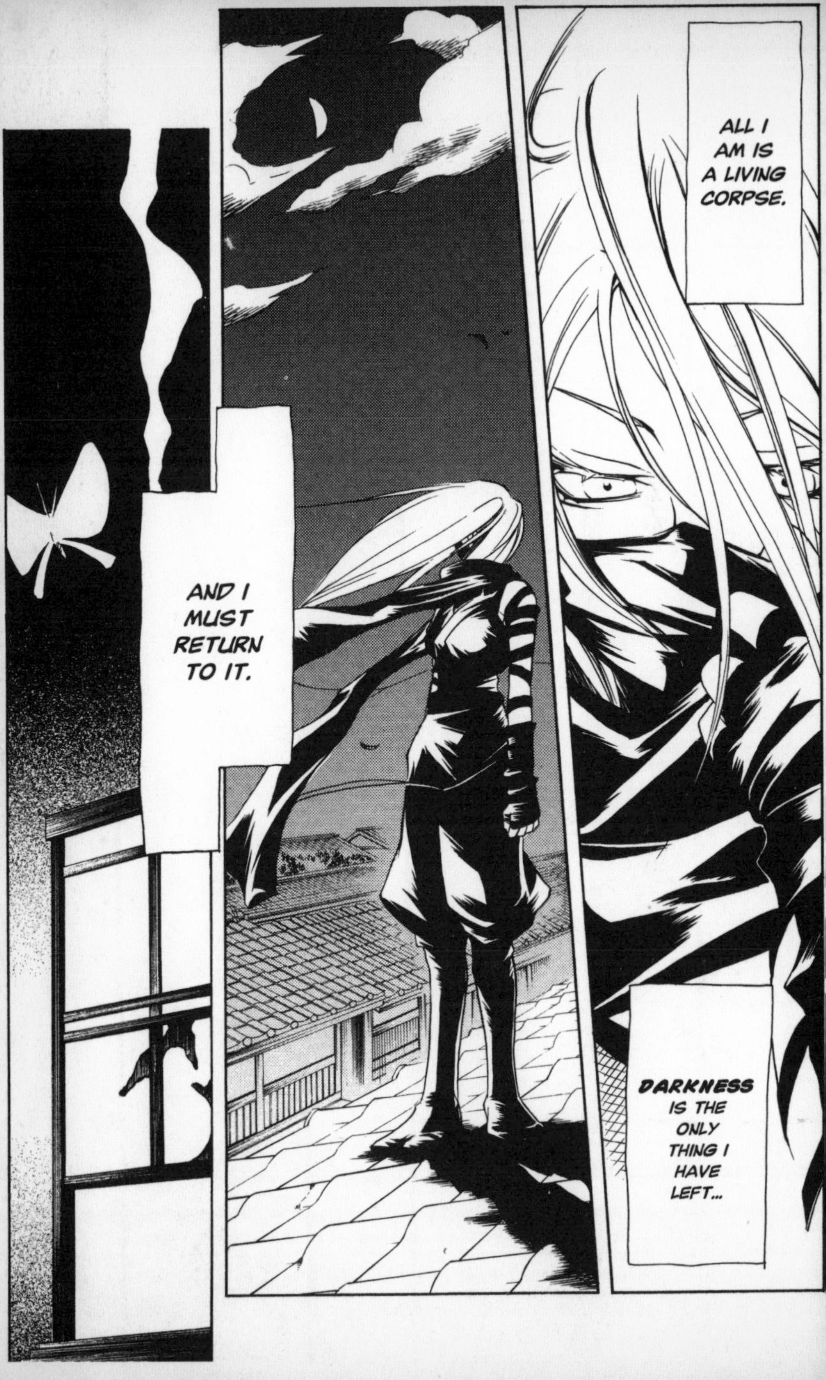
ALL I AM IS A LIVING CORPSE.
DARKNESS IS THE ONLY THING I HAVE LEFT...
AND I MUST RETURN TO IT.

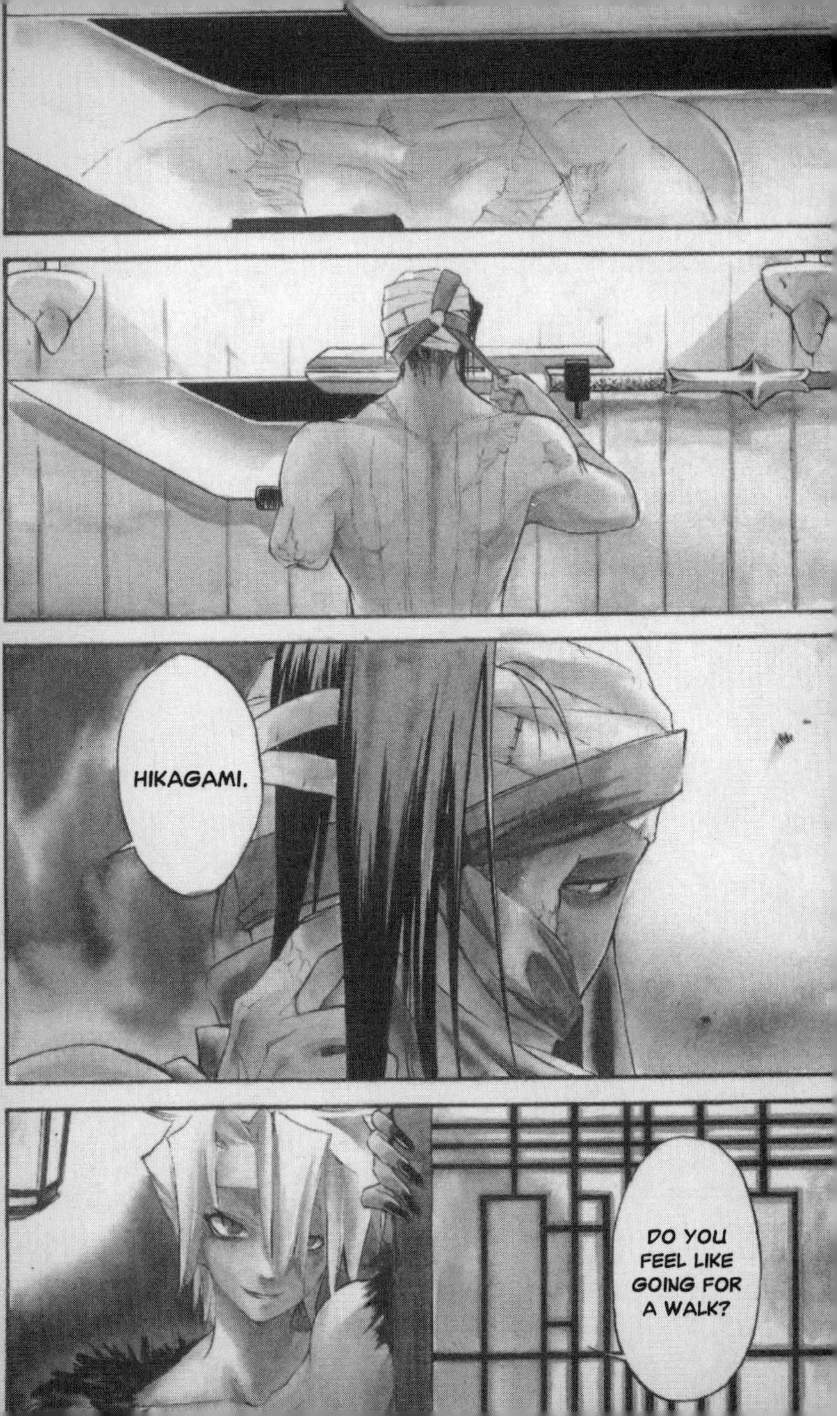
HIKAGAMI.
DO YOU FEEL LIKE GOING FOR A WALK?

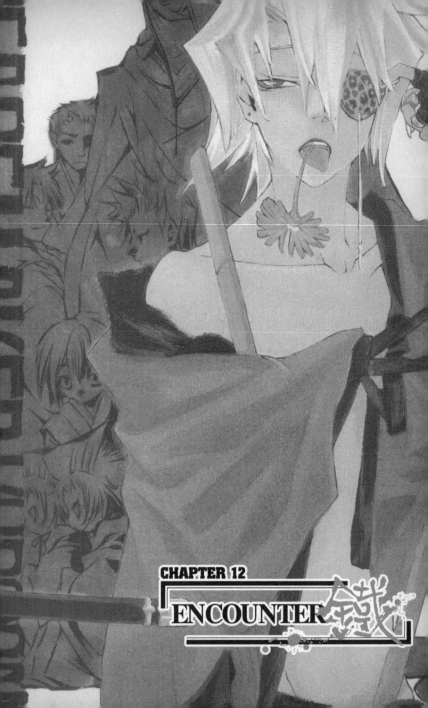

CHAPTER 12
ENCOUNTER 鉄

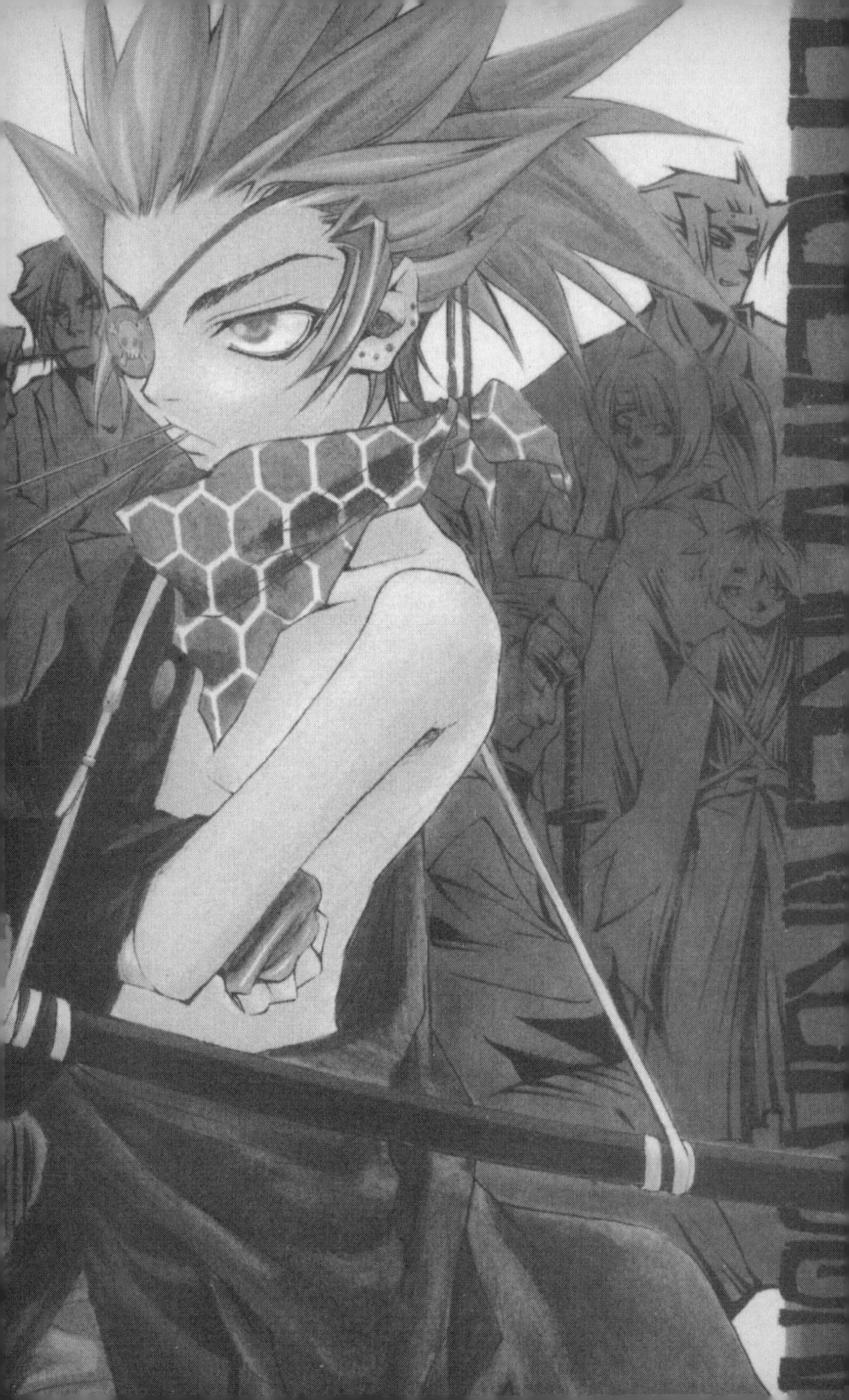

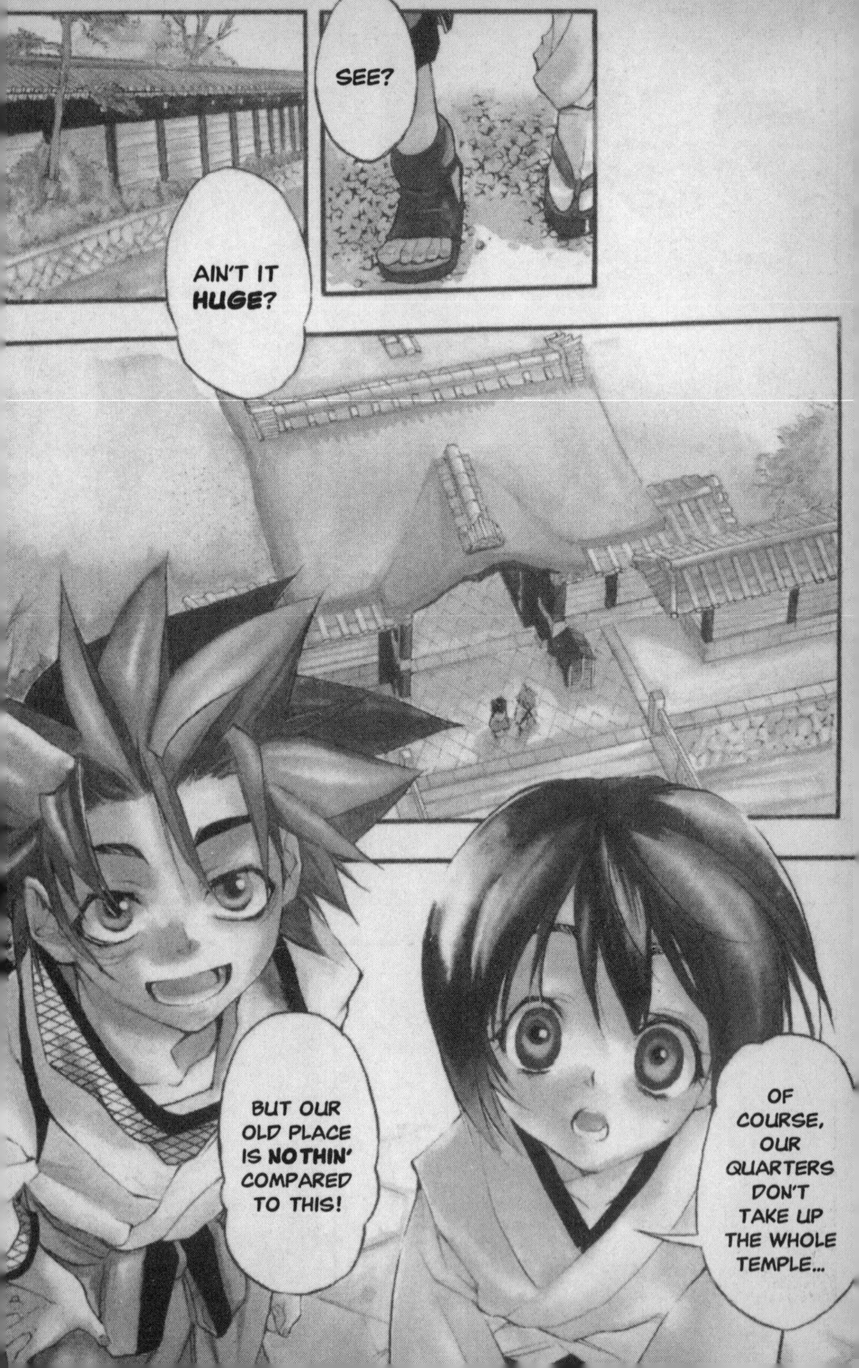
SEE?
AIN'T IT **HUGE**?
BUT OUR OLD PLACE IS **NOTHIN'** COMPARED TO THIS!
OF COURSE, OUR QUARTERS DON'T TAKE UP THE WHOLE TEMPLE...

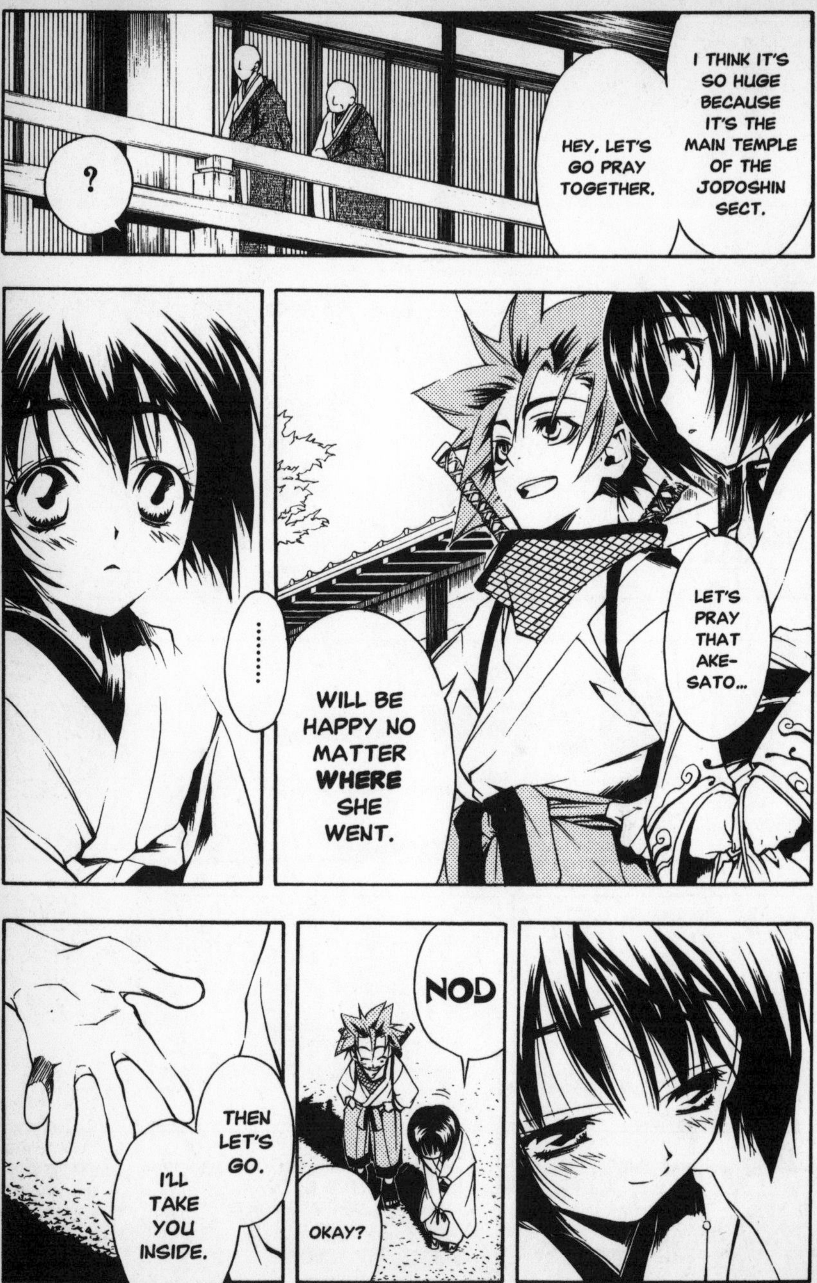
I THINK IT'S SO HUGE BECAUSE IT'S THE MAIN TEMPLE OF THE JODOSHIN SECT.
HEY, LET'S GO PRAY TOGETHER.
?
LET'S PRAY THAT AKE-SATO...
WILL BE HAPPY NO MATTER **WHERE** SHE WENT.
....
NOD
OKAY?
THEN LET'S GO.
I'LL TAKE YOU INSIDE.

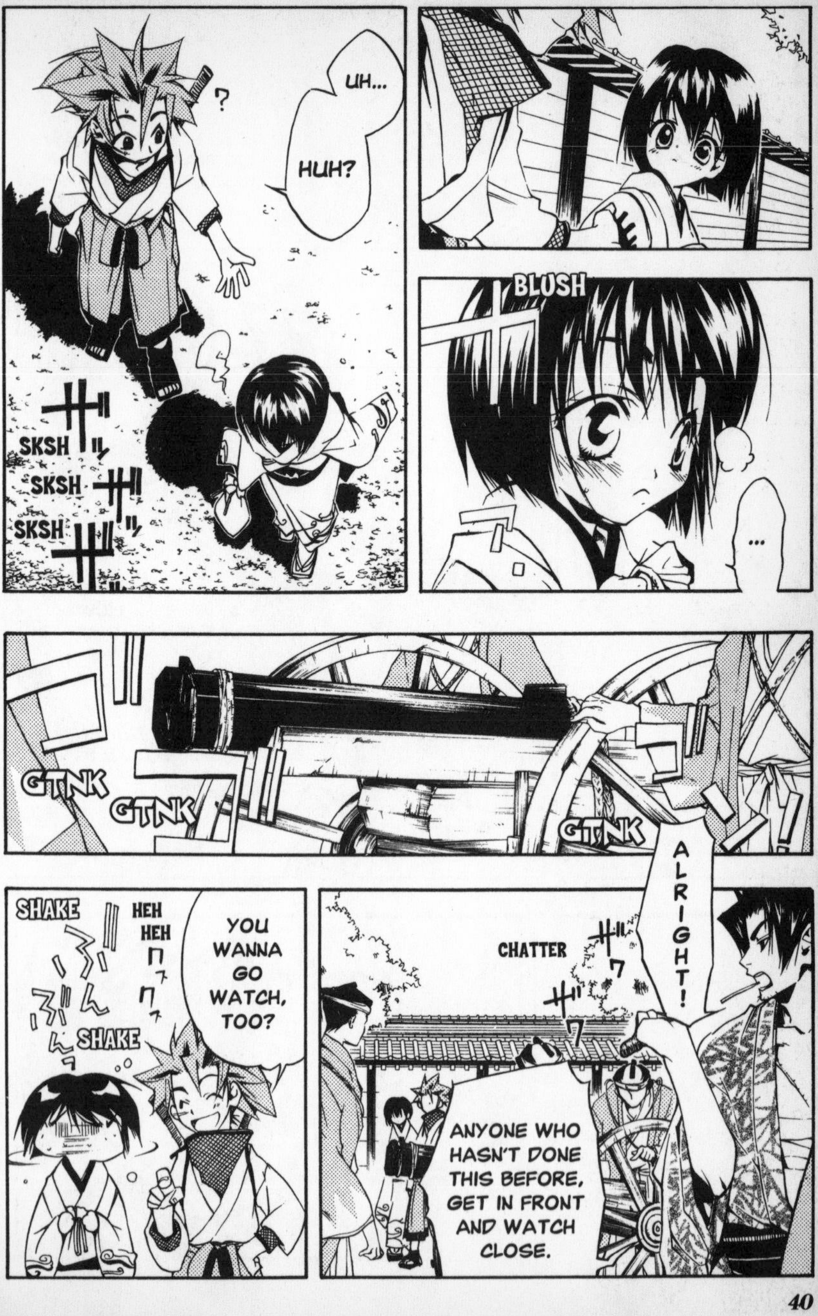
?
UH...
HUH?
SKSH
SKSH
SKSH
BLUSH
...
GTNK
GTNK
GTNK
ALRIGHT!
CHATTER
ANYONE WHO HASN'T DONE THIS BEFORE, GET IN FRONT AND WATCH CLOSE.
SHAKE
HEH HEH
YOU WANNA GO WATCH, TOO?
SHAKE

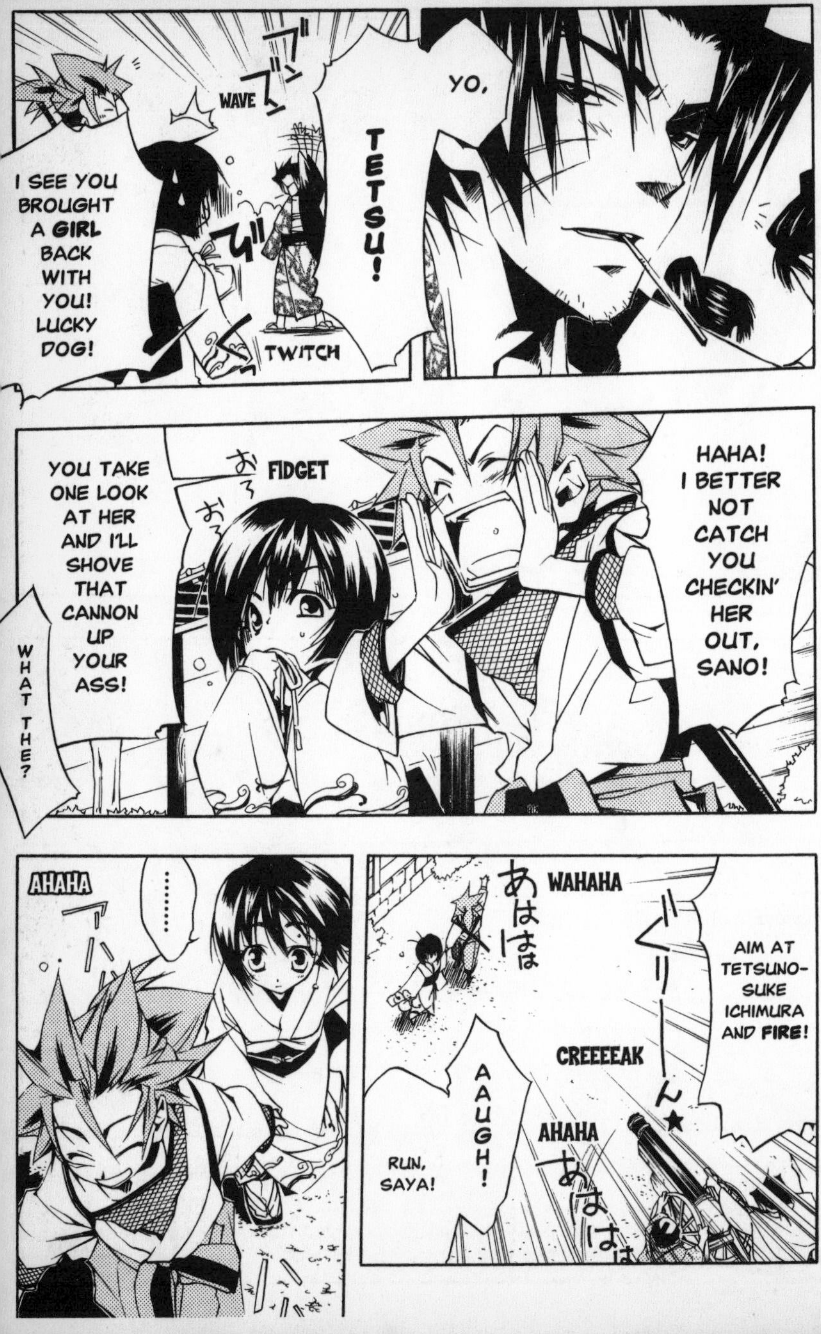
YO,
TETSU!
WAVE
ブンブン
I SEE YOU BROUGHT A GIRL BACK WITH YOU! LUCKY DOG!
びく
TWITCH
HAHA! I BETTER NOT CATCH YOU CHECKIN' HER OUT, SANO!
おろおろ
FIDGET
YOU TAKE ONE LOOK AT HER AND I'LL SHOVE THAT CANNON UP YOUR ASS!
WHAT THE?
AIM AT TETSUNOSUKE ICHIMURA AND FIRE!
ぎりーん★
CREEEEAK
あはは
WAHAHA
AAUGH!
RUN, SAYA!
あははは
AHAHA
......
アハハ
AHAHA

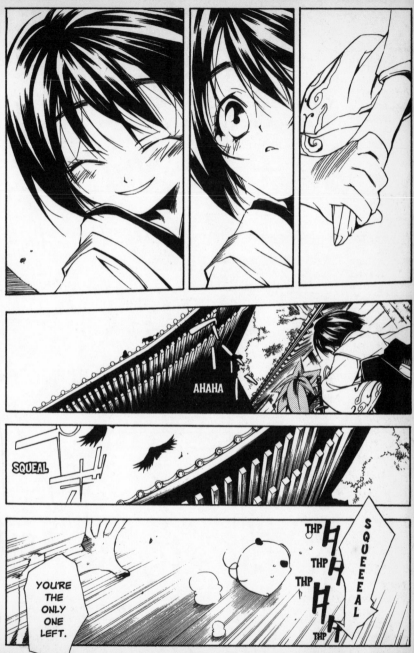

AHAHA

SQUEAL

YOU'RE THE ONLY ONE LEFT.

THP THP THP THP

SQUEEEAL

42

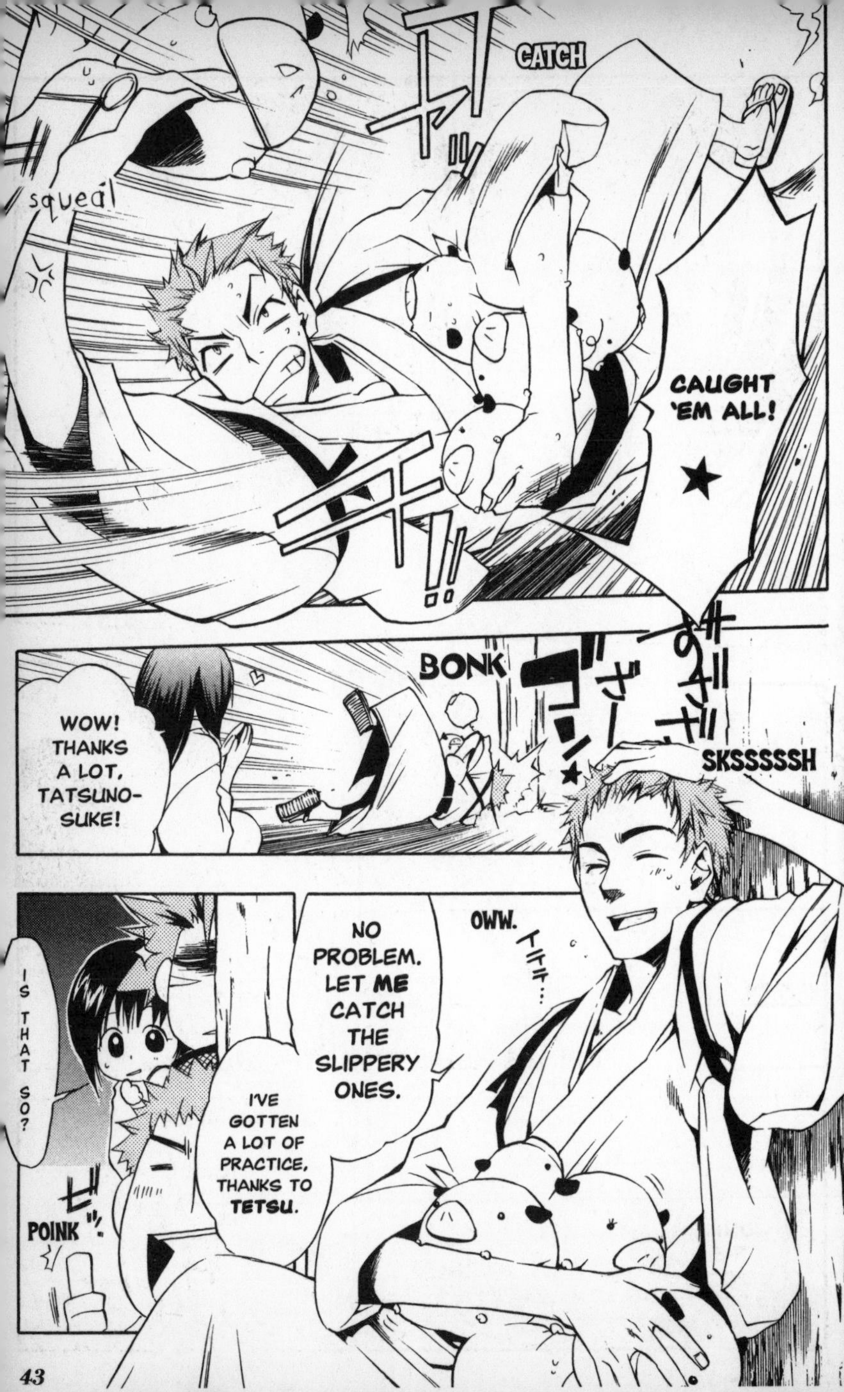
CATCH
squeal
CAUGHT 'EM ALL! ★
SKSSSSSH
BONK
WOW! THANKS A LOT, TATSUNOSUKE!
OWW.
NO PROBLEM. LET ME CATCH THE SLIPPERY ONES.
I'VE GOTTEN A LOT OF PRACTICE, THANKS TO TETSU.
IS THAT SO?
POINK

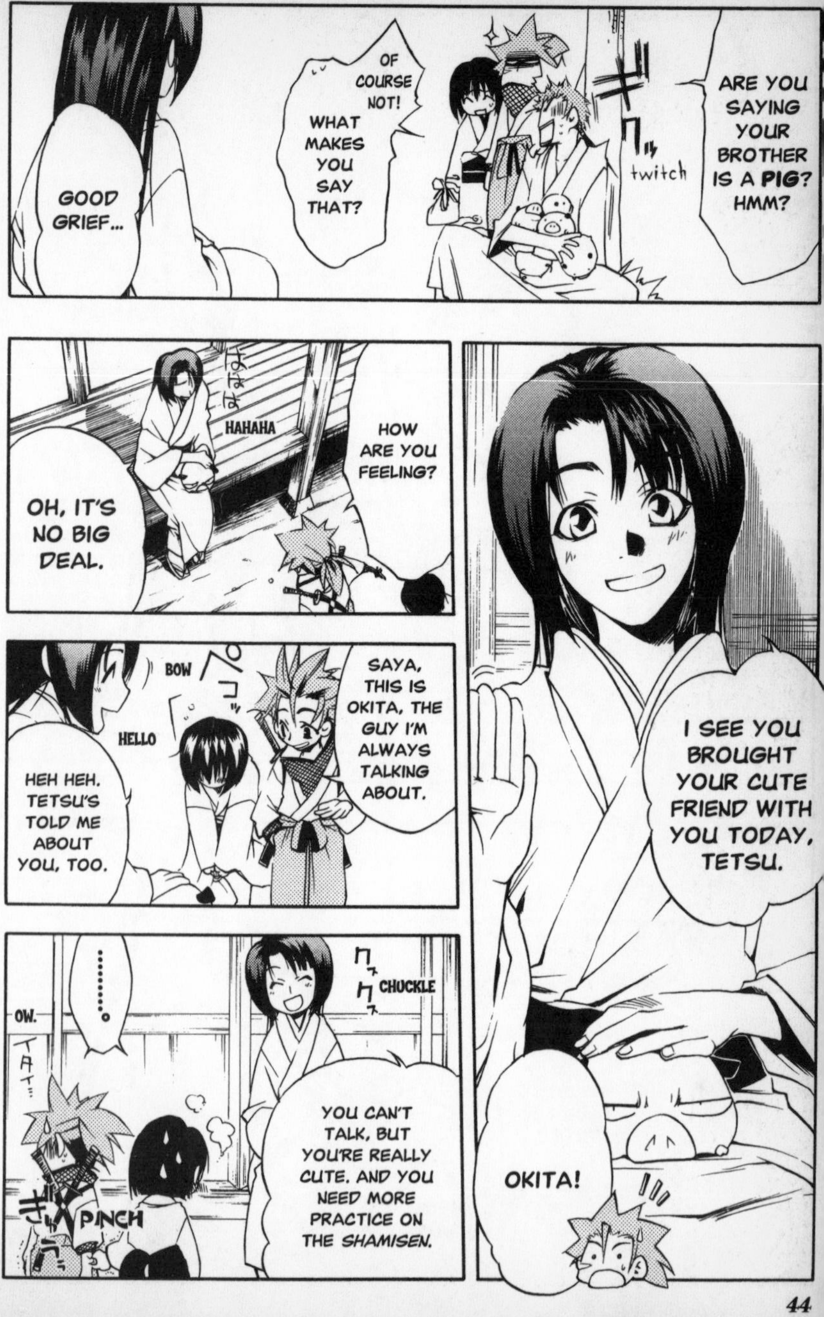
ARE YOU SAYING YOUR BROTHER IS A PIG? HMM?
twitch
OF COURSE NOT! WHAT MAKES YOU SAY THAT?
GOOD GRIEF...
I SEE YOU BROUGHT YOUR CUTE FRIEND WITH YOU TODAY, TETSU.
OKITA!
HOW ARE YOU FEELING?
HAHAHA
OH, IT'S NO BIG DEAL.
SAYA, THIS IS OKITA, THE GUY I'M ALWAYS TALKING ABOUT.
BOW
HELLO
HEH HEH. TETSU'S TOLD ME ABOUT YOU, TOO.
CHUCKLE
YOU CAN'T TALK, BUT YOU'RE REALLY CUTE. AND YOU NEED MORE PRACTICE ON THE SHAMISEN.
....
OW.
PINCH

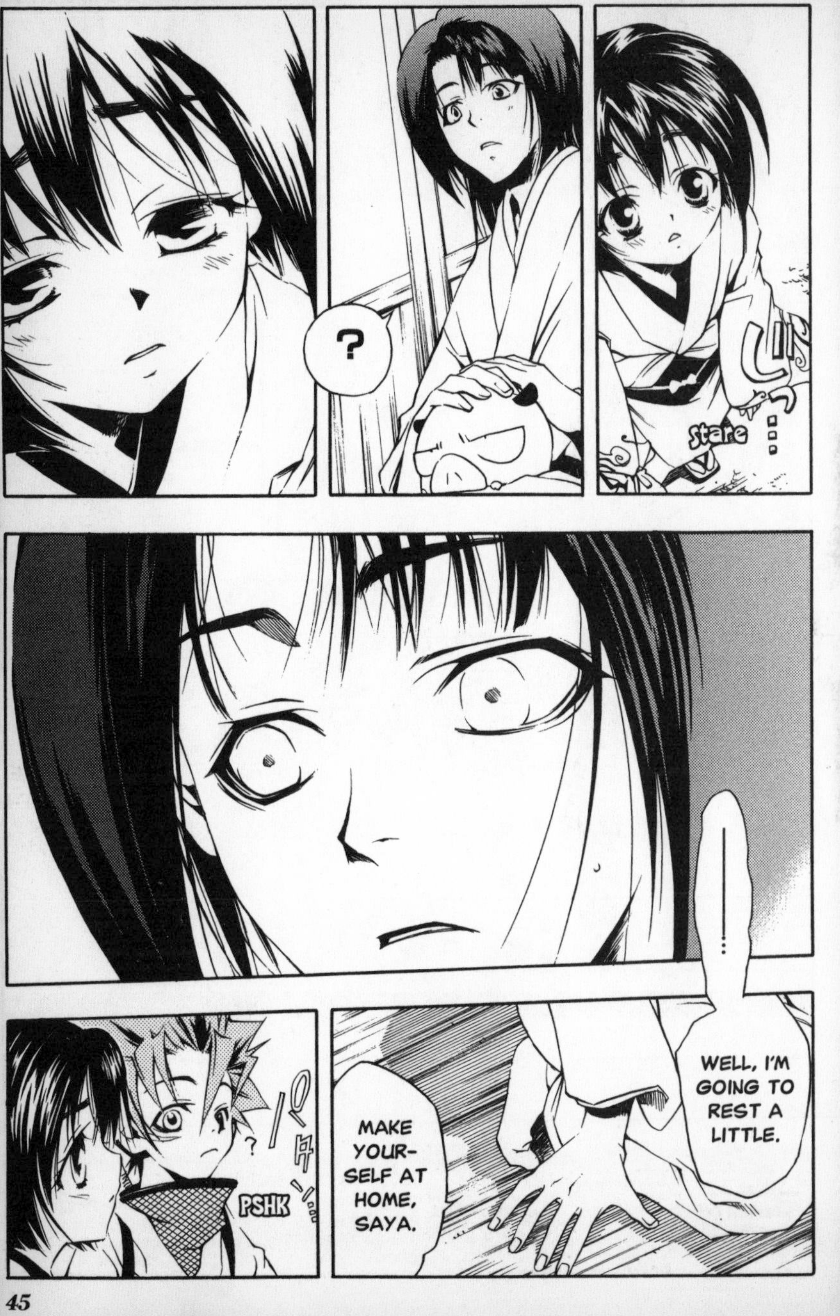
stare
?
WELL, I'M GOING TO REST A LITTLE.
MAKE YOUR-SELF AT HOME, SAYA.
PSHK

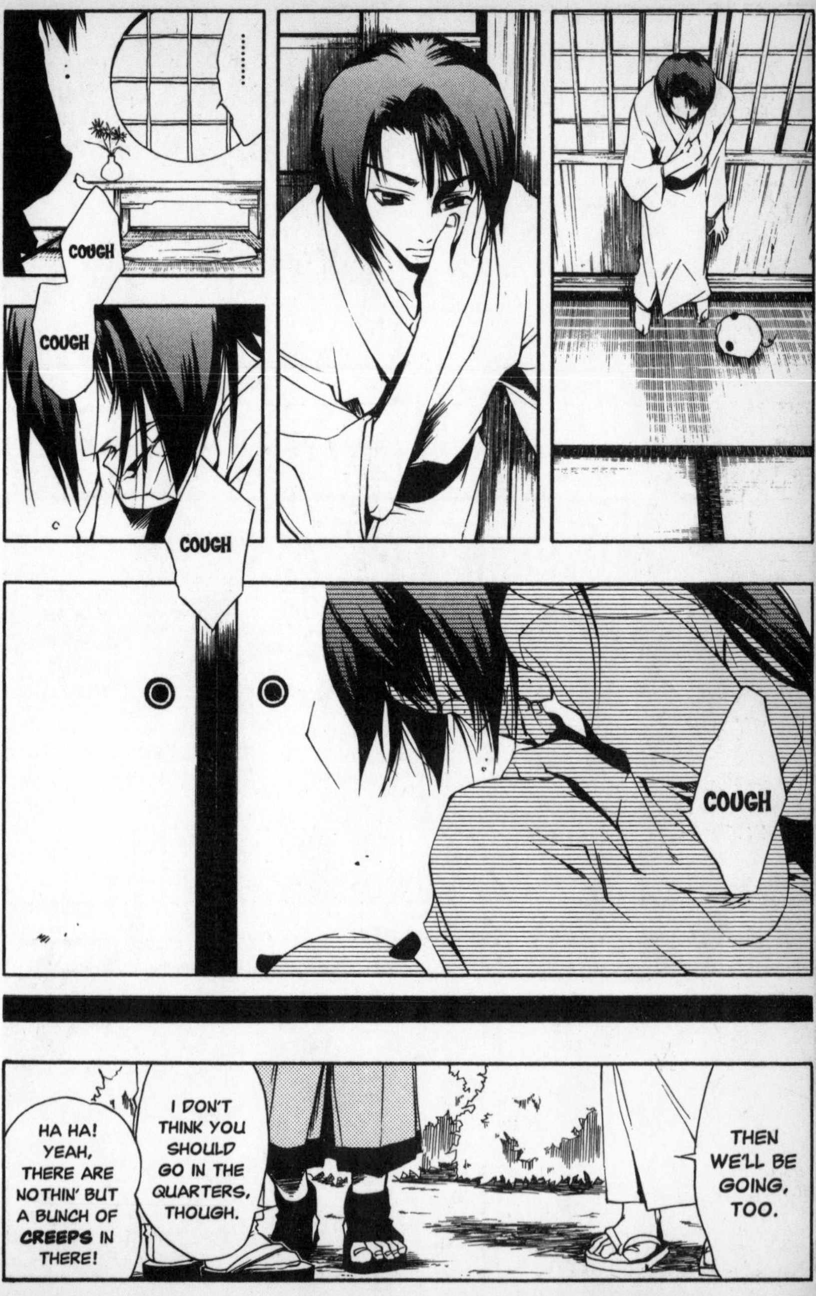
COUGH
COUGH
COUGH
COUGH
THEN WE'LL BE GOING, TOO.
I DON'T THINK YOU SHOULD GO IN THE QUARTERS, THOUGH.
HA HA! YEAH, THERE ARE NOTHIN' BUT A BUNCH OF CREEPS IN THERE!

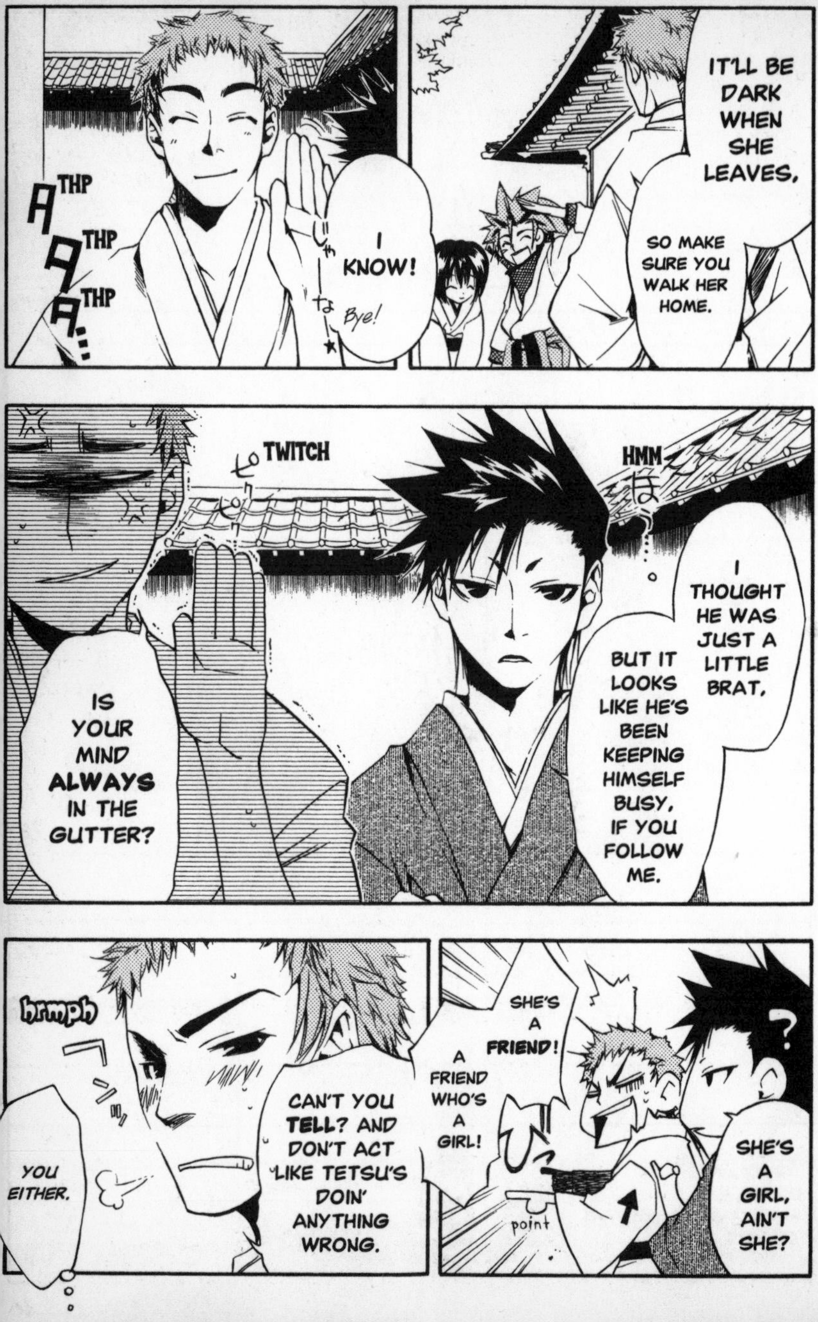
IT'LL BE DARK WHEN SHE LEAVES,
SO MAKE SURE YOU WALK HER HOME.
I KNOW!
Bye!
THP
THP
THP
HMM
I THOUGHT HE WAS JUST A LITTLE BRAT,
BUT IT LOOKS LIKE HE'S BEEN KEEPING HIMSELF BUSY, IF YOU FOLLOW ME.
TWITCH
IS YOUR MIND ALWAYS IN THE GUTTER?
SHE'S A GIRL, AIN'T SHE?
SHE'S A FRIEND!
A FRIEND WHO'S A GIRL!
point
CAN'T YOU TELL? AND DON'T ACT LIKE TETSU'S DOIN' ANYTHING WRONG.
hrmph
YOU EITHER.

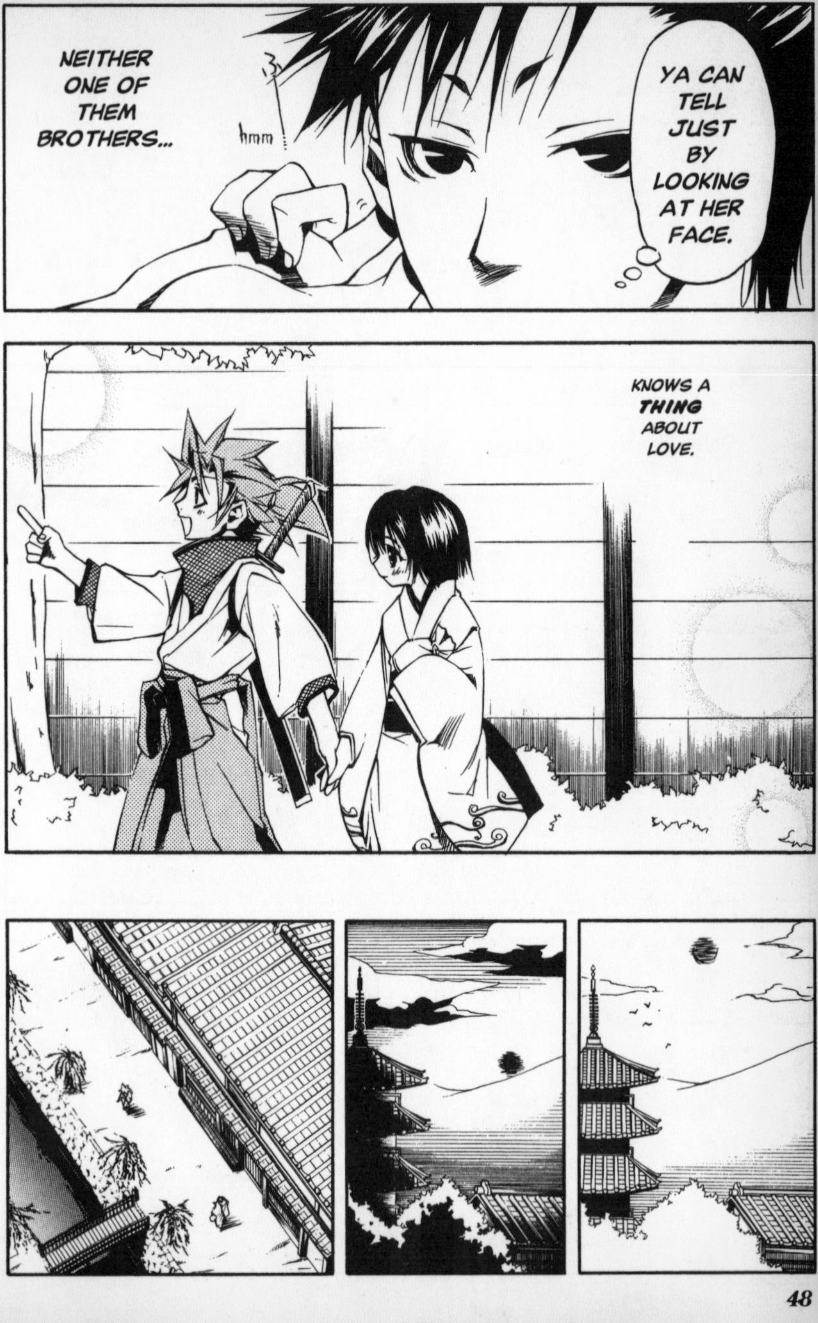
YA CAN TELL JUST BY LOOKING AT HER FACE.
hmm
NEITHER ONE OF THEM BROTHERS...
KNOWS A THING ABOUT LOVE.

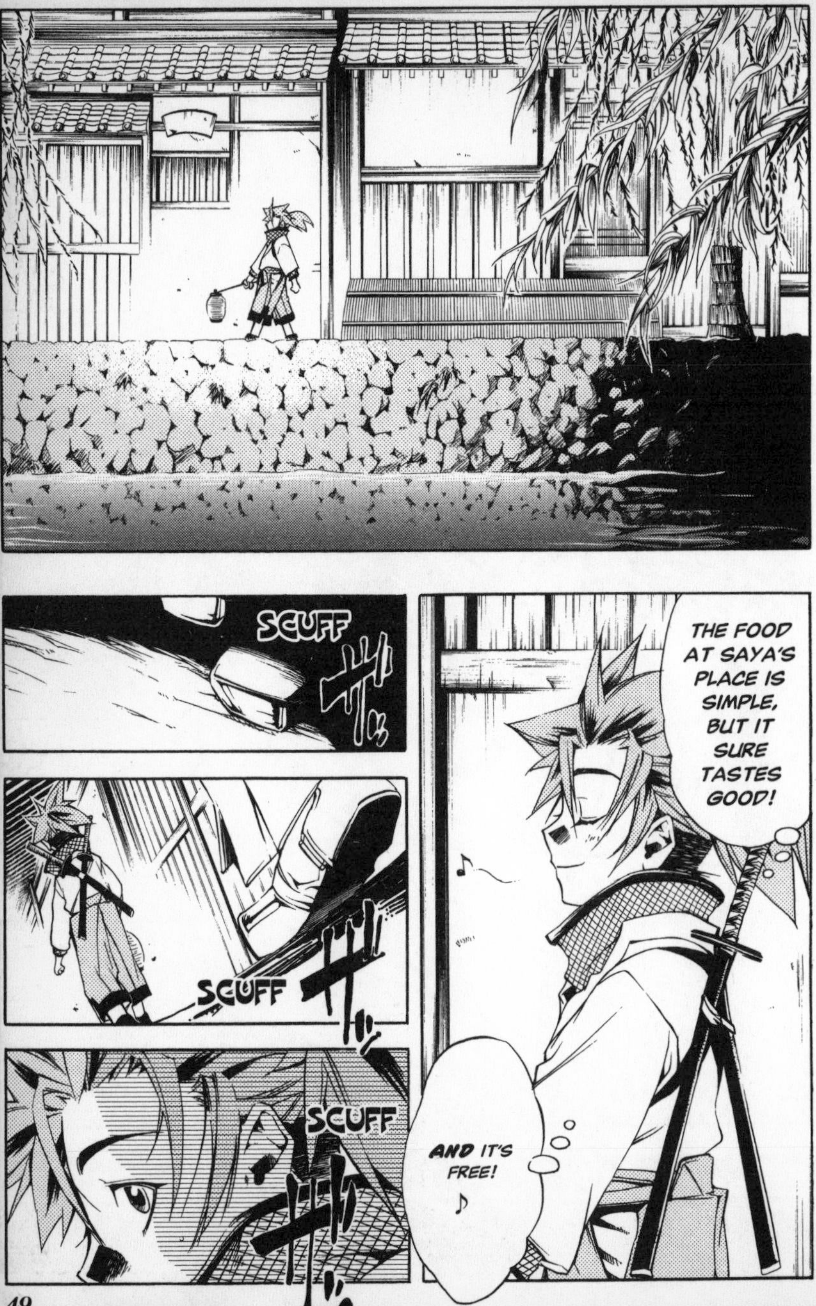
THE FOOD AT SAYA'S PLACE IS SIMPLE, BUT IT SURE TASTES GOOD!
AND IT'S FREE! ♪
SCUFF
SCUFF
SCUFF

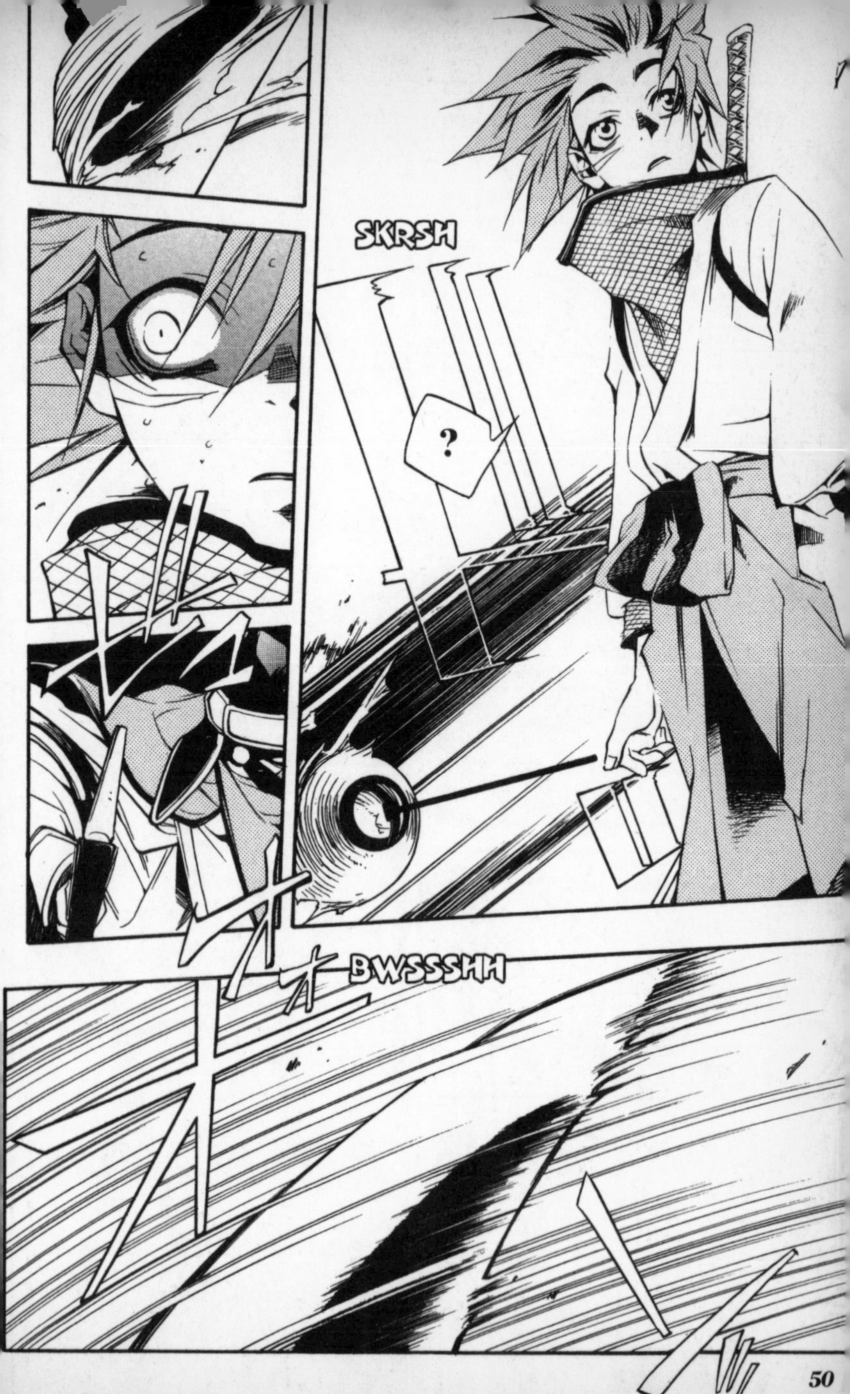
SKRSH
?
BWSSSHH

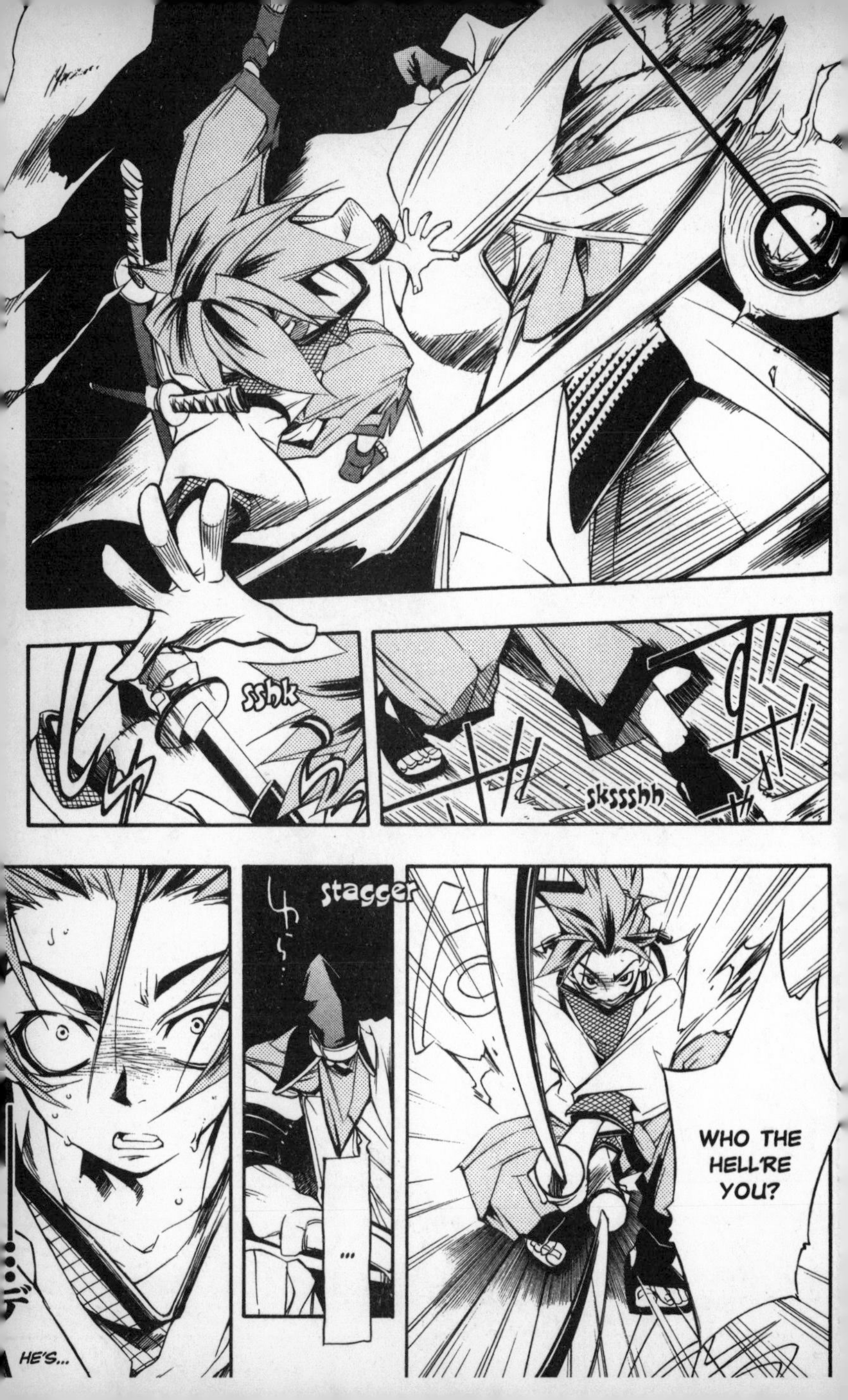
sksssshh
sshk
WHO THE HELL'RE YOU?
stagger
...
HE'S...

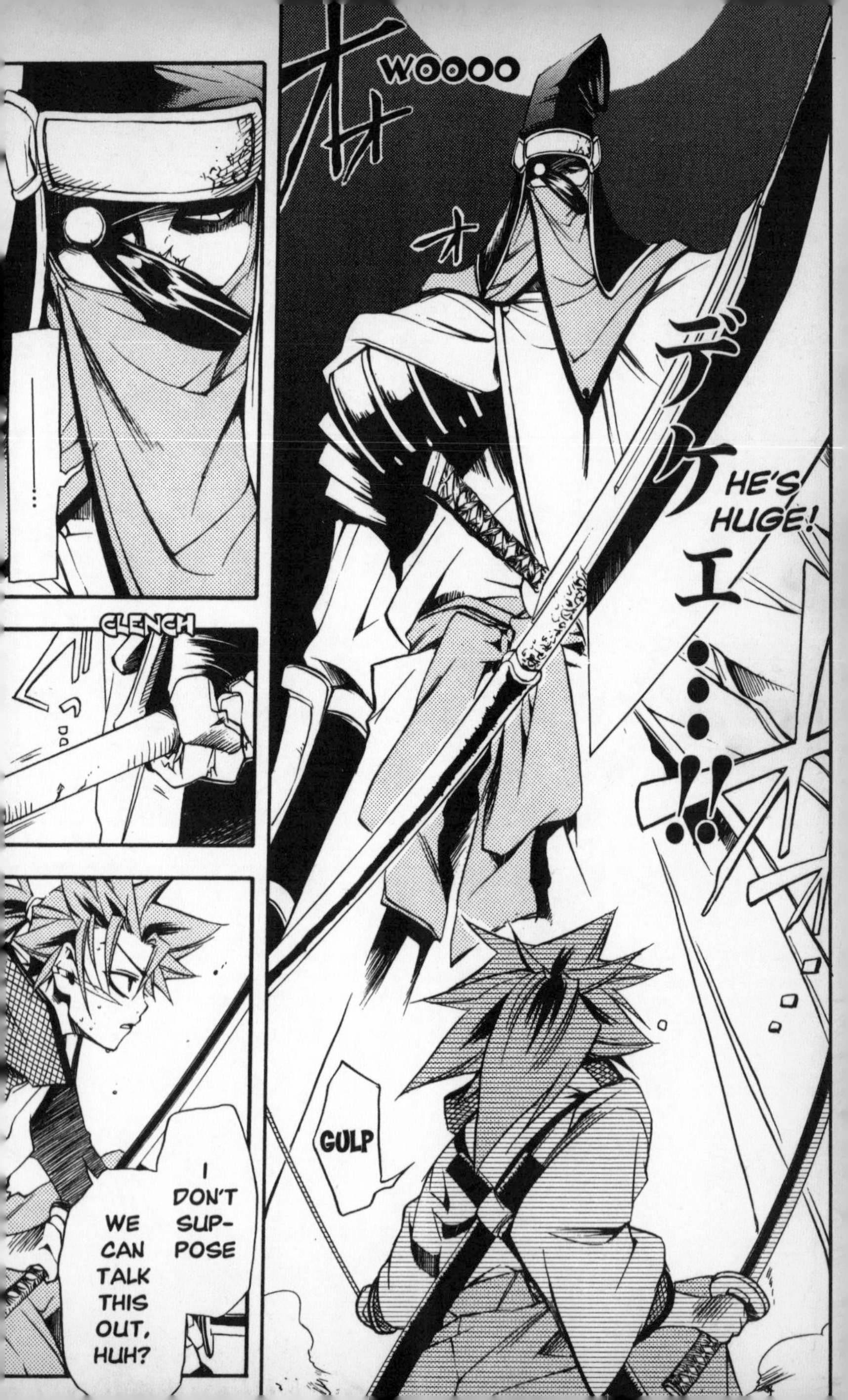
WOOOO
HE'S HUGE!
GULP
......
CLENCH
I DON'T SUPPOSE WE CAN TALK THIS OUT, HUH?

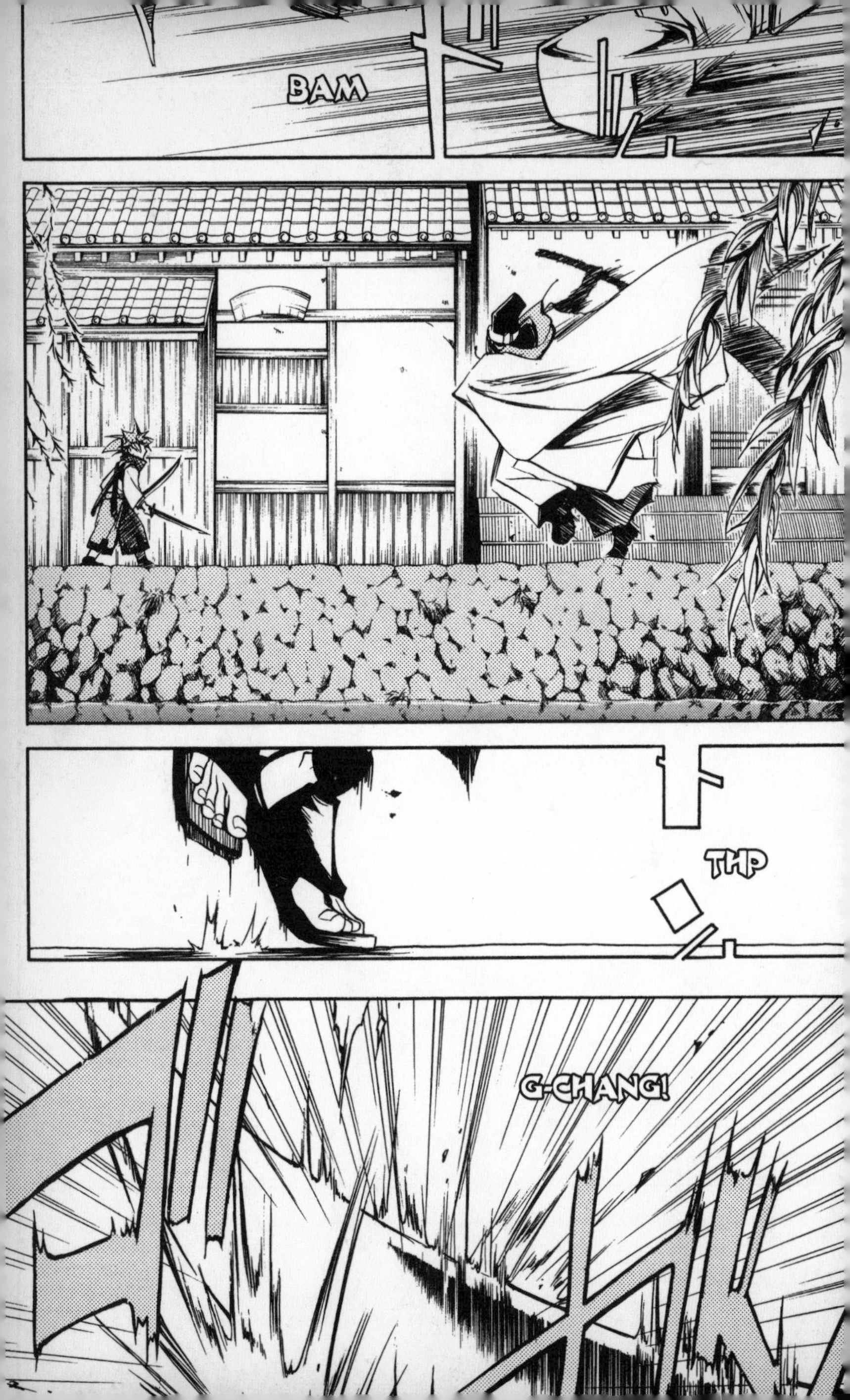
BAM
THP
G-CHANG!

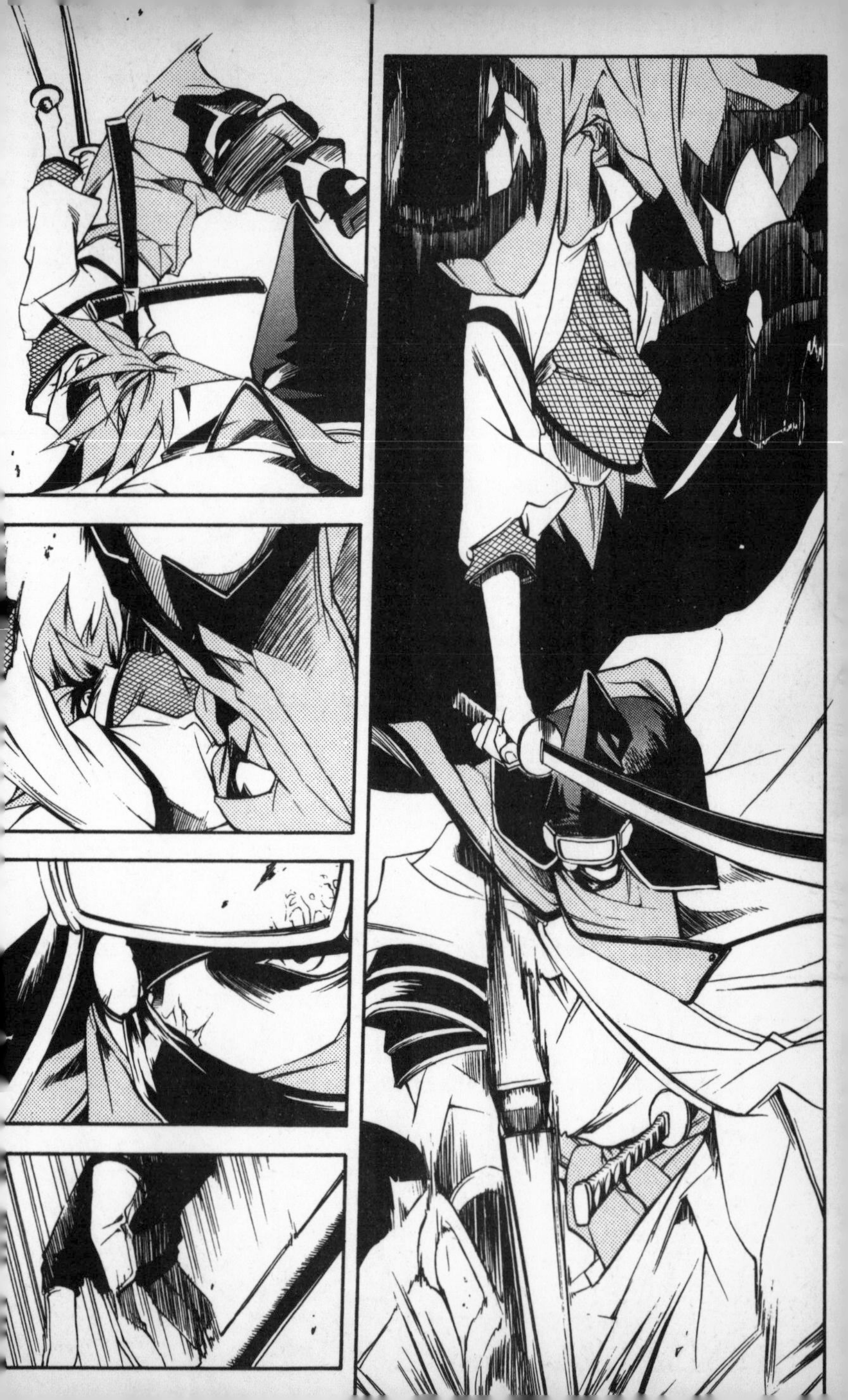

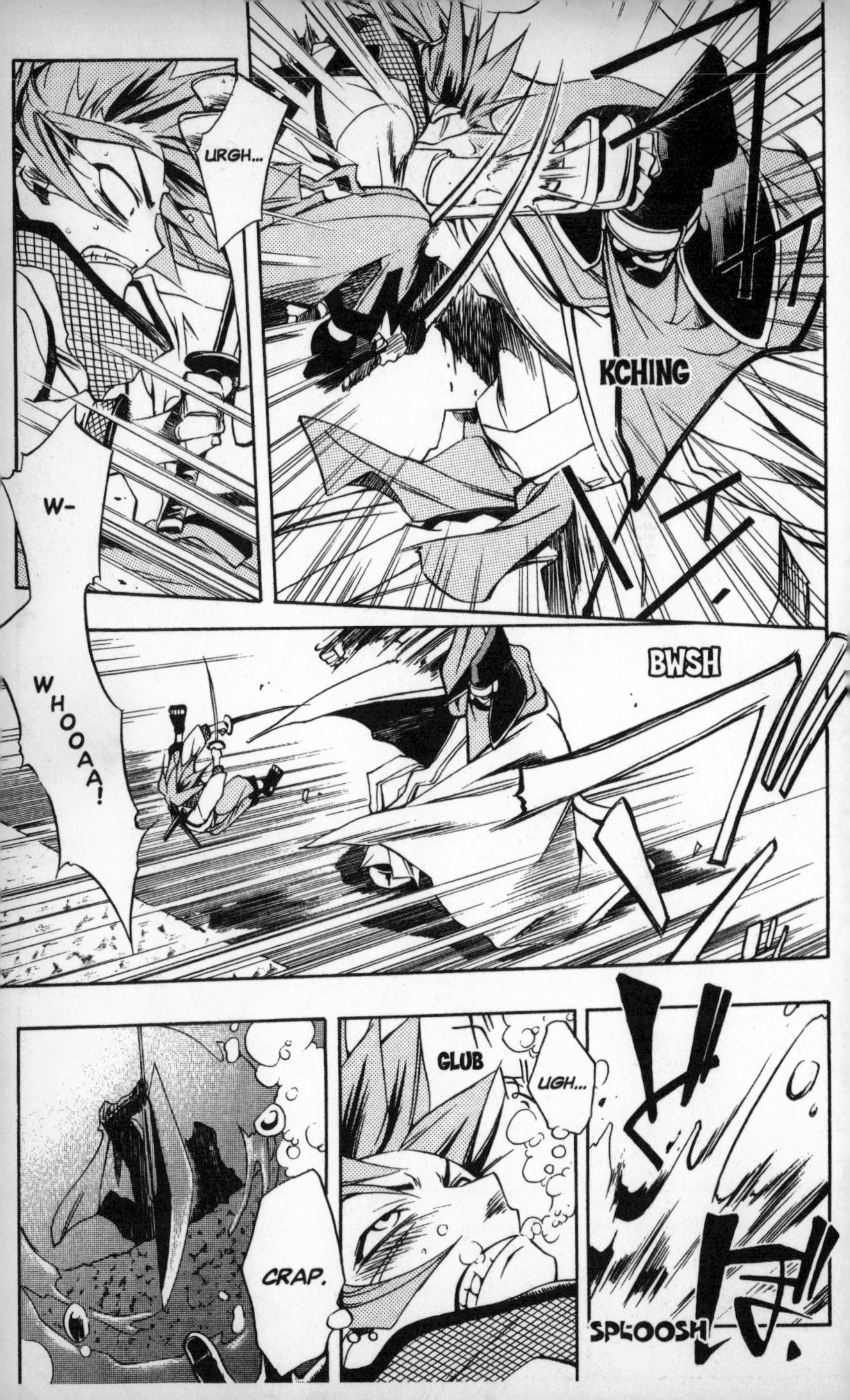
KCHING
URGH...
W-
BWSH
WHOOAA!
SPLOOSH
GLUB
UGH...
CRAP.

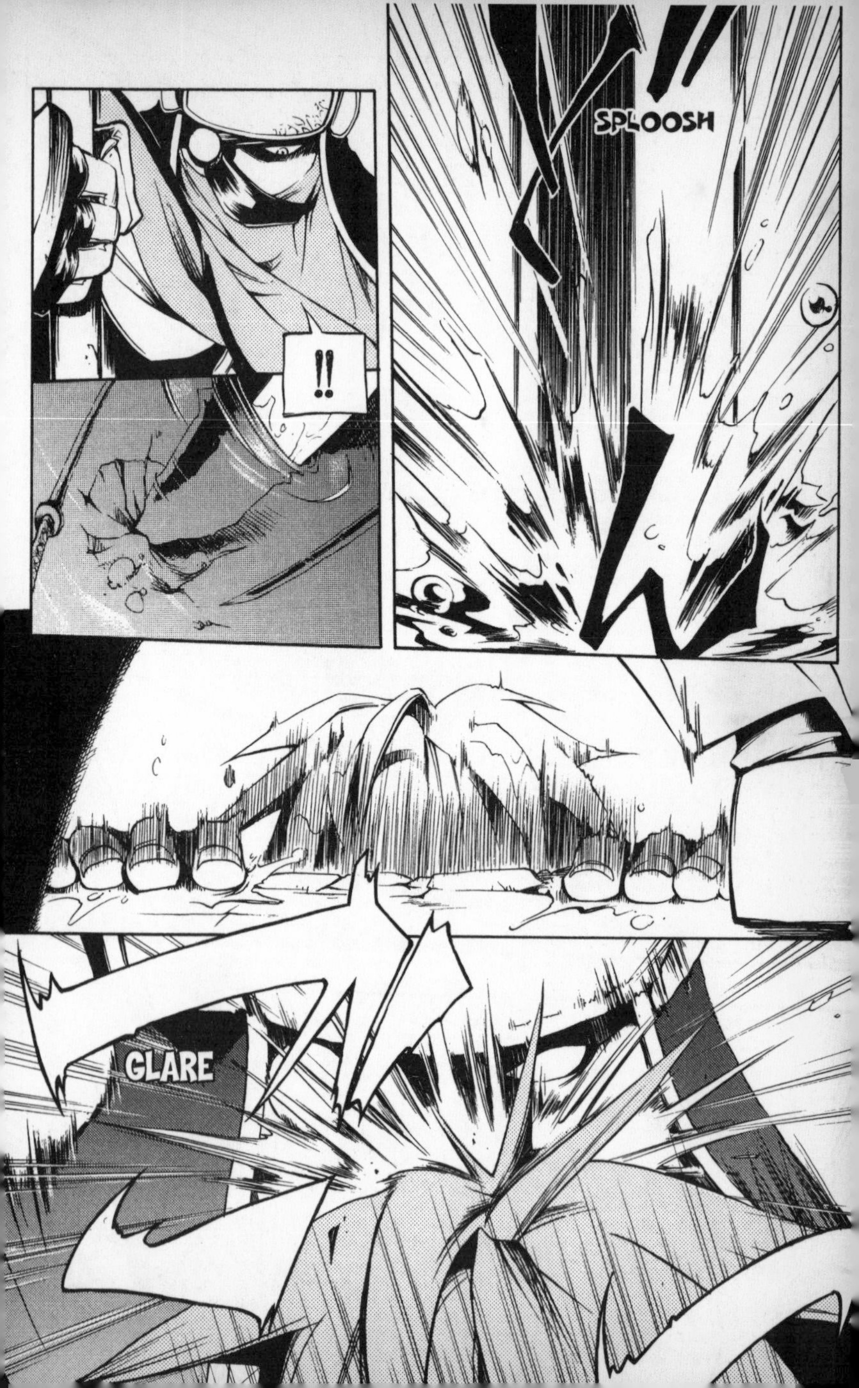
SPLOOSH
!!
GLARE

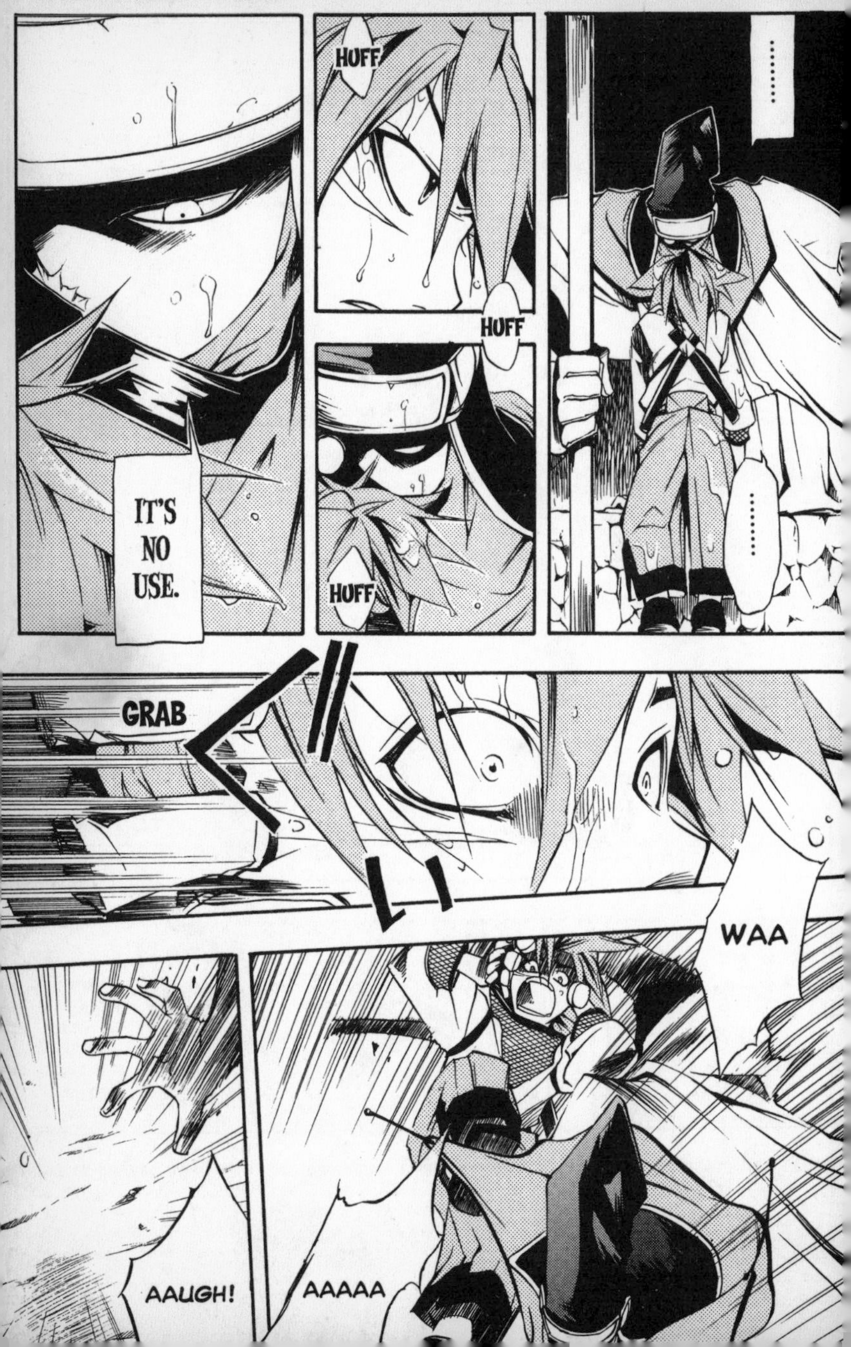
......
HUFF
HUFF
IT'S NO USE.
HUFF
......
GRAB
WAA
AAAAA
AAUGH!

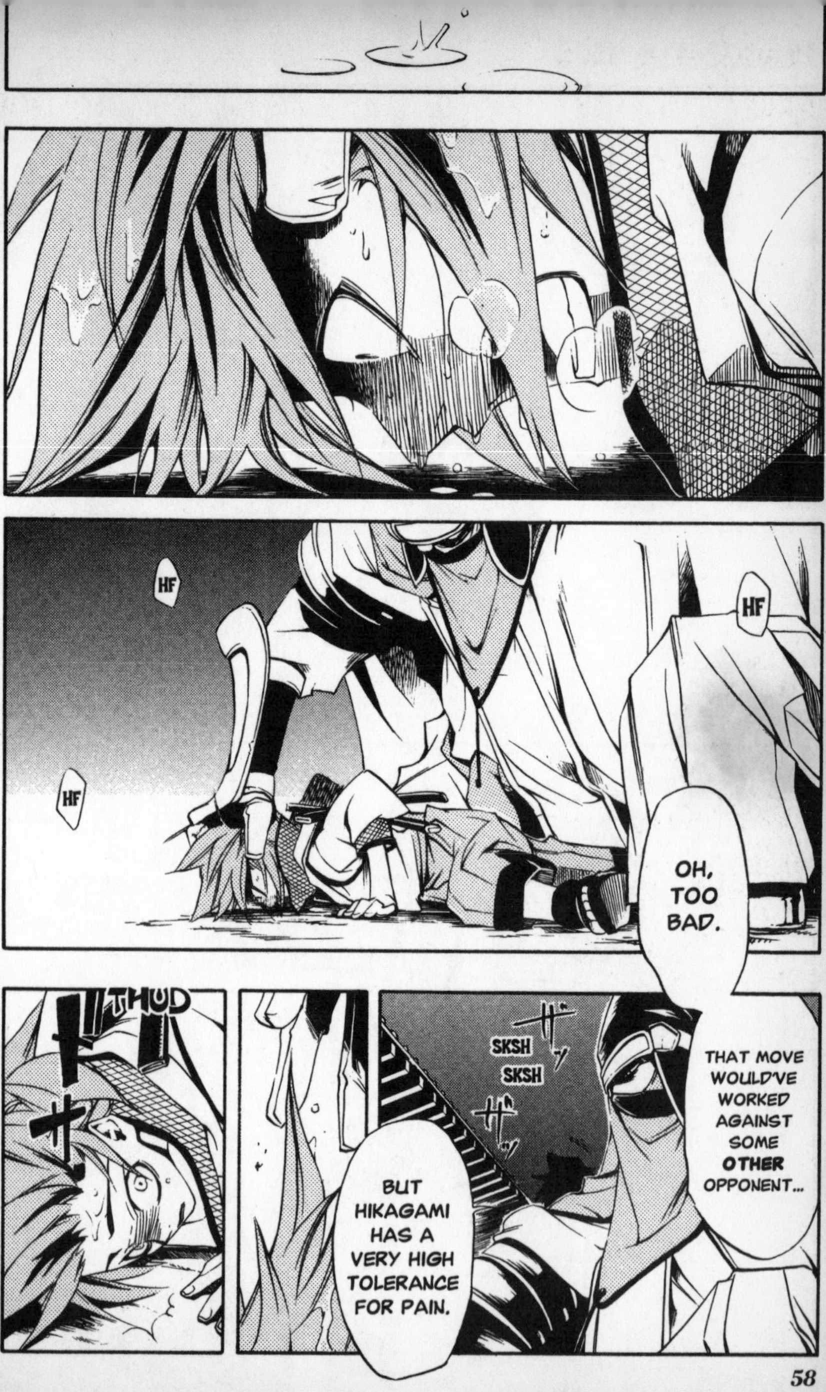
HF
HF
HF
OH, TOO BAD.
THAT MOVE WOULD'VE WORKED AGAINST SOME OTHER OPPONENT...
SKSH SKSH
BUT HIKAGAMI HAS A VERY HIGH TOLERANCE FOR PAIN.
THUD

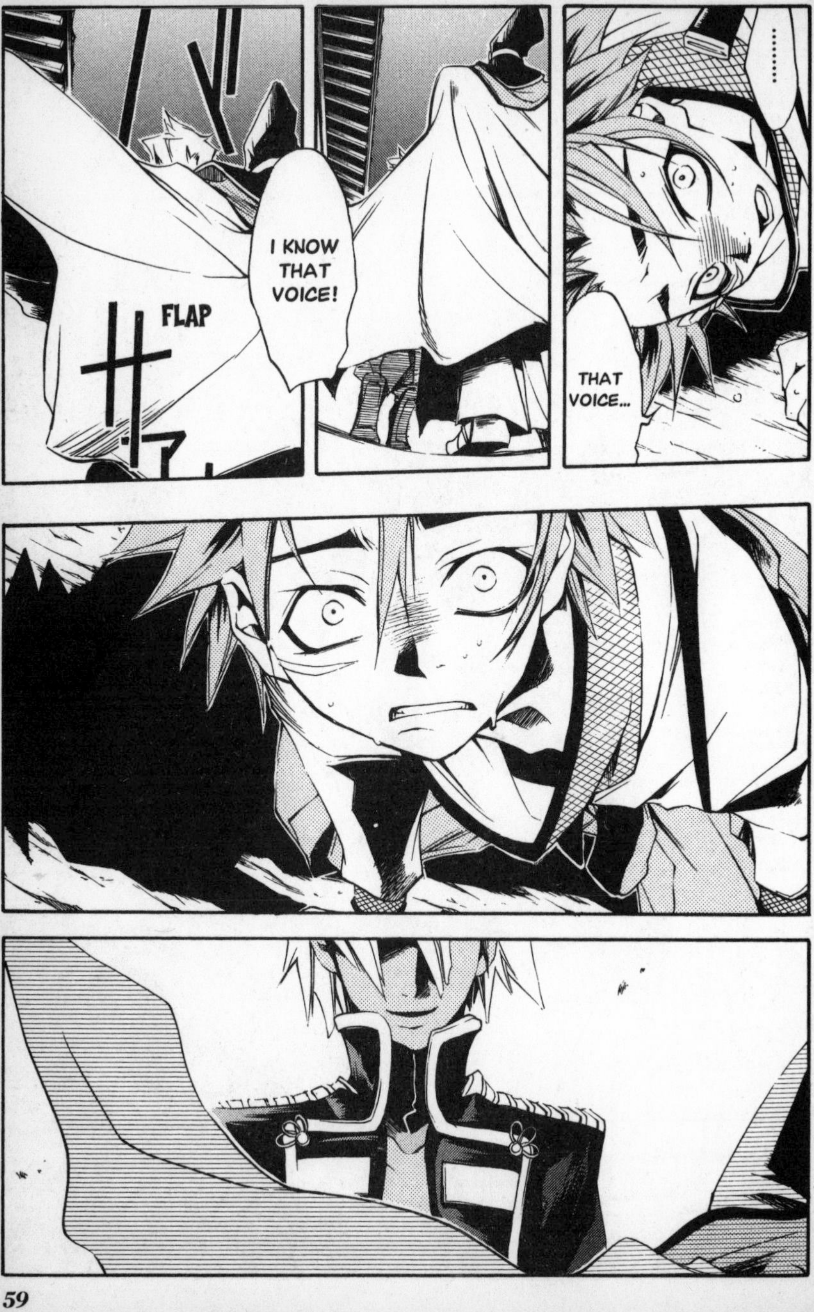
......
THAT VOICE...
I KNOW THAT VOICE!
FLAP

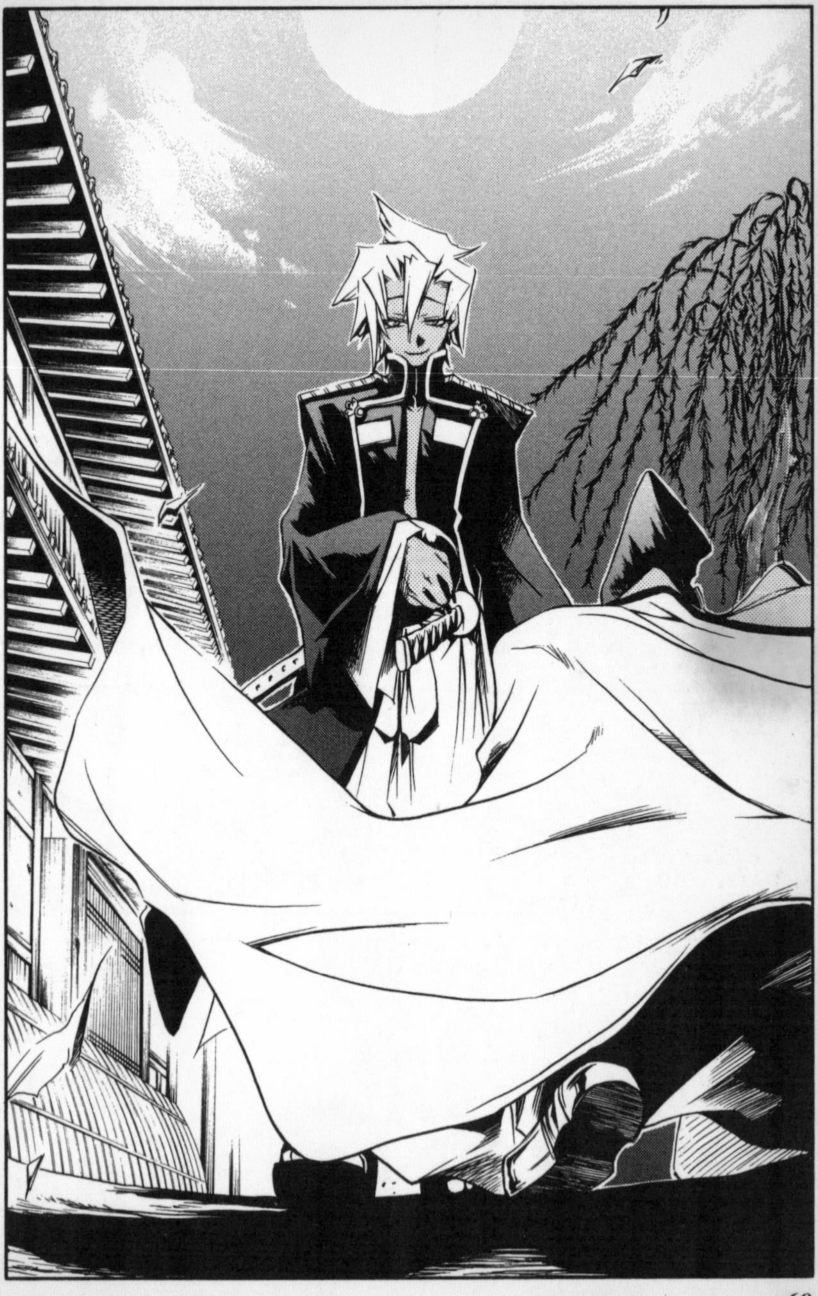

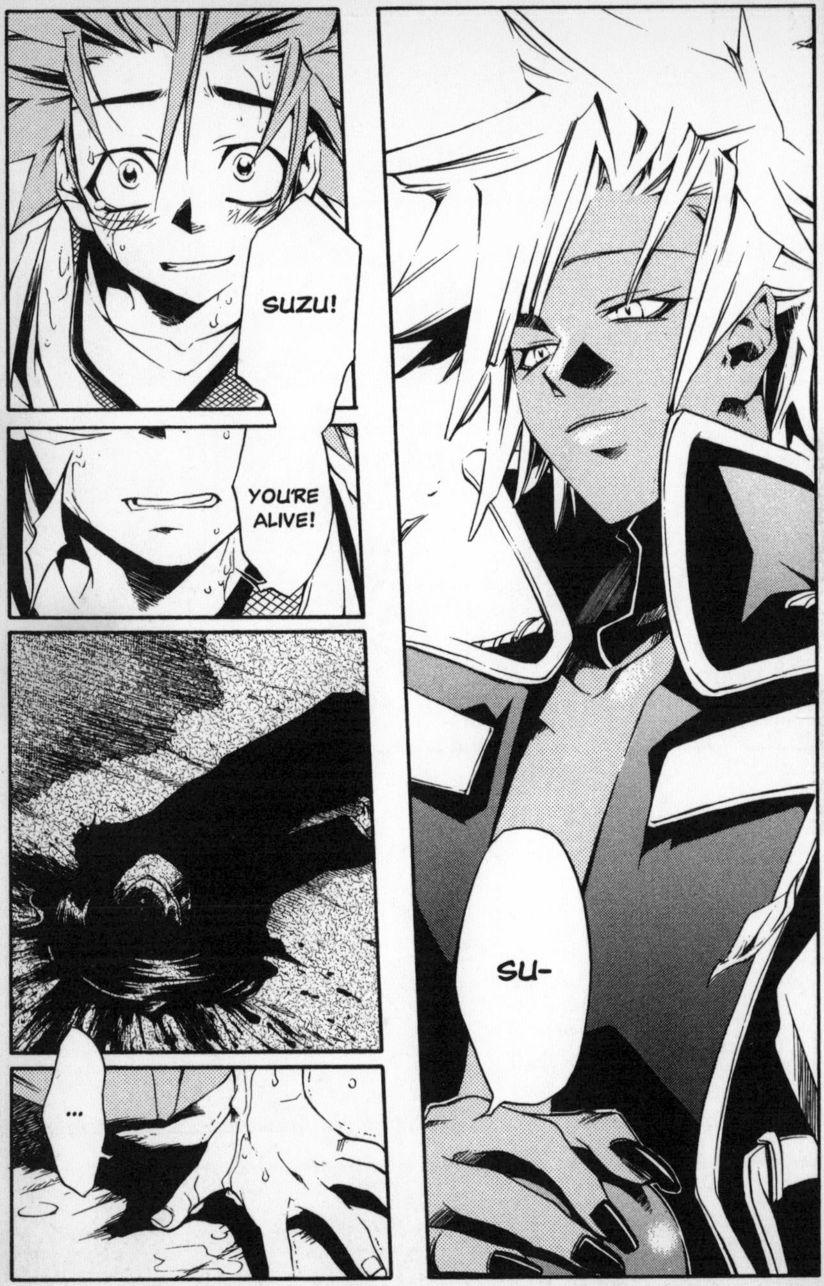
SUZU!
YOU'RE ALIVE!
SU-
...

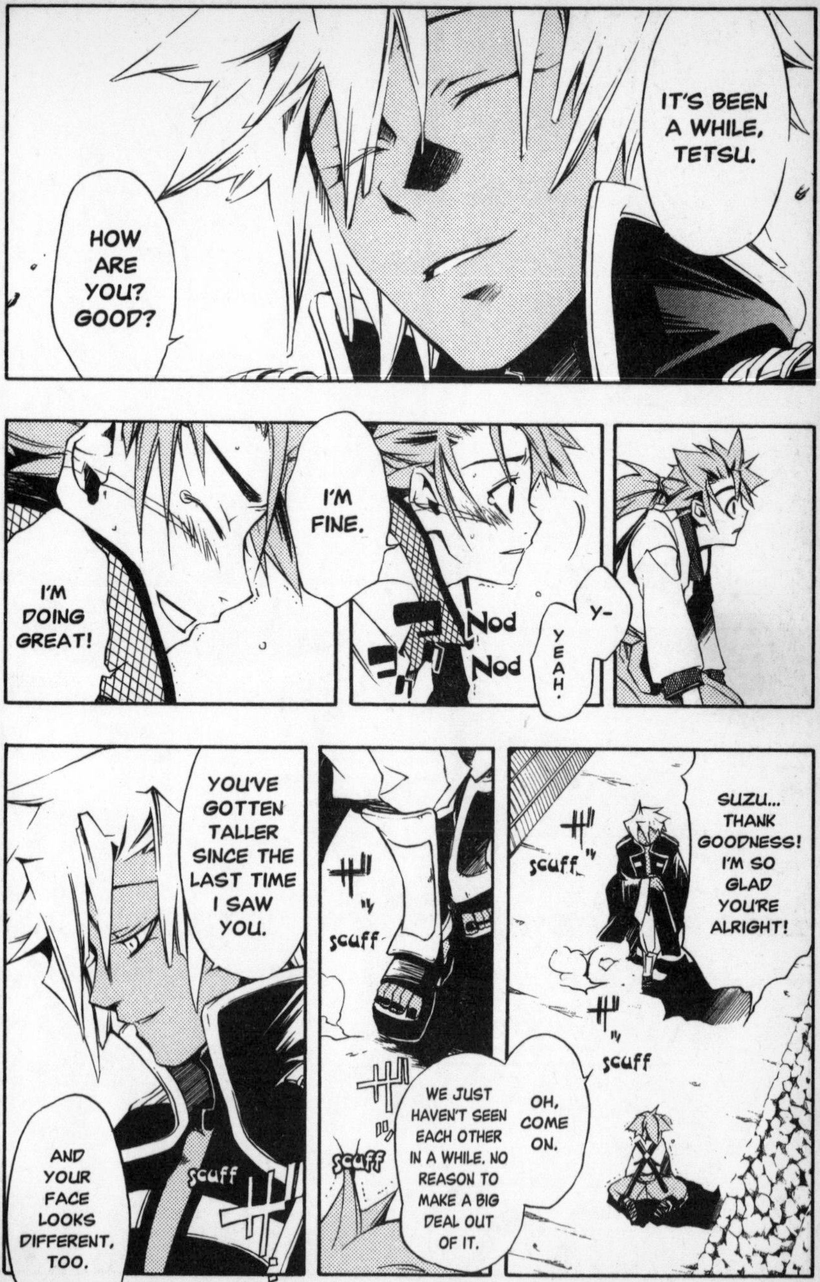
IT'S BEEN A WHILE, TETSU.
HOW ARE YOU? GOOD?
Y- YEAH.
I'M FINE.
Nod
Nod
I'M DOING GREAT!
SUZU... THANK GOODNESS! I'M SO GLAD YOU'RE ALRIGHT!
scuff
scuff
OH, COME ON.
WE JUST HAVEN'T SEEN EACH OTHER IN A WHILE. NO REASON TO MAKE A BIG DEAL OUT OF IT.
scuff
scuff
YOU'VE GOTTEN TALLER SINCE THE LAST TIME I SAW YOU.
scuff
AND YOUR FACE LOOKS DIFFERENT, TOO.

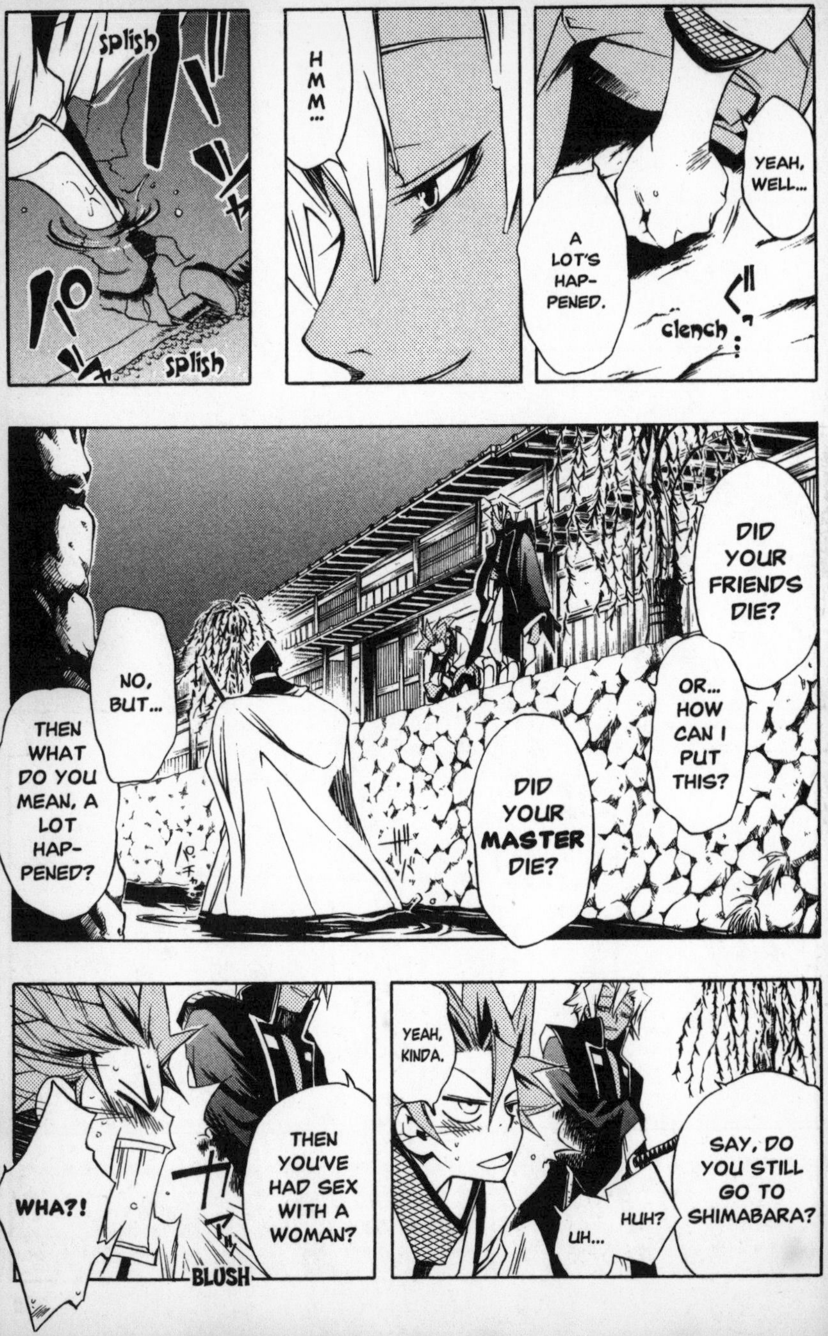
YEAH, WELL...
A LOT'S HAPPENED.
clench
HMM...
splish
splish
DID YOUR FRIENDS DIE?
OR... HOW CAN I PUT THIS?
DID YOUR MASTER DIE?
NO, BUT...
THEN WHAT DO YOU MEAN, A LOT HAPPENED?
SAY, DO YOU STILL GO TO SHIMABARA?
HUH?
UH...
YEAH, KINDA.
THEN YOU'VE HAD SEX WITH A WOMAN?
WHA?!
BLUSH

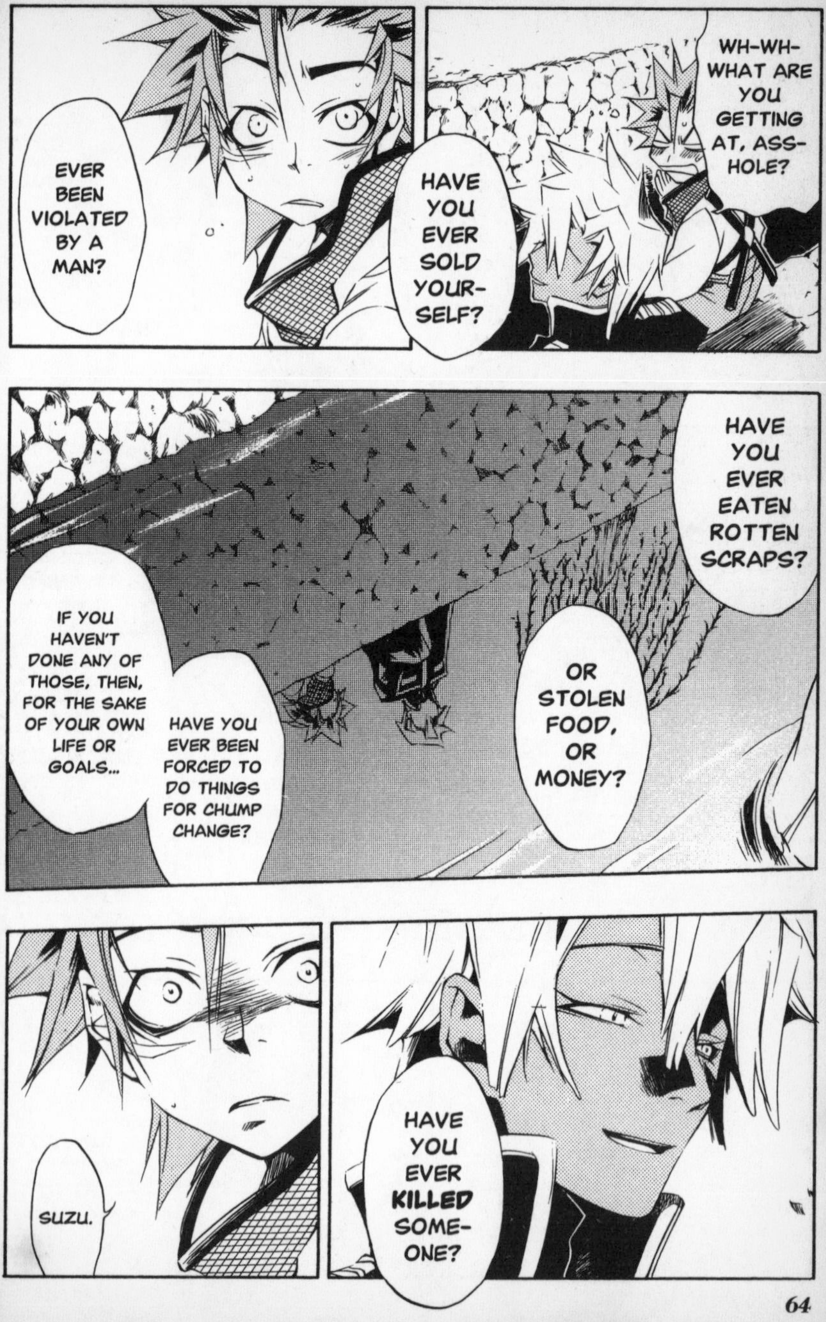
WH-WH-WHAT ARE YOU GETTING AT, ASS-HOLE?
HAVE YOU EVER SOLD YOUR-SELF?
EVER BEEN VIOLATED BY A MAN?
HAVE YOU EVER EATEN ROTTEN SCRAPS?
OR STOLEN FOOD, OR MONEY?
HAVE YOU EVER BEEN FORCED TO DO THINGS FOR CHUMP CHANGE?
IF YOU HAVEN'T DONE ANY OF THOSE, THEN, FOR THE SAKE OF YOUR OWN LIFE OR GOALS...
HAVE YOU EVER **KILLED** SOME-ONE?
SUZU.

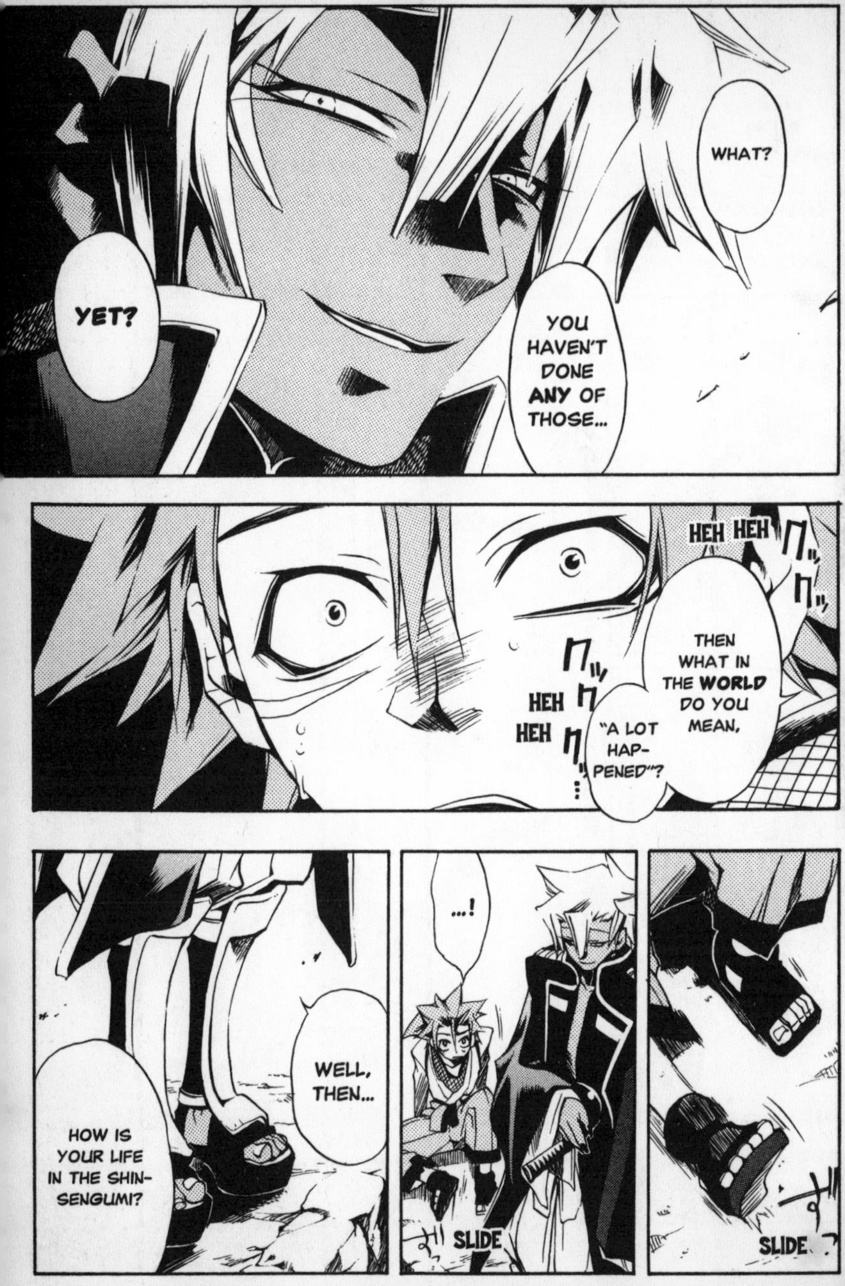
WHAT?
YOU HAVEN'T DONE ANY OF THOSE...
YET?
HEH HEH
THEN WHAT IN THE WORLD DO YOU MEAN,
"A LOT HAP-PENED"?
HEH HEH
SLIDE
...!
SLIDE
WELL, THEN...
HOW IS YOUR LIFE IN THE SHIN-SENGUMI?

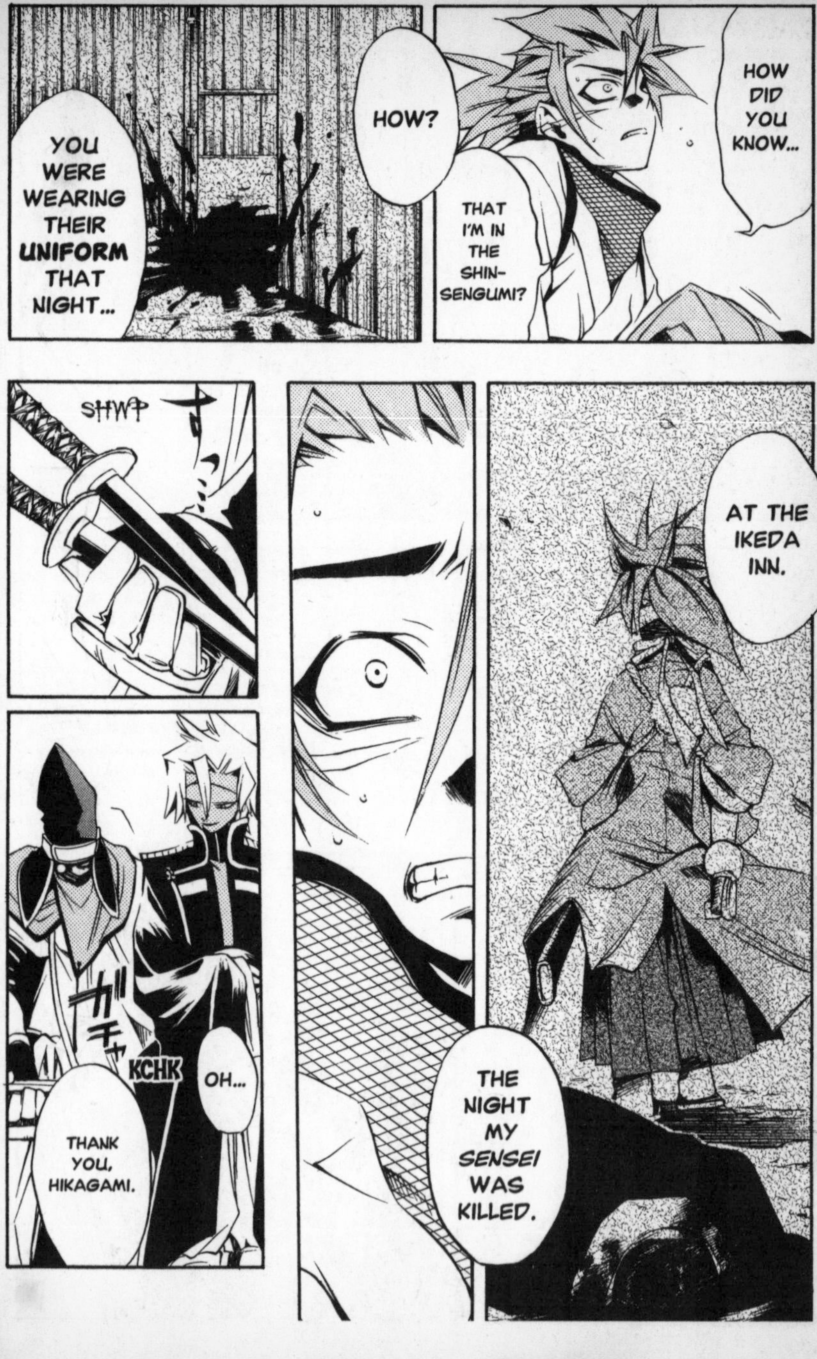
HOW DID YOU KNOW...
HOW?
THAT I'M IN THE SHIN-SENGUMI?
YOU WERE WEARING THEIR **UNIFORM** THAT NIGHT...
AT THE IKEDA INN.
THE NIGHT MY *SENSEI* WAS KILLED.
SHWP
ガチャ
KCHK
OH...
THANK YOU, HIKAGAMI.

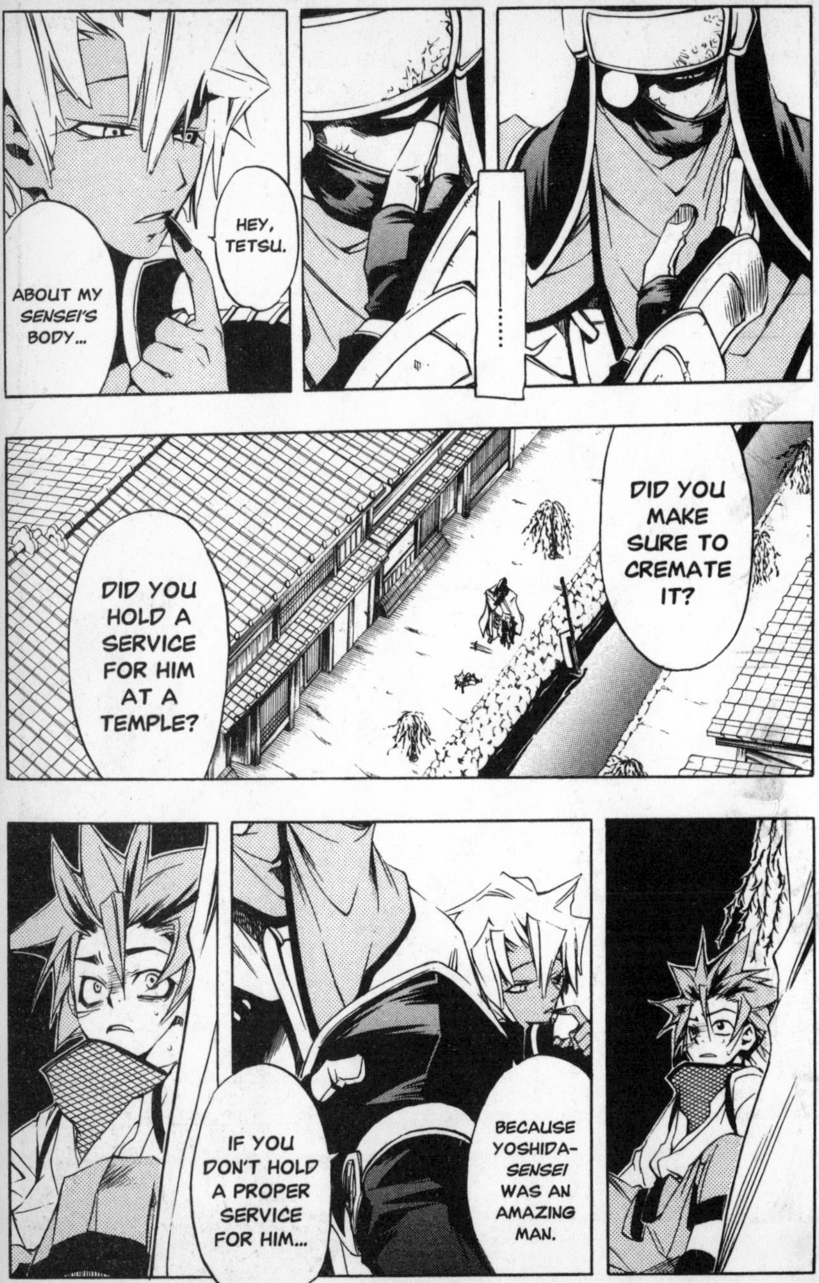
......
HEY, TETSU.
ABOUT MY SENSEI'S BODY...
DID YOU MAKE SURE TO CREMATE IT?
DID YOU HOLD A SERVICE FOR HIM AT A TEMPLE?
BECAUSE YOSHIDA-SENSEI WAS AN AMAZING MAN.
IF YOU DON'T HOLD A PROPER SERVICE FOR HIM...

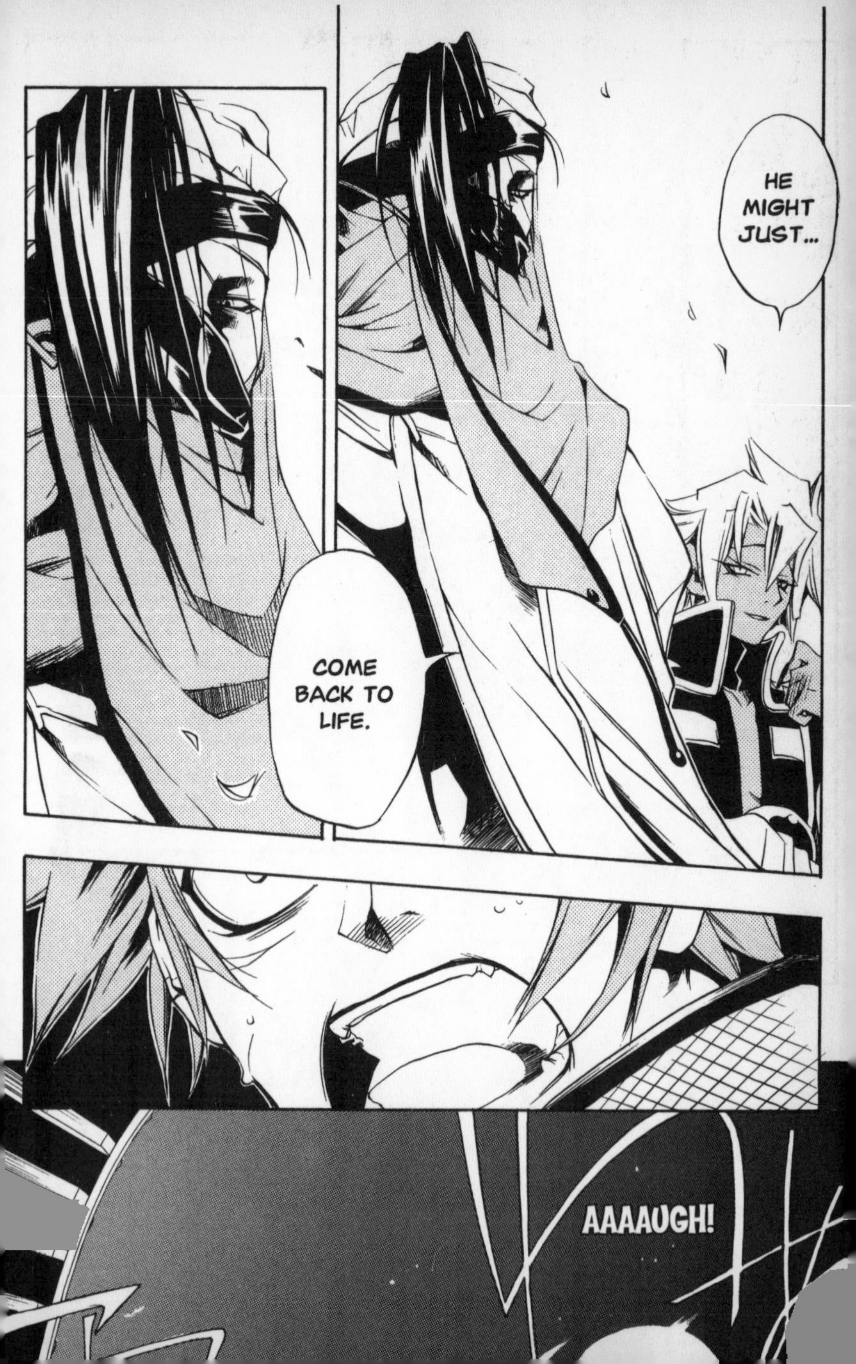
HE MIGHT JUST...
COME BACK TO LIFE.
AAAAUGH!

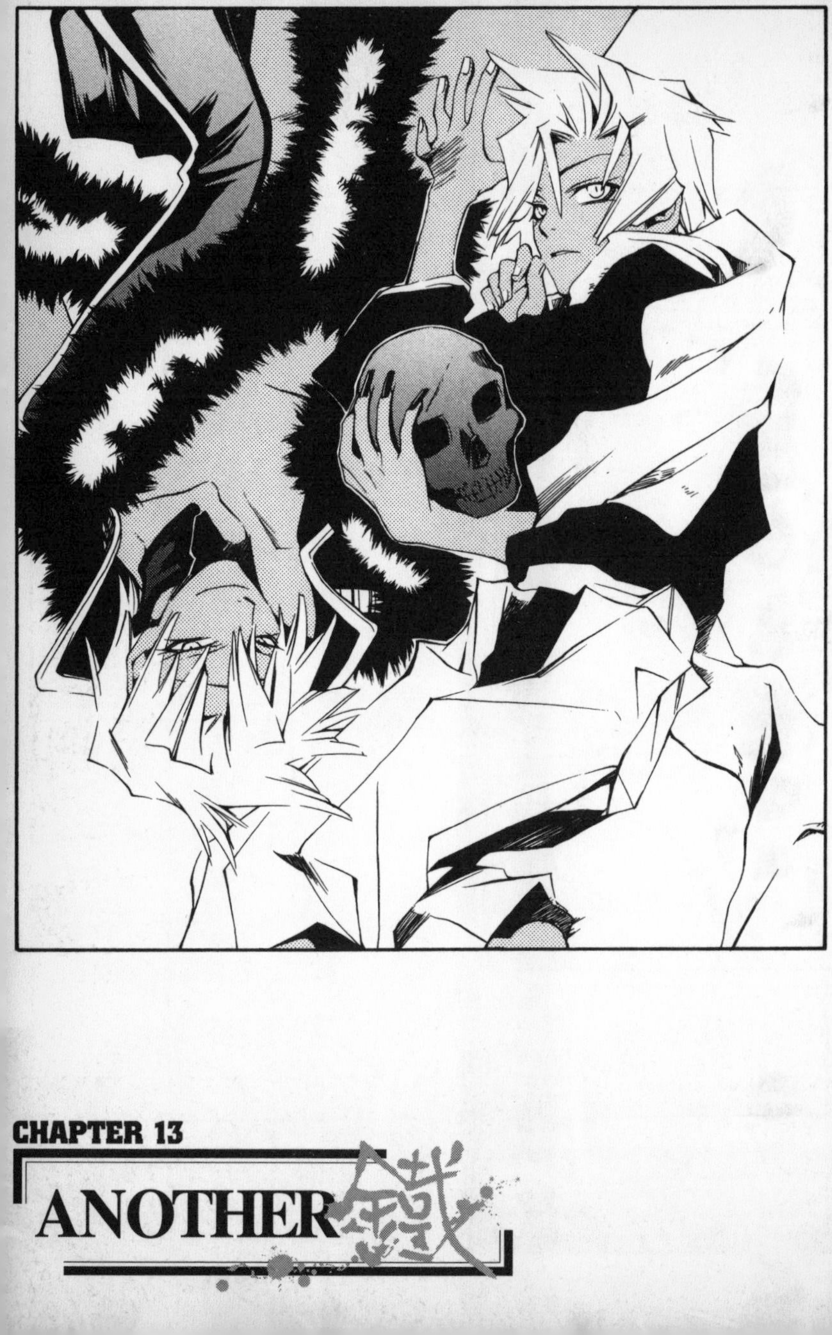

CHAPTER 13

ANOTHER 織

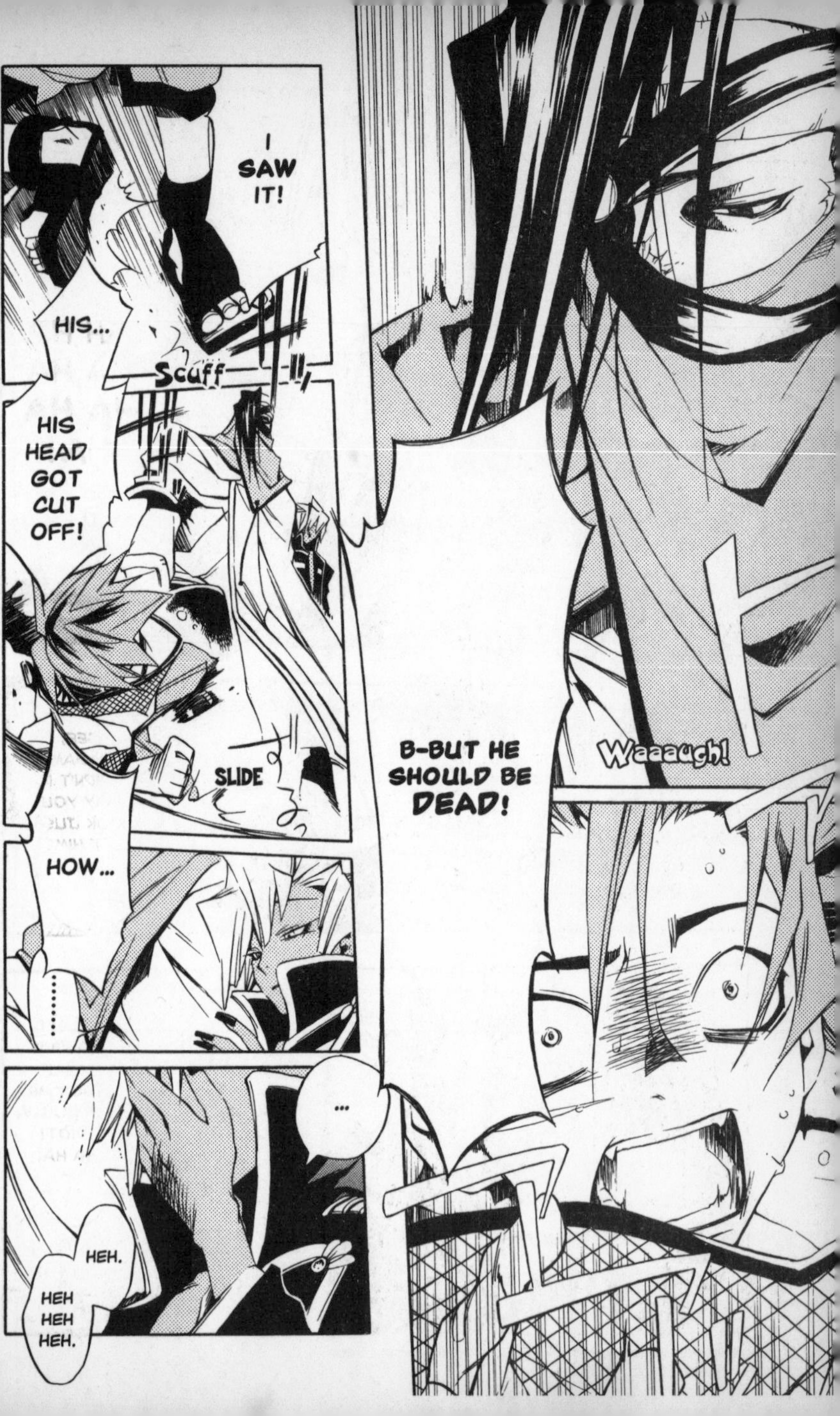
I SAW IT!
HIS...
Scuff
HIS HEAD GOT CUT OFF!
SLIDE
HOW...
......
B-BUT HE SHOULD BE DEAD!
Waaaugh!
...
HEH.
HEH HEH HEH.

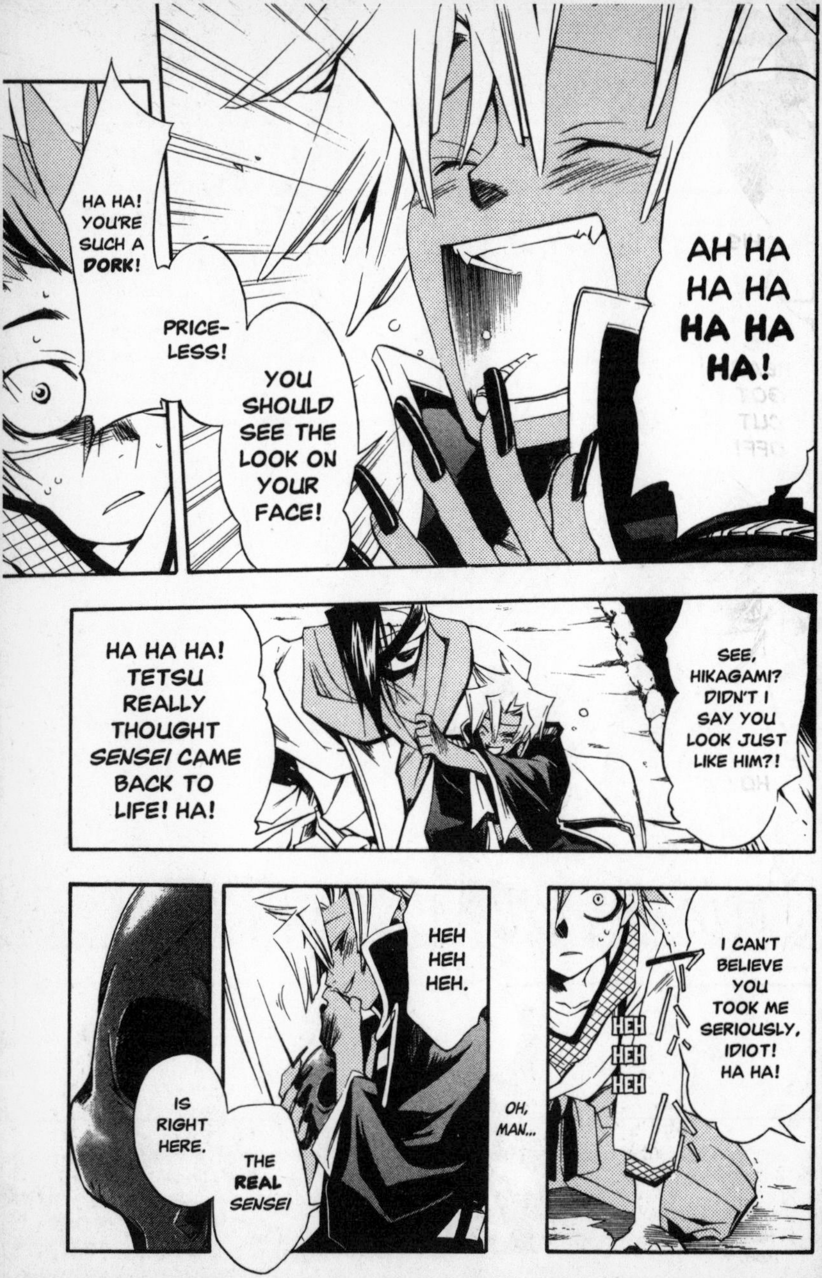
AH HA HA HA HA HA HA!
YOU SHOULD SEE THE LOOK ON YOUR FACE!
PRICE-LESS!
HA HA! YOU'RE SUCH A DORK!
SEE, HIKAGAMI? DIDN'T I SAY YOU LOOK JUST LIKE HIM?!
HA HA HA! TETSU REALLY THOUGHT SENSEI CAME BACK TO LIFE! HA!
I CAN'T BELIEVE YOU TOOK ME SERIOUSLY, IDIOT! HA HA!
HEH HEH HEH
OH, MAN...
HEH HEH HEH.
THE REAL SENSEI
IS RIGHT HERE.

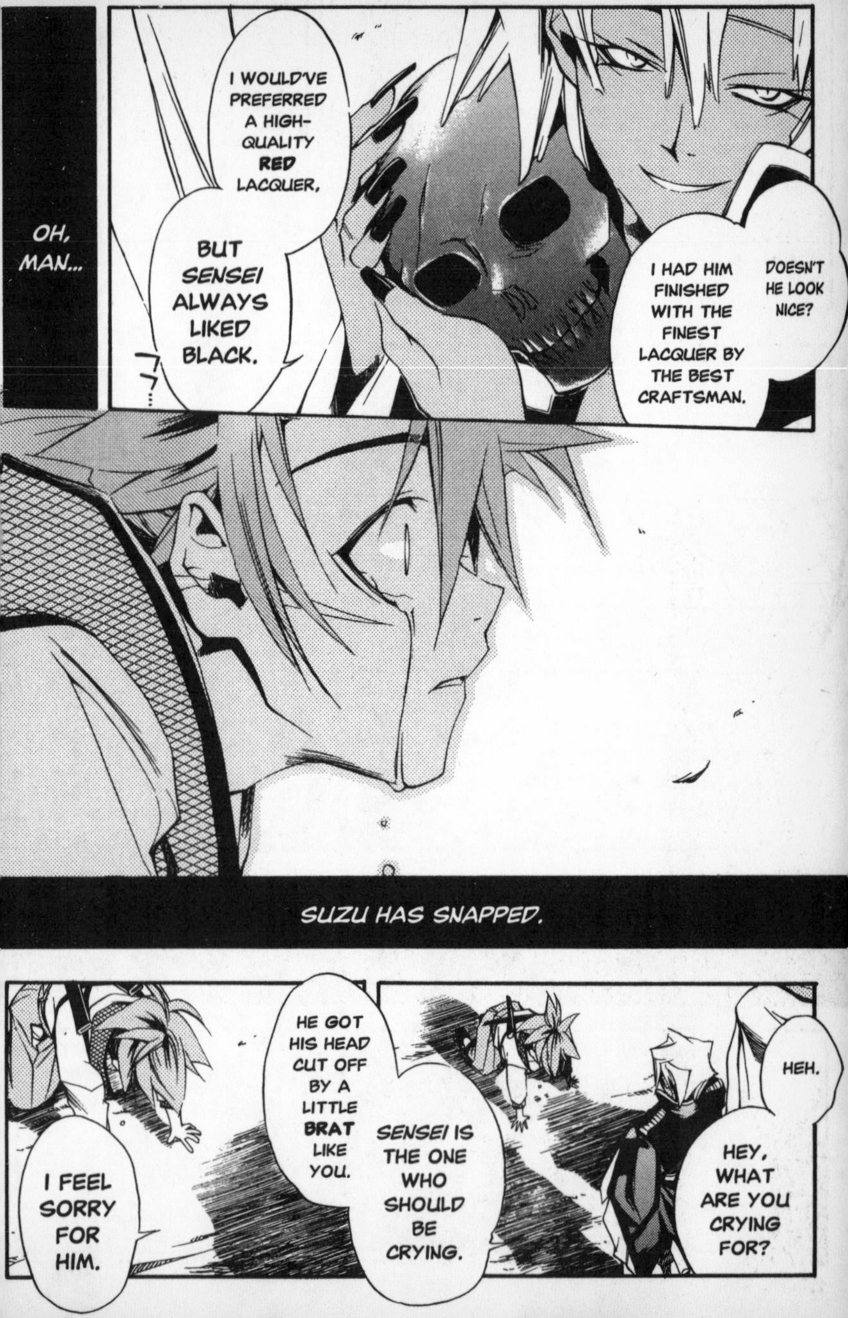
DOESN'T HE LOOK NICE?
I HAD HIM FINISHED WITH THE FINEST LACQUER BY THE BEST CRAFTSMAN.
I WOULD'VE PREFERRED A HIGH-QUALITY RED LACQUER,
BUT SENSEI ALWAYS LIKED BLACK.
OH, MAN...
SUZU HAS SNAPPED.
HEH.
HEY, WHAT ARE YOU CRYING FOR?
SENSEI IS THE ONE WHO SHOULD BE CRYING.
HE GOT HIS HEAD CUT OFF BY A LITTLE BRAT LIKE YOU.
I FEEL SORRY FOR HIM.

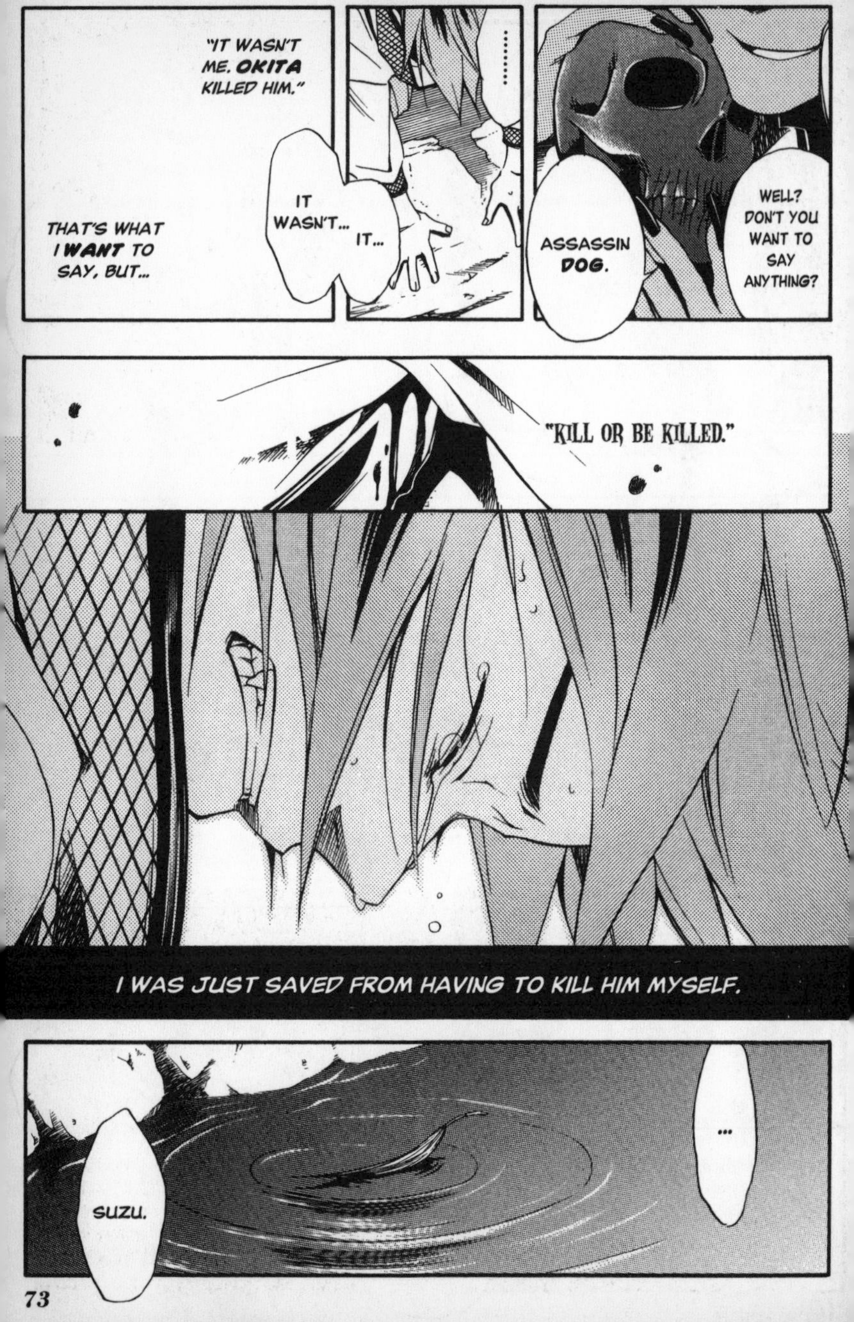
"IT WASN'T ME. OKITA KILLED HIM."
THAT'S WHAT I WANT TO SAY, BUT...
IT WASN'T... IT...
......
WELL? DON'T YOU WANT TO SAY ANYTHING?
ASSASSIN DOG.
"KILL OR BE KILLED."
I WAS JUST SAVED FROM HAVING TO KILL HIM MYSELF.
...
SUZU.

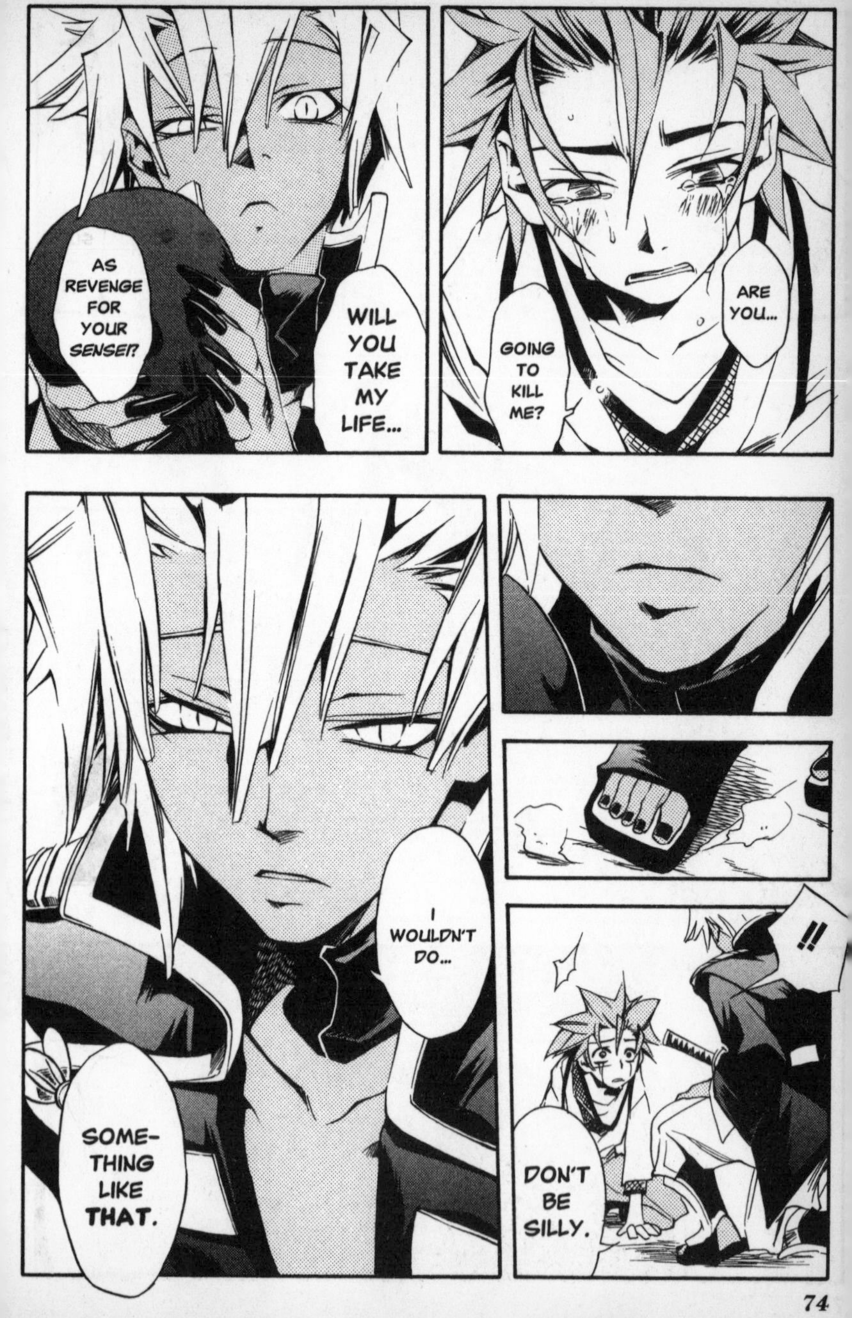
ARE YOU...
GOING TO KILL ME?
WILL YOU TAKE MY LIFE...
AS REVENGE FOR YOUR SENSEI?
!!
DON'T BE SILLY.
I WOULDN'T DO...
SOME-THING LIKE THAT.

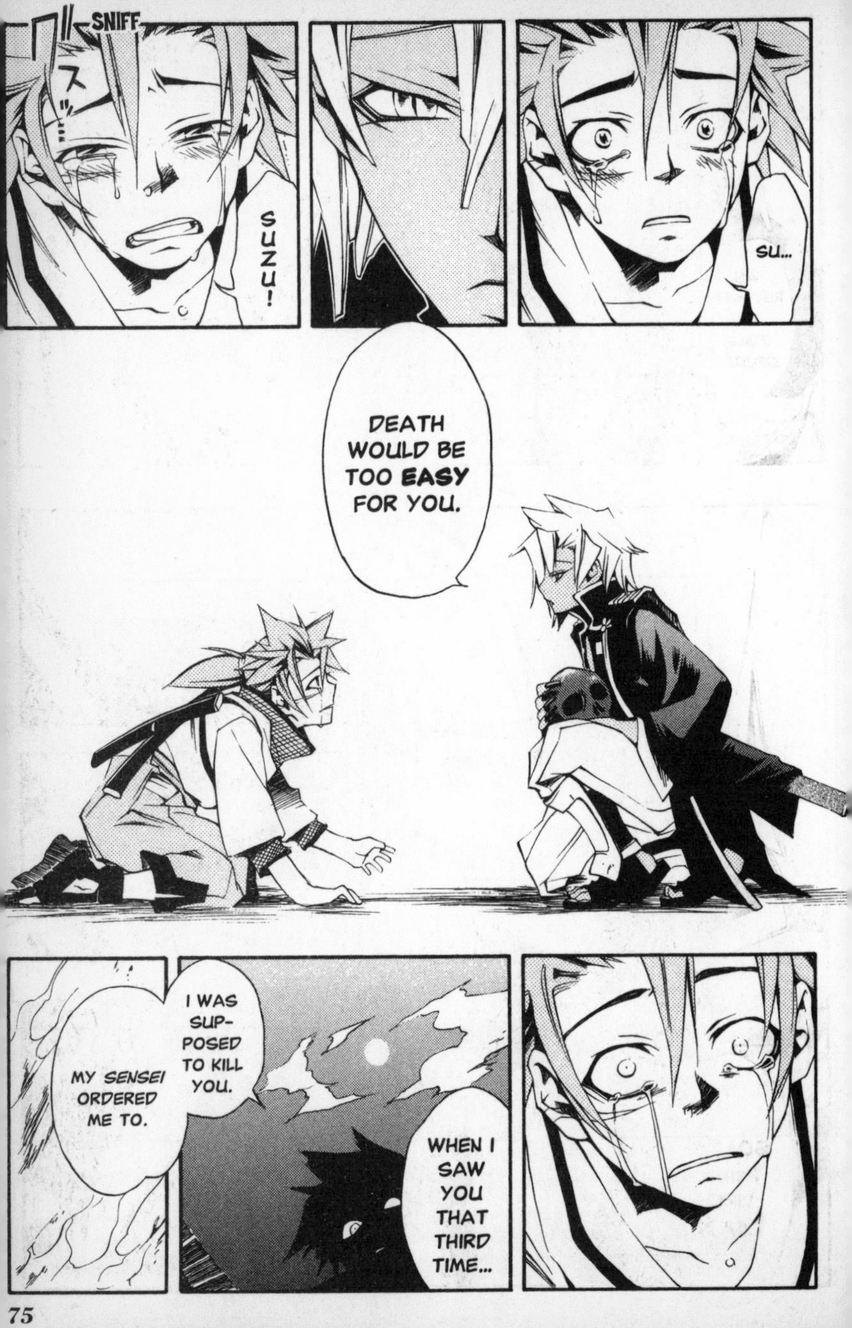
SU...
SNIFF
スッ
SUZU!
DEATH WOULD BE TOO EASY FOR YOU.
I WAS SUP-POSED TO KILL YOU.
WHEN I SAW YOU THAT THIRD TIME...
MY SENSEI ORDERED ME TO.

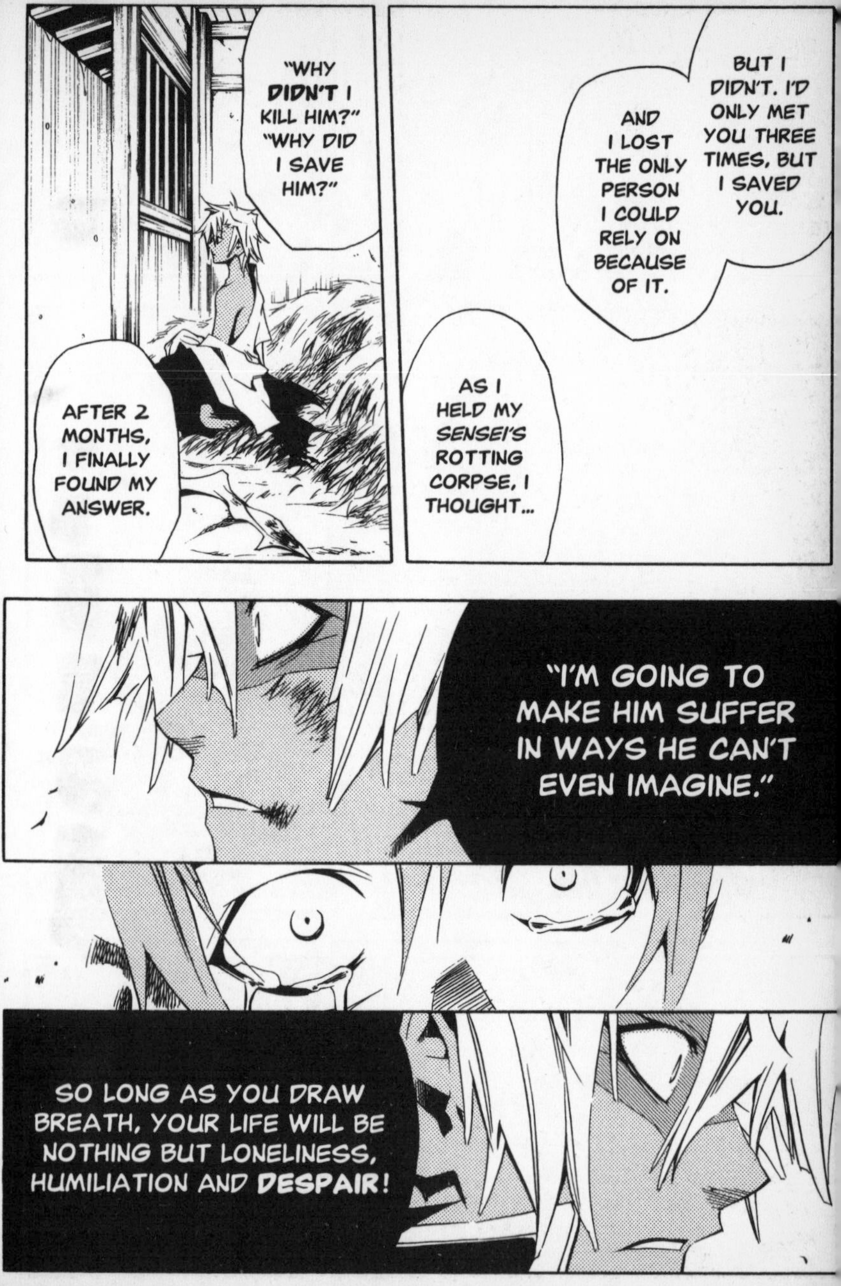

BUT I DIDN'T. I'D ONLY MET YOU THREE TIMES, BUT I SAVED YOU.
AND I LOST THE ONLY PERSON I COULD RELY ON BECAUSE OF IT.
AS I HELD MY *SENSEI'S* ROTTING CORPSE, I THOUGHT...
"WHY **DIDN'T** I KILL HIM?" "WHY DID I SAVE HIM?"
AFTER 2 MONTHS, I FINALLY FOUND MY ANSWER.
"I'M GOING TO MAKE HIM SUFFER IN WAYS HE CAN'T EVEN IMAGINE."
SO LONG AS YOU DRAW BREATH, YOUR LIFE WILL BE NOTHING BUT LONELINESS, HUMILIATION AND **DESPAIR**!

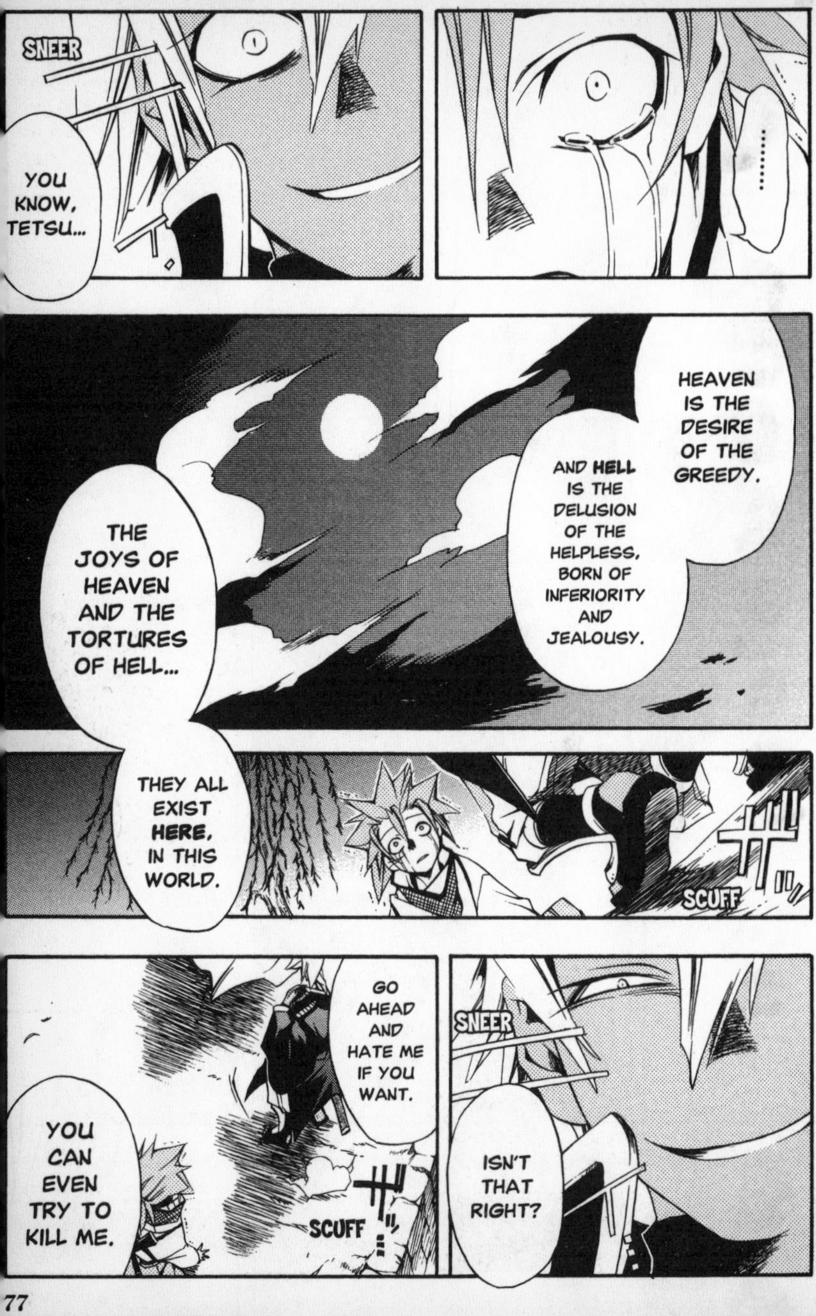
......
SNEER
YOU KNOW, TETSU...
HEAVEN IS THE DESIRE OF THE GREEDY.
AND HELL IS THE DELUSION OF THE HELPLESS, BORN OF INFERIORITY AND JEALOUSY.
THE JOYS OF HEAVEN AND THE TORTURES OF HELL...
SCUFF
THEY ALL EXIST HERE, IN THIS WORLD.
SNEER
ISN'T THAT RIGHT?
GO AHEAD AND HATE ME IF YOU WANT.
SCUFF
YOU CAN EVEN TRY TO KILL ME.

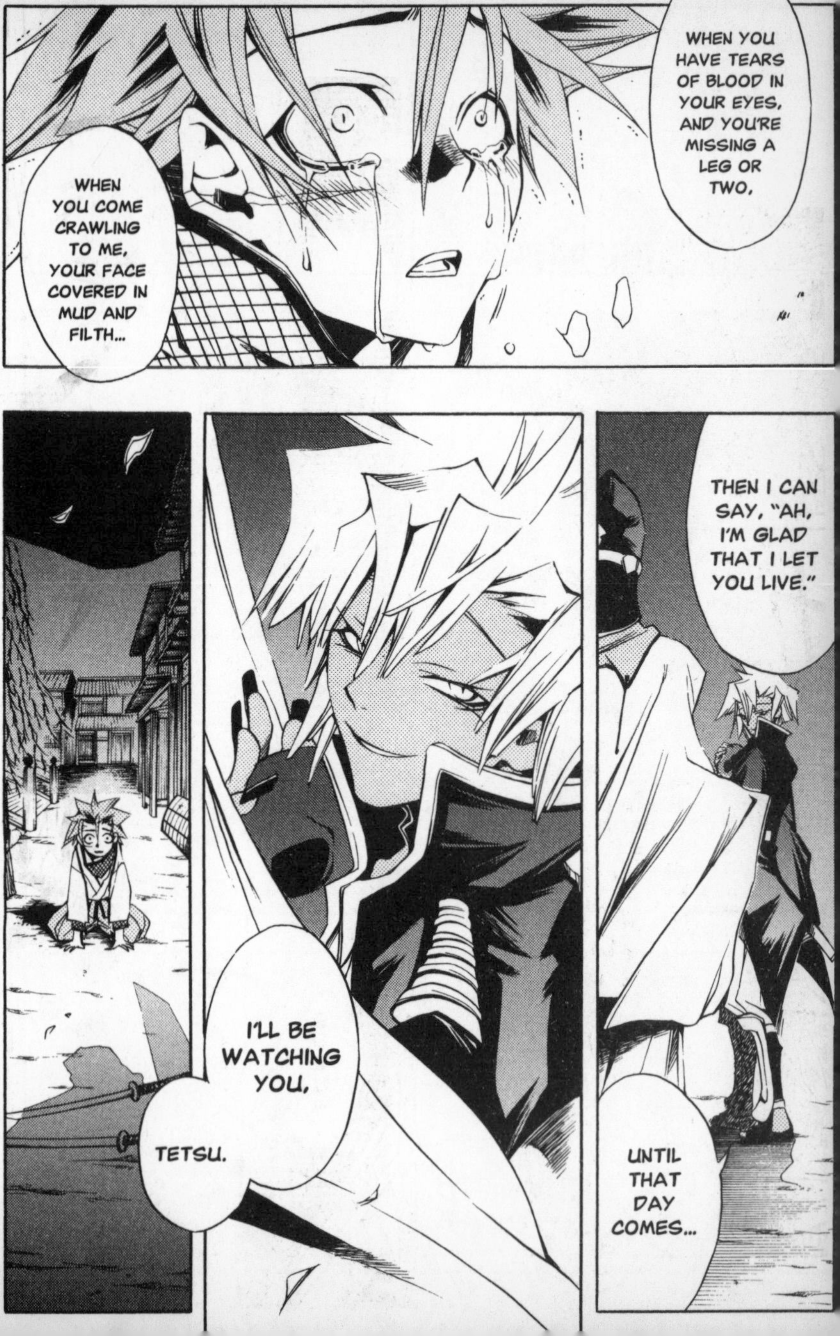
WHEN YOU HAVE TEARS OF BLOOD IN YOUR EYES, AND YOU'RE MISSING A LEG OR TWO,
WHEN YOU COME CRAWLING TO ME, YOUR FACE COVERED IN MUD AND FILTH...
THEN I CAN SAY, "AH, I'M GLAD THAT I LET YOU LIVE."
UNTIL THAT DAY COMES...
I'LL BE WATCHING YOU,
TETSU.

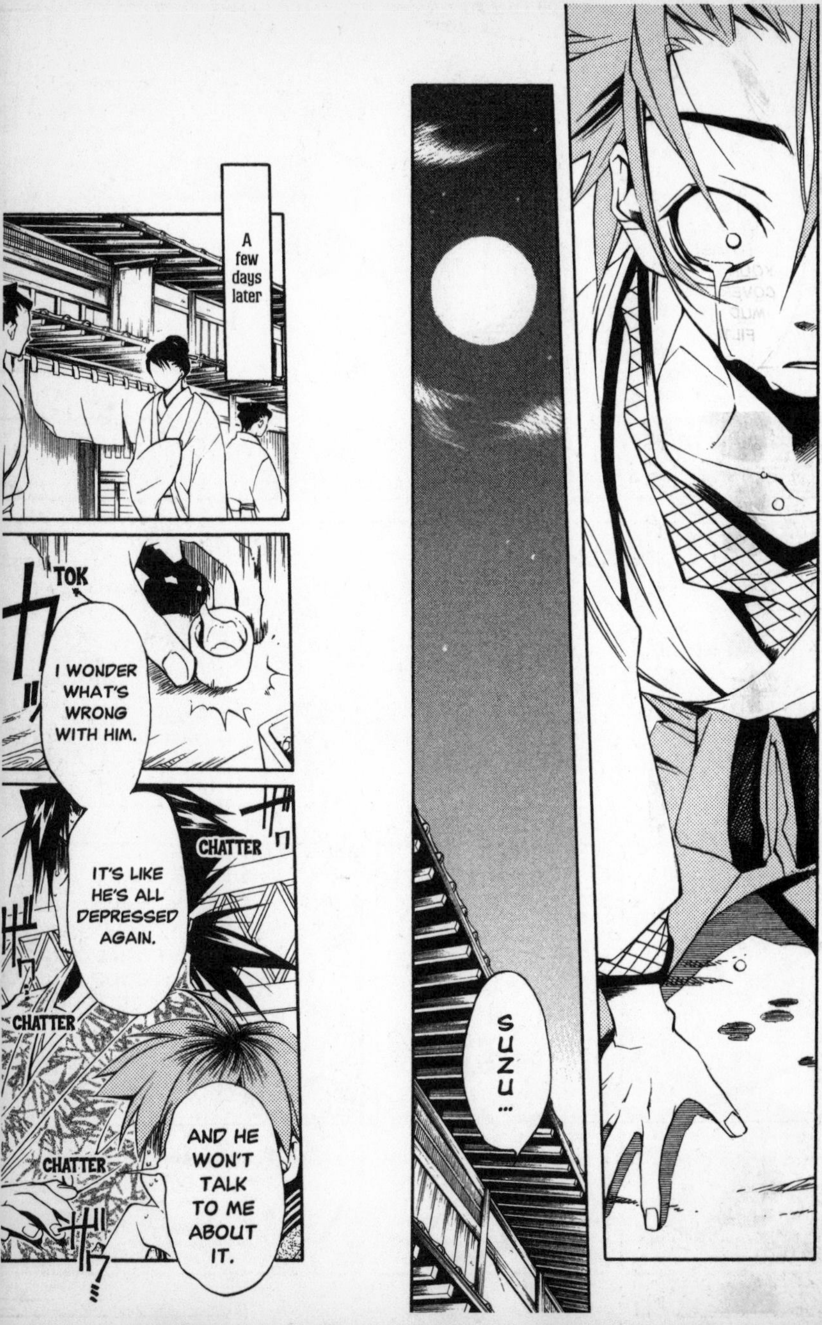
SUZU...
A few days later
TOK
I WONDER WHAT'S WRONG WITH HIM.
CHATTER
IT'S LIKE HE'S ALL DEPRESSED AGAIN.
CHATTER
CHATTER
AND HE WON'T TALK TO ME ABOUT IT.

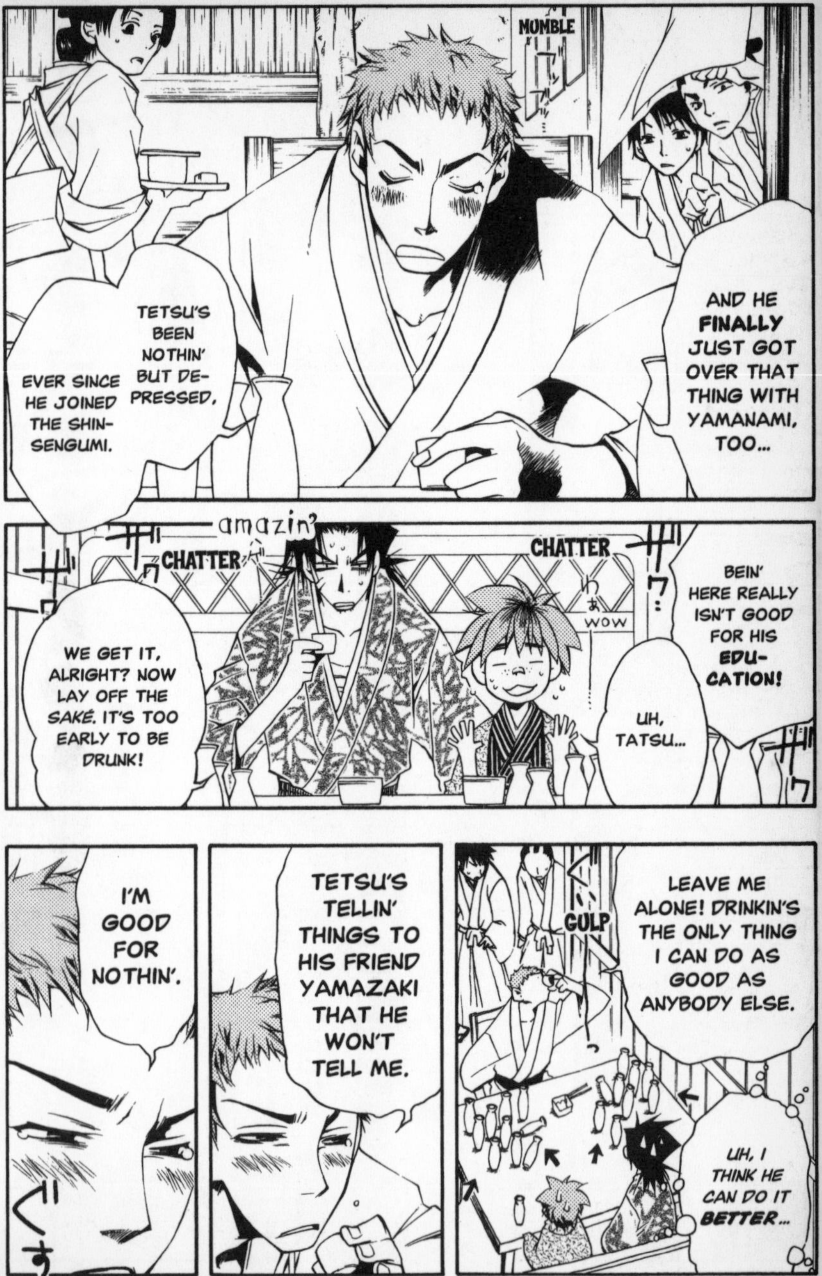
MUMBLE
TETSU'S BEEN NOTHIN' BUT DE-PRESSED,
EVER SINCE HE JOINED THE SHIN-SENGUMI.
AND HE FINALLY JUST GOT OVER THAT THING WITH YAMANAMI, TOO...
CHATTER
BEIN' HERE REALLY ISN'T GOOD FOR HIS EDU-CATION!
WOW
UH, TATSU...
amazin'
CHATTER
WE GET IT, ALRIGHT? NOW LAY OFF THE SAKÉ. IT'S TOO EARLY TO BE DRUNK!
LEAVE ME ALONE! DRINKIN'S THE ONLY THING I CAN DO AS GOOD AS ANYBODY ELSE.
GULP
UH, I THINK HE CAN DO IT BETTER...
TETSU'S TELLIN' THINGS TO HIS FRIEND YAMAZAKI THAT HE WON'T TELL ME.
I'M GOOD FOR NOTHIN'.
SNIFF

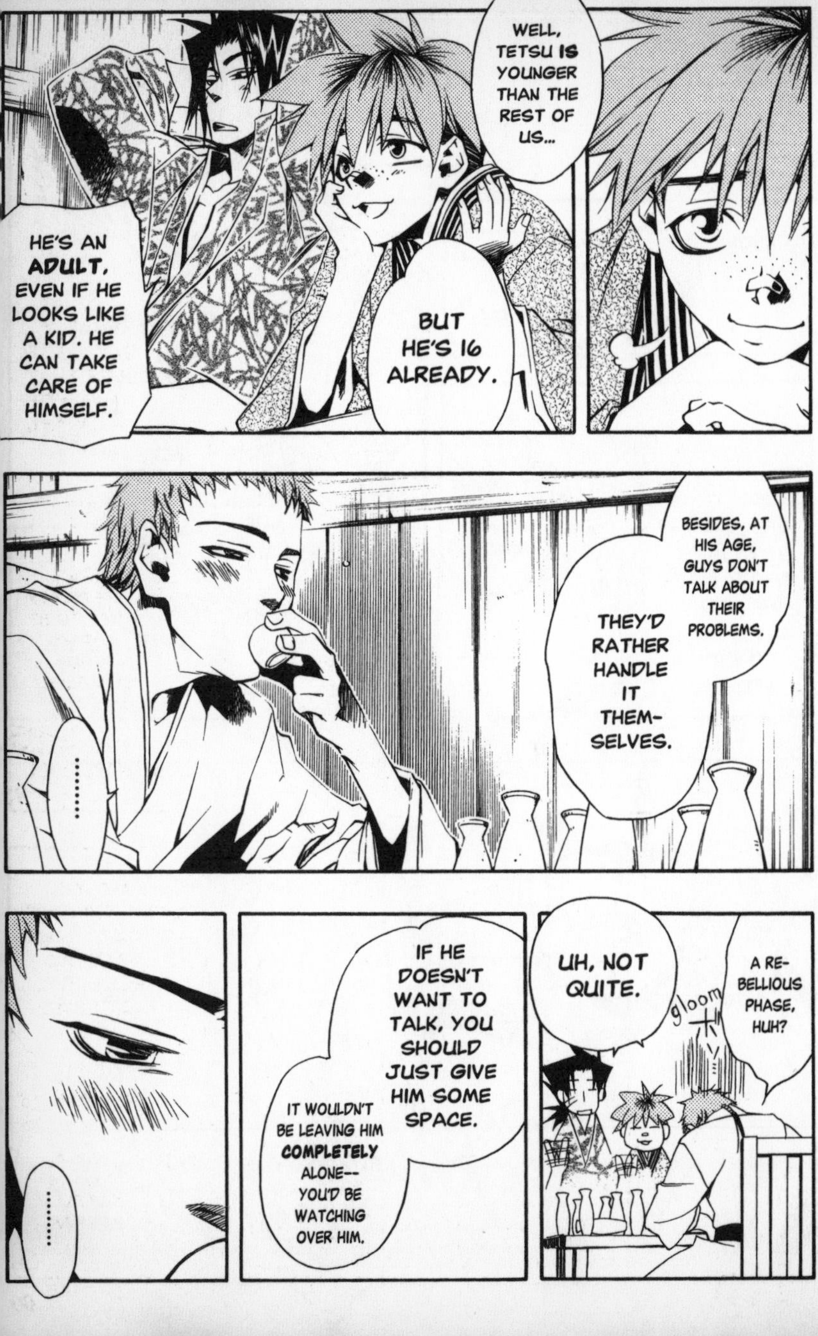
WELL, TETSU IS YOUNGER THAN THE REST OF US...
BUT HE'S 16 ALREADY.
HE'S AN ADULT, EVEN IF HE LOOKS LIKE A KID. HE CAN TAKE CARE OF HIMSELF.
BESIDES, AT HIS AGE, GUYS DON'T TALK ABOUT THEIR PROBLEMS.
THEY'D RATHER HANDLE IT THEM-SELVES.
....
A RE-BELLIOUS PHASE, HUH?
gloom
UH, NOT QUITE.
IF HE DOESN'T WANT TO TALK, YOU SHOULD JUST GIVE HIM SOME SPACE.
IT WOULDN'T BE LEAVING HIM COMPLETELY ALONE-- YOU'D BE WATCHING OVER HIM.
....

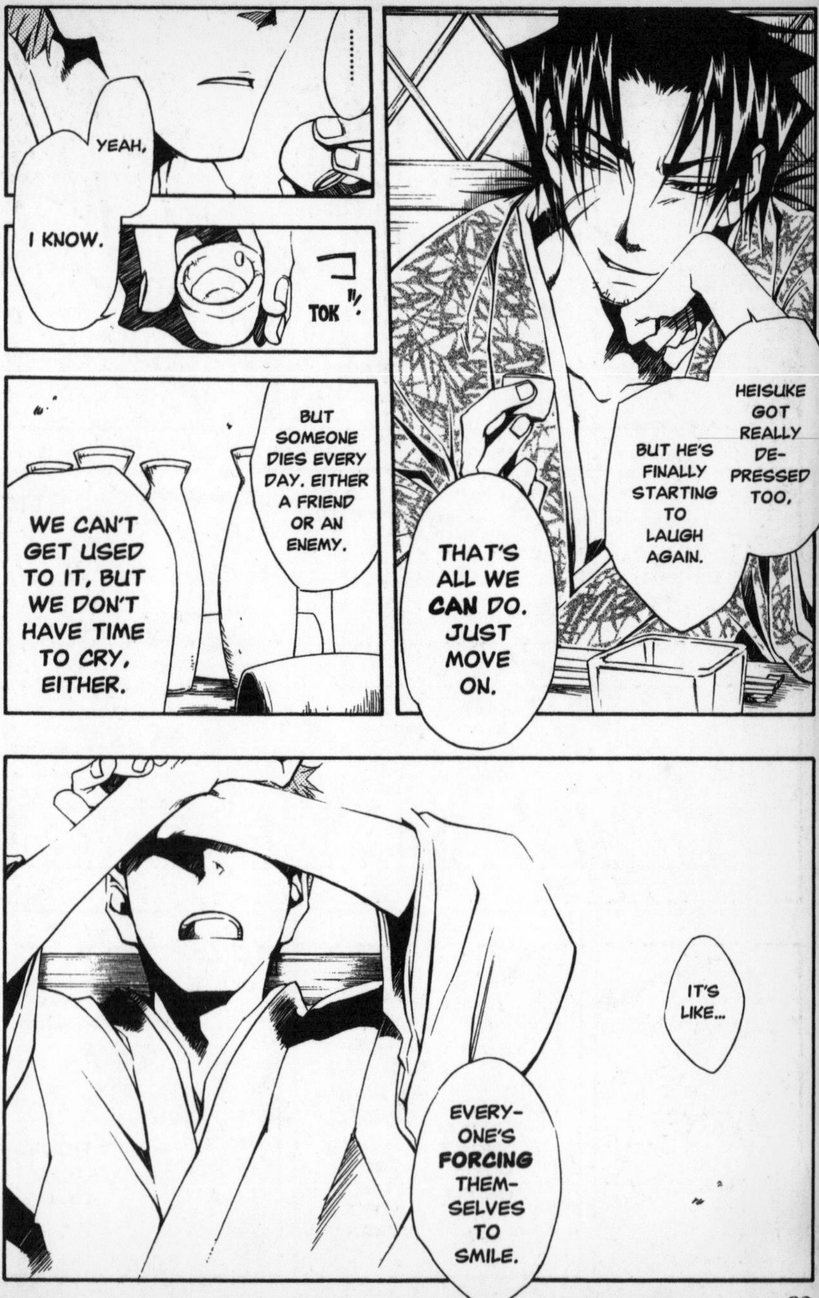
HEISUKE GOT REALLY DE-PRESSED TOO,
BUT HE'S FINALLY STARTING TO LAUGH AGAIN.
THAT'S ALL WE CAN DO. JUST MOVE ON.
......
YEAH,
I KNOW.
TOK
BUT SOMEONE DIES EVERY DAY. EITHER A FRIEND OR AN ENEMY.
WE CAN'T GET USED TO IT, BUT WE DON'T HAVE TIME TO CRY, EITHER.
IT'S LIKE...
EVERY-ONE'S FORCING THEM-SELVES TO SMILE.

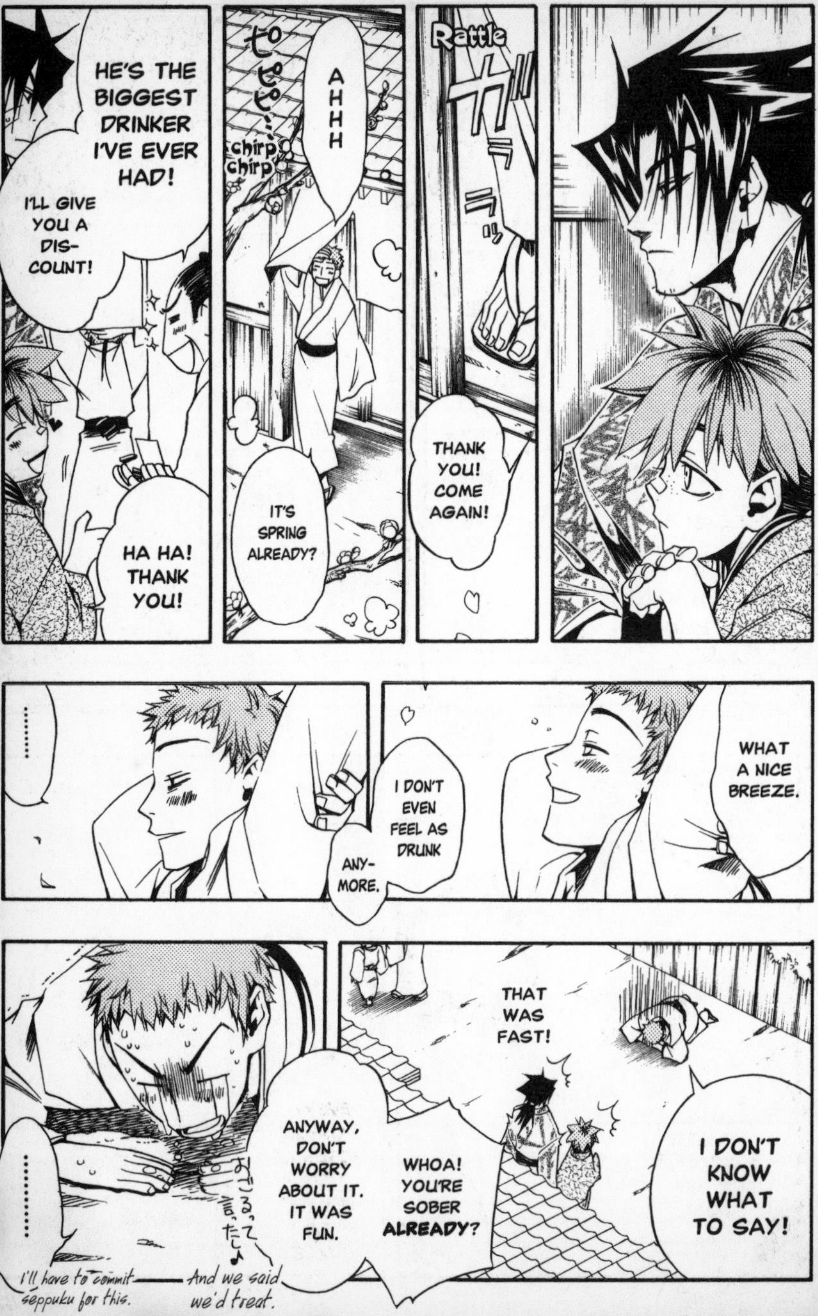
Rattle
THANK YOU! COME AGAIN!
AHHH
chirp chirp
IT'S SPRING ALREADY?
HE'S THE BIGGEST DRINKER I'VE EVER HAD!
I'LL GIVE YOU A DIS-COUNT!
HA HA! THANK YOU!
WHAT A NICE BREEZE.
I DON'T EVEN FEEL AS DRUNK ANYMORE.
......
I DON'T KNOW WHAT TO SAY!
THAT WAS FAST!
WHOA! YOU'RE SOBER ALREADY?
ANYWAY, DON'T WORRY ABOUT IT. IT WAS FUN.
And we said we'd treat.
......
I'll have to commit seppuku for this.

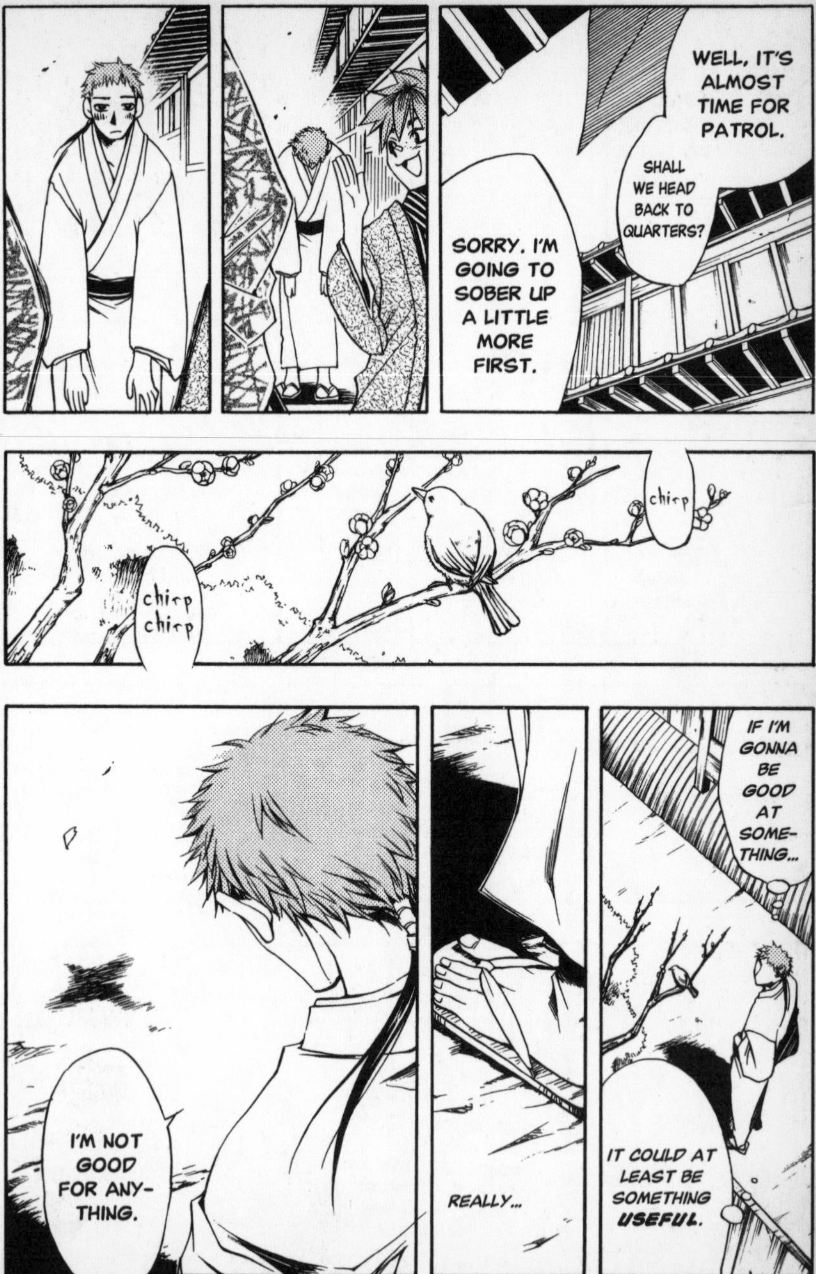
WELL, IT'S ALMOST TIME FOR PATROL.
SHALL WE HEAD BACK TO QUARTERS?
SORRY. I'M GOING TO SOBER UP A LITTLE MORE FIRST.
chirp
chirp chirp
IF I'M GONNA BE GOOD AT SOME-THING...
IT COULD AT LEAST BE SOMETHING USEFUL.
REALLY...
I'M NOT GOOD FOR ANY-THING.

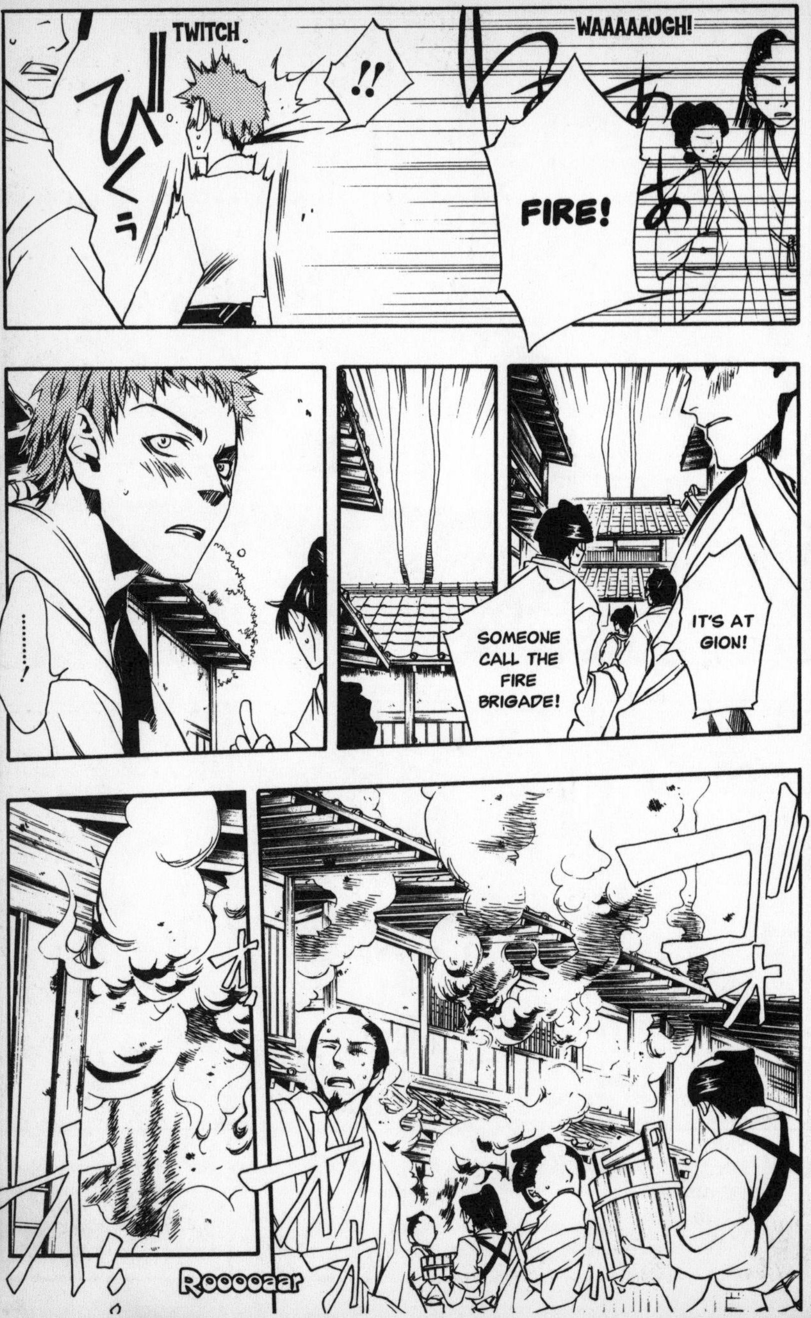
WAAAAAUGH!
FIRE!
!!
TWITCH
IT'S AT GION!
SOMEONE CALL THE FIRE BRIGADE!
.........!
Roooaar

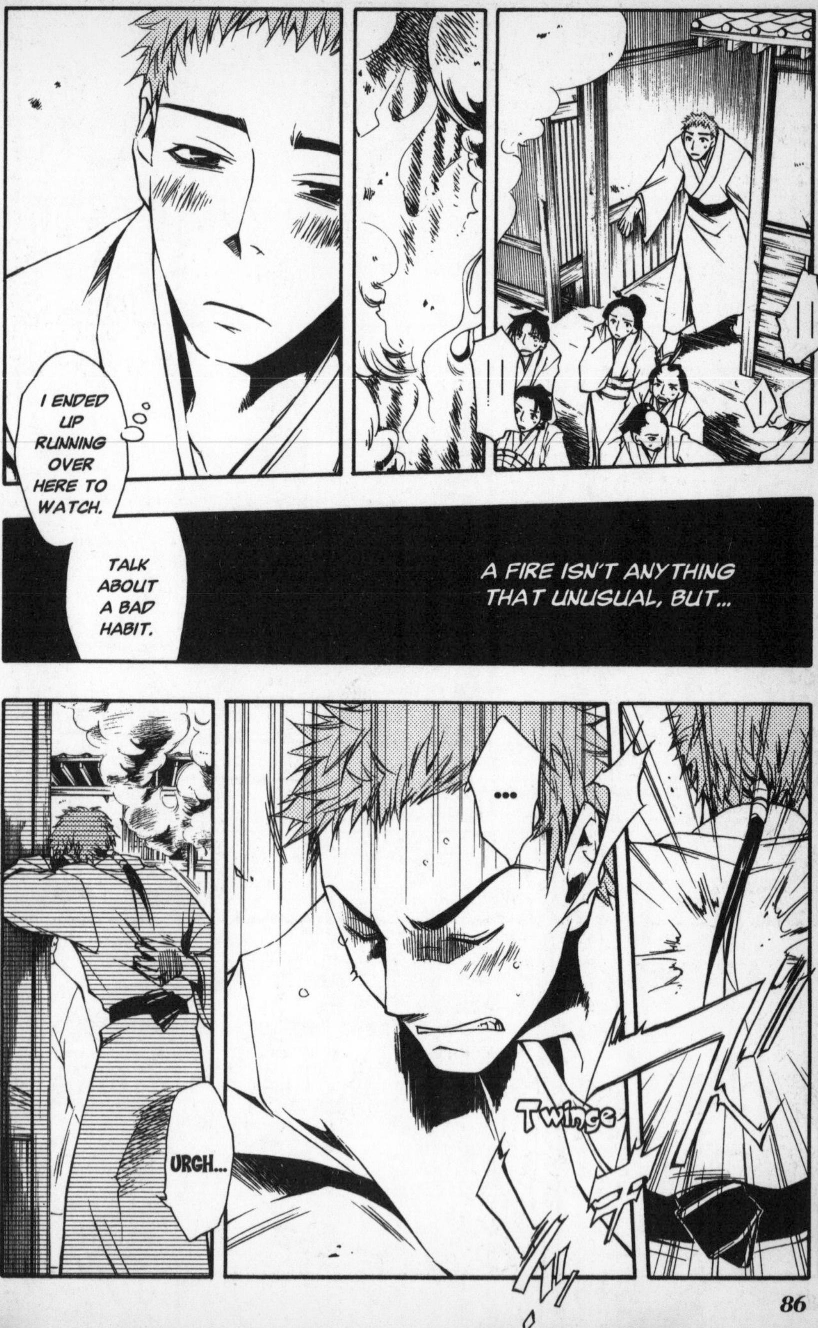
I ENDED UP RUNNING OVER HERE TO WATCH.
TALK ABOUT A BAD HABIT.
A FIRE ISN'T ANYTHING THAT UNUSUAL, BUT...
URGH...
...
Twinge

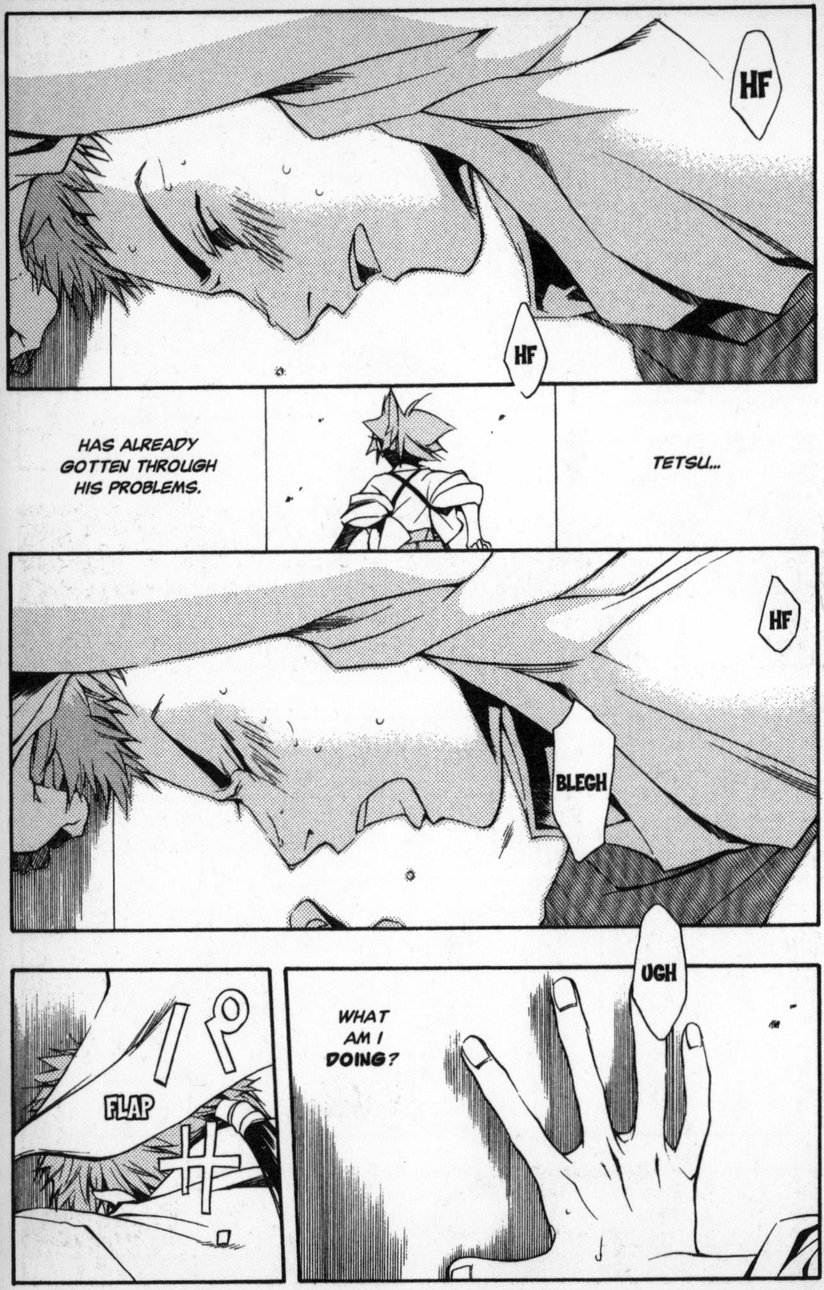
HF
HF
TETSU...
HAS ALREADY GOTTEN THROUGH HIS PROBLEMS.
HF
BLEGH
UGH
WHAT AM I DOING?
FLAP

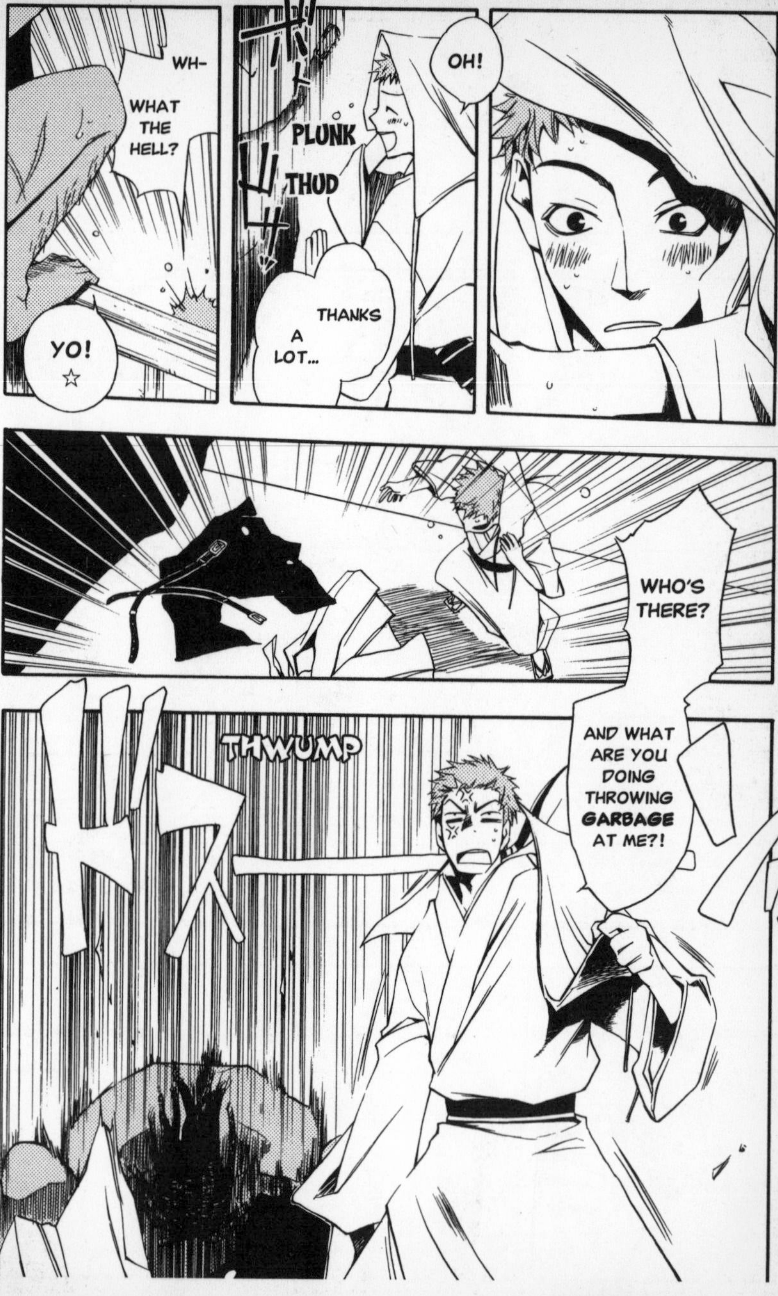
OH!
PLUNK
THUD
THANKS A LOT...
WH-
WHAT THE HELL?
YO! ☆
WHO'S THERE?
THWUMP
AND WHAT ARE YOU DOING THROWING **GARBAGE** AT ME?!

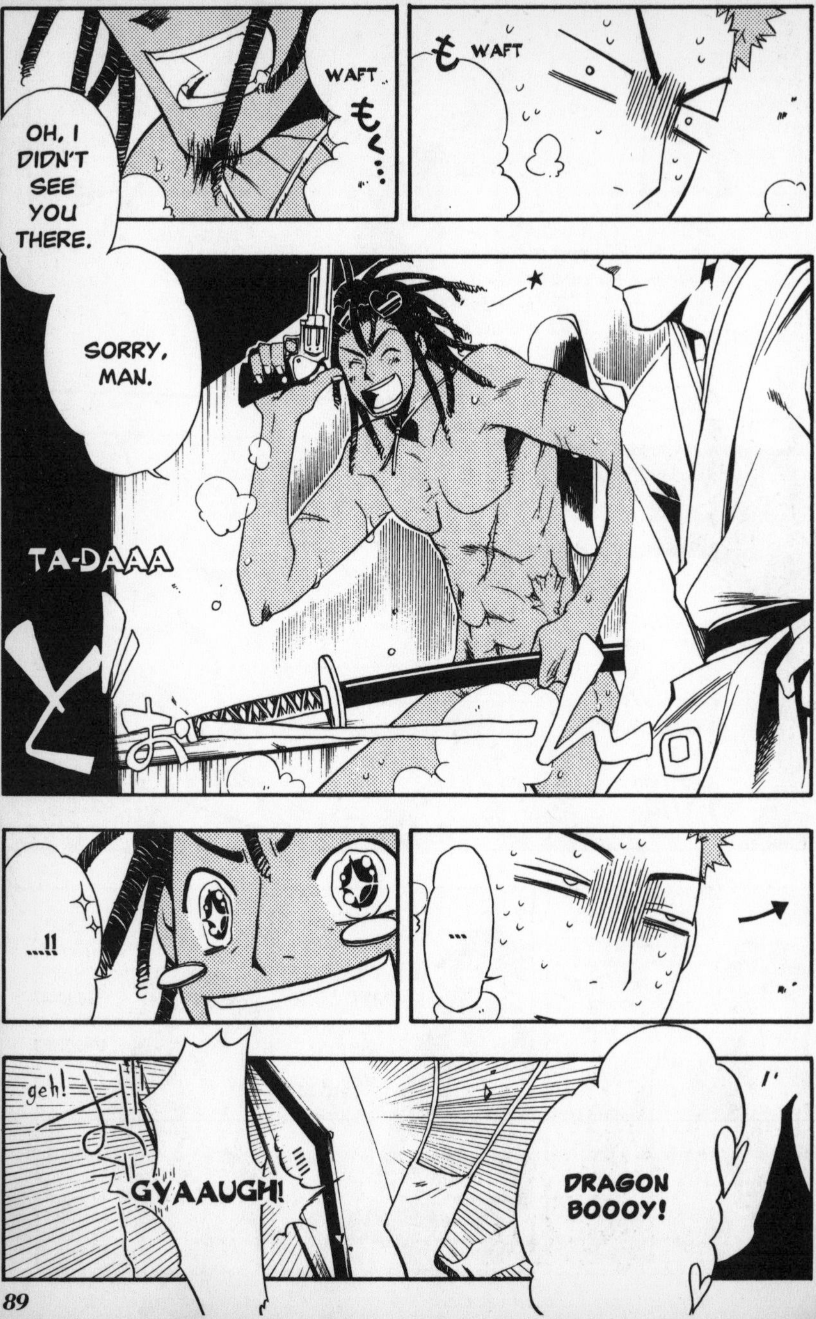
もく...
WAFT
も WAFT
OH, I DIDN'T SEE YOU THERE.
SORRY, MAN.
TA-DAAA
...!!
...
geh!
GYAAUGH!
DRAGON BOOOY!

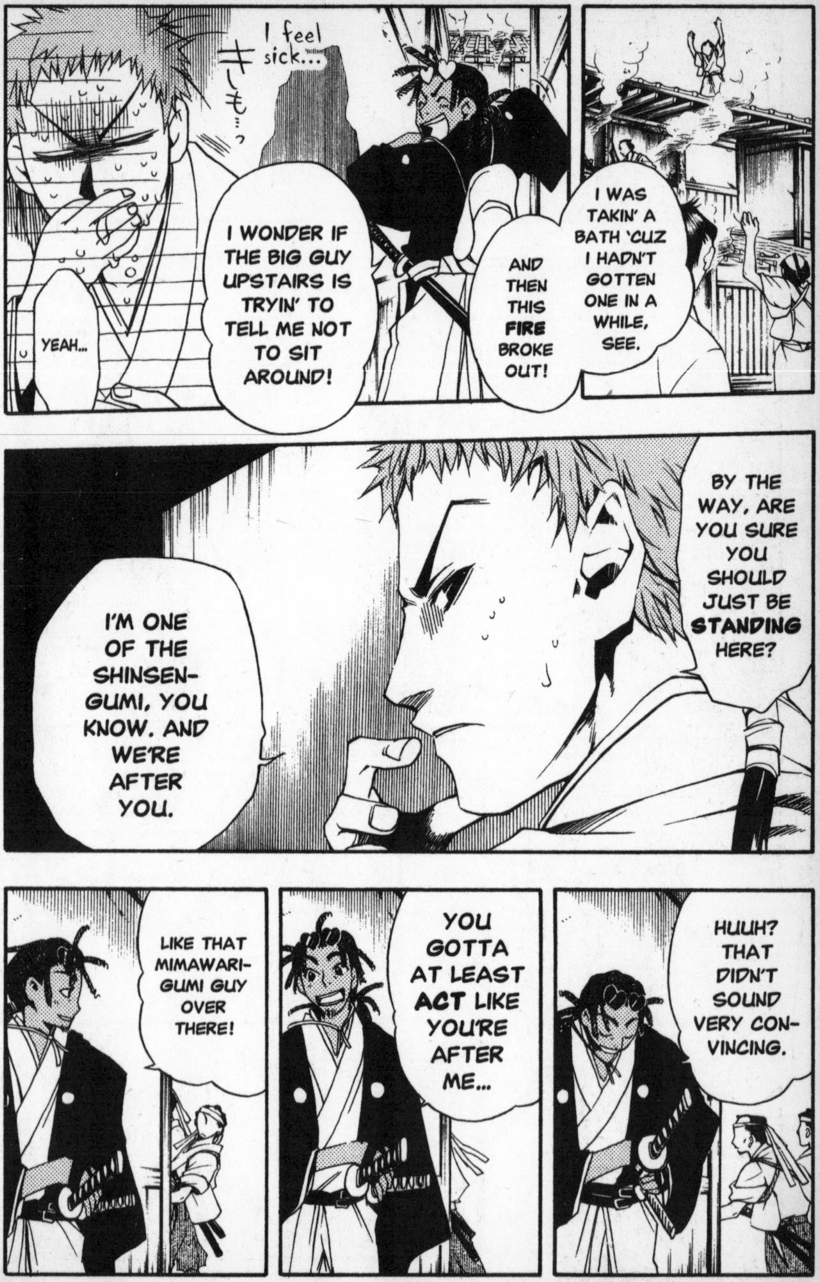
I WAS TAKIN' A BATH 'CUZ I HADN'T GOTTEN ONE IN A WHILE, SEE.
AND THEN THIS FIRE BROKE OUT!
I WONDER IF THE BIG GUY UPSTAIRS IS TRYIN' TO TELL ME NOT TO SIT AROUND!
I feel sick...
YEAH...
BY THE WAY, ARE YOU SURE YOU SHOULD JUST BE STANDING HERE?
I'M ONE OF THE SHINSEN-GUMI, YOU KNOW. AND WE'RE AFTER YOU.
HUUH? THAT DIDN'T SOUND VERY CON-VINCING.
YOU GOTTA AT LEAST ACT LIKE YOU'RE AFTER ME...
LIKE THAT MIMAWARI-GUMI GUY OVER THERE!

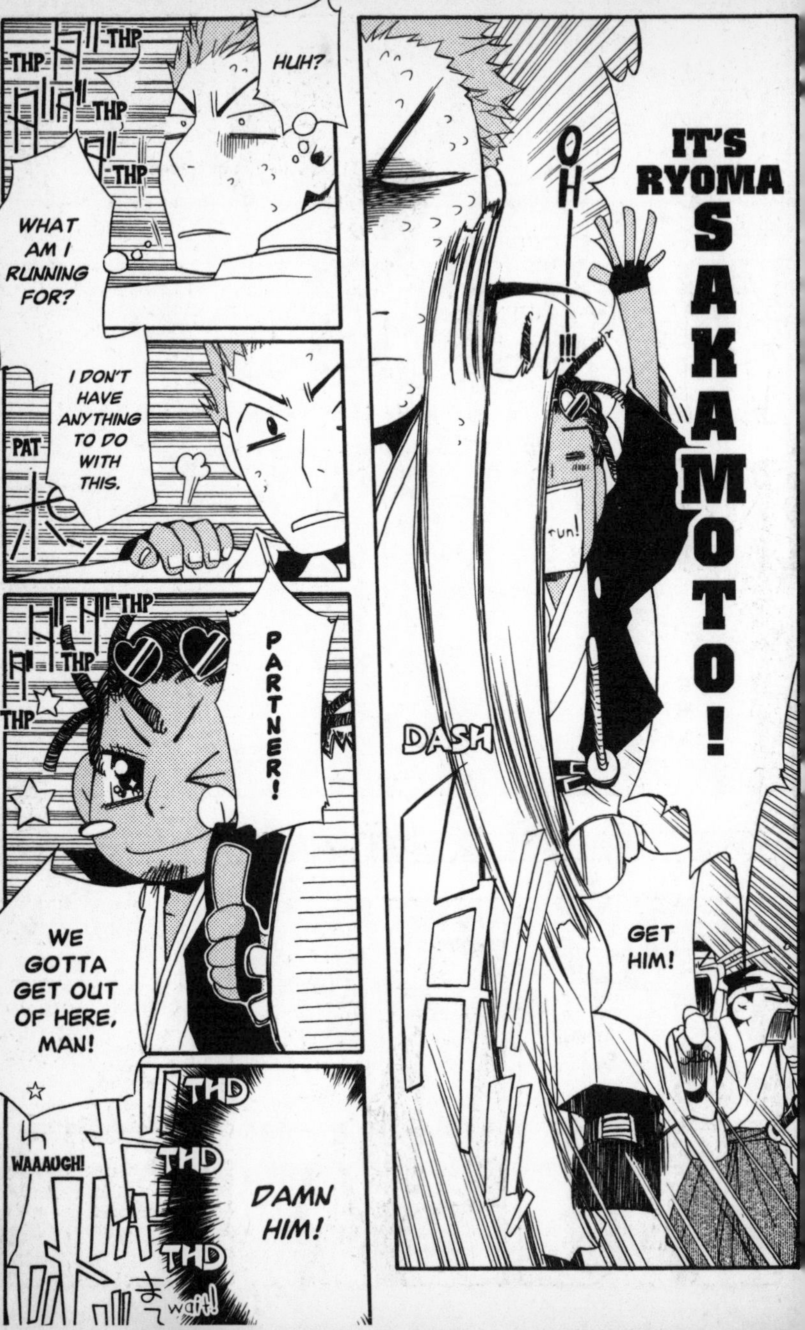

OH--!!!
IT'S RYOMA SAKAMOTO!
run!
DASH
GET HIM!
THP THP THP THP
HUH?
WHAT AM I RUNNING FOR?
I DON'T HAVE ANYTHING TO DO WITH THIS.
PAT
THP THP THP
PARTNER!
WE GOTTA GET OUT OF HERE, MAN! ☆
THD THD THD
WAAAUGH!
DAMN HIM!
wait!

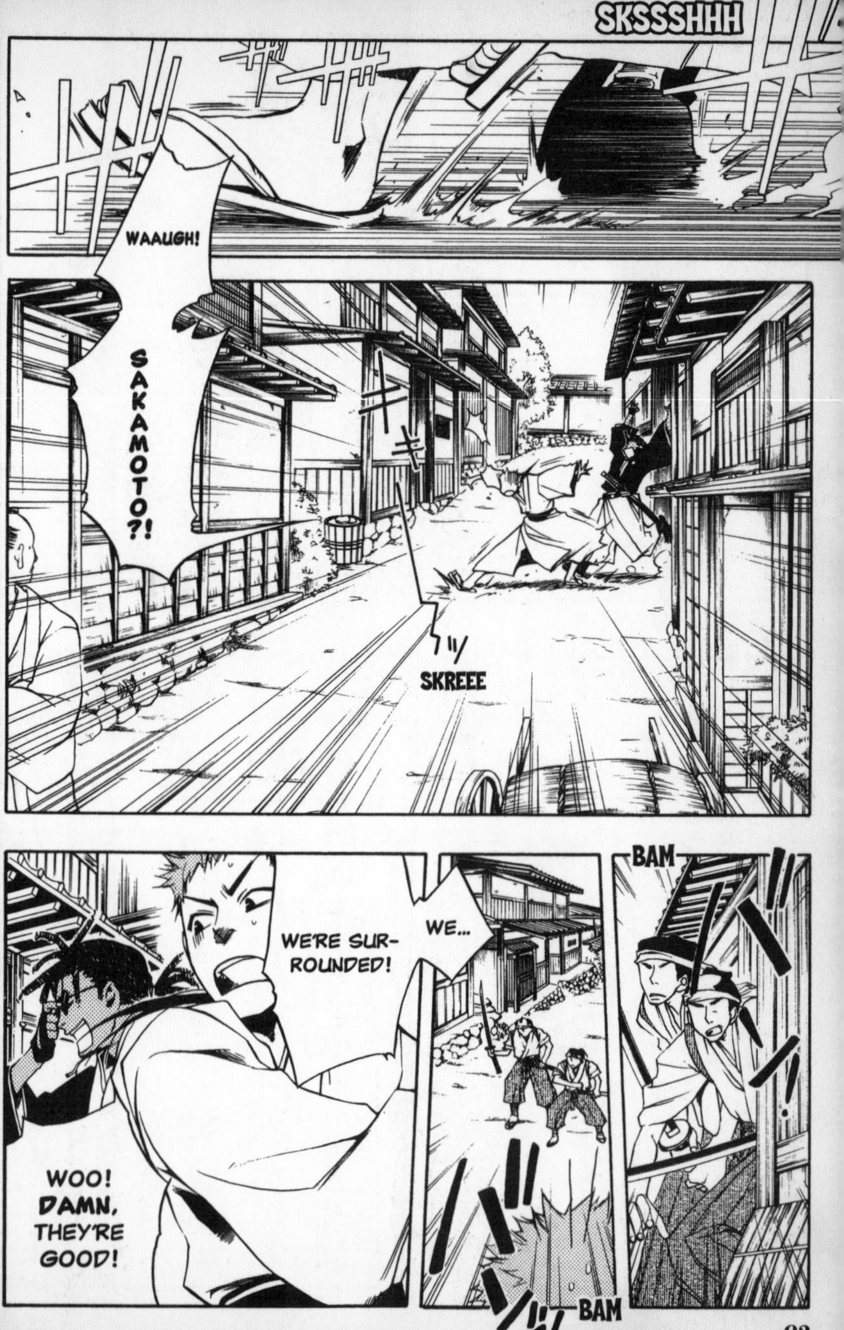
SKSSSHHH
WAAUGH!
SAKAMOTO?!
SKREEE
BAM
WE...
BAM
WE'RE SUR-
ROUNDED!
WOO!
DAMN,
THEY'RE
GOOD!

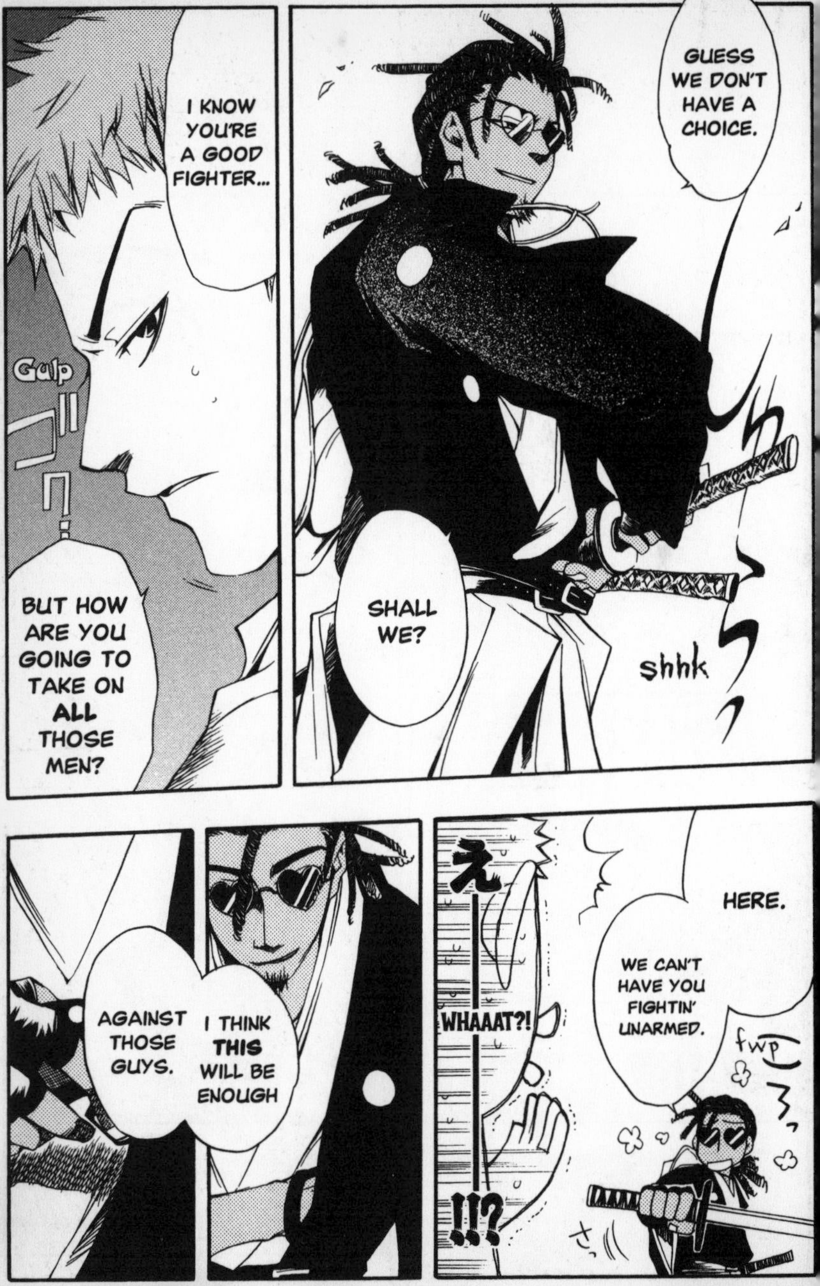
GUESS WE DON'T HAVE A CHOICE.
SHALL WE?
shhk
I KNOW YOU'RE A GOOD FIGHTER...
Gulp
BUT HOW ARE YOU GOING TO TAKE ON **ALL** THOSE MEN?
HERE.
WE CAN'T HAVE YOU FIGHTIN' UNARMED.
fwp
え WHAAAT?!!!?
I THINK **THIS** WILL BE ENOUGH
AGAINST THOSE GUYS.

whoosh

DRAGON BOY!

RUN FOR THE CART!

R-

RIGHT!

kchk

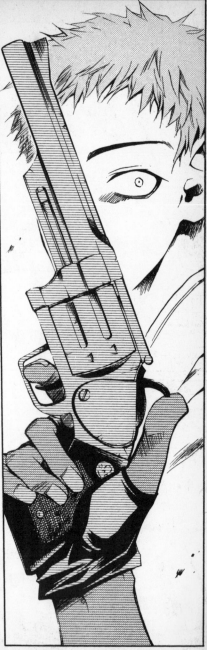

94

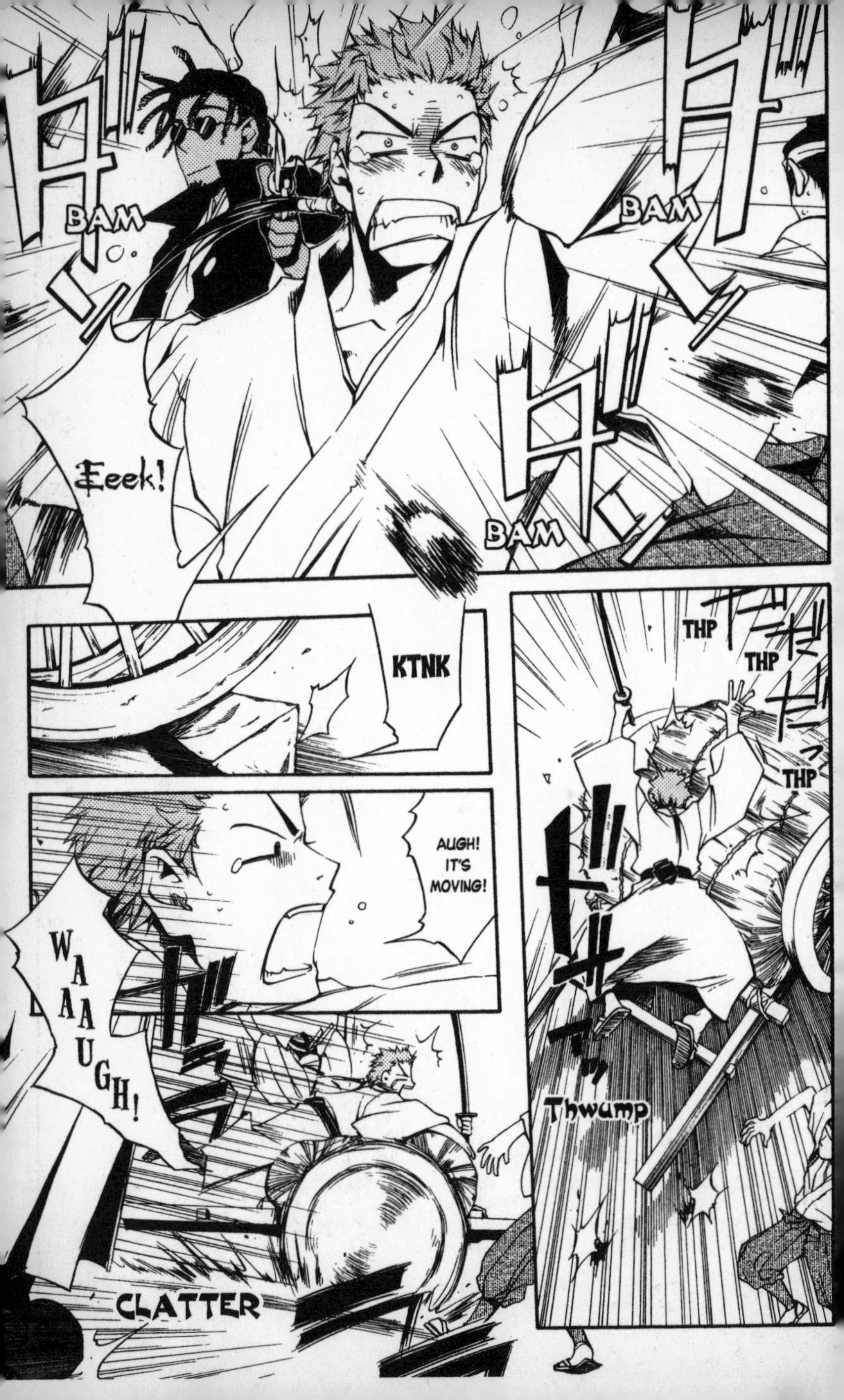
BAM
BAM
BAM
Eeek!
THP
THP
THP
KTNK
Thwump
AUGH! IT'S MOVING!
WAAAUGH!
CLATTER

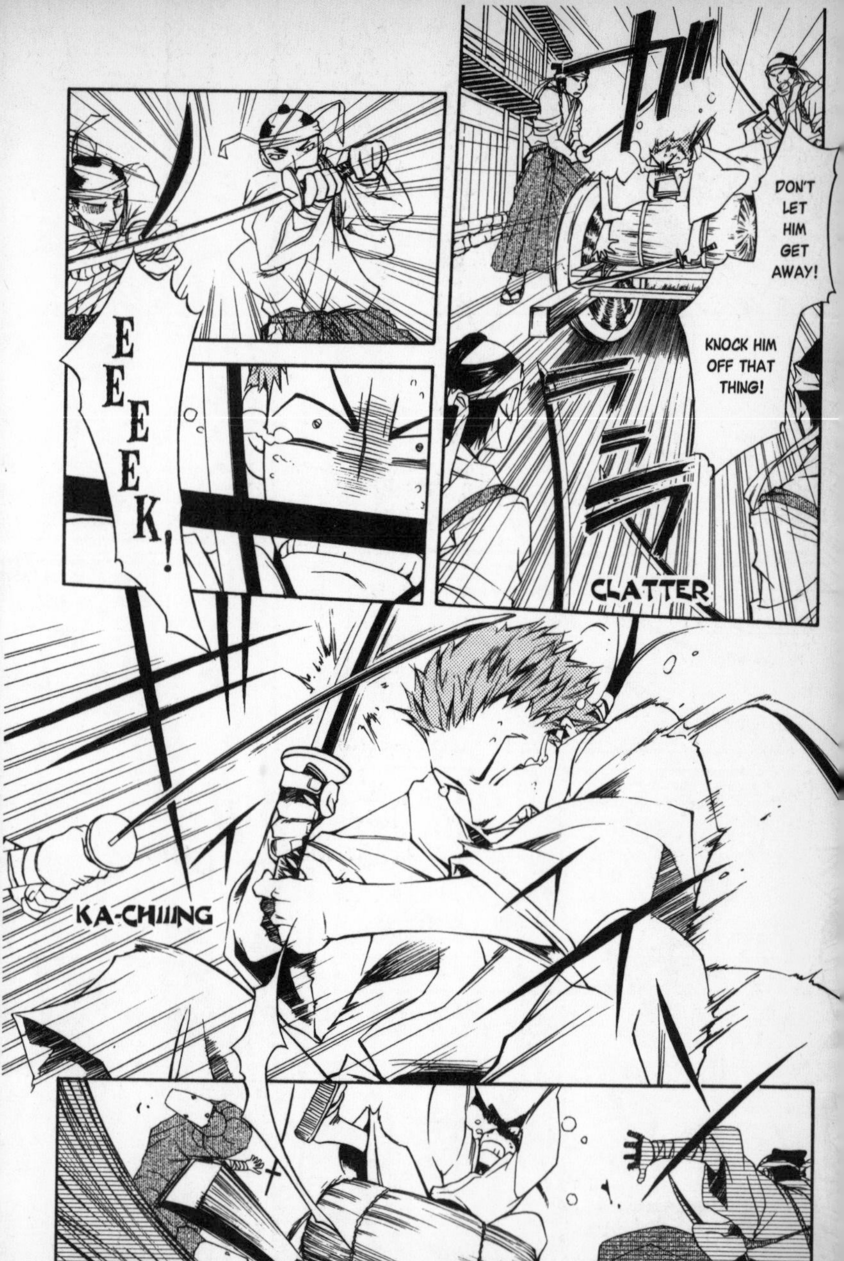
DON'T LET HIM GET AWAY!
KNOCK HIM OFF THAT THING!
CLATTER
EEEEK!
KA-CHIIING

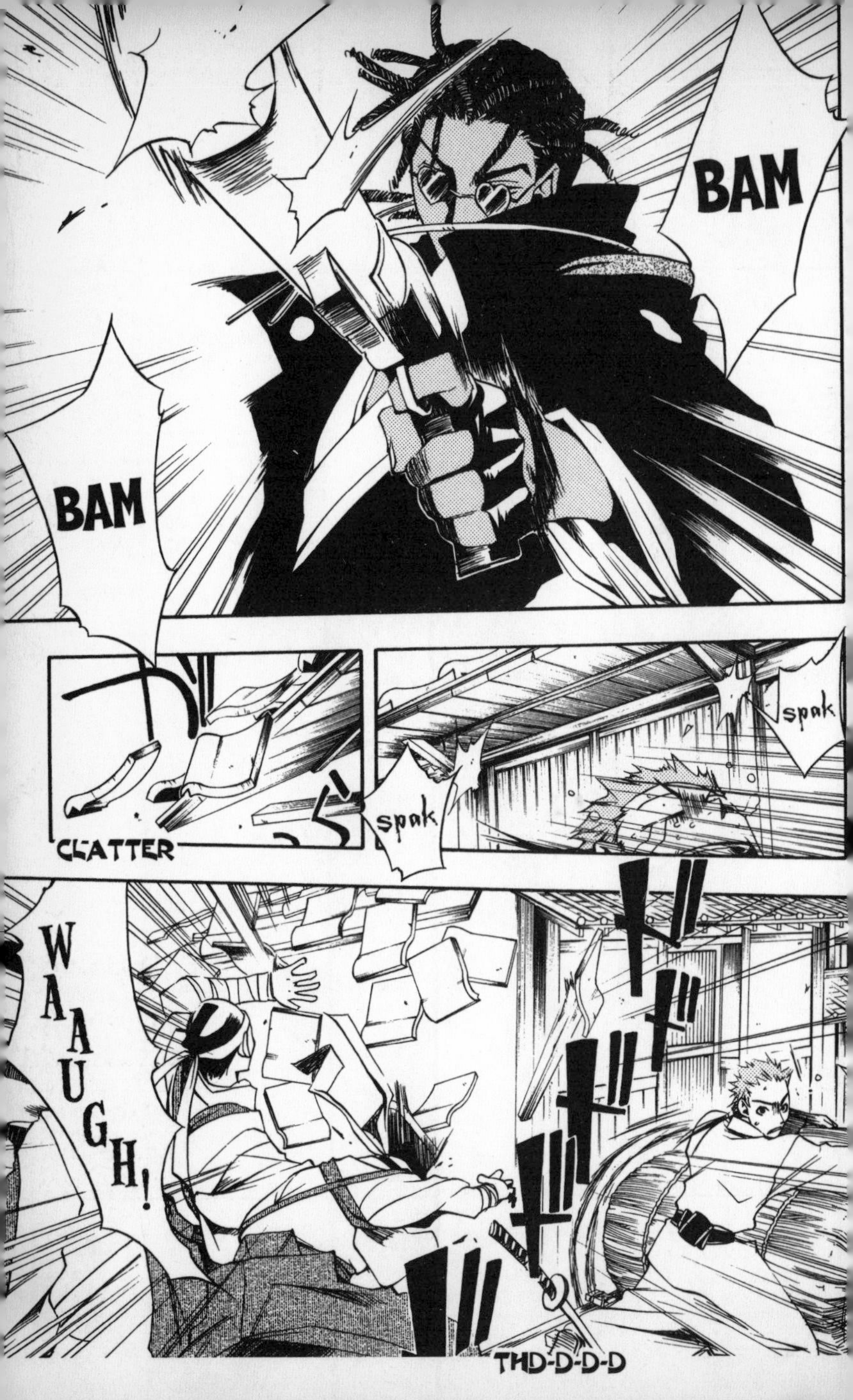
BAM
BAM
spak
spak
CLATTER
WAAUGH!
THD-D-D-D

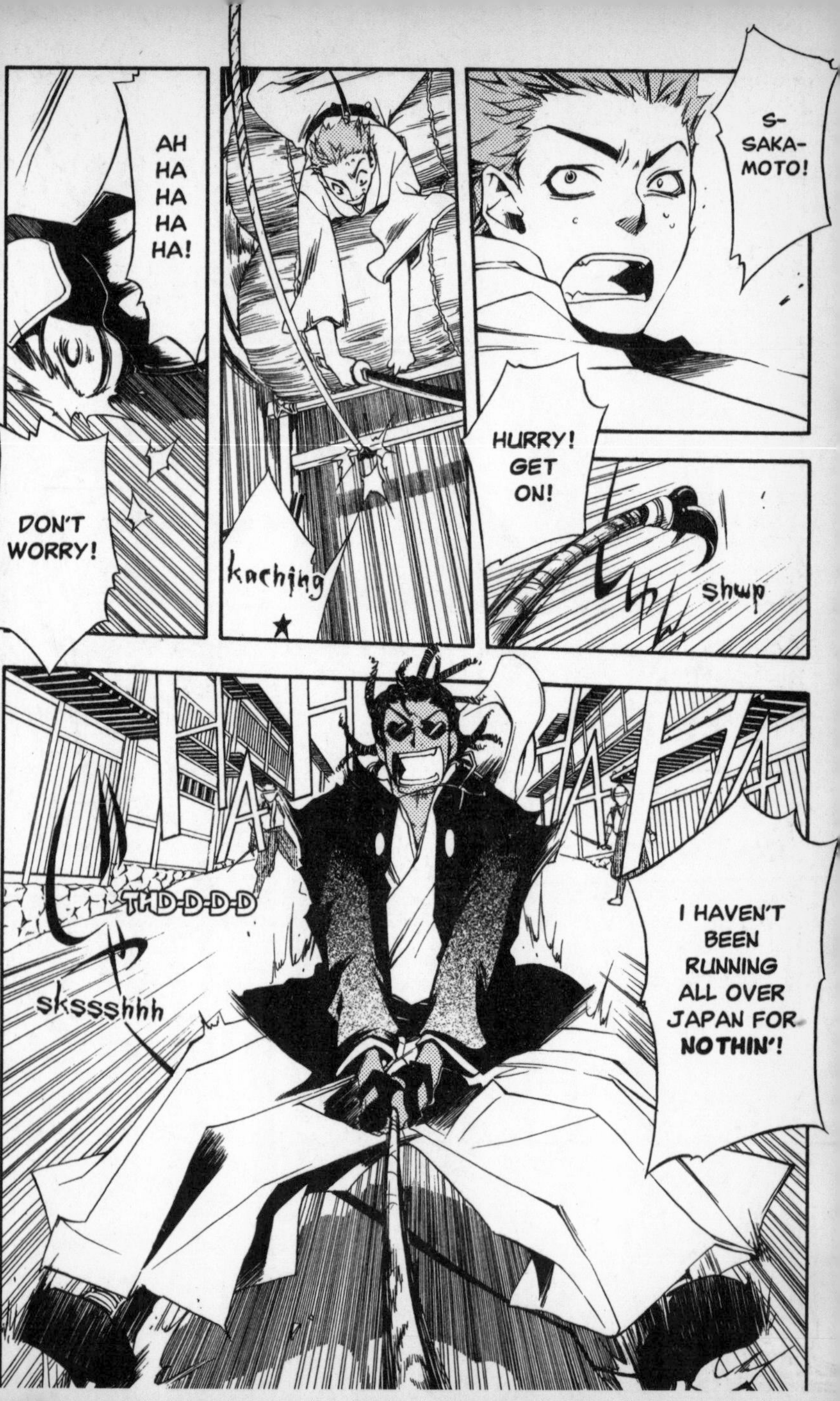
S-SAKAMOTO!
HURRY! GET ON!
shwp
kaching
AH HA HA HA HA!
DON'T WORRY!
I HAVEN'T BEEN RUNNING ALL OVER JAPAN FOR **NOTHIN'**!
THD-D-D-D
sksssshhh

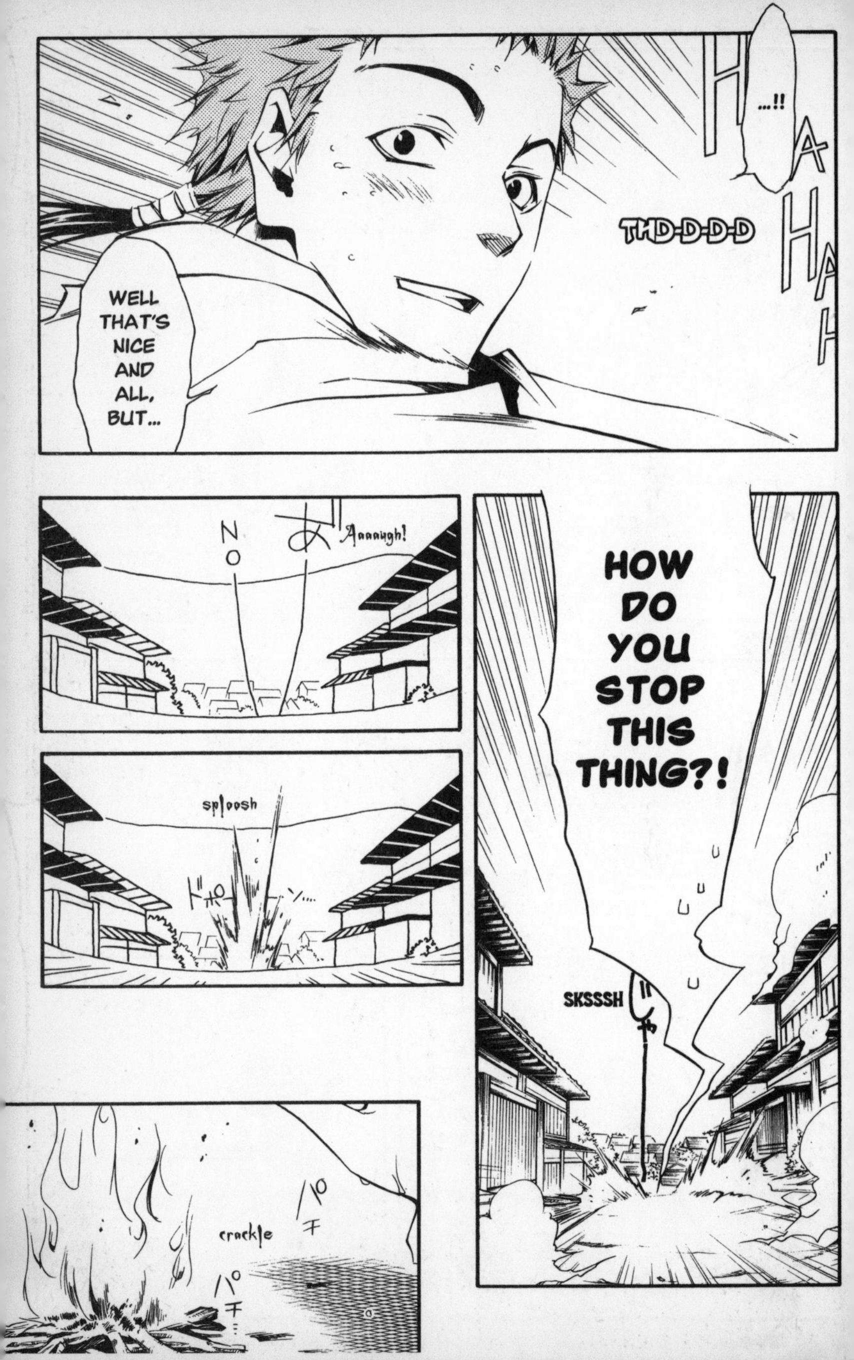
HAHAH
...!!
THD-D-D-D
WELL THAT'S NICE AND ALL, BUT...
HOW DO YOU STOP THIS THING?!
SKSSSH
NO
Aaaaugh!
sploosh
ドボーン...
crackle
パチ
パチ...

PHEEEW.
MAN, WE'RE LUCKY WE LANDED IN A RIVER!
shiver
shiver
I THINK MY HEART SKIPPED A BEAT WHEN WE FELL.
shiver
shiver
crackle
ONCE I GET WARMED UP, I'M LEAVING.
IF I STAY WITH YOU, THEY MIGHT GET THE WRONG IDEA AND TRY TO KILL ME AGAIN.
SIGH
COME ON, MAN! YOU NEED A LITTLE EXCITEMENT ONCE IN A WHILE! LETS YOU KNOW YOU'RE ALIVE!
I FEEL ALIVE ENOUGH AS IT IS, THANK YOU.
WHO ASKED YOU?
STILL, I MADE THE RIGHT CHOICE GIVING YOU THAT
SWORD, HUH? YOU CAN'T PROTECT YOURSELF UNARMED!
FLAT OUT
I'M BETTER OFF WITHOUT IT. THEY WOULDN'T KILL AN UNARMED MAN.

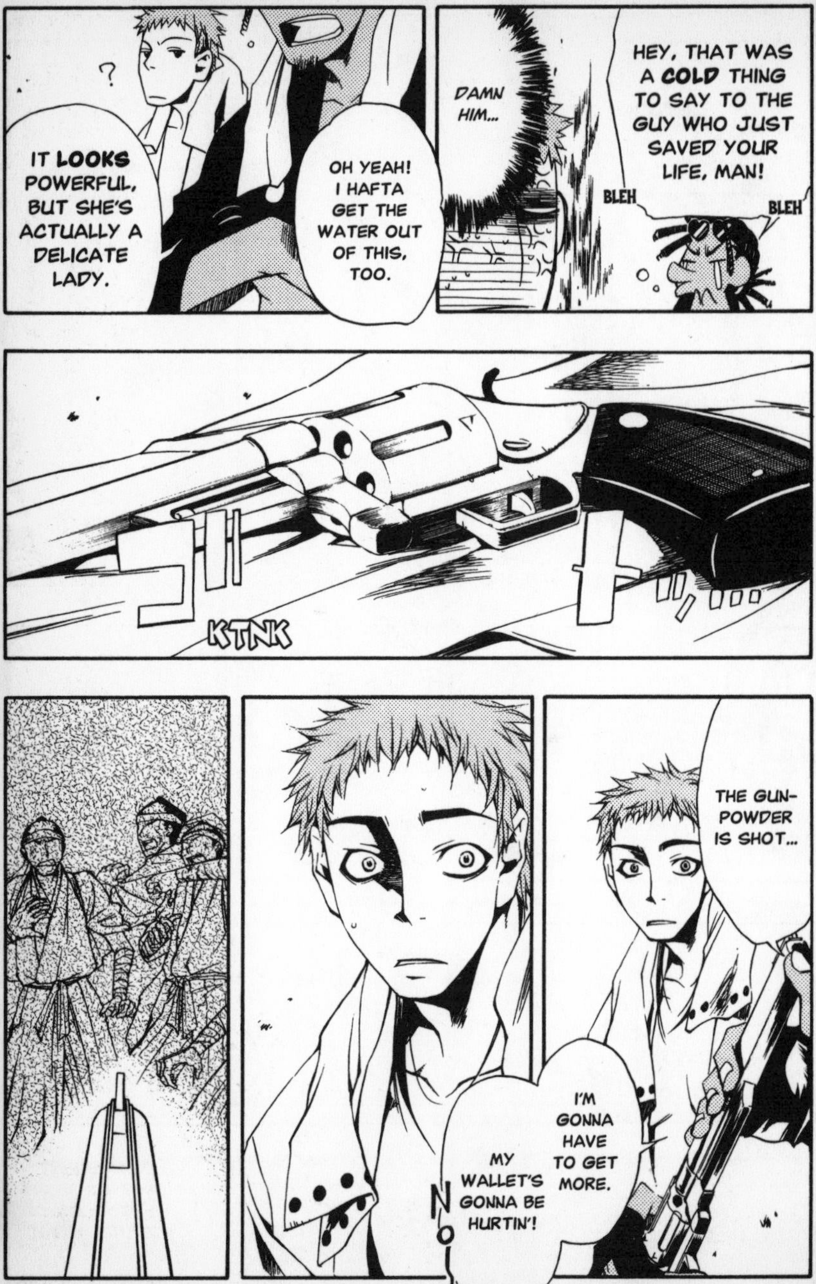
HEY, THAT WAS A **COLD** THING TO SAY TO THE GUY WHO JUST SAVED YOUR LIFE, MAN!
DAMN HIM...
BLEH
BLEH
?
OH YEAH! I HAFTA GET THE WATER OUT OF THIS, TOO.
IT **LOOKS** POWERFUL, BUT SHE'S ACTUALLY A DELICATE LADY.
KTNK
THE GUN-POWDER IS SHOT...
I'M GONNA HAVE TO GET MORE.
MY WALLET'S GONNA BE HURTIN'!
NO...!

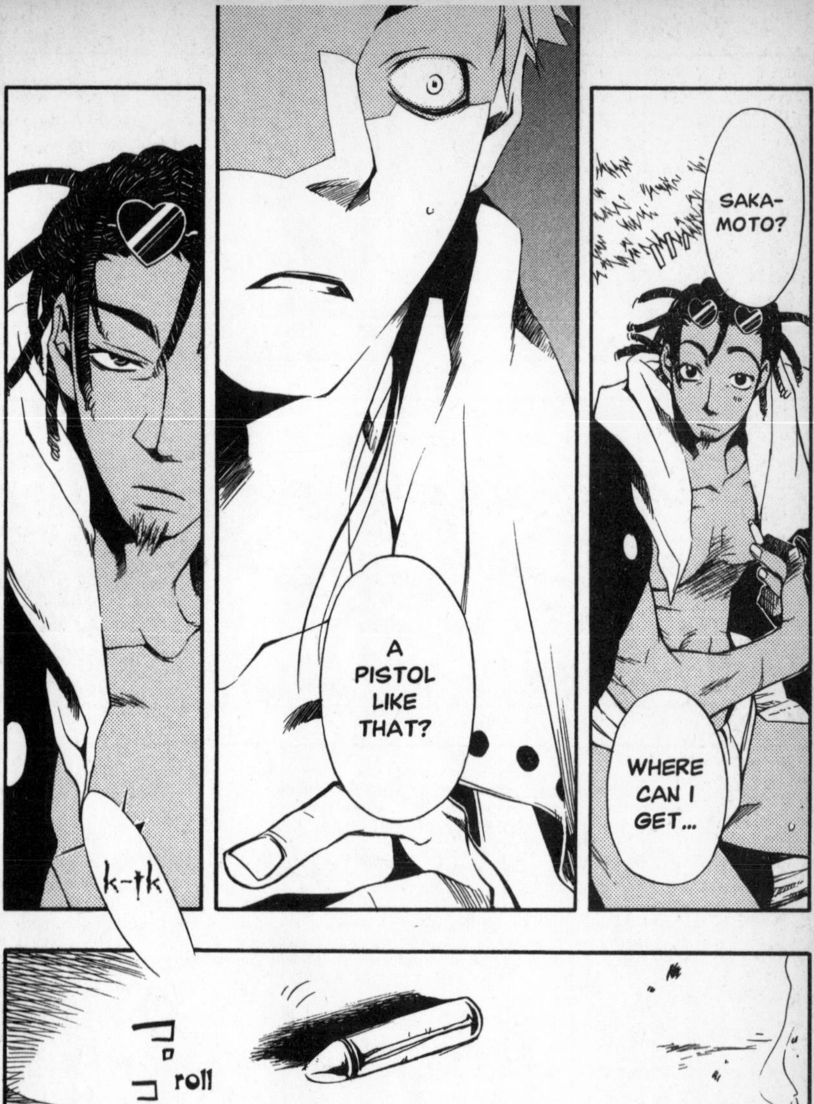
SAKA-MOTO?
WHERE CAN I GET...
A PISTOL LIKE THAT?
k-tk
コロ roll コロ...

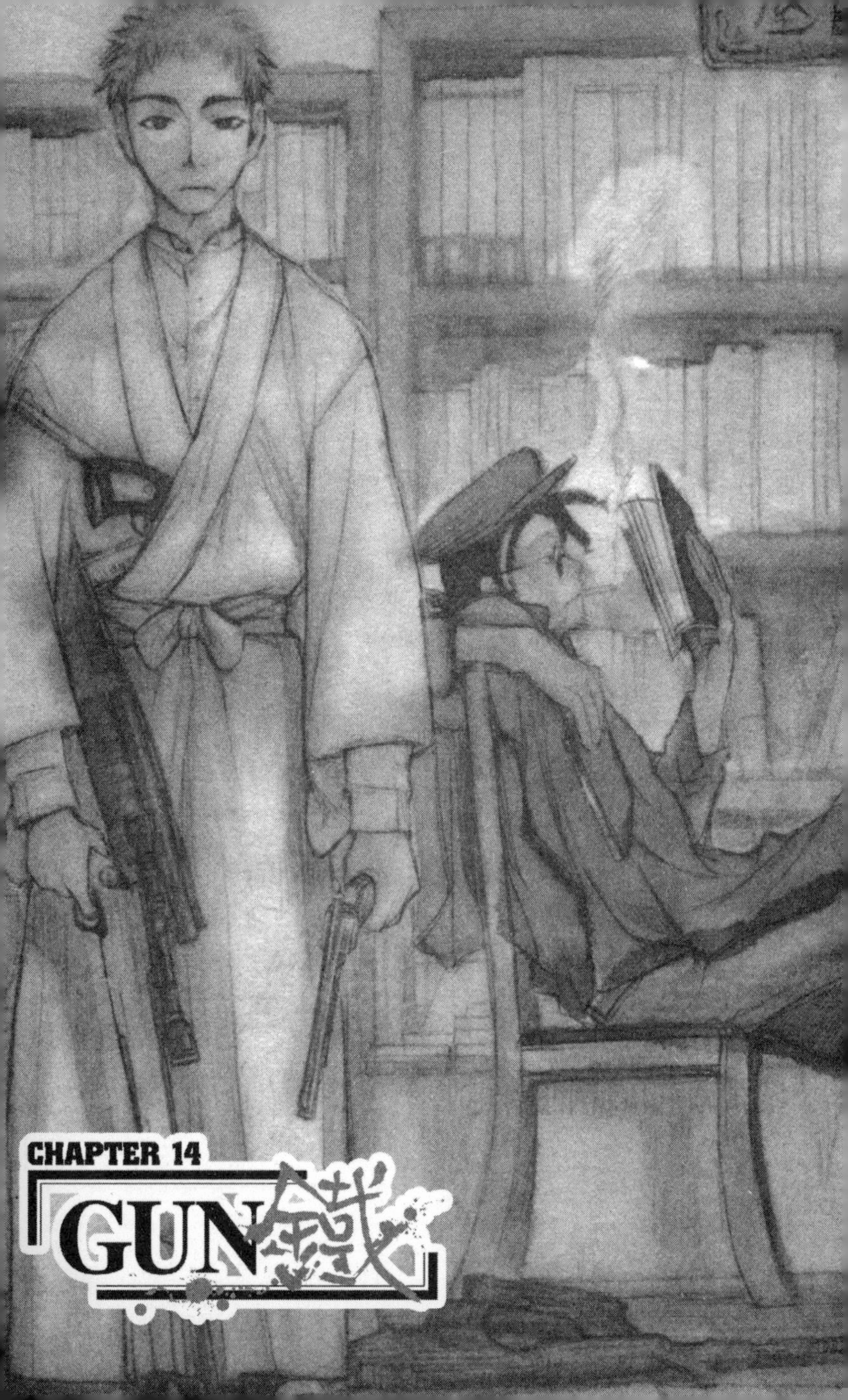
CHAPTER 14
GUN鐵

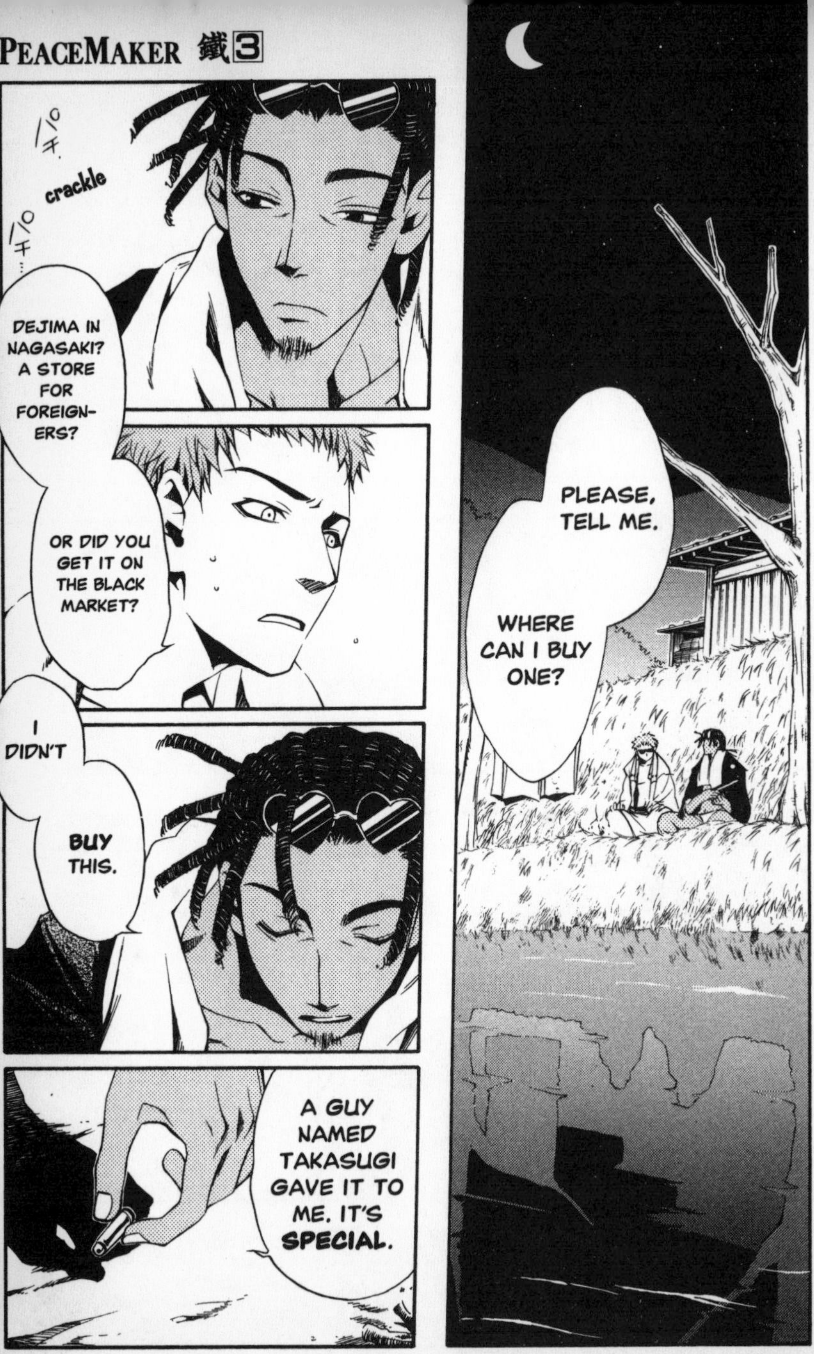
PLEASE, TELL ME.
WHERE CAN I BUY ONE?
パチ
crackle
パチ…
DEJIMA IN NAGASAKI? A STORE FOR FOREIGN-ERS?
OR DID YOU GET IT ON THE BLACK MARKET?
I DIDN'T
BUY THIS.
A GUY NAMED TAKASUGI GAVE IT TO ME. IT'S SPECIAL.

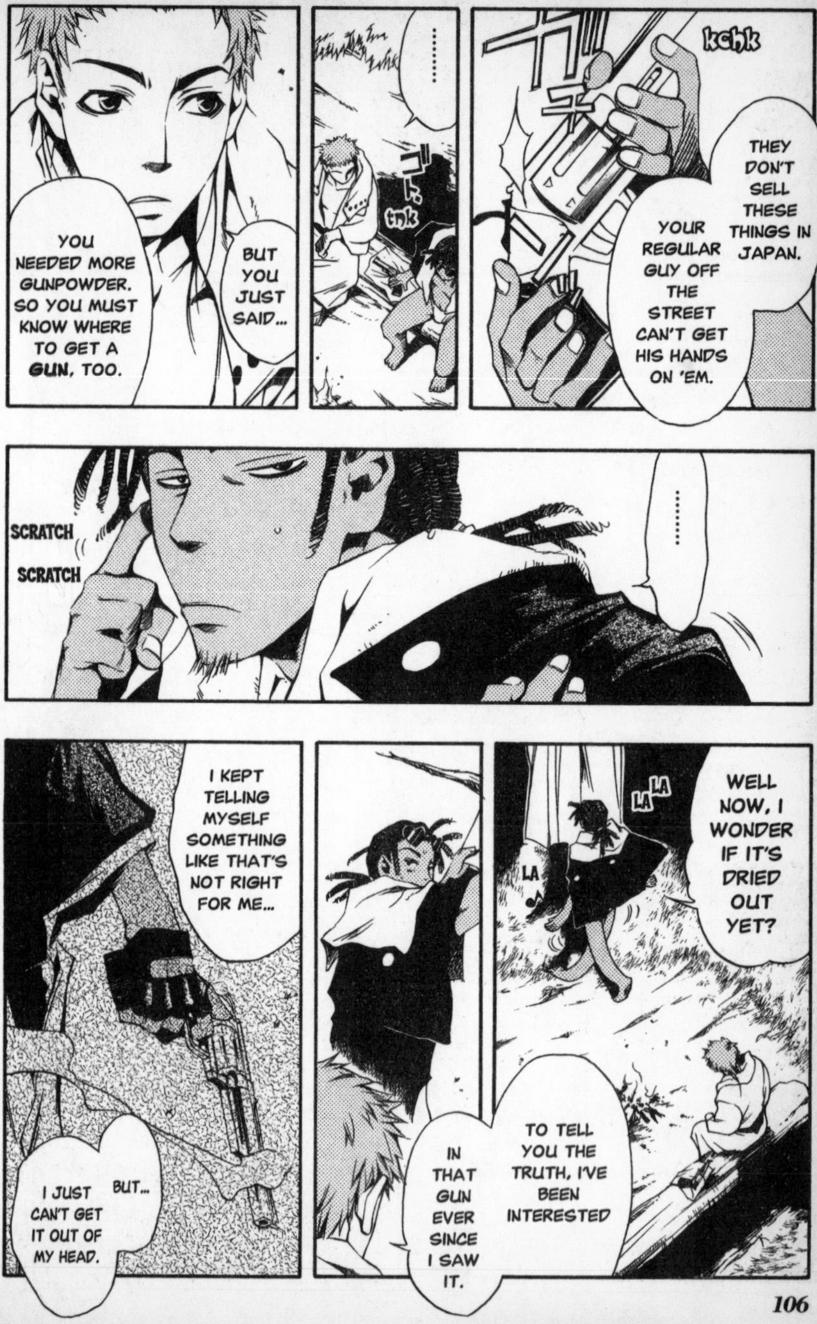
kchk
THEY DON'T SELL THESE THINGS IN JAPAN.
YOUR REGULAR GUY OFF THE STREET CAN'T GET HIS HANDS ON 'EM.
......
tnk
BUT YOU JUST SAID...
YOU NEEDED MORE GUNPOWDER. SO YOU MUST KNOW WHERE TO GET A GUN, TOO.
......
SCRATCH
SCRATCH
LA LA
LA
WELL NOW, I WONDER IF IT'S DRIED OUT YET?
TO TELL YOU THE TRUTH, I'VE BEEN INTERESTED
IN THAT GUN EVER SINCE I SAW IT.
I KEPT TELLING MYSELF SOMETHING LIKE THAT'S NOT RIGHT FOR ME...
BUT...
I JUST CAN'T GET IT OUT OF MY HEAD.

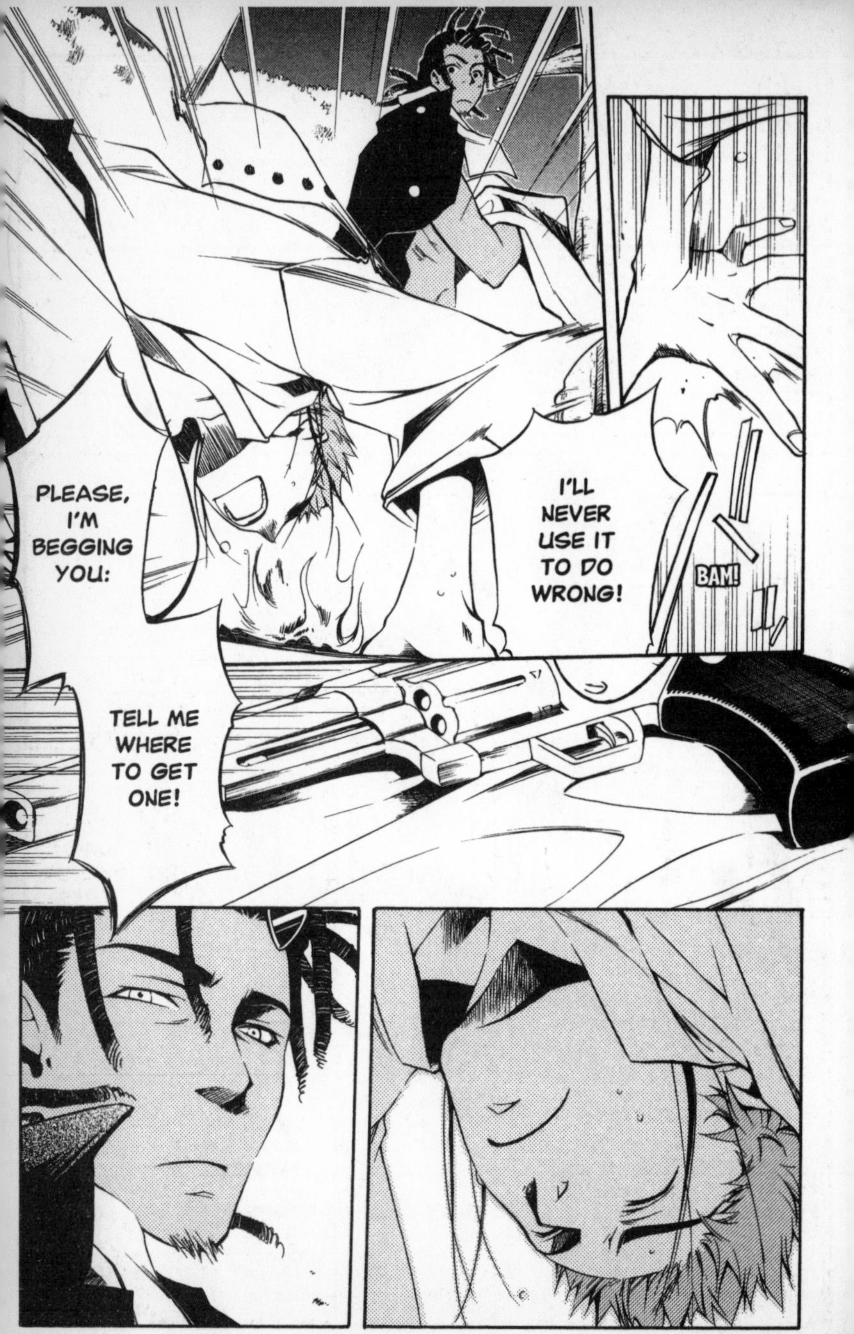
BAM!
I'LL NEVER USE IT TO DO WRONG!
PLEASE, I'M BEGGING YOU:
TELL ME WHERE TO GET ONE!

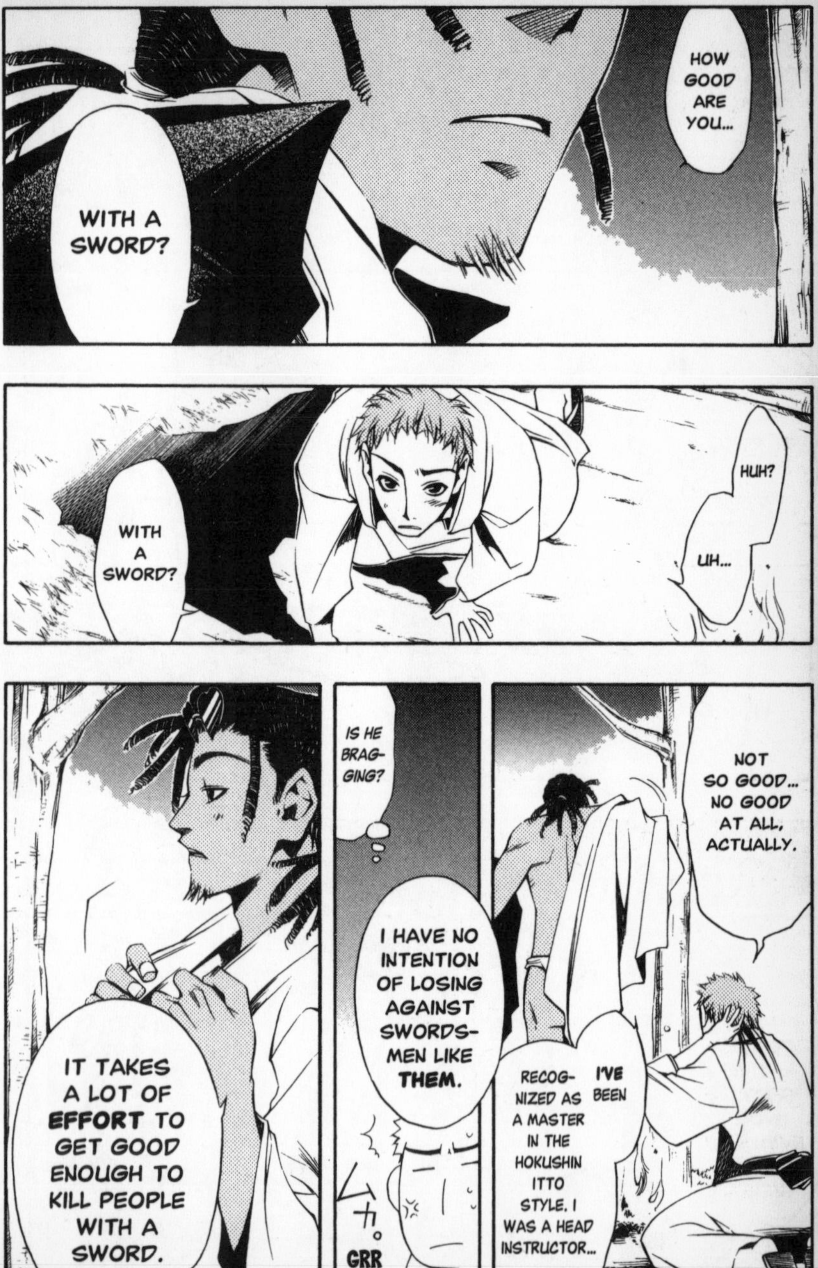
HOW GOOD ARE YOU...
WITH A SWORD?
HUH?
UH...
WITH A SWORD?
NOT SO GOOD... NO GOOD AT ALL, ACTUALLY.
I'VE BEEN RECOGNIZED AS A MASTER IN THE HOKUSHIN ITTO STYLE. I WAS A HEAD INSTRUCTOR...
IS HE BRAGGING?
I HAVE NO INTENTION OF LOSING AGAINST SWORDSMEN LIKE THEM.
GRR
IT TAKES A LOT OF EFFORT TO GET GOOD ENOUGH TO KILL PEOPLE WITH A SWORD.

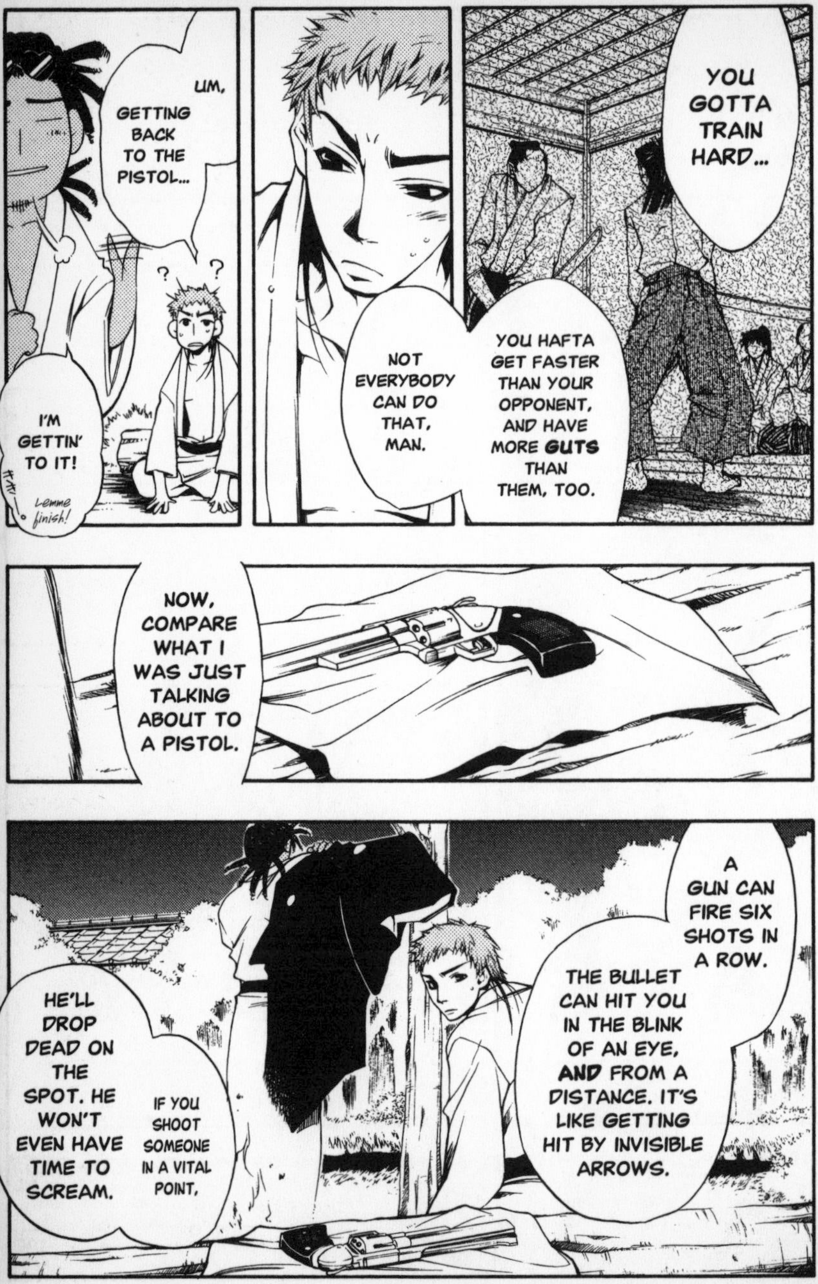
YOU GOTTA TRAIN HARD...
YOU HAFTA GET FASTER THAN YOUR OPPONENT, AND HAVE MORE **GUTS** THAN THEM, TOO.
NOT EVERYBODY CAN DO THAT, MAN.
UM, GETTING BACK TO THE PISTOL...
I'M GETTIN' TO IT!
Lemme finish!
NOW, COMPARE WHAT I WAS JUST TALKING ABOUT TO A PISTOL.
A GUN CAN FIRE SIX SHOTS IN A ROW.
THE BULLET CAN HIT YOU IN THE BLINK OF AN EYE, **AND** FROM A DISTANCE. IT'S LIKE GETTING HIT BY INVISIBLE ARROWS.
IF YOU SHOOT SOMEONE IN A VITAL POINT,
HE'LL DROP DEAD ON THE SPOT. HE WON'T EVEN HAVE TIME TO SCREAM.

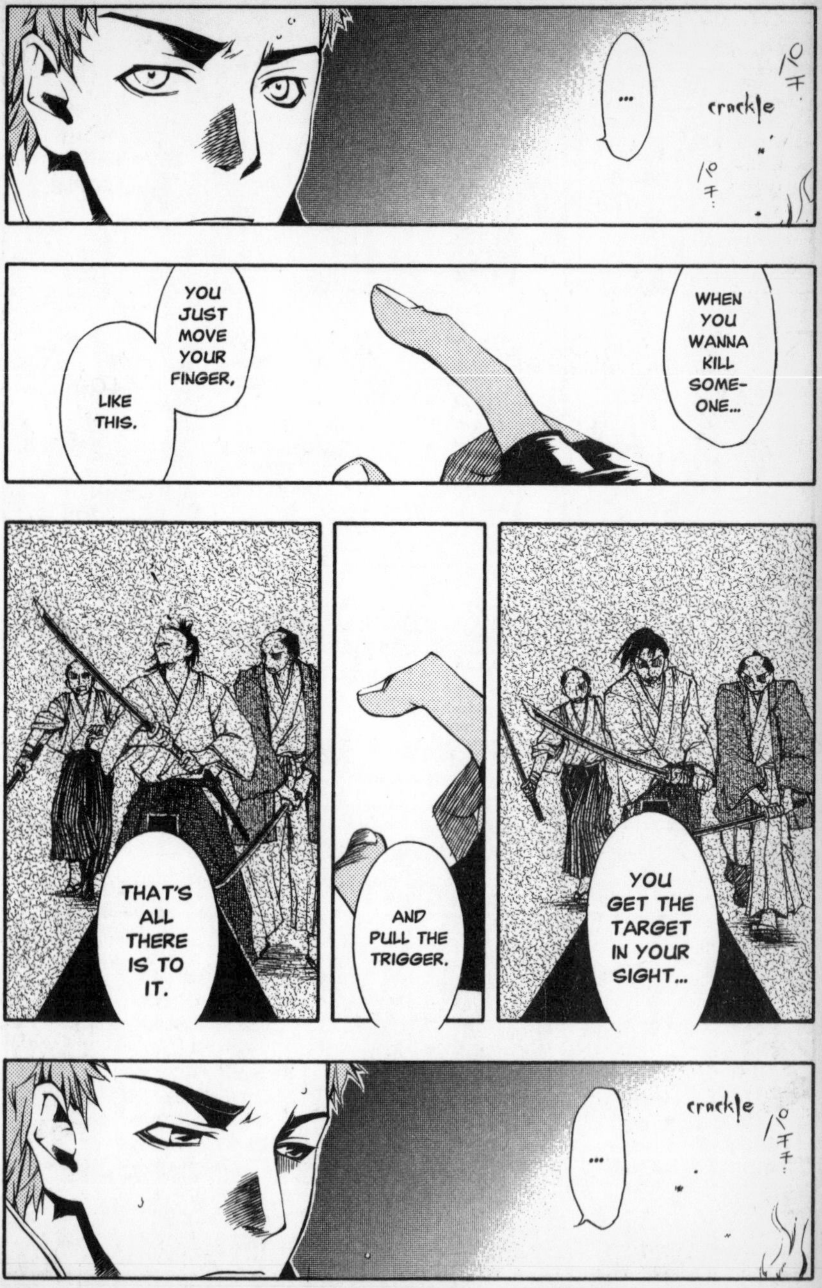

パチ・
crackle
パチ…
...
WHEN YOU WANNA KILL SOMEONE...
YOU JUST MOVE YOUR FINGER,
LIKE THIS.
YOU GET THE TARGET IN YOUR SIGHT...
AND PULL THE TRIGGER.
THAT'S ALL THERE IS TO IT.
crackle
パチチ…
...

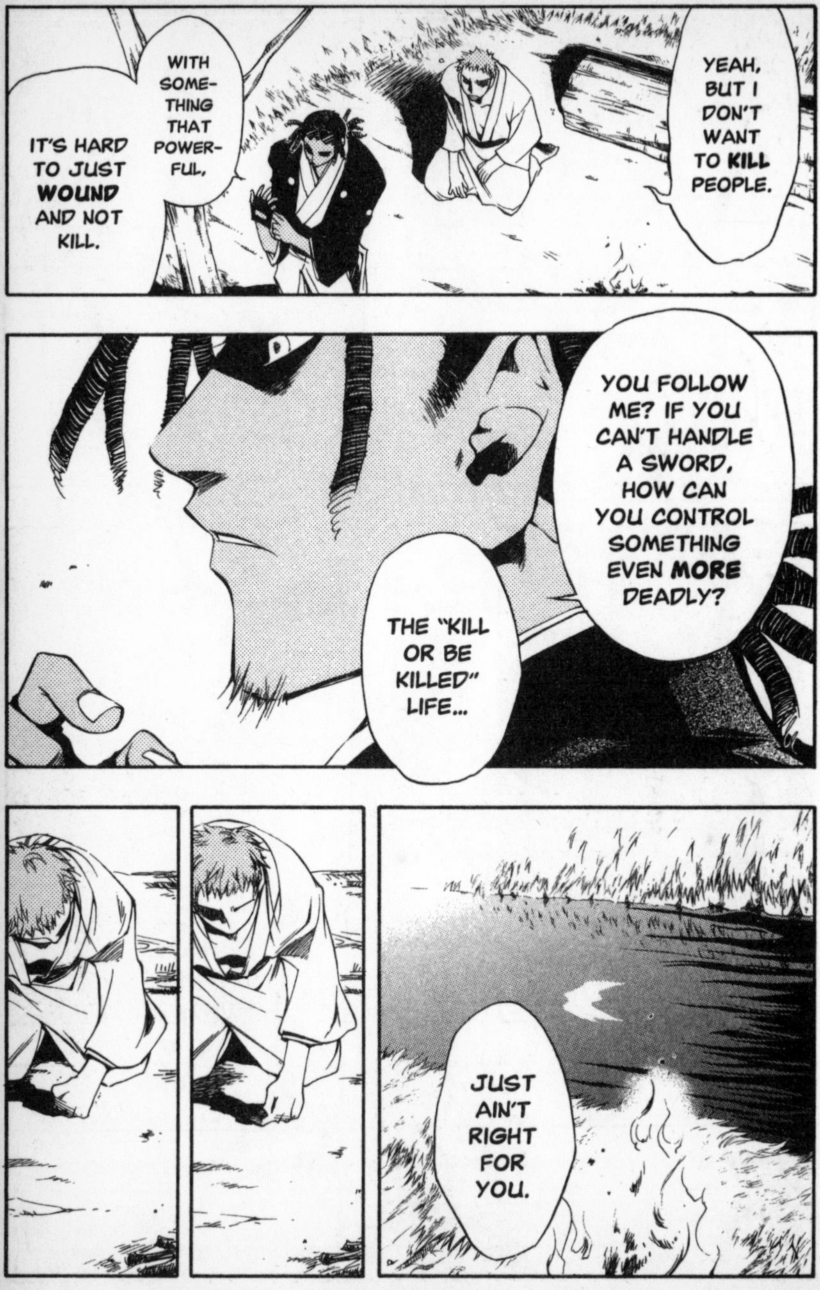
YEAH, BUT I DON'T WANT TO **KILL** PEOPLE.
WITH SOMETHING THAT POWERFUL,
IT'S HARD TO JUST **WOUND** AND NOT KILL.
YOU FOLLOW ME? IF YOU CAN'T HANDLE A SWORD, HOW CAN YOU CONTROL SOMETHING EVEN **MORE** DEADLY?
THE "KILL OR BE KILLED" LIFE...
JUST AIN'T RIGHT FOR YOU.

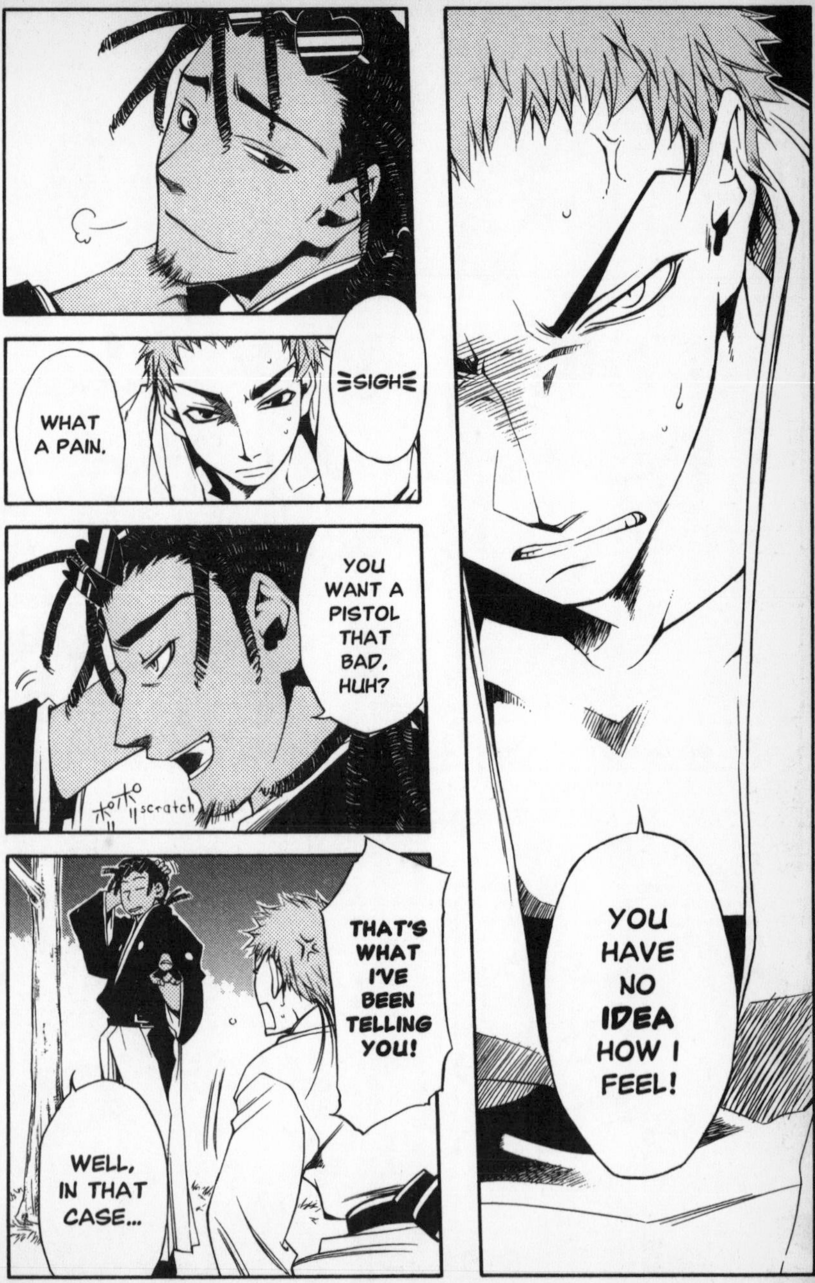
SIGH
WHAT A PAIN.
YOU WANT A PISTOL THAT BAD, HUH?
scratch
THAT'S WHAT I'VE BEEN TELLING YOU!
YOU HAVE NO IDEA HOW I FEEL!
WELL, IN THAT CASE...

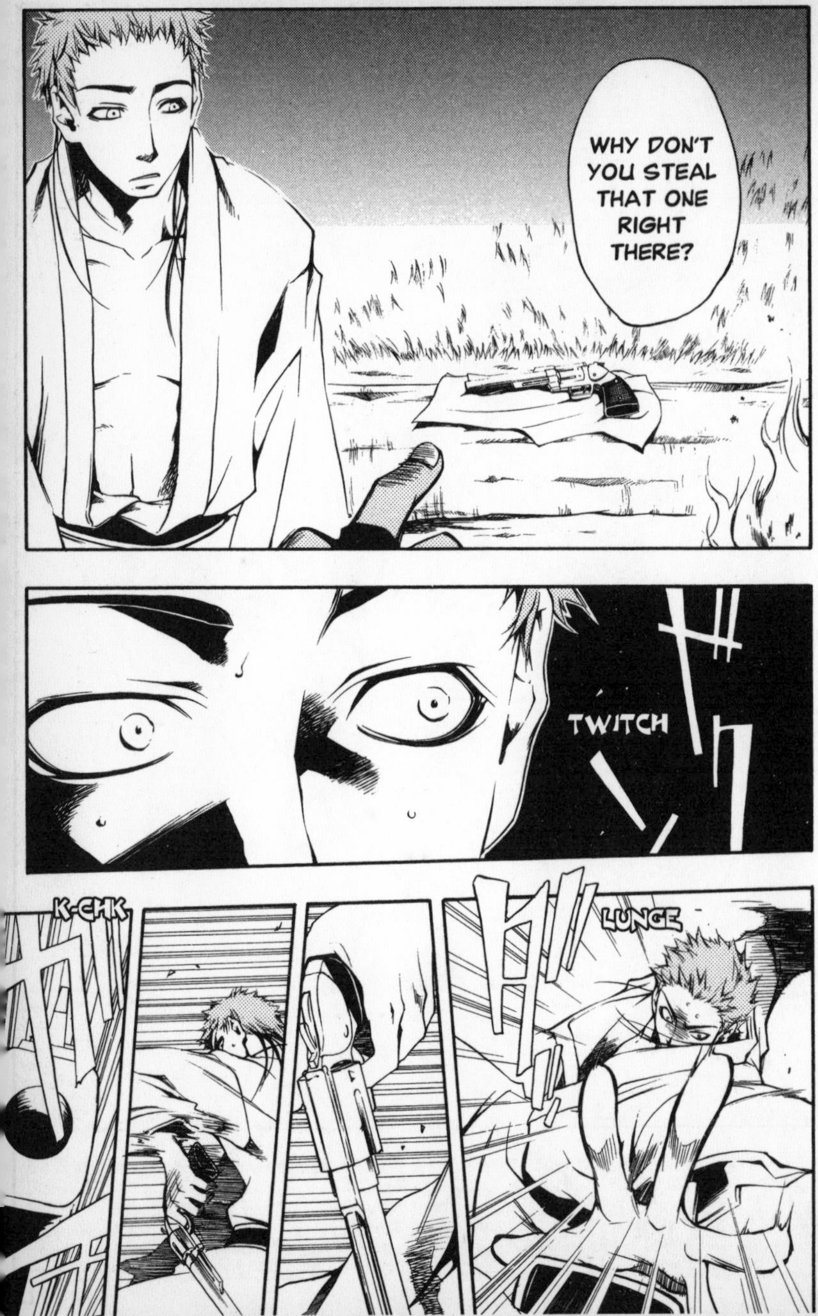

WHY DON'T YOU STEAL THAT ONE RIGHT THERE?
TWITCH
LUNGE
K-CHK

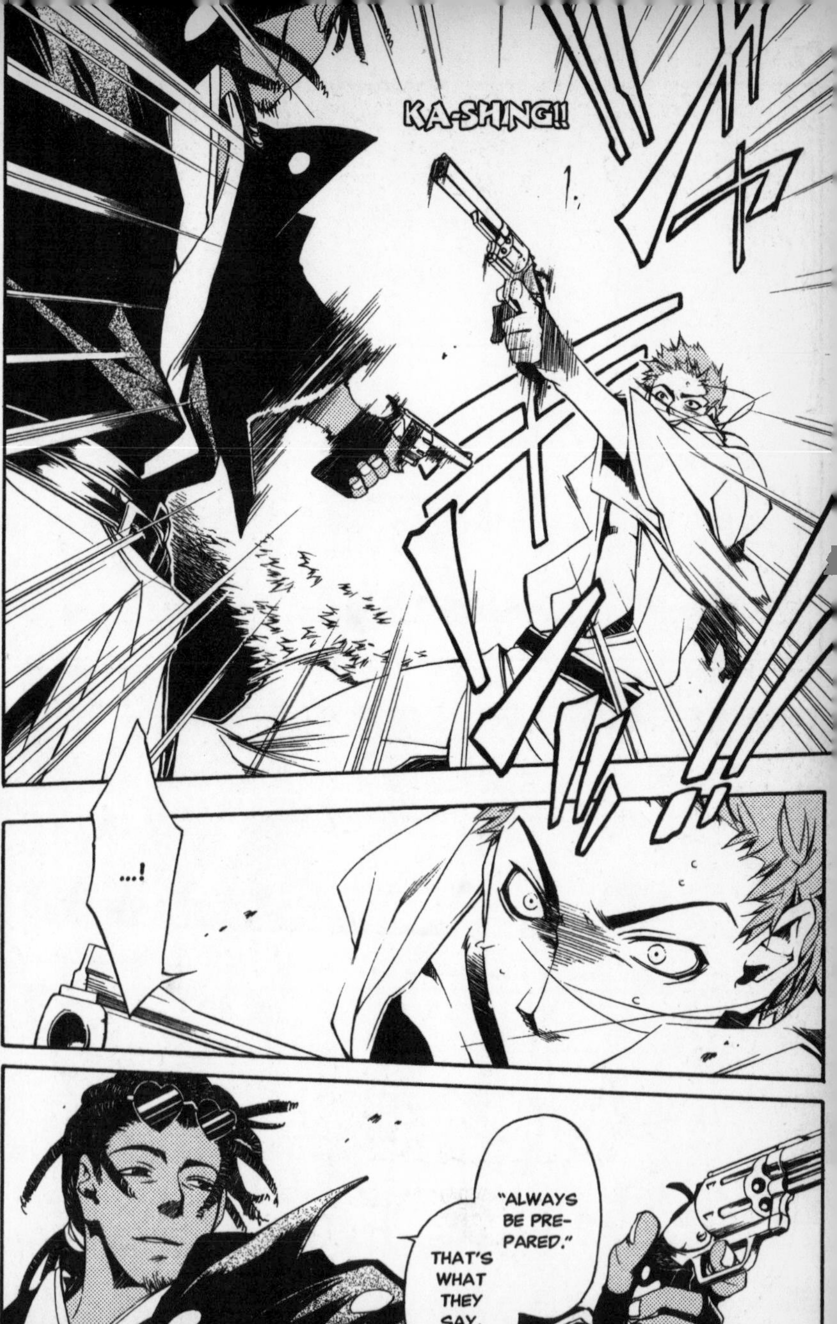
KA-SHING!!
...!
"ALWAYS BE PRE-PARED."
THAT'S WHAT THEY SAY, RIGHT?

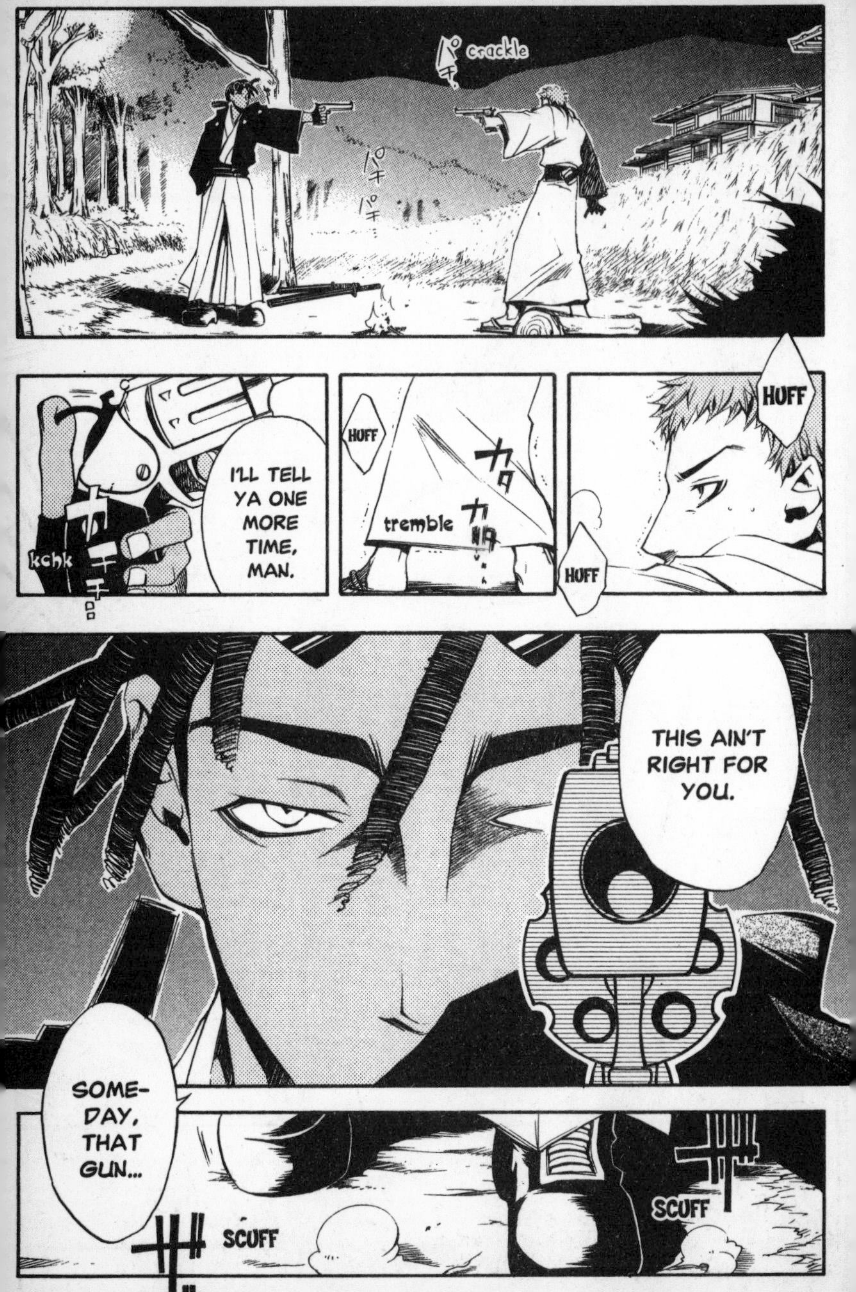
crackle
HUFF
HUFF
HUFF
tremble
I'LL TELL YA ONE MORE TIME, MAN.
kchk
THIS AIN'T RIGHT FOR YOU.
SOME-DAY, THAT GUN...
SCUFF
SCUFF

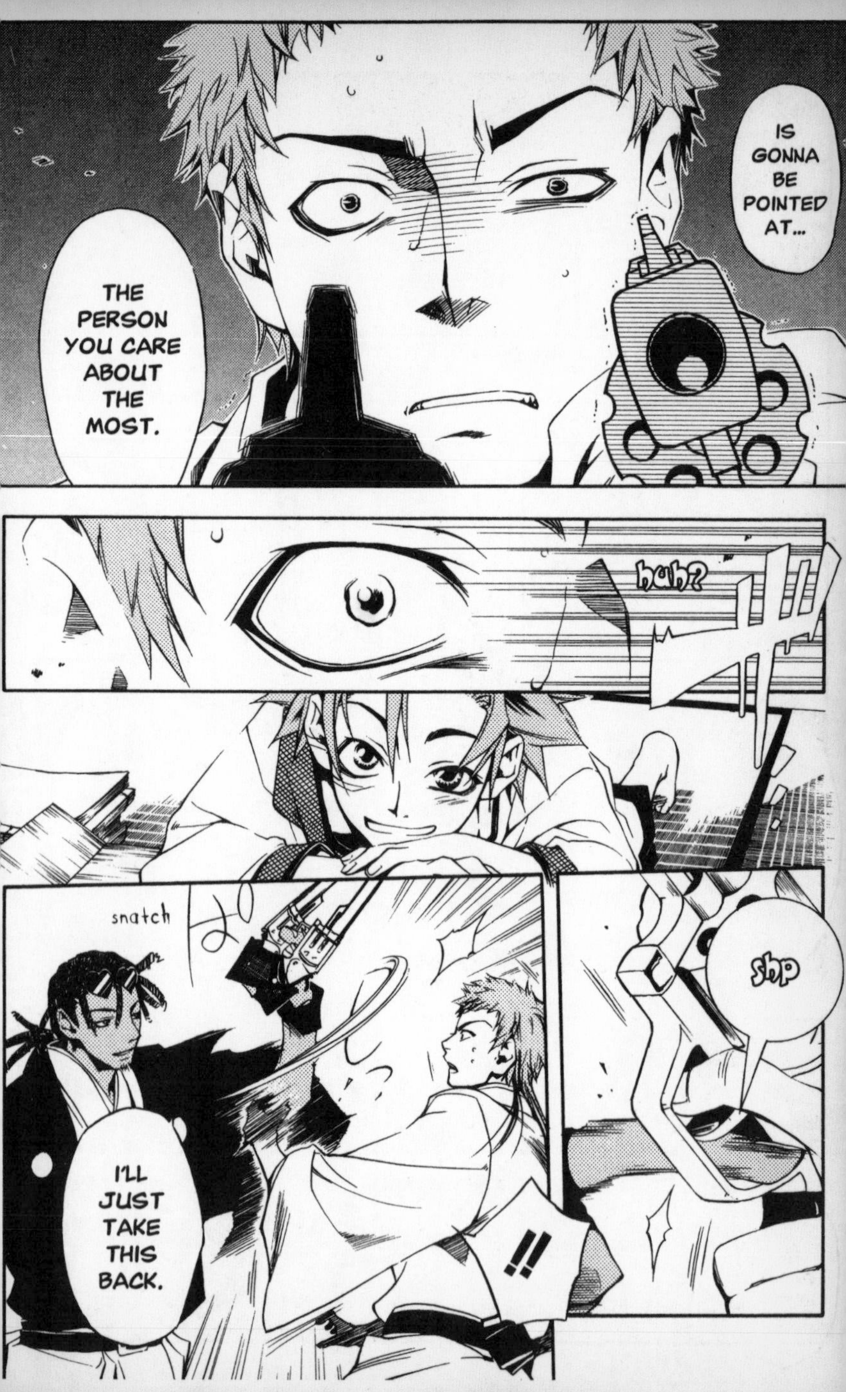
IS GONNA BE POINTED AT...
THE PERSON YOU CARE ABOUT THE MOST.
huh?
shp
snatch
I'LL JUST TAKE THIS BACK.
!!

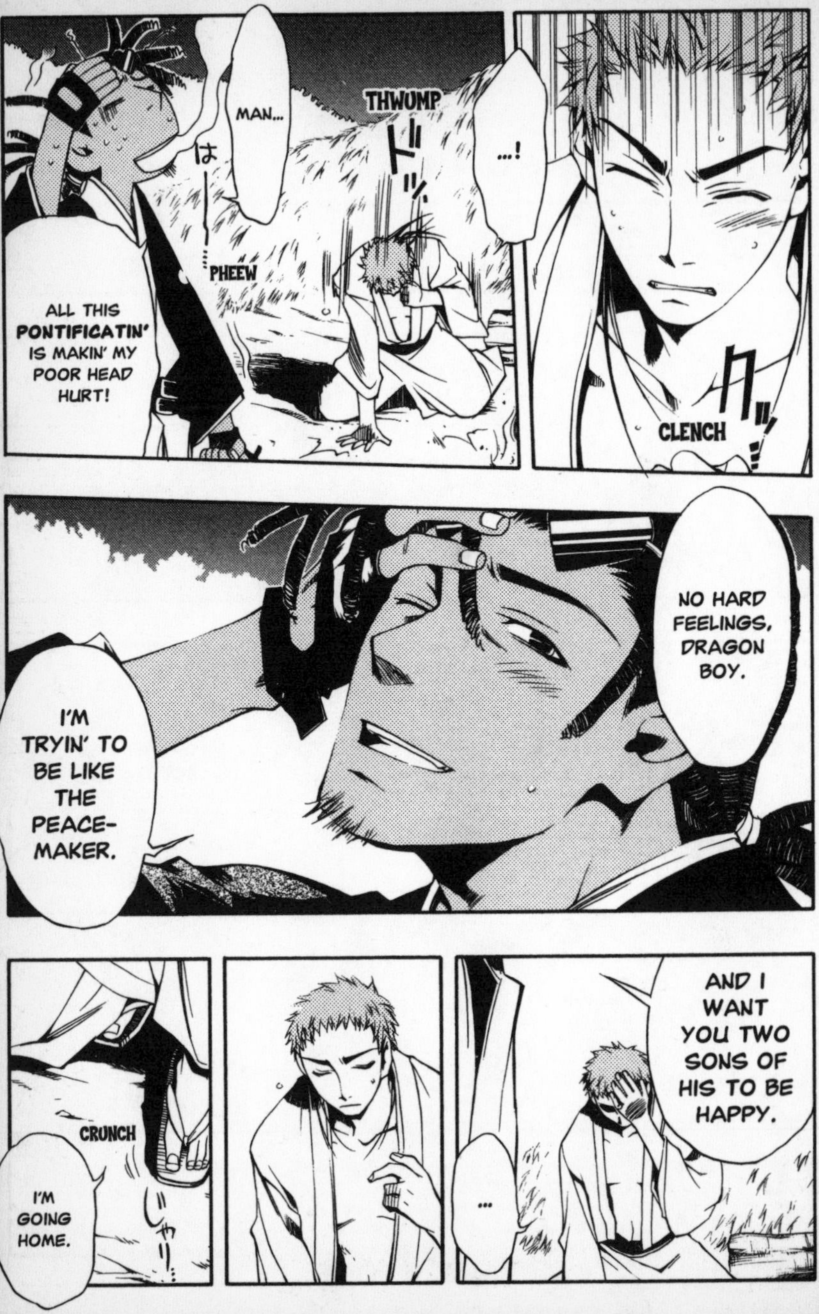

...!
CLENCH
クッ
MAN...
THWOMP
ドッ
PHEEW
はー…
ALL THIS **PONTIFICATIN'** IS MAKIN' MY POOR HEAD HURT!
NO HARD FEELINGS, DRAGON BOY.
I'M TRYIN' TO BE LIKE THE PEACE-MAKER.
AND I WANT YOU TWO SONS OF HIS TO BE HAPPY.
...
CRUNCH
じゃり…
I'M GOING HOME.

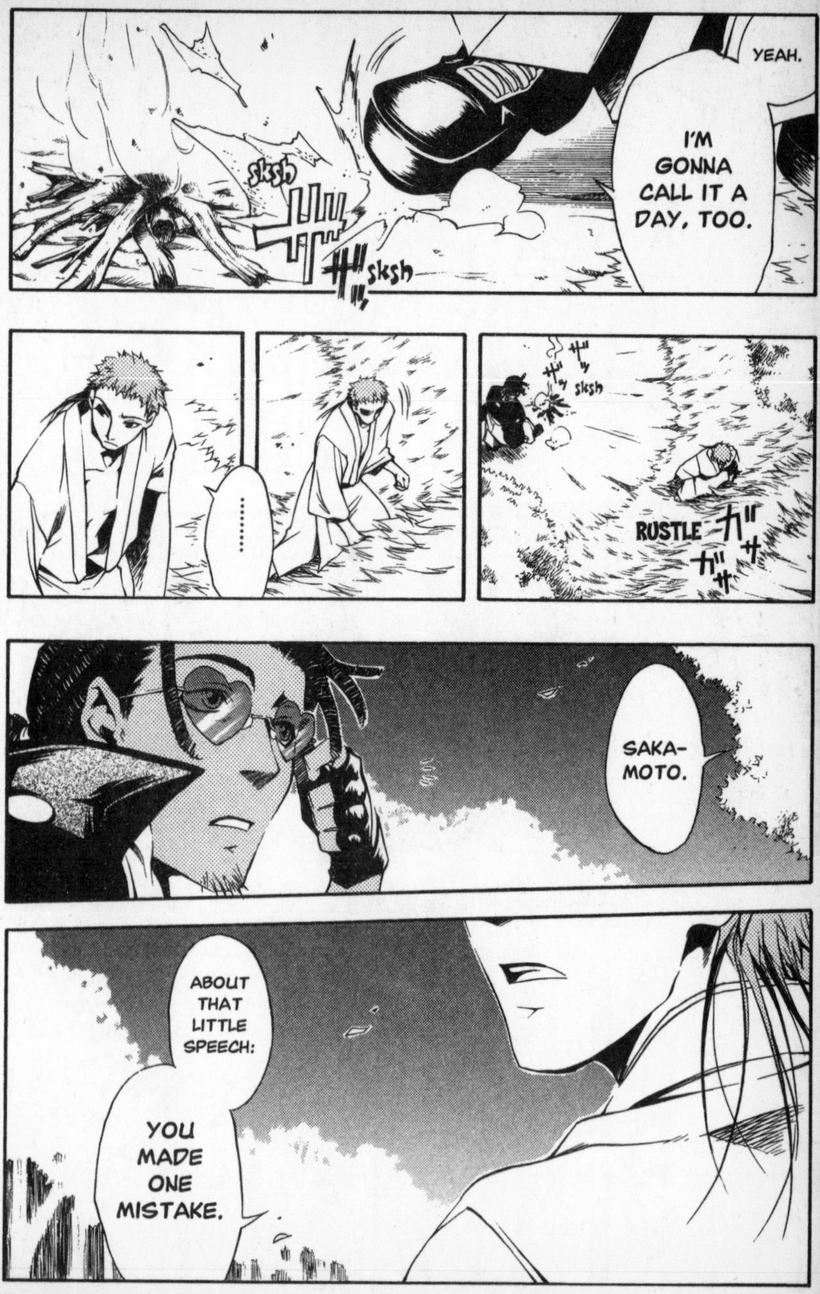
YEAH.
I'M GONNA CALL IT A DAY, TOO.
sksh
sksh
sksh
RUSTLE
ガサ
ガサ
....
SAKA-MOTO.
ABOUT THAT LITTLE SPEECH:
YOU MADE ONE MISTAKE.

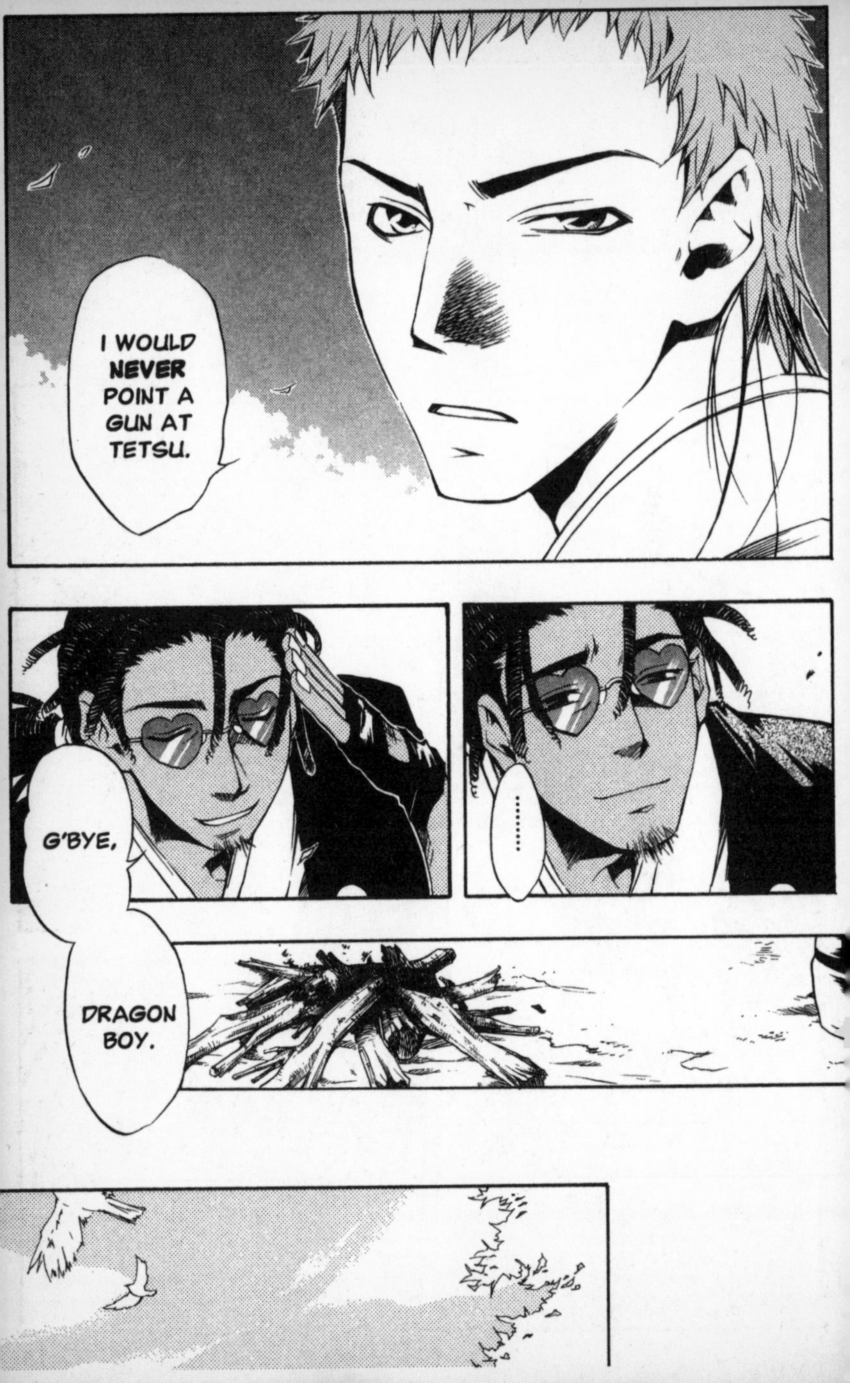
I WOULD NEVER POINT A GUN AT TETSU.
......
G'BYE,
DRAGON BOY.

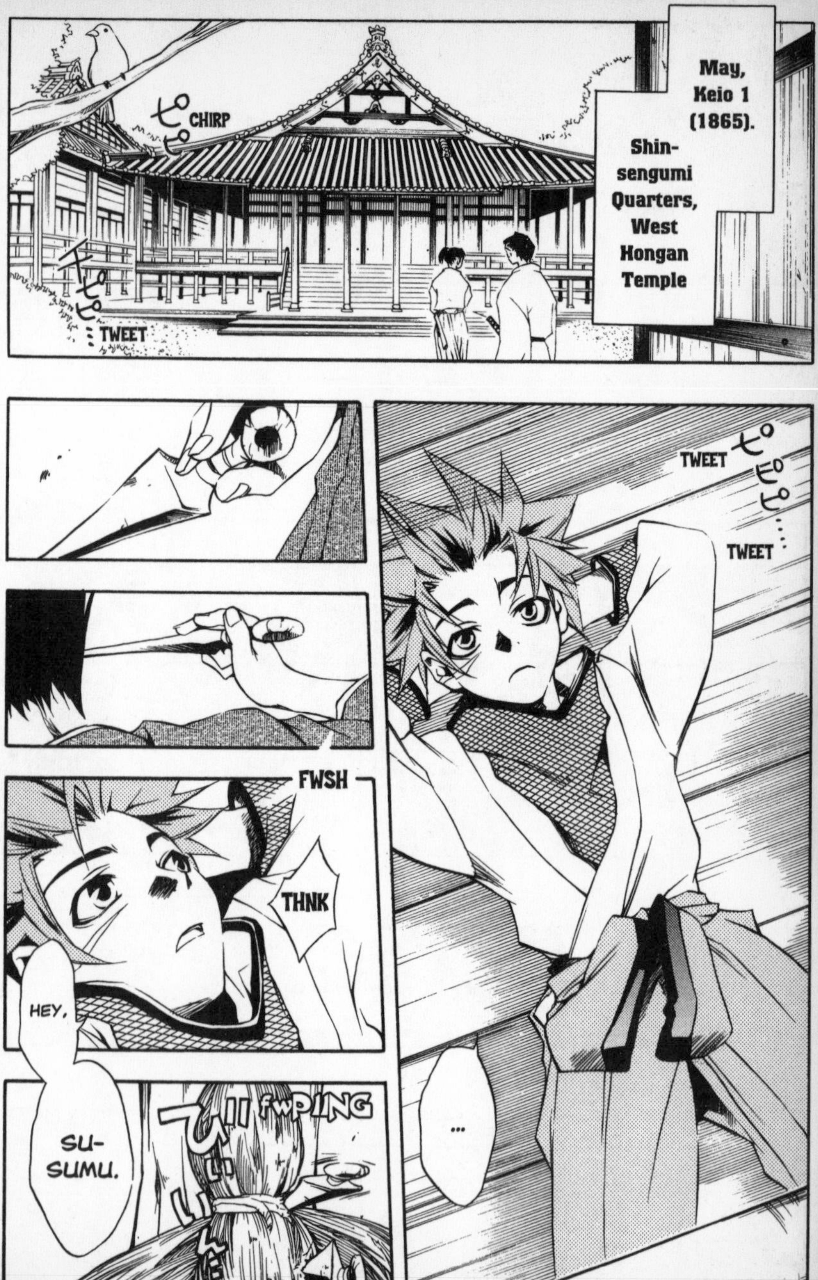
May, Keio 1 (1865).
Shin-sengumi Quarters, West Hongan Temple
CHIRP
TWEET
TWEET
TWEET
FWSH
THNK
HEY,
SU-SUMU.
fwPING
...

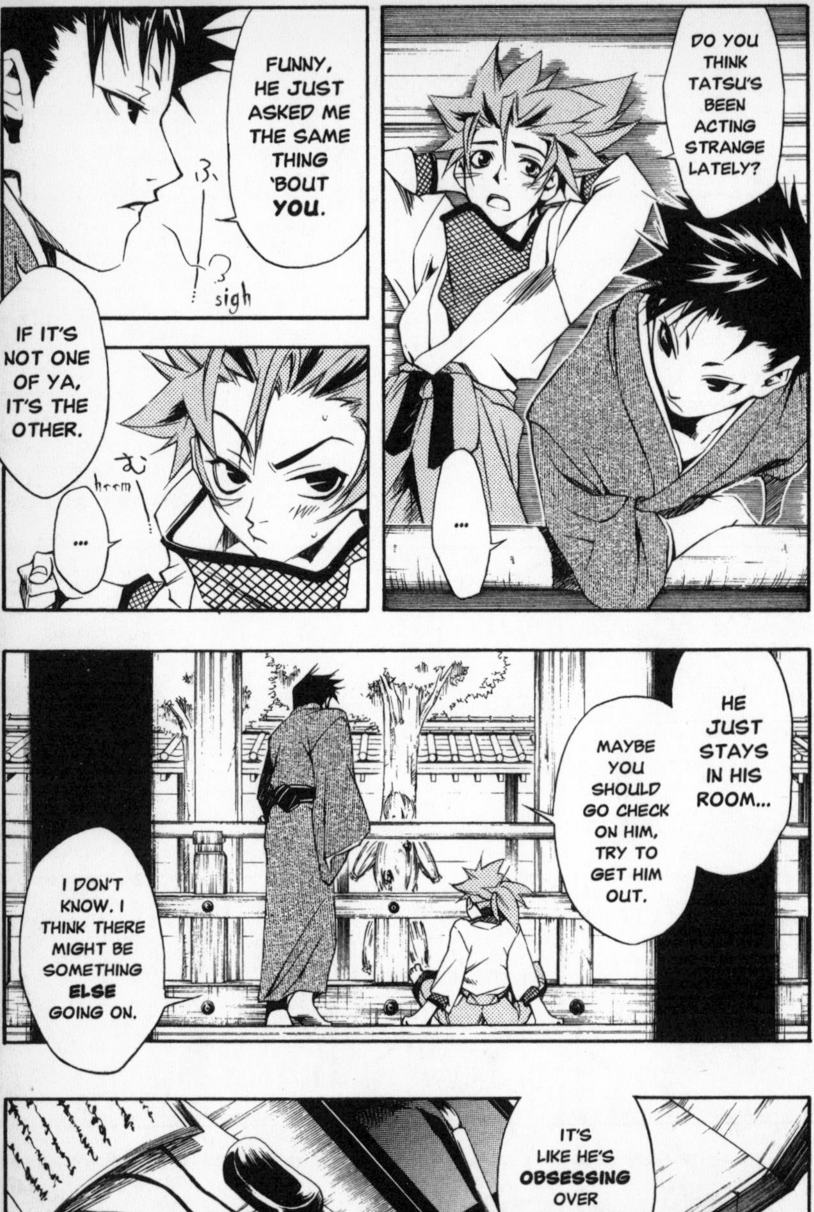
DO YOU THINK TATSU'S BEEN ACTING STRANGE LATELY?
...
FUNNY, HE JUST ASKED ME THE SAME THING 'BOUT **YOU**.
ふ
ふ
sigh
IF IT'S NOT ONE OF YA, IT'S THE OTHER.
む
hmm
...
HE JUST STAYS IN HIS ROOM...
MAYBE YOU SHOULD GO CHECK ON HIM, TRY TO GET HIM OUT.
I DON'T KNOW. I THINK THERE MIGHT BE SOMETHING **ELSE** GOING ON.
IT'S LIKE HE'S **OBSESSING** OVER SOMETHING.

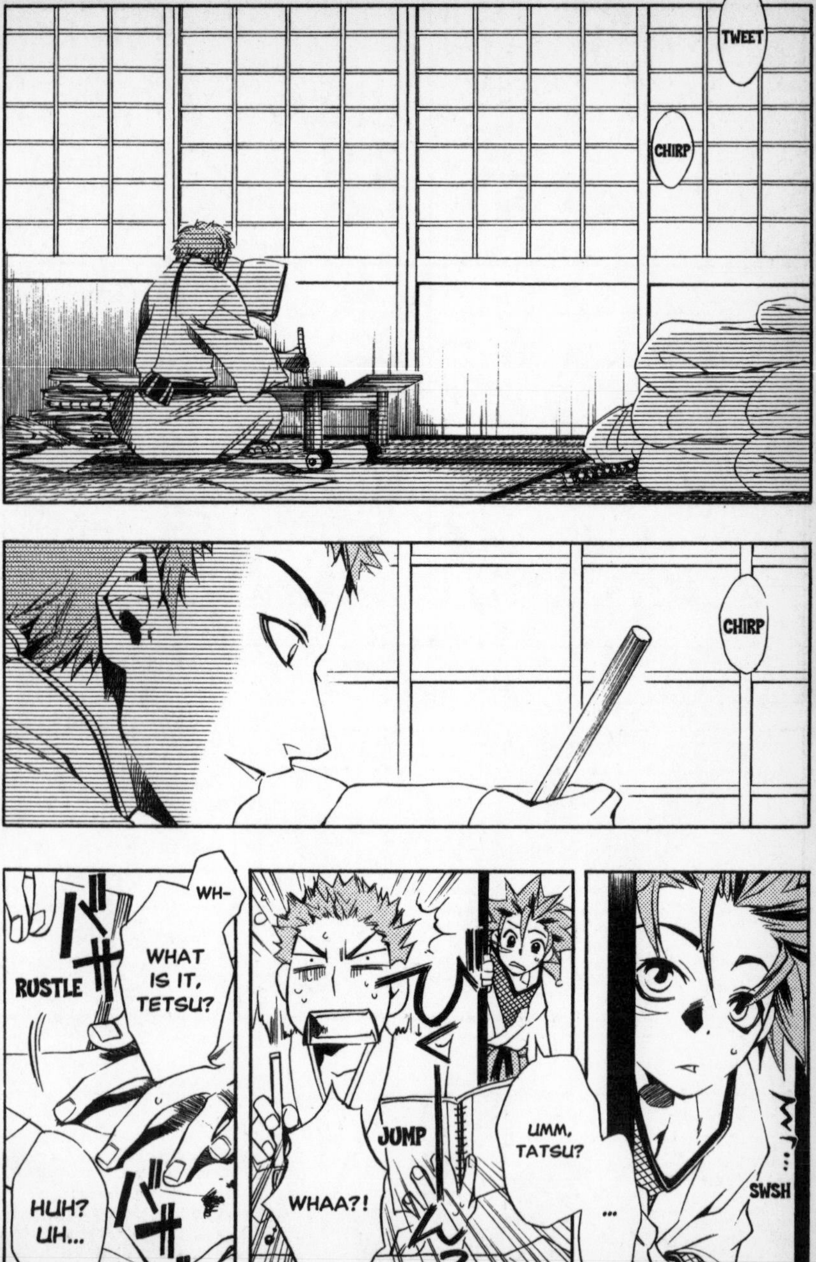
TWEET
CHIRP
CHIRP
SWSH
...
UMM, TATSU?
JUMP
WHAA?!
WH-
WHAT IS IT, TETSU?
RUSTLE
HUH? UH...

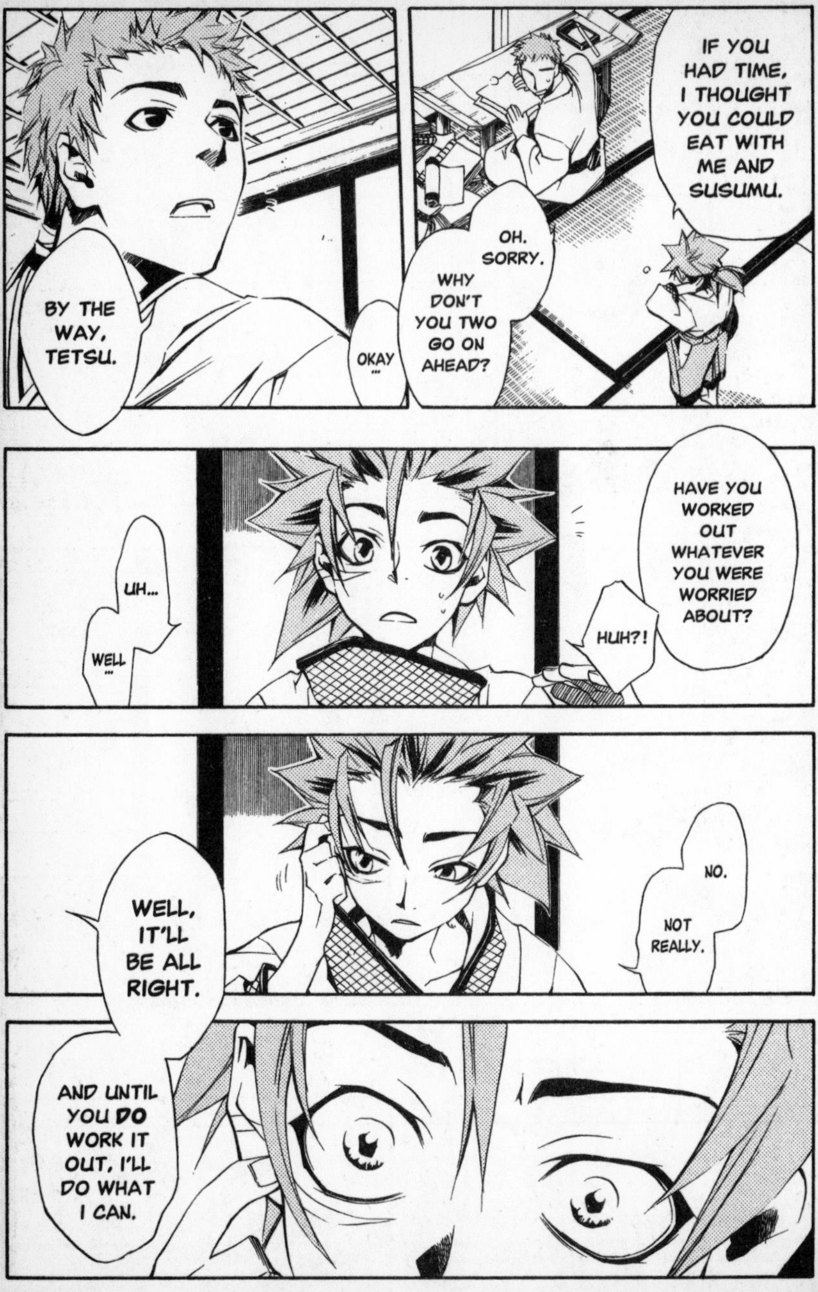
IF YOU HAD TIME, I THOUGHT YOU COULD EAT WITH ME AND SUSUMU.
OH. SORRY.
WHY DON'T YOU TWO GO ON AHEAD?
OKAY...
BY THE WAY, TETSU.
HAVE YOU WORKED OUT WHATEVER YOU WERE WORRIED ABOUT?
HUH?!
UH...
WELL...
NO.
NOT REALLY.
WELL, IT'LL BE ALL RIGHT.
AND UNTIL YOU DO WORK IT OUT, I'LL DO WHAT I CAN.

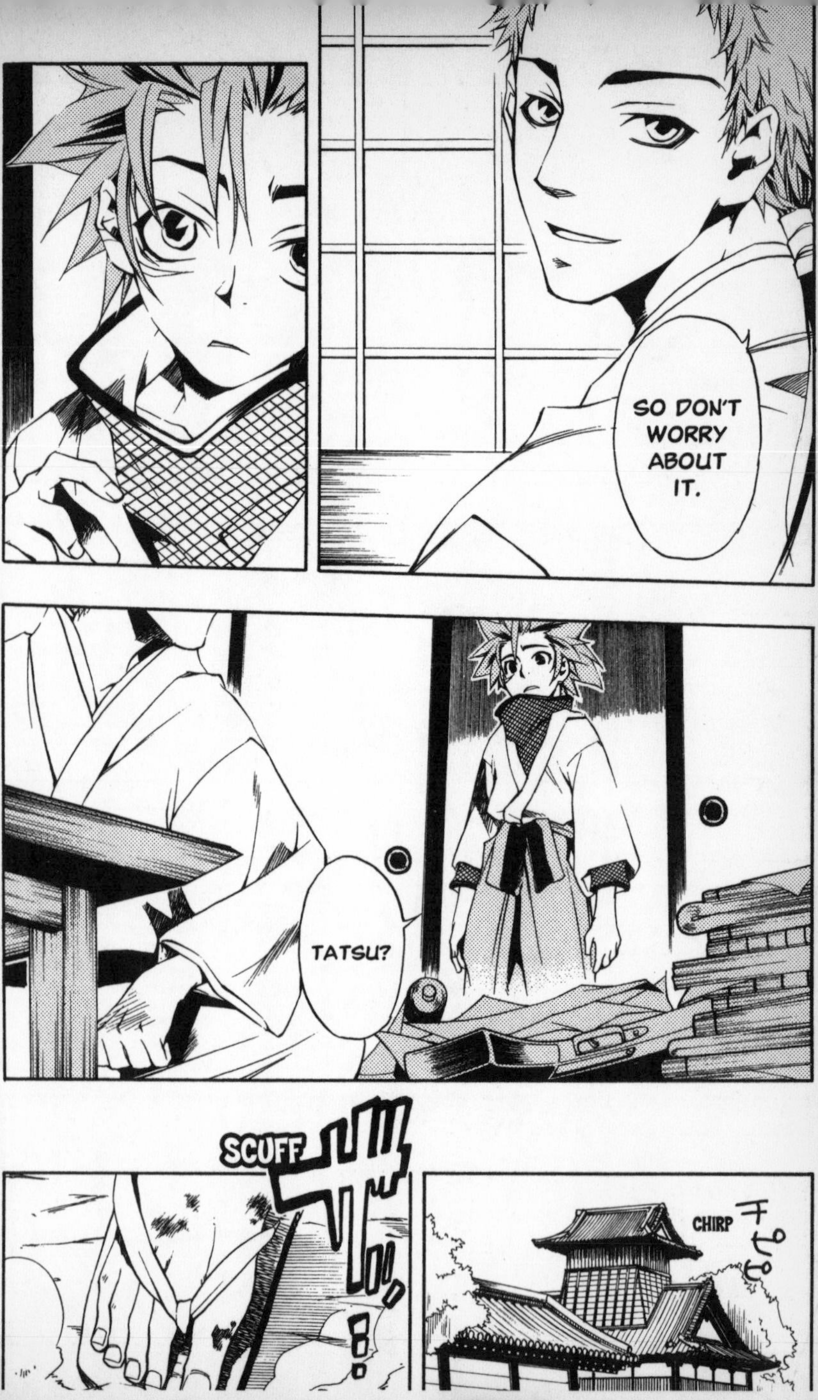
SO DON'T WORRY ABOUT IT.
TATSU?
CHIRP
チピピ
SCUFF

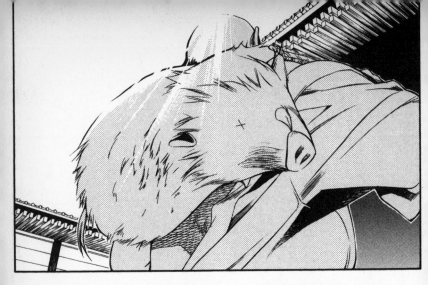

SO THE CHICK WHO DRAGGED ME THERE WAS REALLY A **GUY**. AN' WHEN HE RAN AT ME, I FENDED 'IM OFF WITH MY SPEAR, LIKE **THIS**!

ARE YOU FOR REAL, SANO? THIS STORY SOUNDS A LITTLE **TOO** GOOD...

HEY, IT'S THE TRUTH! AND WHEN I CHASED HIM DOWN, FOUR OF HIS BUDDIES SHOWED UP WITH PARASOLS, AND...

AHAHA!

ボ　DUOOOH

WASN'T THAT IN A **PLAY** WE JUST SAW?

THP THP THP THP THP THP

CAPTAIN!

CAPTAIN!

?

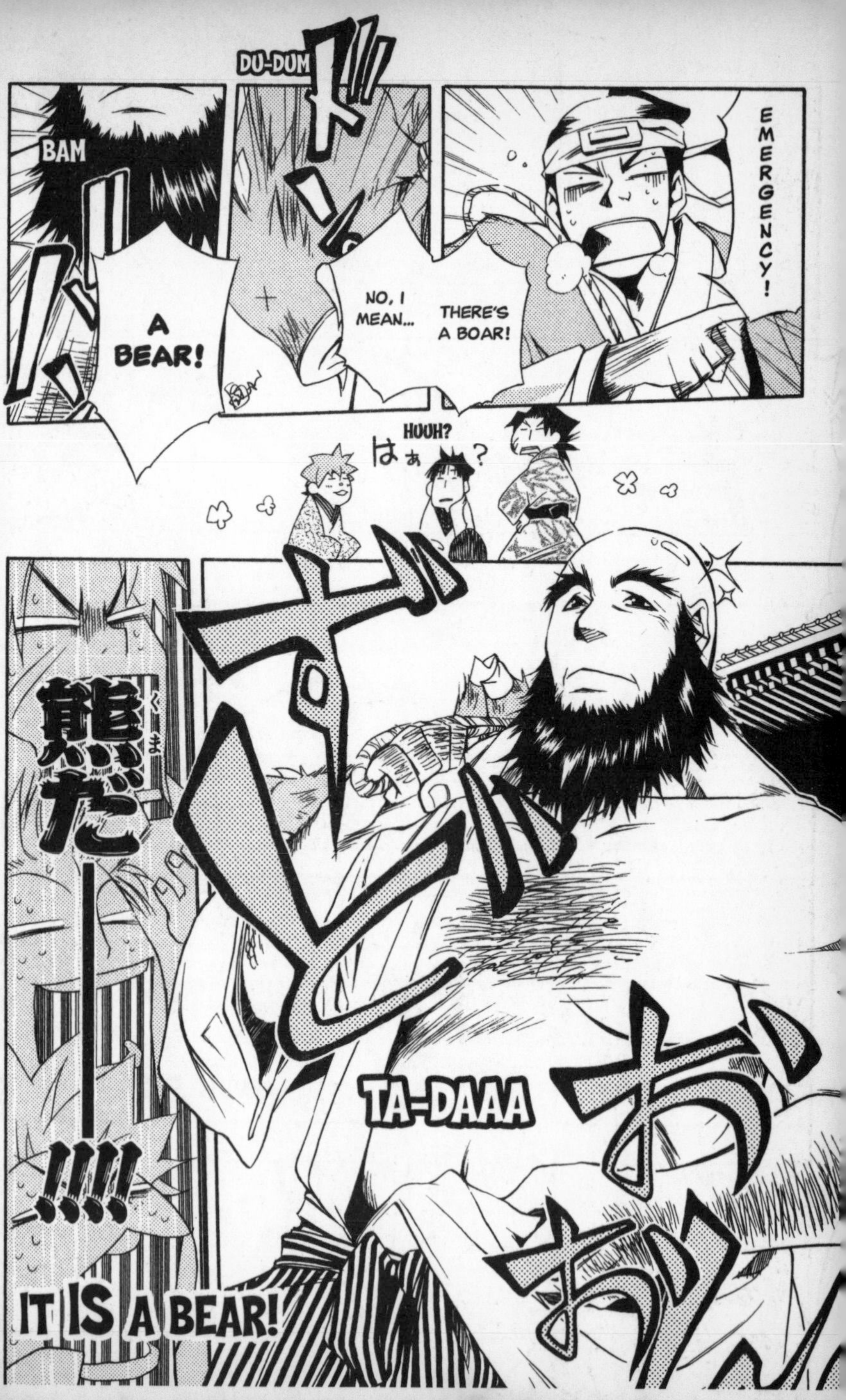

EMERGENCY!
THERE'S A BOAR!
NO, I MEAN...
DU-DUM
A BEAR!
BAM
HUUH?
はぁ？
TA-DAAA
熊だー!!!!
IT IS A BEAR!

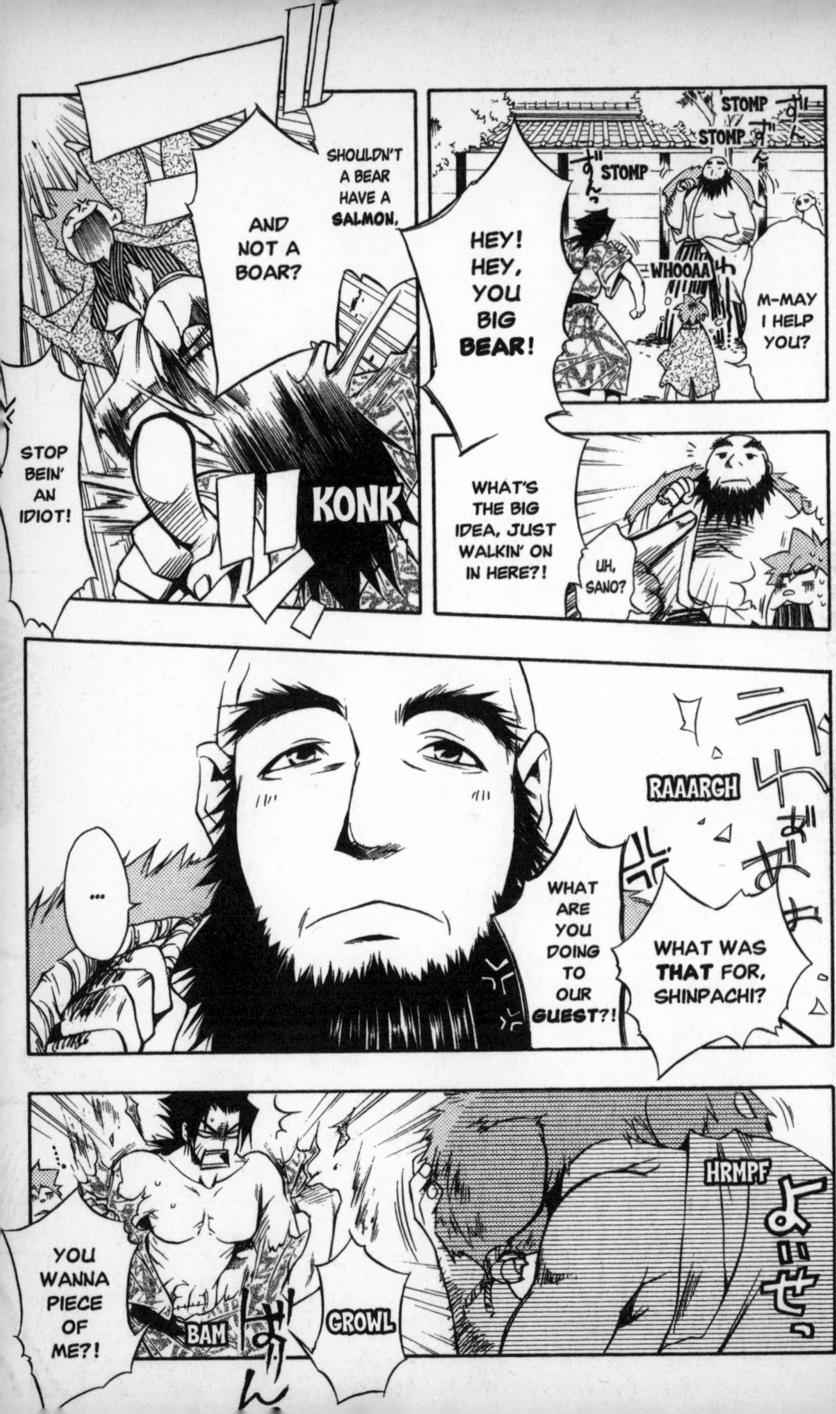
STOMP
STOMP
STOMP
WHOOAA
M-MAY I HELP YOU?
HEY! HEY, YOU BIG BEAR!
WHAT'S THE BIG IDEA, JUST WALKIN' ON IN HERE?!
UH, SANO?
SHOULDN'T A BEAR HAVE A SALMON,
AND NOT A BOAR?
KONK
STOP BEIN' AN IDIOT!
WHAT WAS THAT FOR, SHINPACHI?
RAAARGH
WHAT ARE YOU DOING TO OUR GUEST?!
...
HRMPF
GROWL
BAM
YOU WANNA PIECE OF ME?!

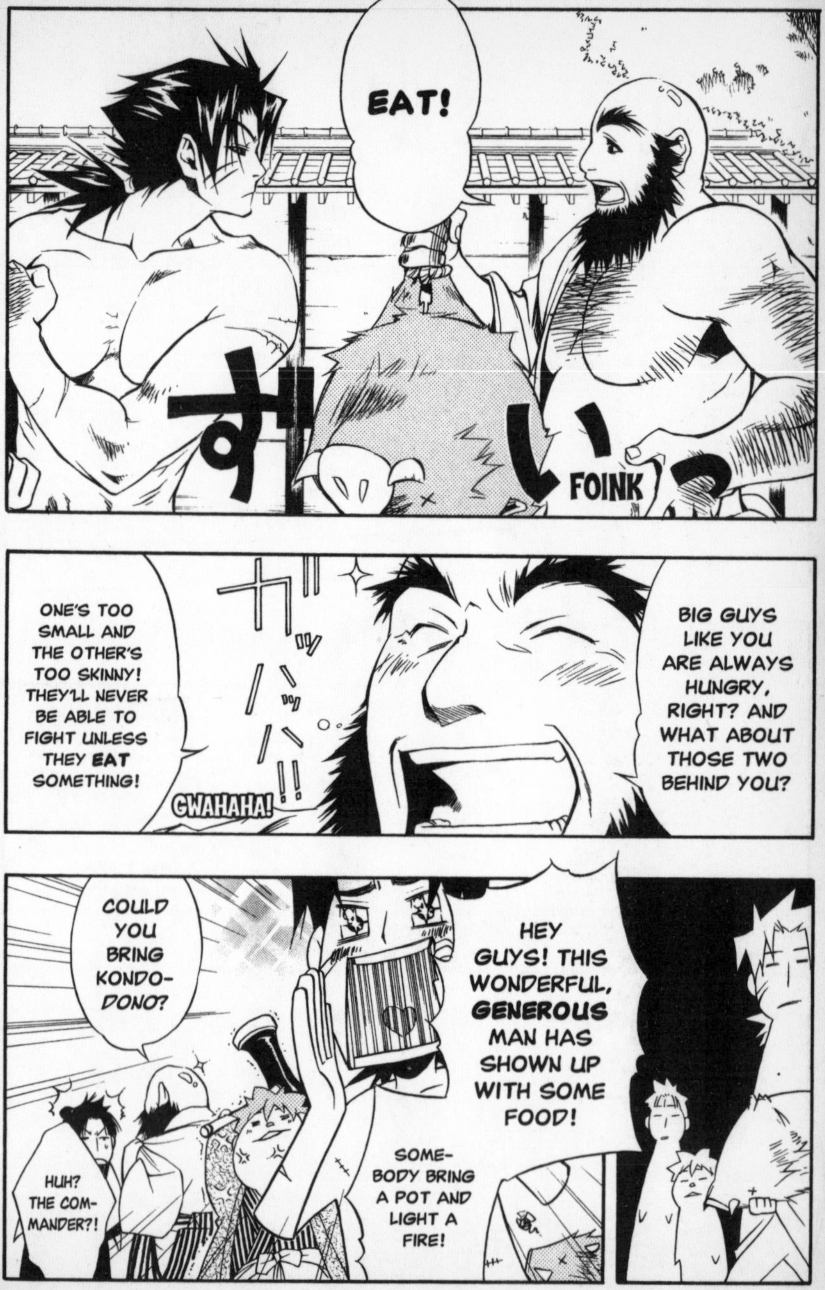

EAT!
すいっ
FOINK
BIG GUYS LIKE YOU ARE ALWAYS HUNGRY, RIGHT? AND WHAT ABOUT THOSE TWO BEHIND YOU?
ガッハッハ!!
GWAHAHA!
ONE'S TOO SMALL AND THE OTHER'S TOO SKINNY! THEY'LL NEVER BE ABLE TO FIGHT UNLESS THEY EAT SOMETHING!
HEY GUYS! THIS WONDERFUL, GENEROUS MAN HAS SHOWN UP WITH SOME FOOD!
SOME-BODY BRING A POT AND LIGHT A FIRE!
COULD YOU BRING KONDO-DONO?
HUH? THE COM-MANDER?!

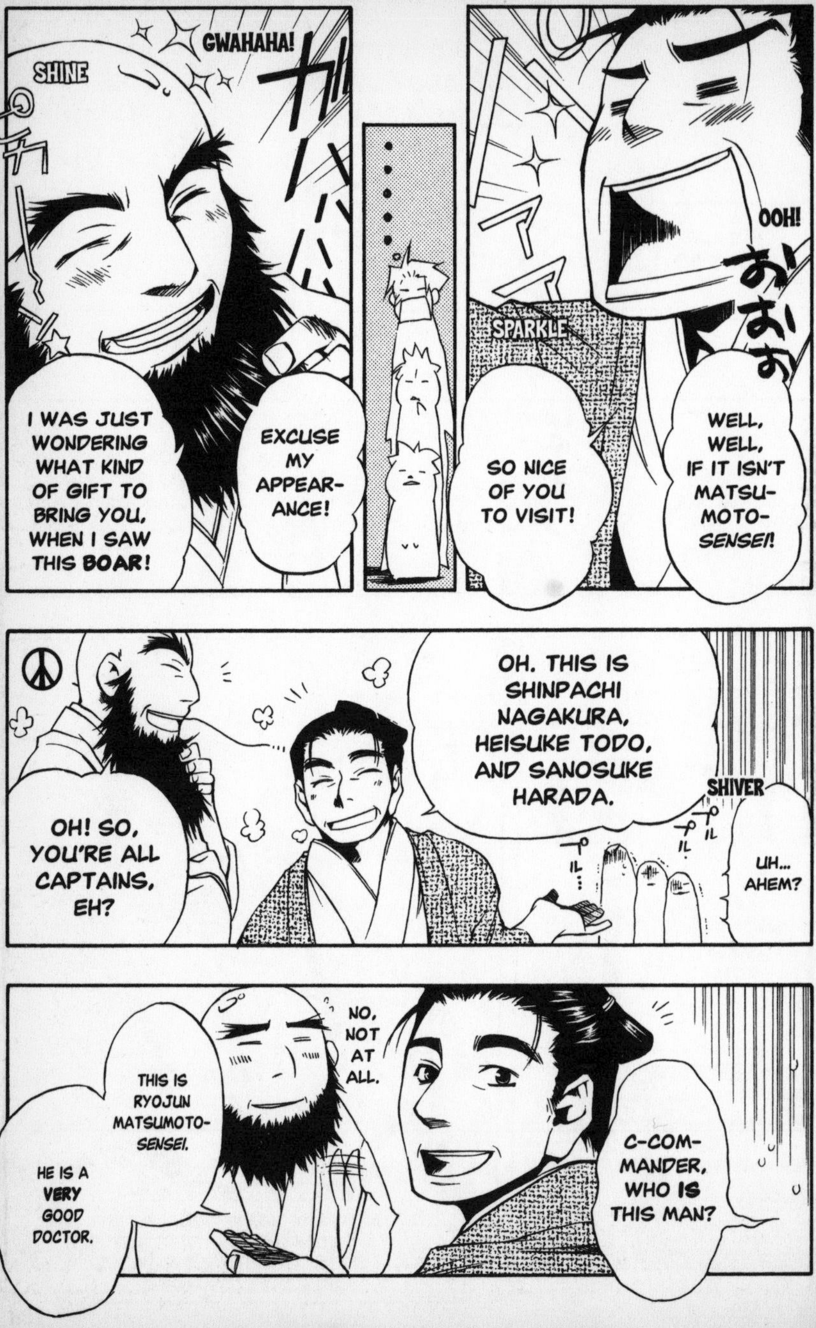
OOH!
おおお
WELL, WELL, IF IT ISN'T MATSUMOTO-SENSEI!
SPARKLE
SO NICE OF YOU TO VISIT!
......
EXCUSE MY APPEARANCE!
GWAHAHA!
SHINE
I WAS JUST WONDERING WHAT KIND OF GIFT TO BRING YOU, WHEN I SAW THIS **BOAR**!
UH... AHEM?
SHIVER
OH. THIS IS SHINPACHI NAGAKURA, HEISUKE TODO, AND SANOSUKE HARADA.
OH! SO, YOU'RE ALL CAPTAINS, EH?
C-COMMANDER, WHO **IS** THIS MAN?
NO, NOT AT ALL.
THIS IS RYOJUN MATSUMOTO-SENSEI.
HE IS A **VERY** GOOD DOCTOR.

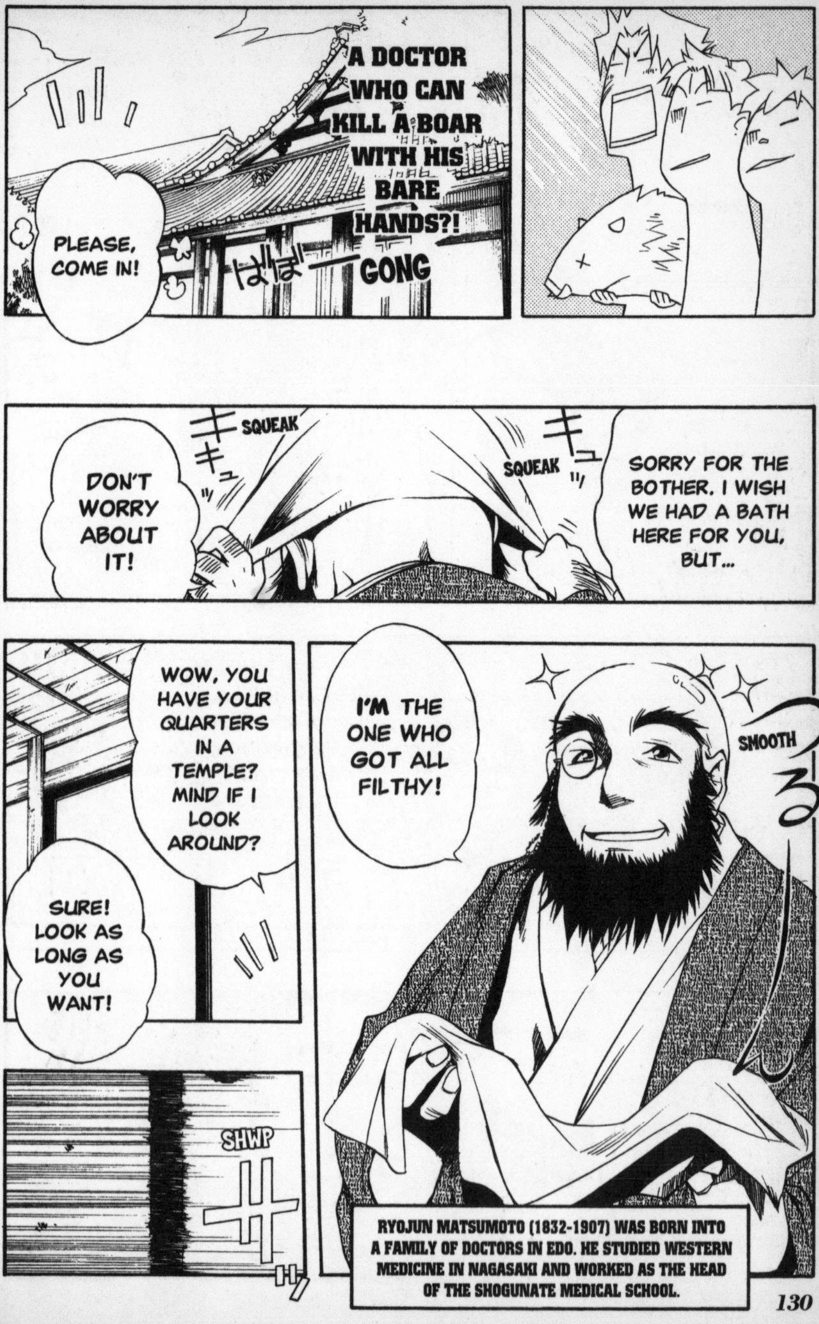

A DOCTOR WHO CAN KILL A BOAR WITH HIS BARE HANDS?!
PLEASE, COME IN!
GONG
SQUEAK
DON'T WORRY ABOUT IT!
SQUEAK
SORRY FOR THE BOTHER. I WISH WE HAD A BATH HERE FOR YOU, BUT...
WOW, YOU HAVE YOUR QUARTERS IN A TEMPLE? MIND IF I LOOK AROUND?
SURE! LOOK AS LONG AS YOU WANT!
SHWP
I'M THE ONE WHO GOT ALL FILTHY!
SMOOTH
RYOJUN MATSUMOTO (1832-1907) WAS BORN INTO A FAMILY OF DOCTORS IN EDO. HE STUDIED WESTERN MEDICINE IN NAGASAKI AND WORKED AS THE HEAD OF THE SHOGUNATE MEDICAL SCHOOL.

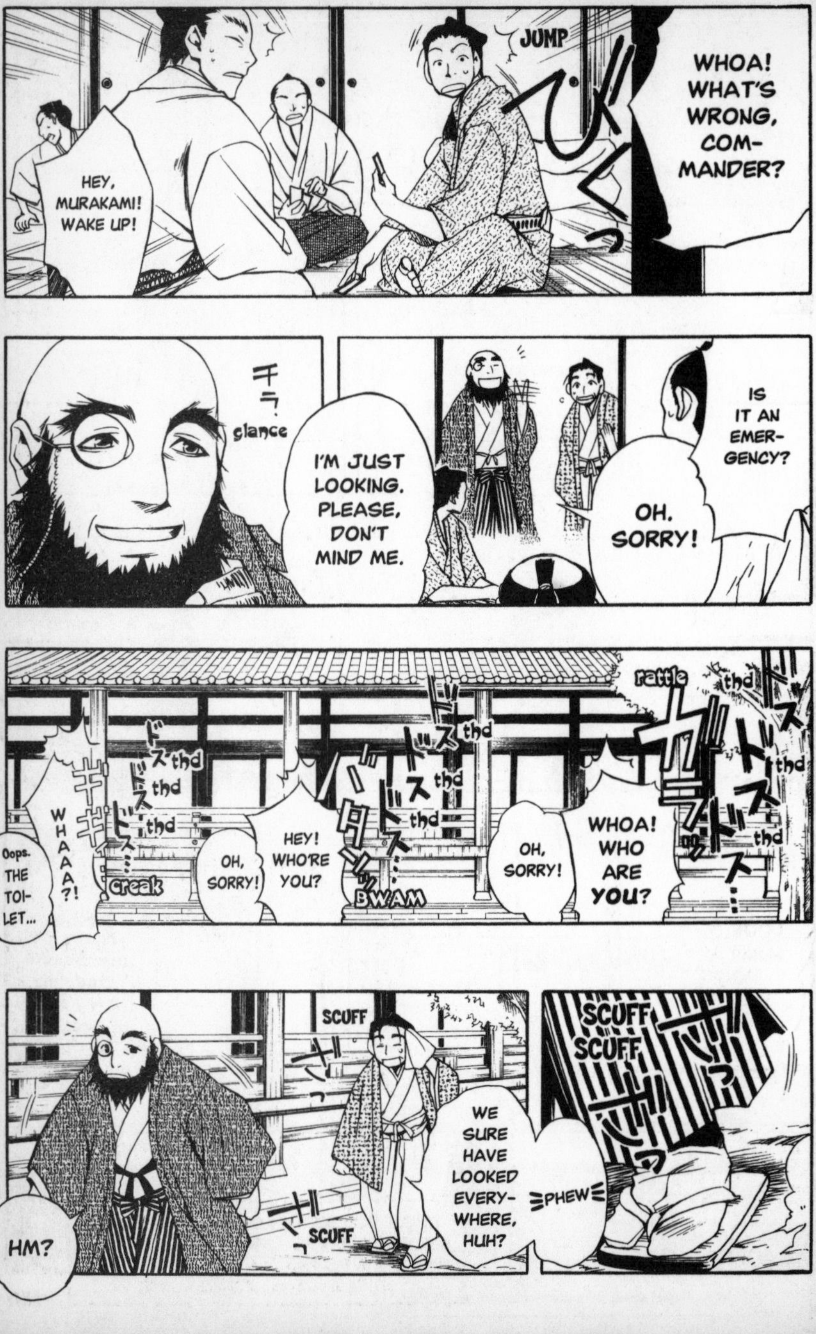
WHOA! WHAT'S WRONG, COM-MANDER?
JUMP
HEY, MURAKAMI! WAKE UP!
IS IT AN EMER-GENCY?
OH. SORRY!
I'M JUST LOOKING. PLEASE, DON'T MIND ME.
glance
rattle
thd
thd
thd
WHOA! WHO ARE YOU?
OH, SORRY!
thd
thd
thd
BWAM
HEY! WHO'RE YOU?
OH, SORRY!
thd
thd
thd
creak
WHAAAA?!
Oops. THE TOI-LET...
SCUFF SCUFF
PHEW
WE SURE HAVE LOOKED EVERY-WHERE, HUH?
SCUFF
SCUFF
HM?

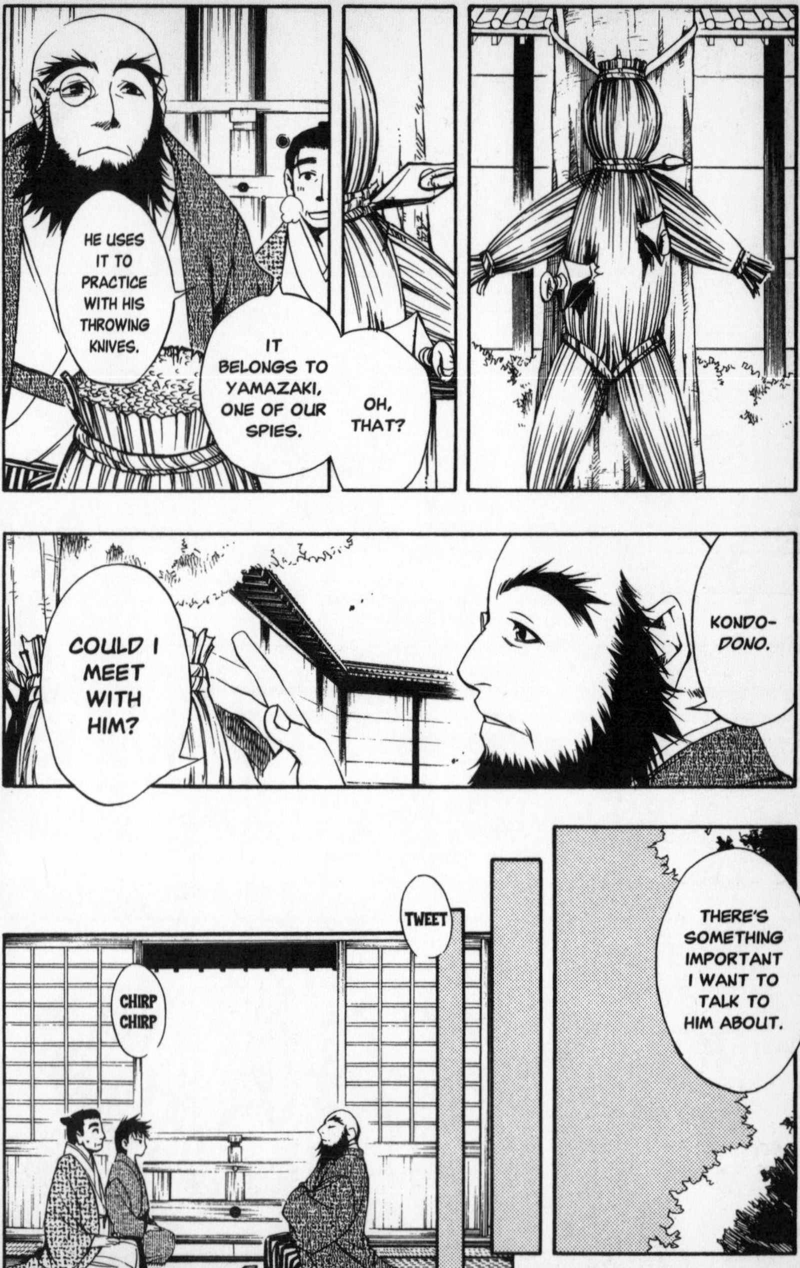
OH, THAT?
IT BELONGS TO YAMAZAKI, ONE OF OUR SPIES.
HE USES IT TO PRACTICE WITH HIS THROWING KNIVES.
KONDO-DONO.
COULD I MEET WITH HIM?
THERE'S SOMETHING IMPORTANT I WANT TO TALK TO HIM ABOUT.
TWEET
CHIRP CHIRP

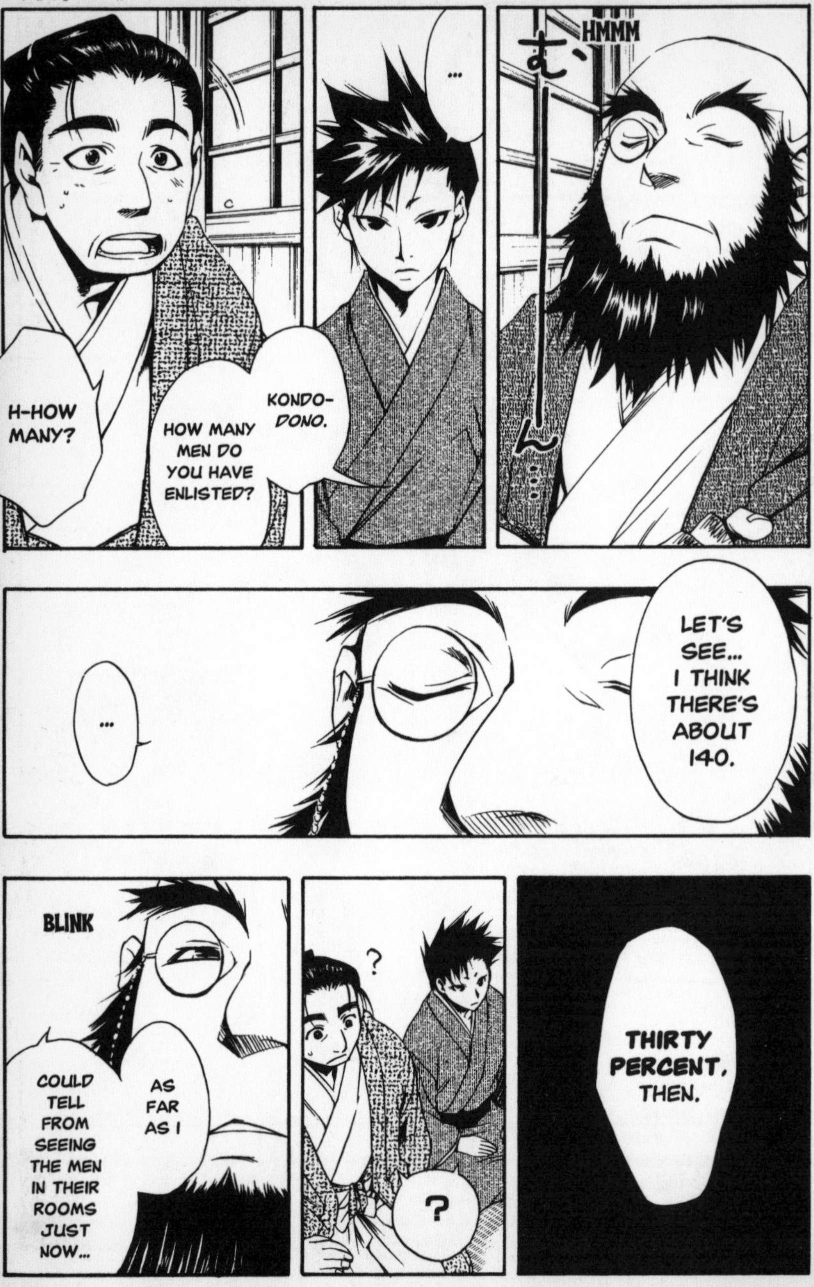
HMMM
む、
ん…
...
KONDO-DONO.
HOW MANY MEN DO YOU HAVE ENLISTED?
H-HOW MANY?
LET'S SEE... I THINK THERE'S ABOUT 140.
...
THIRTY PERCENT, THEN.
?
?
BLINK
AS FAR AS I
COULD TELL FROM SEEING THE MEN IN THEIR ROOMS JUST NOW...

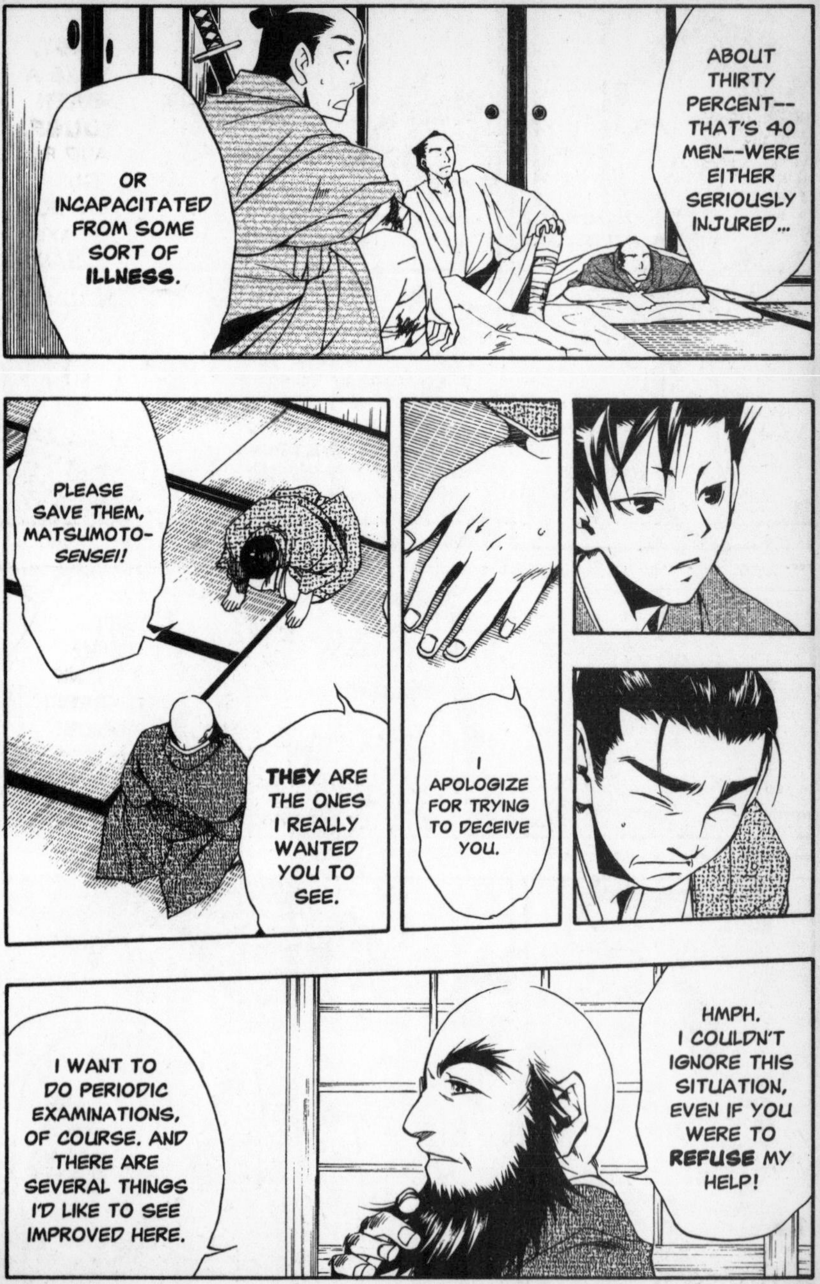
ABOUT THIRTY PERCENT--THAT'S 40 MEN--WERE EITHER SERIOUSLY INJURED...
OR INCAPACITATED FROM SOME SORT OF **ILLNESS.**
I APOLOGIZE FOR TRYING TO DECEIVE YOU.
THEY ARE THE ONES I REALLY WANTED YOU TO SEE.
PLEASE SAVE THEM, MATSUMOTO-SENSEI!
HMPH. I COULDN'T IGNORE THIS SITUATION, EVEN IF YOU WERE TO **REFUSE** MY HELP!
I WANT TO DO PERIODIC EXAMINATIONS, OF COURSE. AND THERE ARE SEVERAL THINGS I'D LIKE TO SEE IMPROVED HERE.

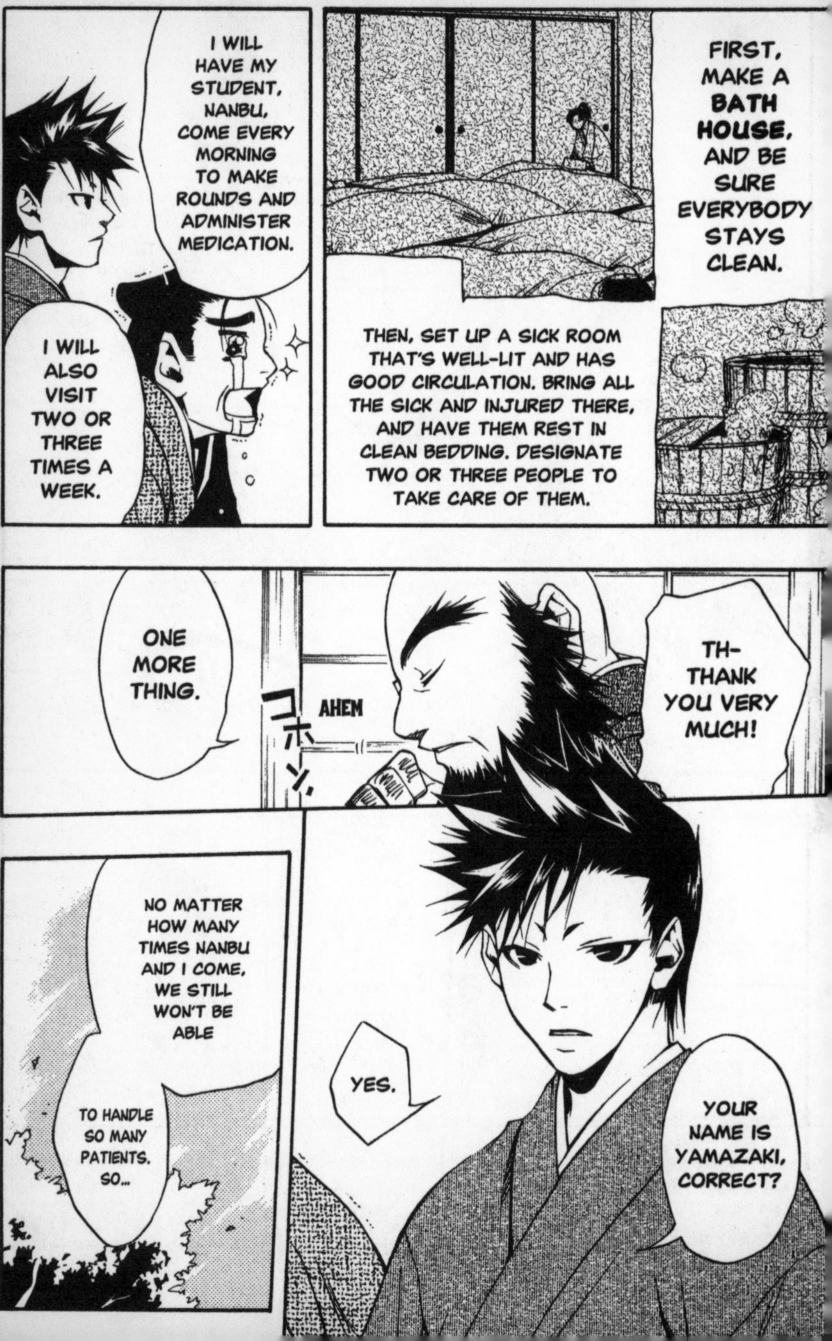
FIRST, MAKE A BATH HOUSE, AND BE SURE EVERYBODY STAYS CLEAN.
THEN, SET UP A SICK ROOM THAT'S WELL-LIT AND HAS GOOD CIRCULATION. BRING ALL THE SICK AND INJURED THERE, AND HAVE THEM REST IN CLEAN BEDDING. DESIGNATE TWO OR THREE PEOPLE TO TAKE CARE OF THEM.
I WILL HAVE MY STUDENT, NANBU, COME EVERY MORNING TO MAKE ROUNDS AND ADMINISTER MEDICATION.
I WILL ALSO VISIT TWO OR THREE TIMES A WEEK.
TH-THANK YOU VERY MUCH!
AHEM
ONE MORE THING.
YOUR NAME IS YAMAZAKI, CORRECT?
YES.
NO MATTER HOW MANY TIMES NANBU AND I COME, WE STILL WON'T BE ABLE
TO HANDLE SO MANY PATIENTS. SO...

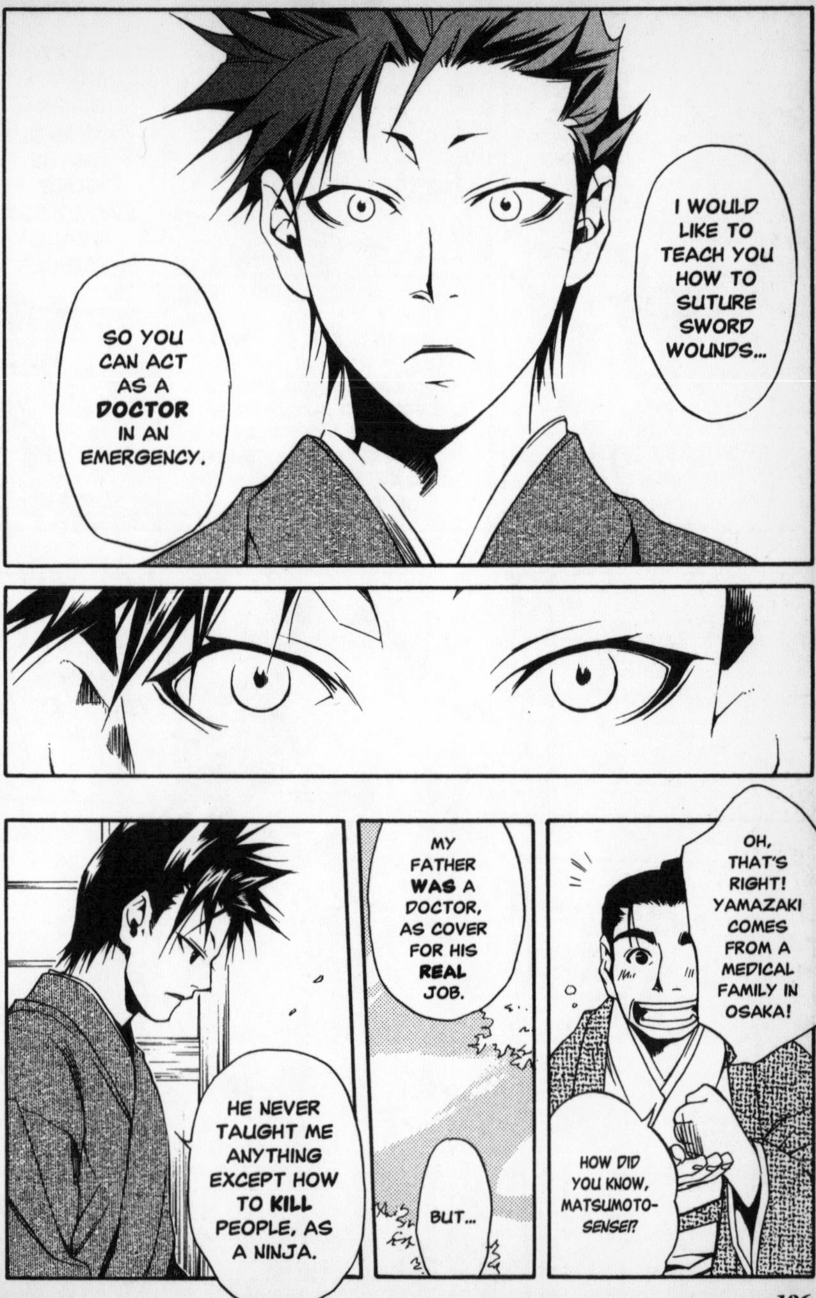
I WOULD LIKE TO TEACH YOU HOW TO SUTURE SWORD WOUNDS...
SO YOU CAN ACT AS A DOCTOR IN AN EMERGENCY.
OH, THAT'S RIGHT! YAMAZAKI COMES FROM A MEDICAL FAMILY IN OSAKA!
HOW DID YOU KNOW, MATSUMOTO-SENSEI?
MY FATHER WAS A DOCTOR, AS COVER FOR HIS REAL JOB.
BUT...
HE NEVER TAUGHT ME ANYTHING EXCEPT HOW TO KILL PEOPLE, AS A NINJA.

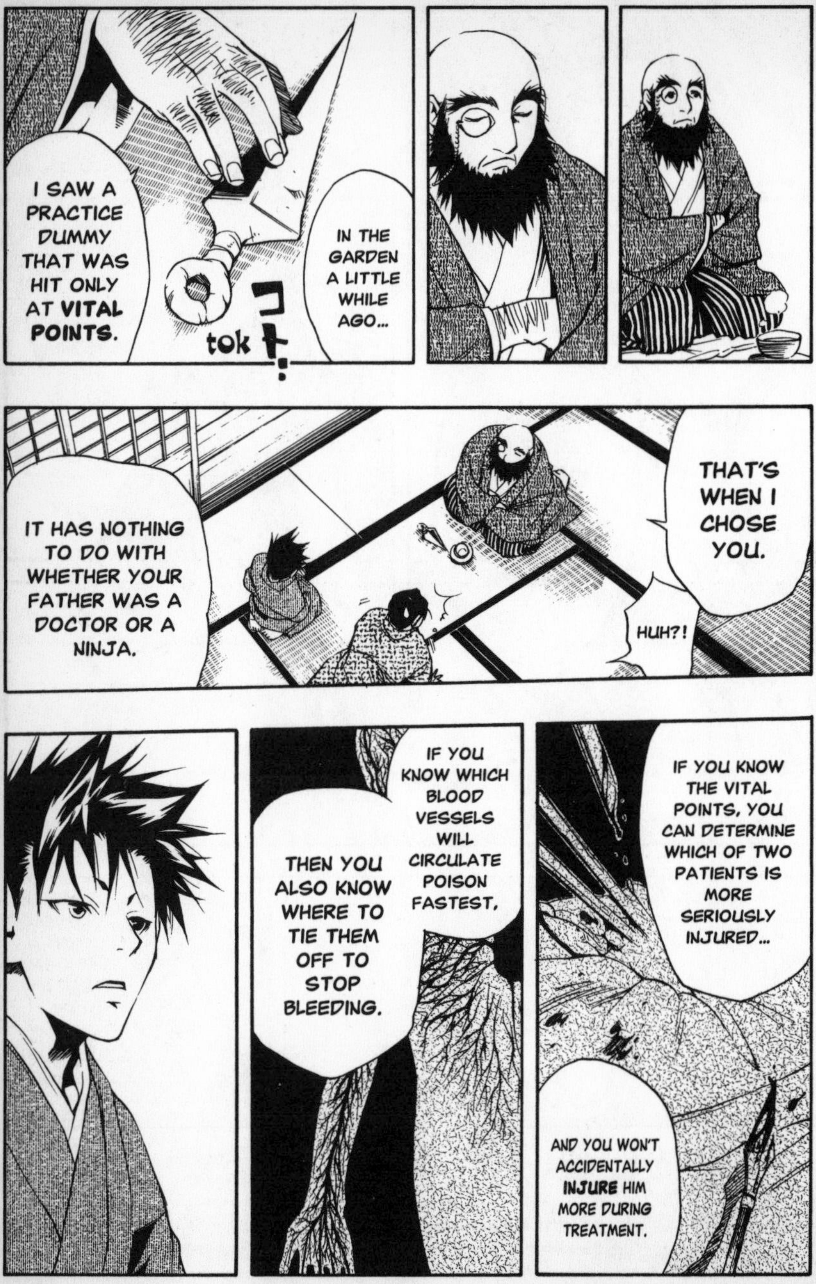
I SAW A PRACTICE DUMMY THAT WAS HIT ONLY AT VITAL POINTS.
IN THE GARDEN A LITTLE WHILE AGO...
tok
コト!
THAT'S WHEN I CHOSE YOU.
IT HAS NOTHING TO DO WITH WHETHER YOUR FATHER WAS A DOCTOR OR A NINJA.
HUH?!
IF YOU KNOW THE VITAL POINTS, YOU CAN DETERMINE WHICH OF TWO PATIENTS IS MORE SERIOUSLY INJURED...
AND YOU WON'T ACCIDENTALLY INJURE HIM MORE DURING TREATMENT.
IF YOU KNOW WHICH BLOOD VESSELS WILL CIRCULATE POISON FASTEST,
THEN YOU ALSO KNOW WHERE TO TIE THEM OFF TO STOP BLEEDING.

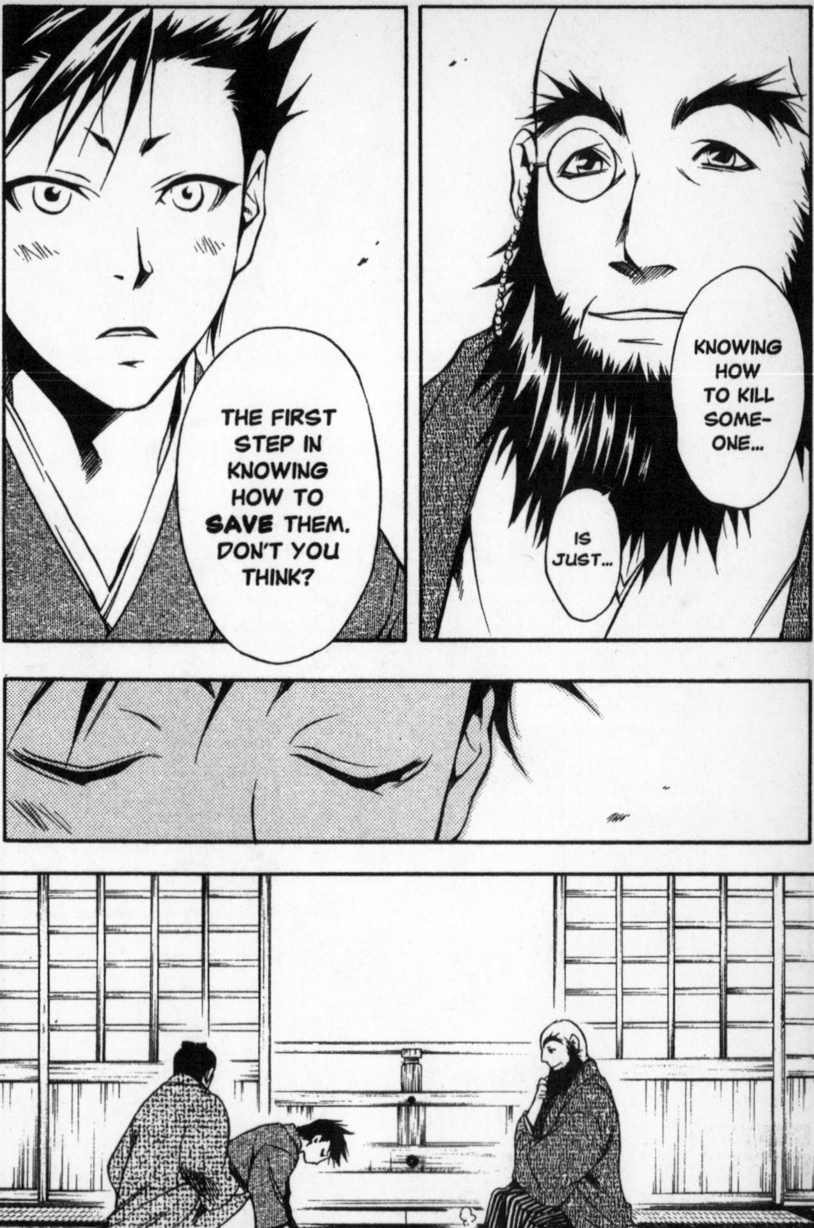
KNOWING HOW TO KILL SOME-ONE...
IS JUST...
THE FIRST STEP IN KNOWING HOW TO SAVE THEM. DON'T YOU THINK?

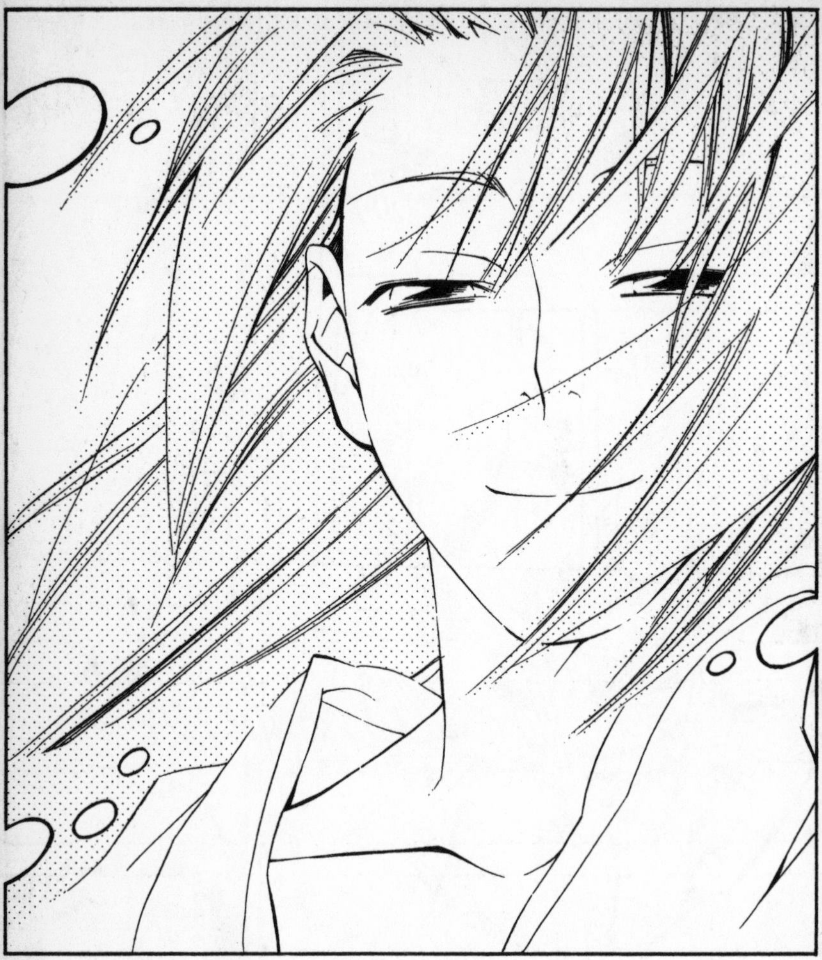

CHAPTER 15

SICKNESS 蝕

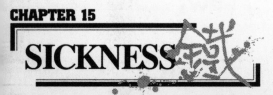

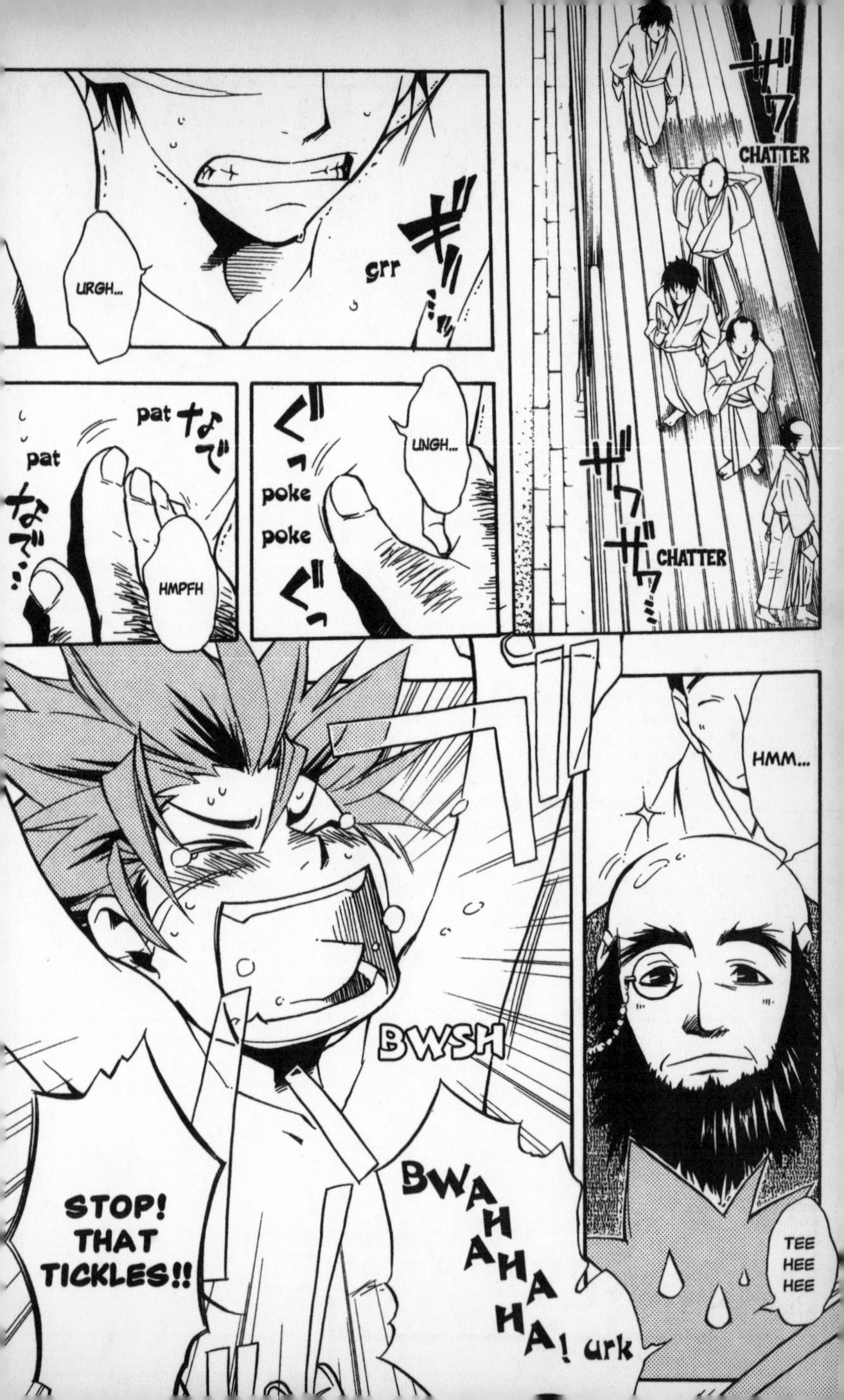

ザワ
CHATTER
ザワ ザワ…
CHATTER
URGH...
grr
ギリ…
UNGH...
ぐっ
poke
poke
ぐっ
pat
なで
pat
なで…
HMPFH
HMM...
BWSH
STOP! THAT TICKLES!!
BWAHAHAHAHA!
urk
TEE HEE HEE

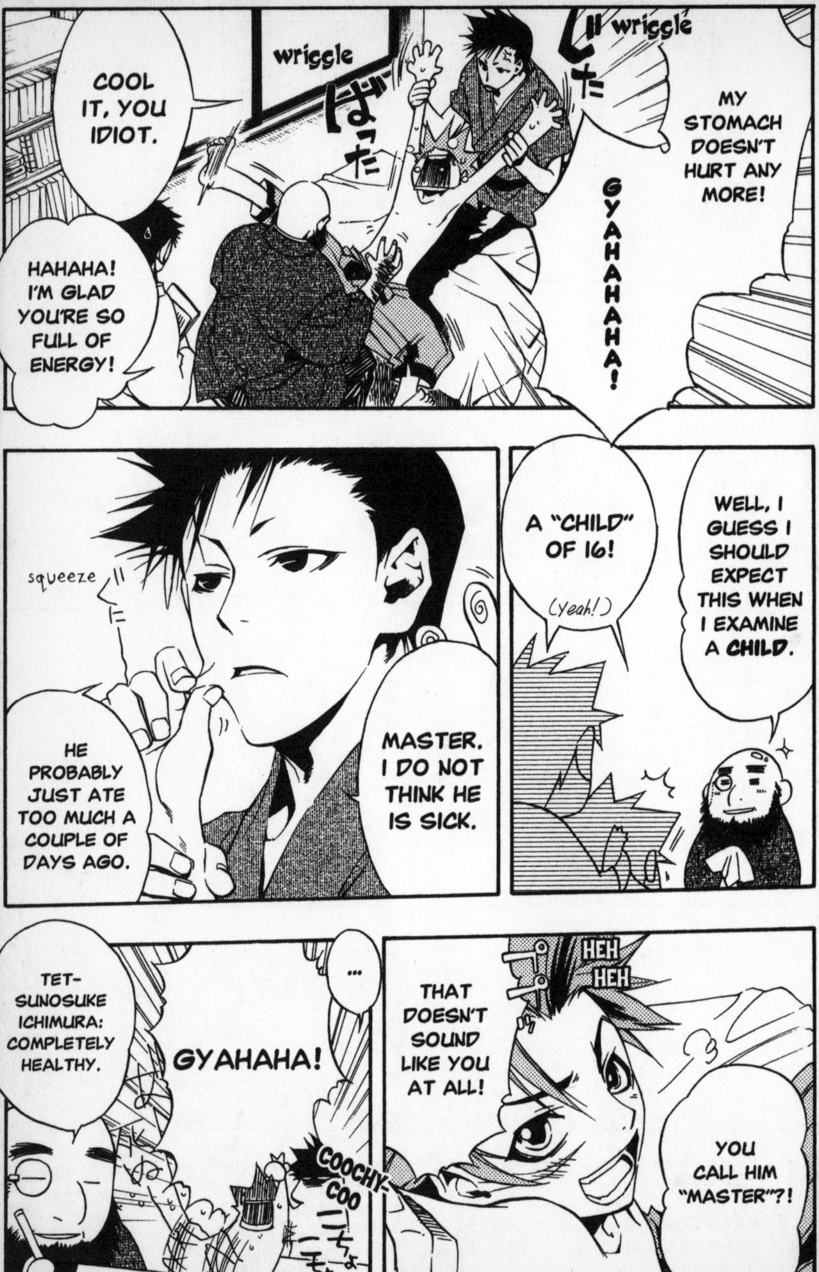
wriggle
MY STOMACH DOESN'T HURT ANY MORE!
GYAHAHAHA!
wriggle
COOL IT, YOU IDIOT.
HAHAHA! I'M GLAD YOU'RE SO FULL OF ENERGY!
WELL, I GUESS I SHOULD EXPECT THIS WHEN I EXAMINE A **CHILD**.
A "CHILD" OF 16!
(yeah!)
MASTER. I DO NOT THINK HE IS SICK.
squeeze
HE PROBABLY JUST ATE TOO MUCH A COUPLE OF DAYS AGO.
HEH HEH
YOU CALL HIM "MASTER"?!
THAT DOESN'T SOUND LIKE YOU AT ALL!
COOCHY-COO
...
GYAHAHA!
TET-SUNOSUKE ICHIMURA: COMPLETELY HEALTHY.
AUGH! I'M GONNA DIE!

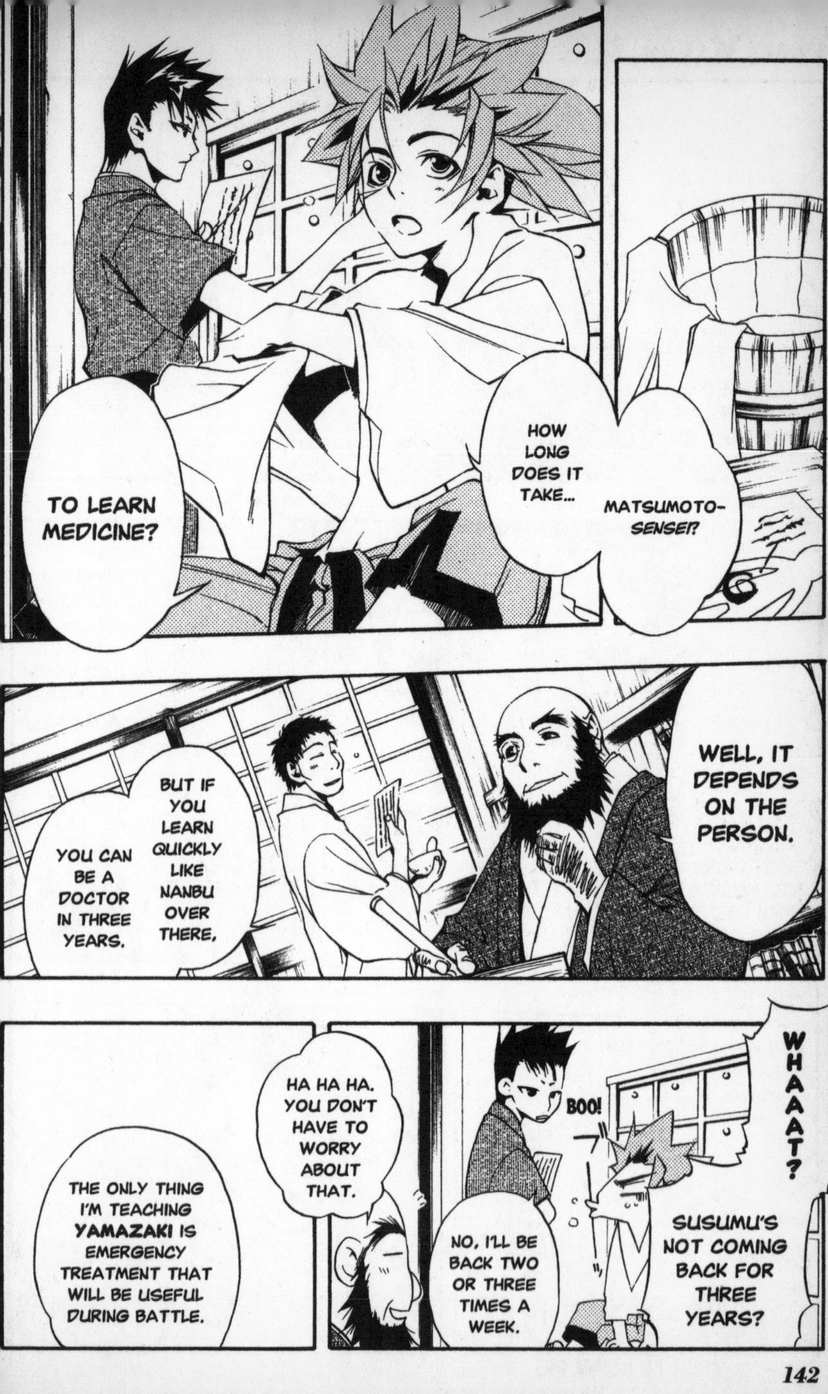
HOW LONG DOES IT TAKE...
MATSUMOTO-SENSEI?
TO LEARN MEDICINE?
WELL, IT DEPENDS ON THE PERSON.
BUT IF YOU LEARN QUICKLY LIKE NANBU OVER THERE,
YOU CAN BE A DOCTOR IN THREE YEARS.
WHAAAT?
BOO!
SUSUMU'S NOT COMING BACK FOR THREE YEARS?
NO, I'LL BE BACK TWO OR THREE TIMES A WEEK.
HA HA HA. YOU DON'T HAVE TO WORRY ABOUT THAT.
THE ONLY THING I'M TEACHING YAMAZAKI IS EMERGENCY TREATMENT THAT WILL BE USEFUL DURING BATTLE.

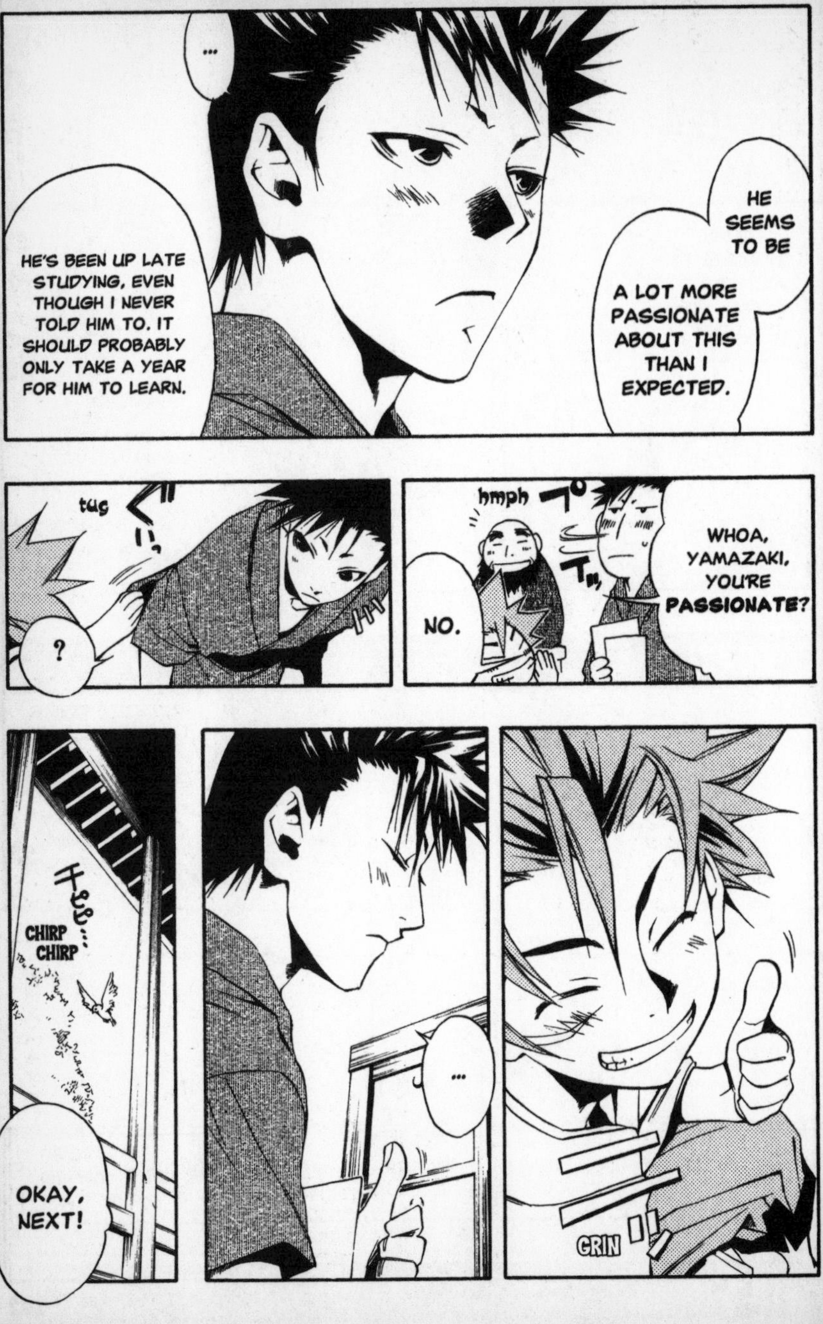
HE SEEMS TO BE
A LOT MORE PASSIONATE ABOUT THIS THAN I EXPECTED.
...
HE'S BEEN UP LATE STUDYING, EVEN THOUGH I NEVER TOLD HIM TO. IT SHOULD PROBABLY ONLY TAKE A YEAR FOR HIM TO LEARN.
WHOA, YAMAZAKI, YOU'RE PASSIONATE?
hmph
NO.
tug
?
GRIN
...
CHIRP CHIRP
OKAY, NEXT!

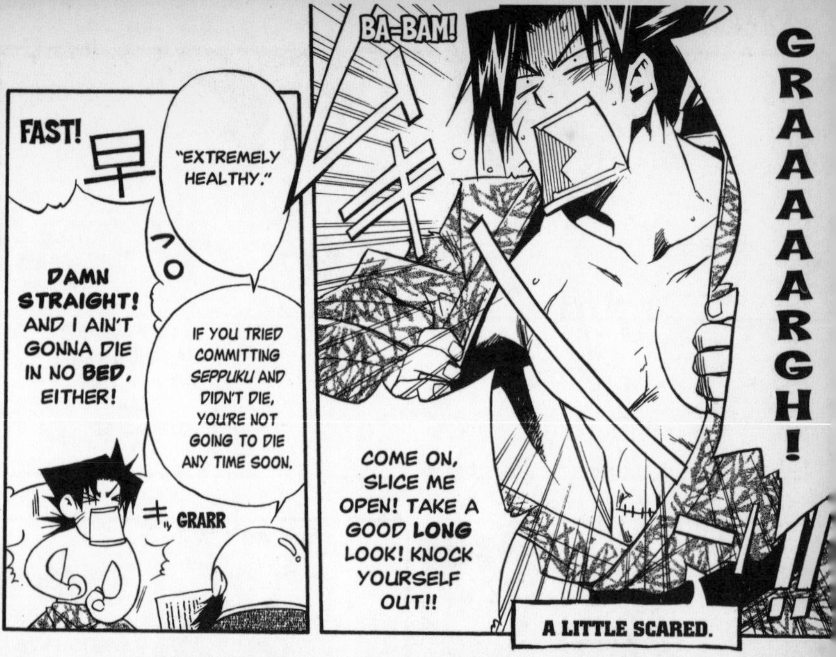
BA-BAM!
GRAAAAARGH!
COME ON, SLICE ME OPEN! TAKE A GOOD LONG LOOK! KNOCK YOURSELF OUT!!
A LITTLE SCARED.
"EXTREMELY HEALTHY."
FAST!
IF YOU TRIED COMMITTING SEPPUKU AND DIDN'T DIE, YOU'RE NOT GOING TO DIE ANY TIME SOON.
DAMN STRAIGHT! AND I AIN'T GONNA DIE IN NO BED, EITHER!
GRARR

NEXT!

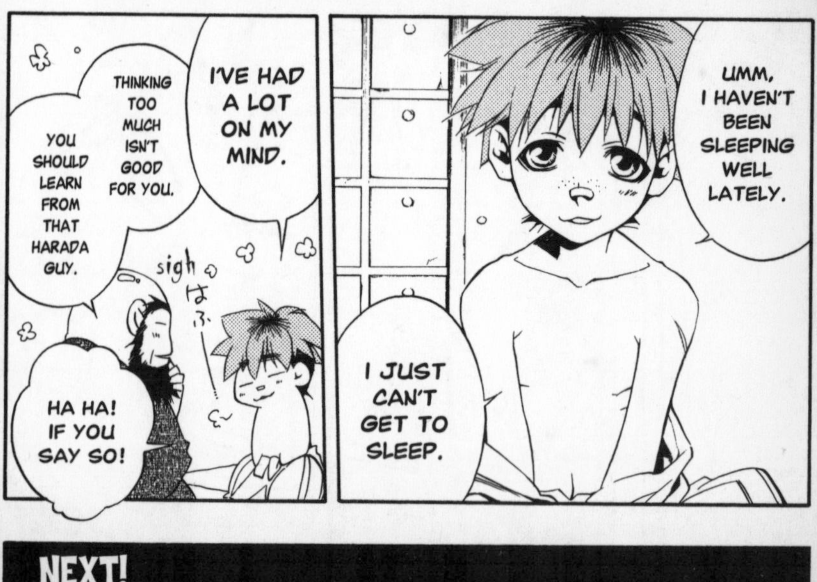
UMM, I HAVEN'T BEEN SLEEPING WELL LATELY.
I JUST CAN'T GET TO SLEEP.
I'VE HAD A LOT ON MY MIND.
THINKING TOO MUCH ISN'T GOOD FOR YOU.
YOU SHOULD LEARN FROM THAT HARADA GUY.
sigh
HA HA! IF YOU SAY SO!

NEXT!

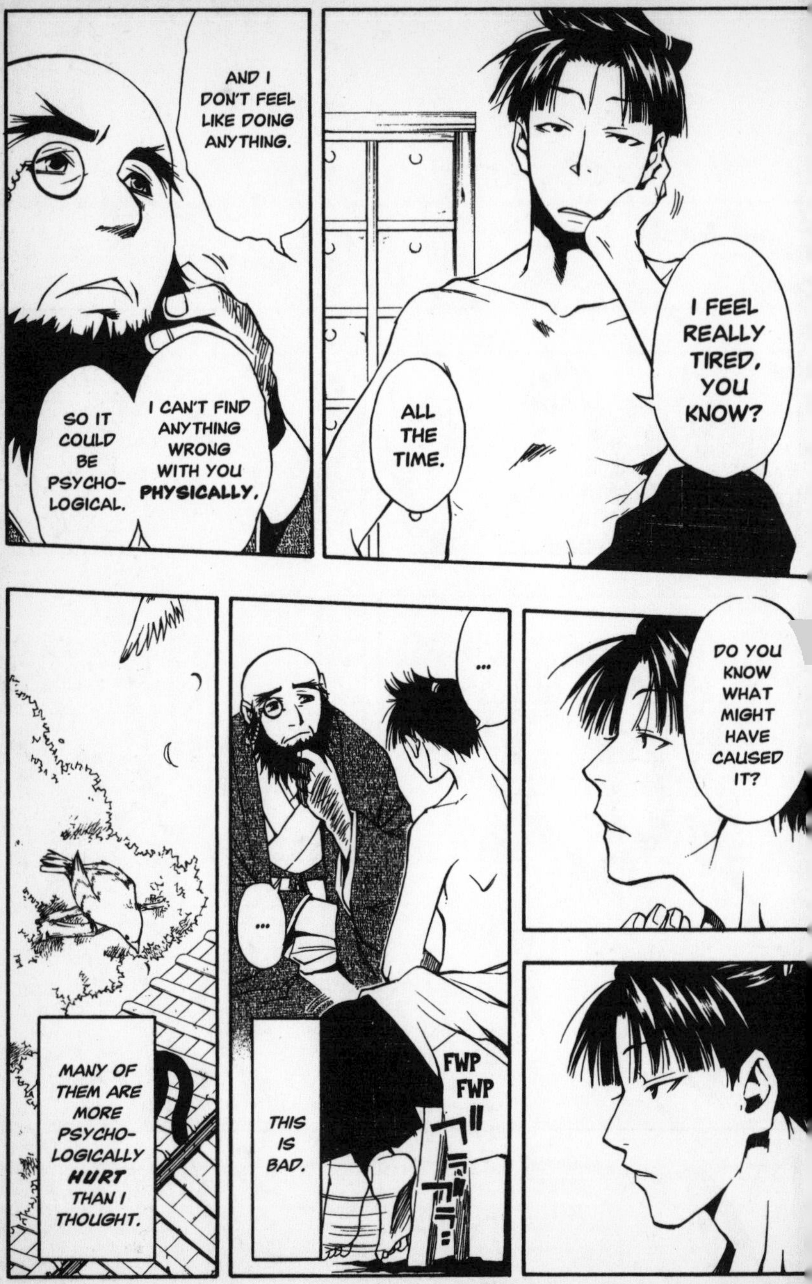
I FEEL REALLY TIRED, YOU KNOW?
ALL THE TIME.
AND I DON'T FEEL LIKE DOING ANYTHING.
I CAN'T FIND ANYTHING WRONG WITH YOU PHYSICALLY.
SO IT COULD BE PSYCHO-LOGICAL.
DO YOU KNOW WHAT MIGHT HAVE CAUSED IT?
...
...
FWP FWP
THIS IS BAD.
MANY OF THEM ARE MORE PSYCHO-LOGICALLY HURT THAN I THOUGHT.

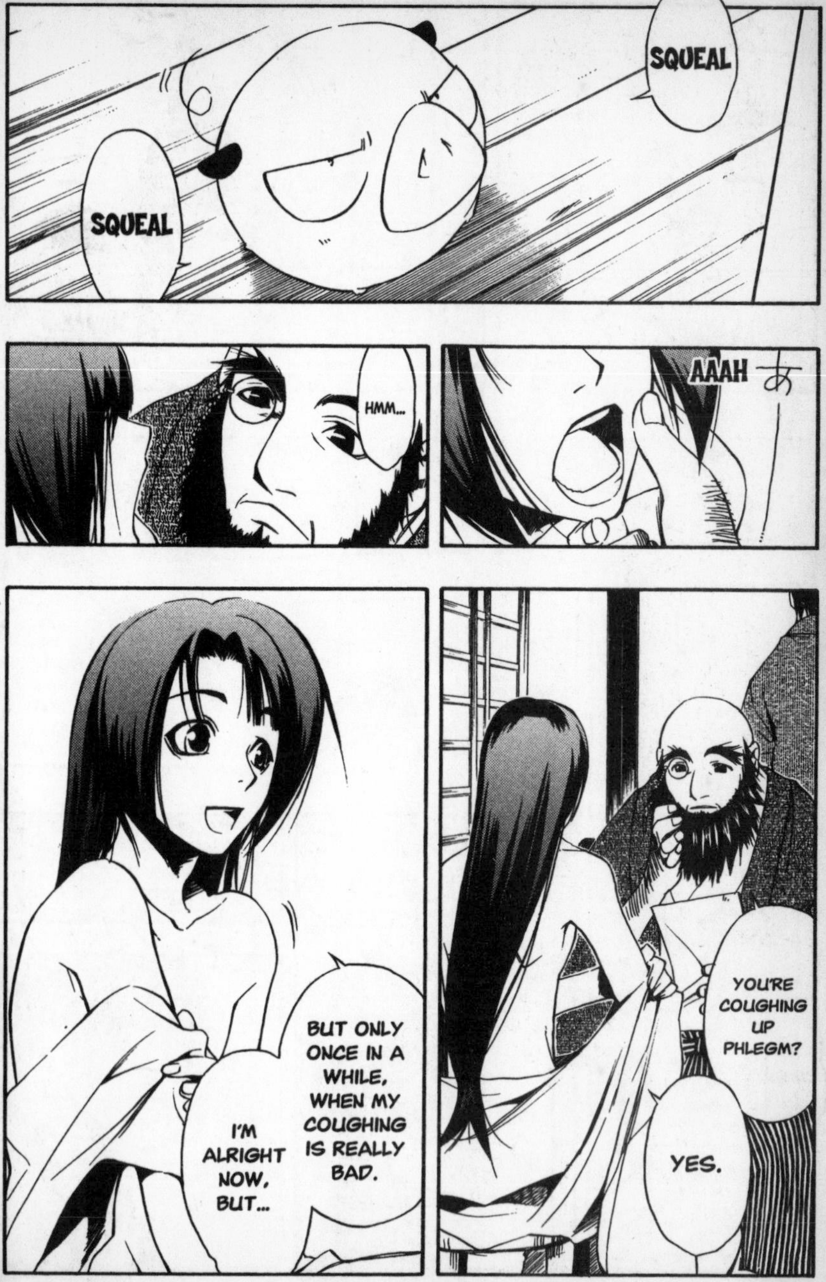
SQUEAL
SQUEAL
AAAH あ
HMM...
YOU'RE COUGHING UP PHLEGM?
YES.
BUT ONLY ONCE IN A WHILE, WHEN MY COUGHING IS REALLY BAD.
I'M ALRIGHT NOW, BUT...

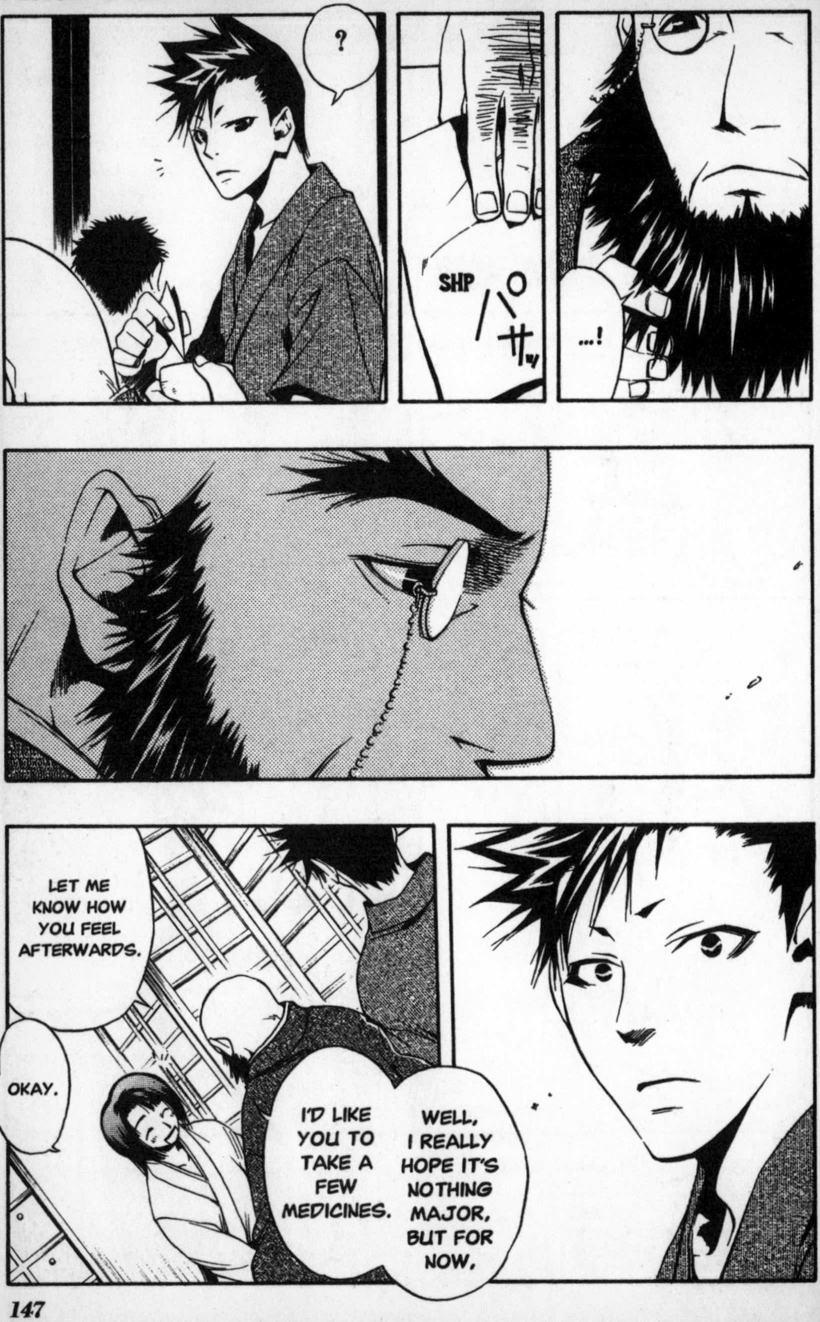
...!
SHP
パサッ
?
WELL, I REALLY HOPE IT'S NOTHING MAJOR, BUT FOR NOW,
I'D LIKE YOU TO TAKE A FEW MEDICINES.
LET ME KNOW HOW YOU FEEL AFTERWARDS.
OKAY.

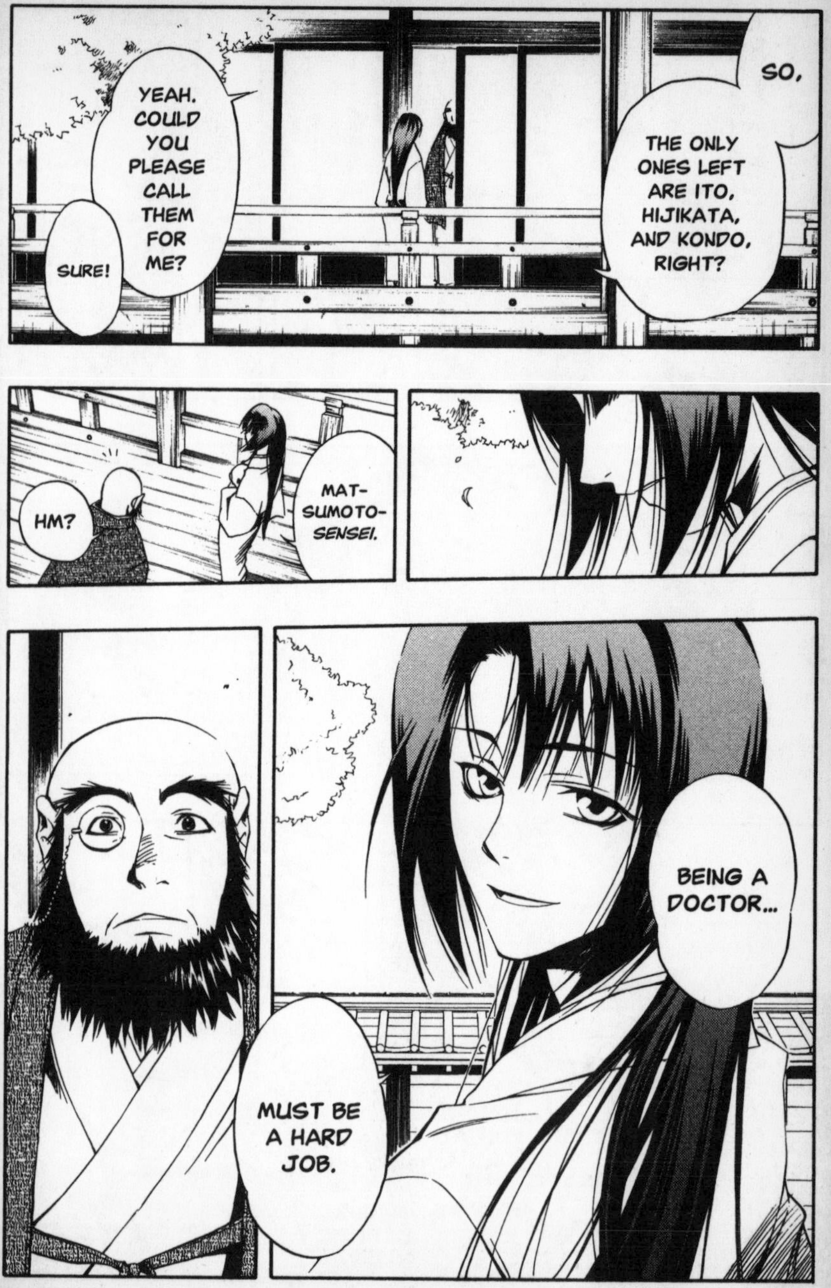
SO,
THE ONLY ONES LEFT ARE ITO, HIJIKATA, AND KONDO, RIGHT?
YEAH. COULD YOU PLEASE CALL THEM FOR ME?
SURE!
MAT-SUMOTO-SENSEI.
HM?
BEING A DOCTOR...
MUST BE A HARD JOB.

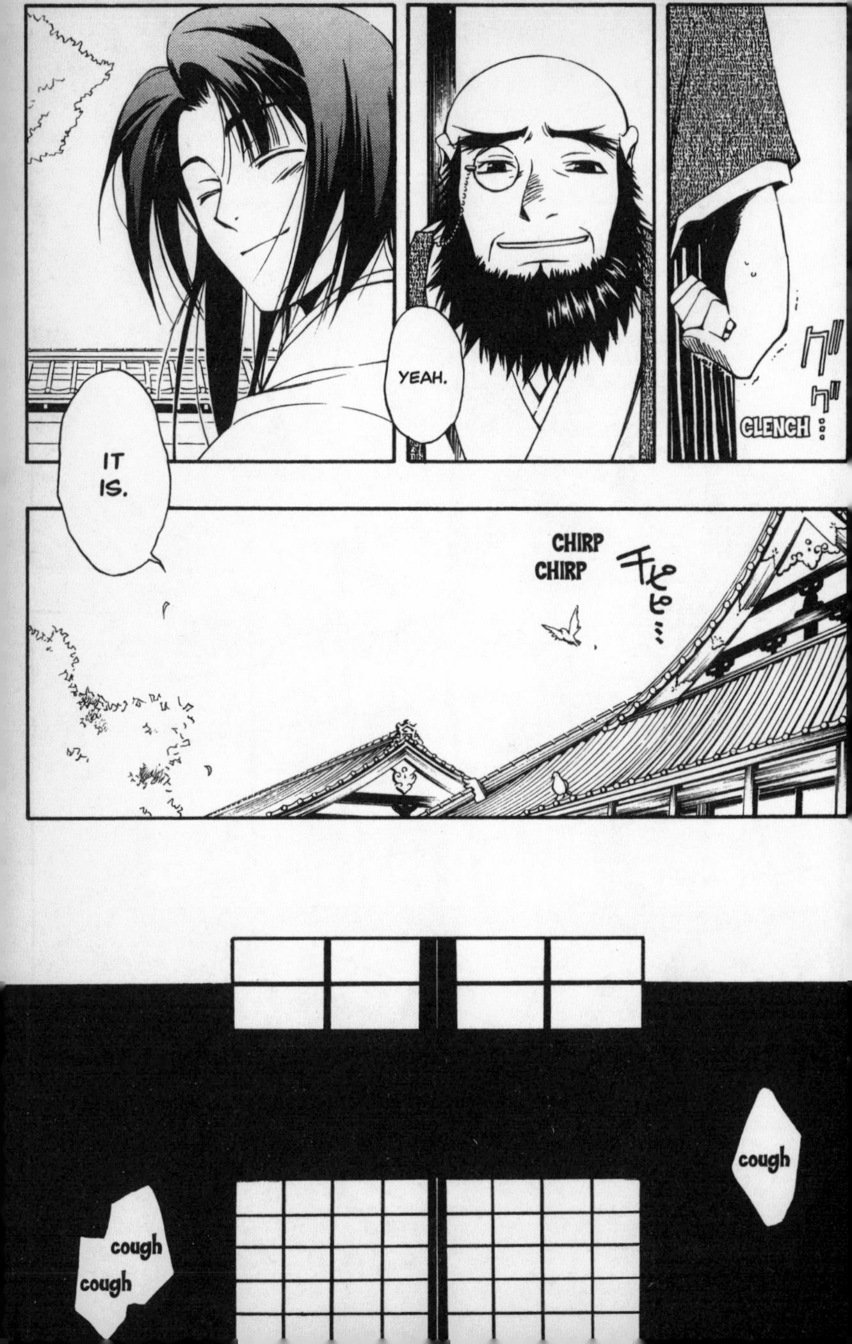
CLENCH
YEAH.
IT IS.
CHIRP
CHIRP
cough
cough
cough

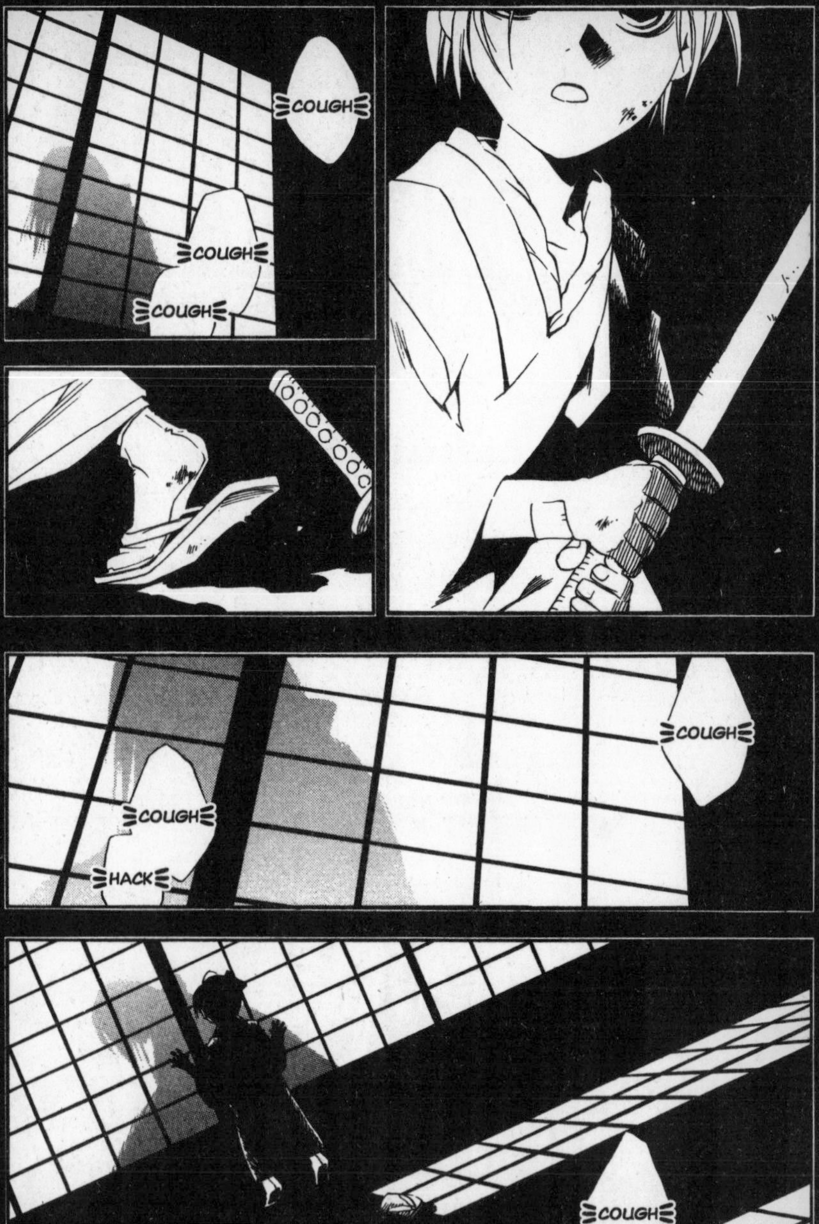
COUGH
COUGH
COUGH
COUGH
COUGH
HACK
COUGH

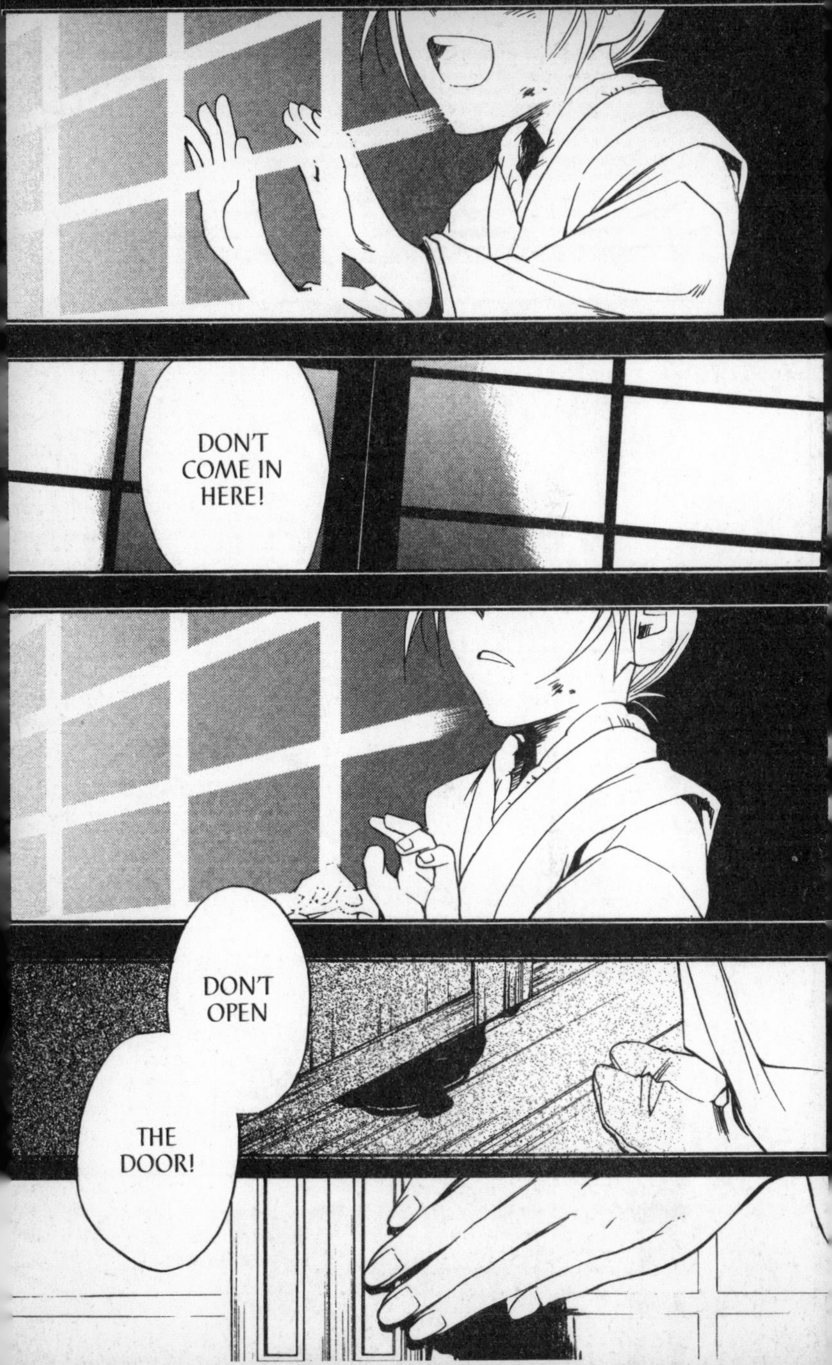
DON'T COME IN HERE!
DON'T OPEN
THE DOOR!

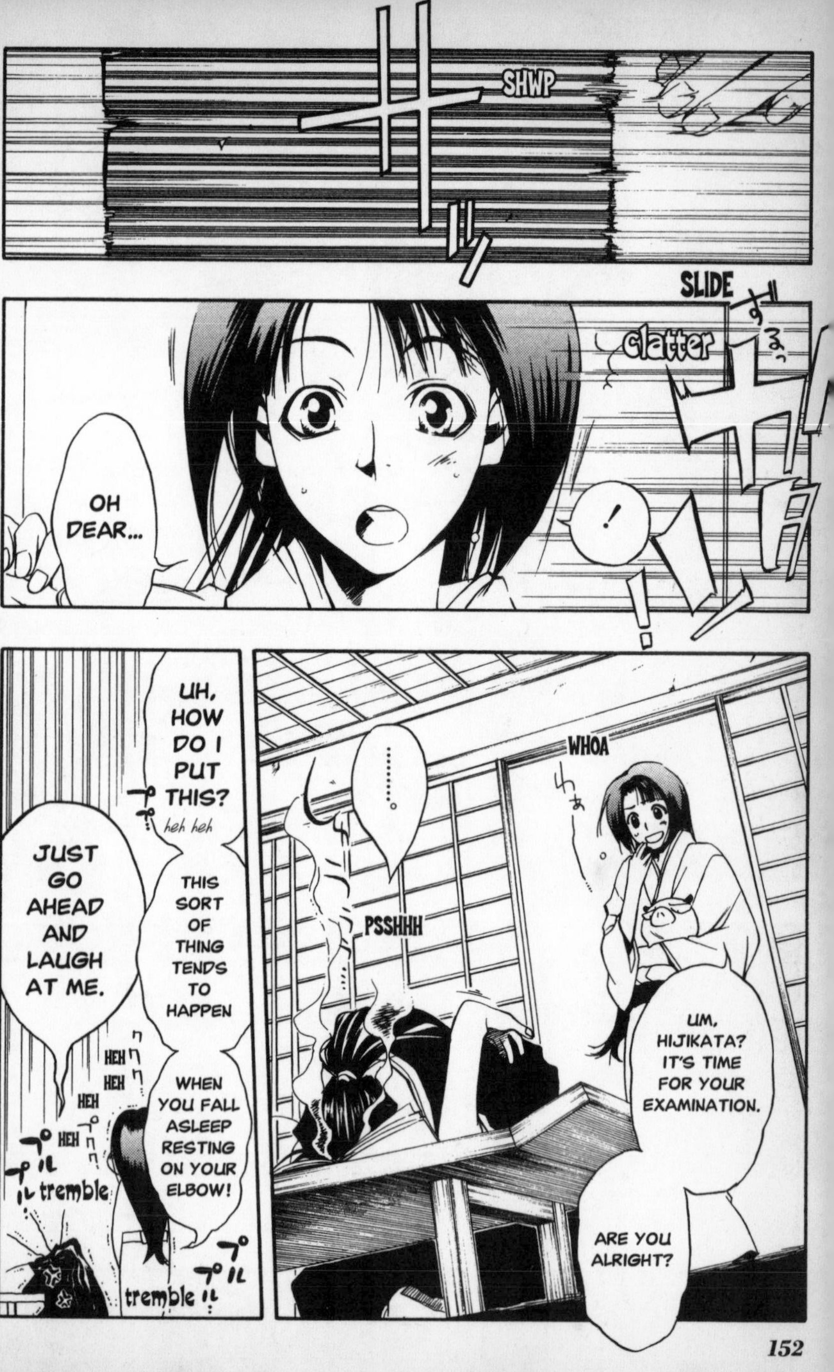
SHWP
SLIDE
clatter
!
OH DEAR...
WHOA
......
PSSHHH
UM, HIJIKATA? IT'S TIME FOR YOUR EXAMINATION.
ARE YOU ALRIGHT?
UH, HOW DO I PUT THIS?
heh heh
THIS SORT OF THING TENDS TO HAPPEN
WHEN YOU FALL ASLEEP RESTING ON YOUR ELBOW!
JUST GO AHEAD AND LAUGH AT ME.
HEH HEH HEH HEH
tremble
tremble

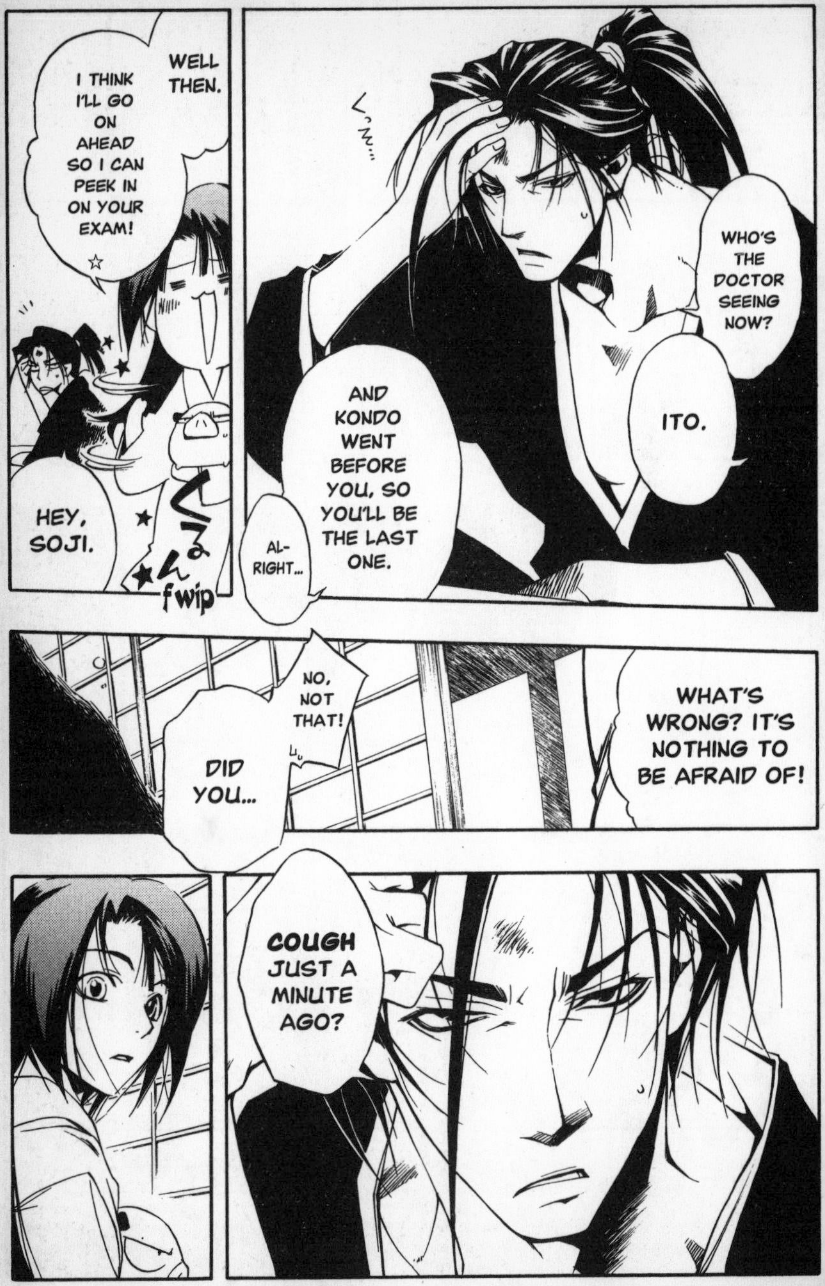
WHO'S THE DOCTOR SEEING NOW?
ITO.
AND KONDO WENT BEFORE YOU, SO YOU'LL BE THE LAST ONE.
AL-RIGHT...
WELL THEN.
I THINK I'LL GO ON AHEAD SO I CAN PEEK IN ON YOUR EXAM! ☆
HEY, SOJI.
くるん
fwip
WHAT'S WRONG? IT'S NOTHING TO BE AFRAID OF!
NO, NOT THAT!
DID YOU...
COUGH JUST A MINUTE AGO?

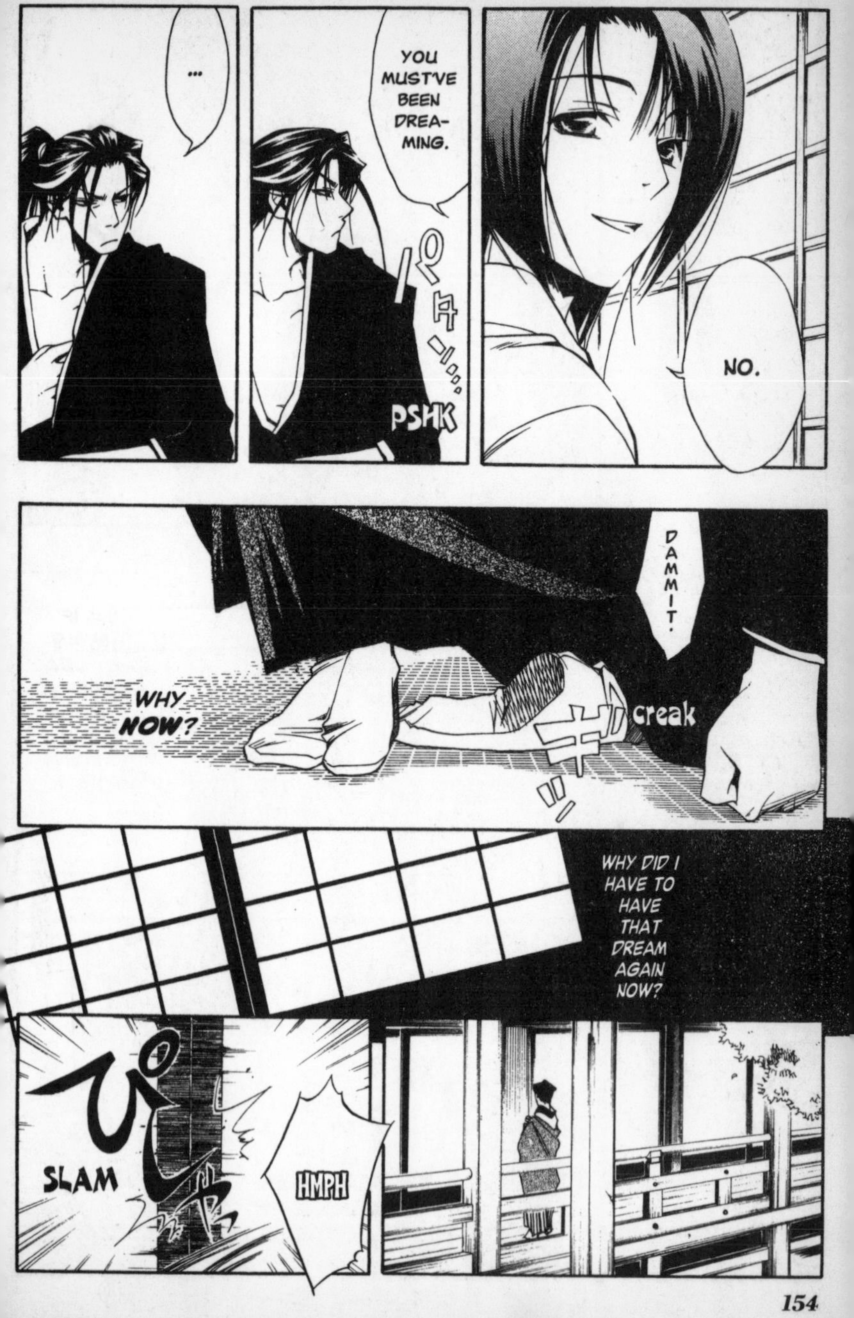

NO.
YOU MUST'VE BEEN DREAMING.
PSHK
...
DAMMIT.
creak
WHY NOW?
WHY DID I HAVE TO HAVE THAT DREAM AGAIN NOW?
HMPH
SLAM

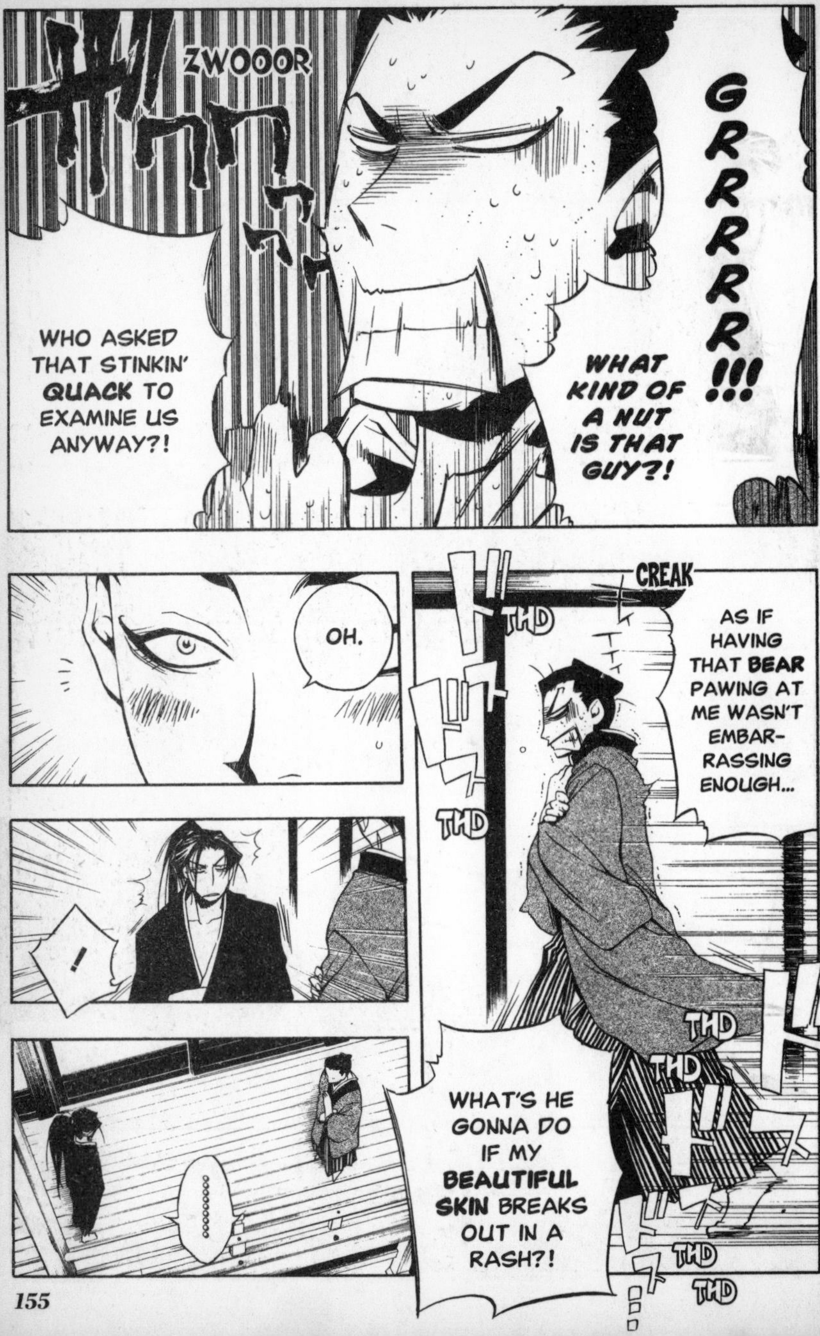
ZWOOOR
GRRRRR!!!
WHAT KIND OF A NUT IS THAT GUY?!
WHO ASKED THAT STINKIN' QUACK TO EXAMINE US ANYWAY?!
CREAK
THD
AS IF HAVING THAT BEAR PAWING AT ME WASN'T EMBARRASSING ENOUGH...
THD
OH.
!
THD
THD
WHAT'S HE GONNA DO IF MY BEAUTIFUL SKIN BREAKS OUT IN A RASH?!
THD
THD
....

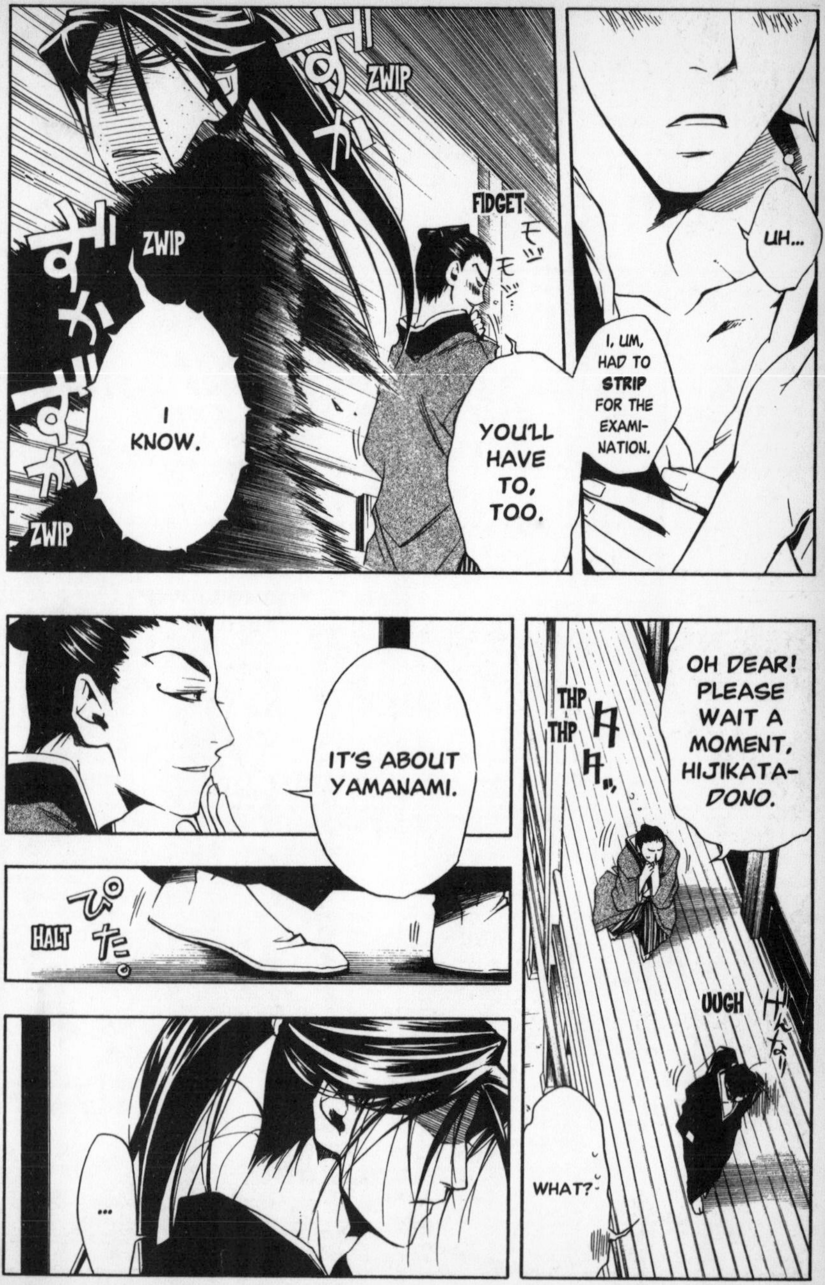
UH...
I, UM, HAD TO STRIP FOR THE EXAMINATION.
YOU'LL HAVE TO, TOO.
FIDGET
ZWIP
ZWIP
ZWIP
I KNOW.
OH DEAR! PLEASE WAIT A MOMENT, HIJIKATA-DONO.
THP
THP
UUGH
WHAT?
IT'S ABOUT YAMANAMI.
HALT
...

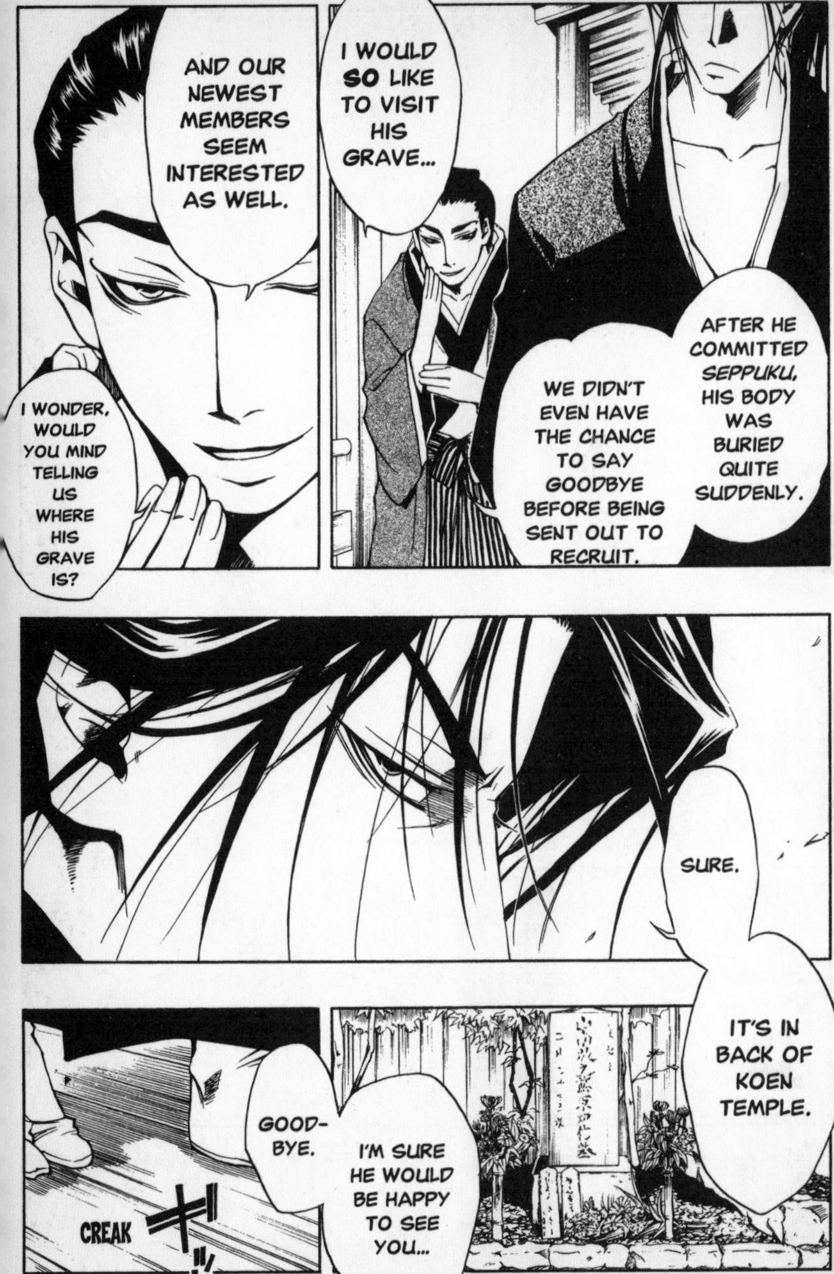
AFTER HE COMMITTED SEPPUKU, HIS BODY WAS BURIED QUITE SUDDENLY.
WE DIDN'T EVEN HAVE THE CHANCE TO SAY GOODBYE BEFORE BEING SENT OUT TO RECRUIT.
I WOULD SO LIKE TO VISIT HIS GRAVE...
AND OUR NEWEST MEMBERS SEEM INTERESTED AS WELL.
I WONDER, WOULD YOU MIND TELLING US WHERE HIS GRAVE IS?
SURE.
IT'S IN BACK OF KOEN TEMPLE.
I'M SURE HE WOULD BE HAPPY TO SEE YOU...
GOOD-BYE.
CREAK

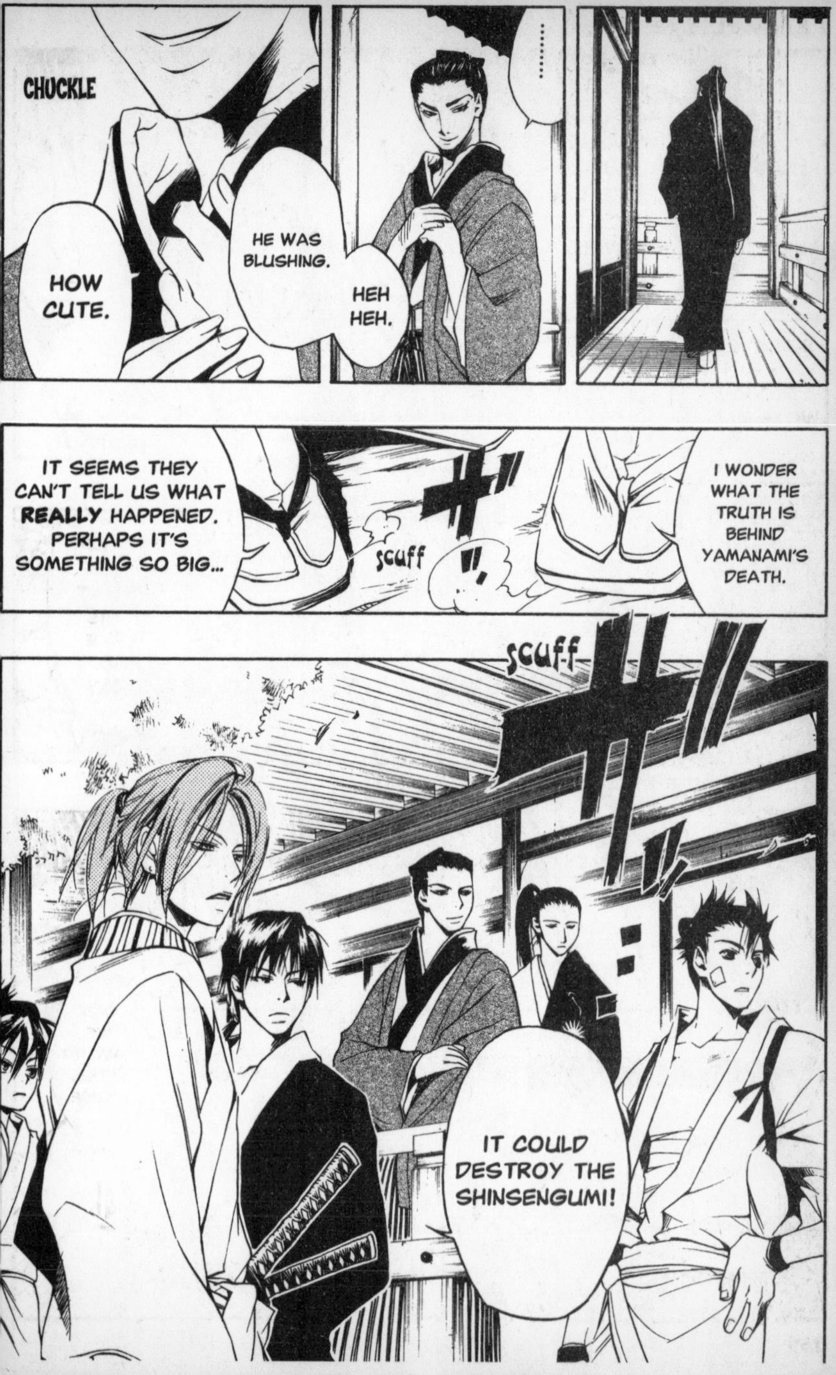
......
HEH HEH.
HE WAS BLUSHING.
HOW CUTE.
CHUCKLE
I WONDER WHAT THE TRUTH IS BEHIND YAMANAMI'S DEATH.
!!
scuff
IT SEEMS THEY CAN'T TELL US WHAT REALLY HAPPENED. PERHAPS IT'S SOMETHING SO BIG...
scuff-f
IT COULD DESTROY THE SHINSENGUMI!

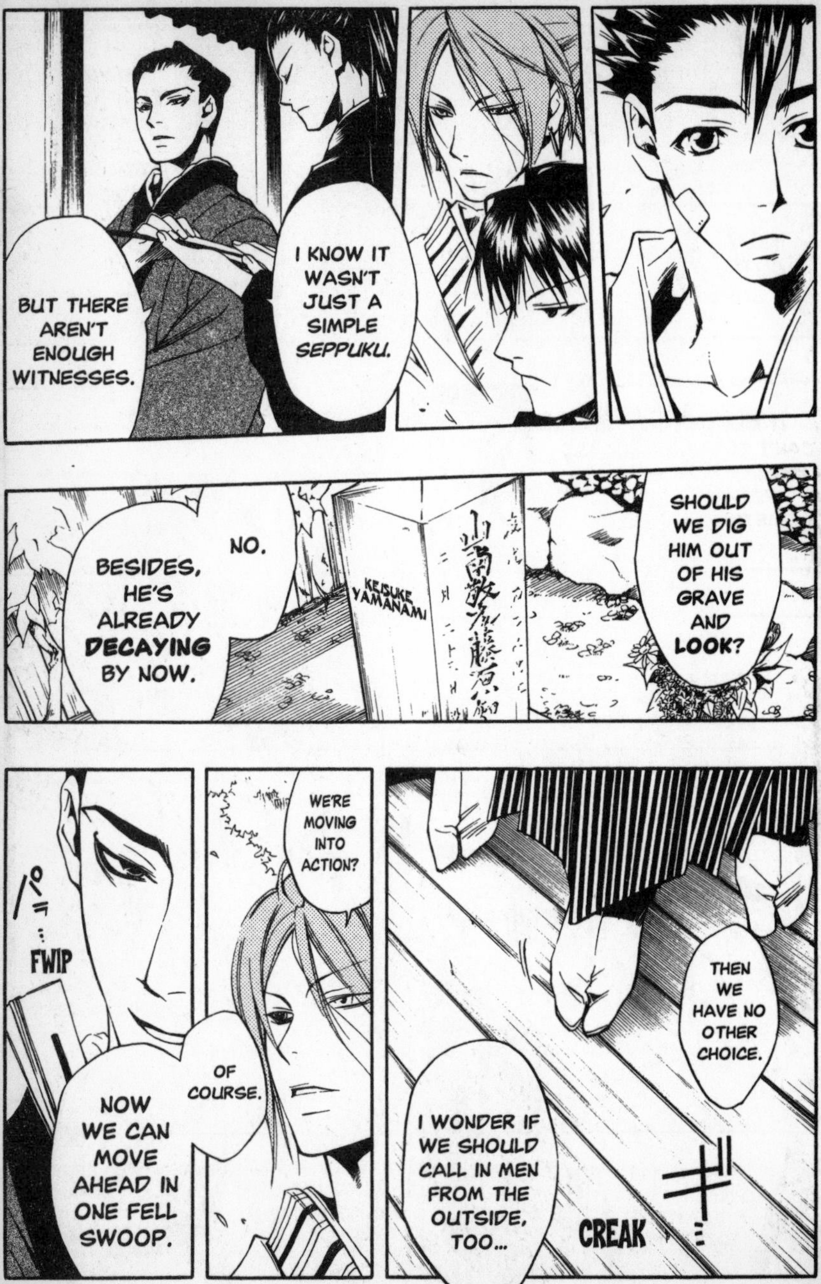
I KNOW IT WASN'T JUST A SIMPLE SEPPUKU.
BUT THERE AREN'T ENOUGH WITNESSES.
SHOULD WE DIG HIM OUT OF HIS GRAVE AND LOOK?
KEISUKE YAMANAMI
NO.
BESIDES, HE'S ALREADY DECAYING BY NOW.
THEN WE HAVE NO OTHER CHOICE.
CREAK
I WONDER IF WE SHOULD CALL IN MEN FROM THE OUTSIDE, TOO...
WE'RE MOVING INTO ACTION?
OF COURSE.
FWIP
NOW WE CAN MOVE AHEAD IN ONE FELL SWOOP.

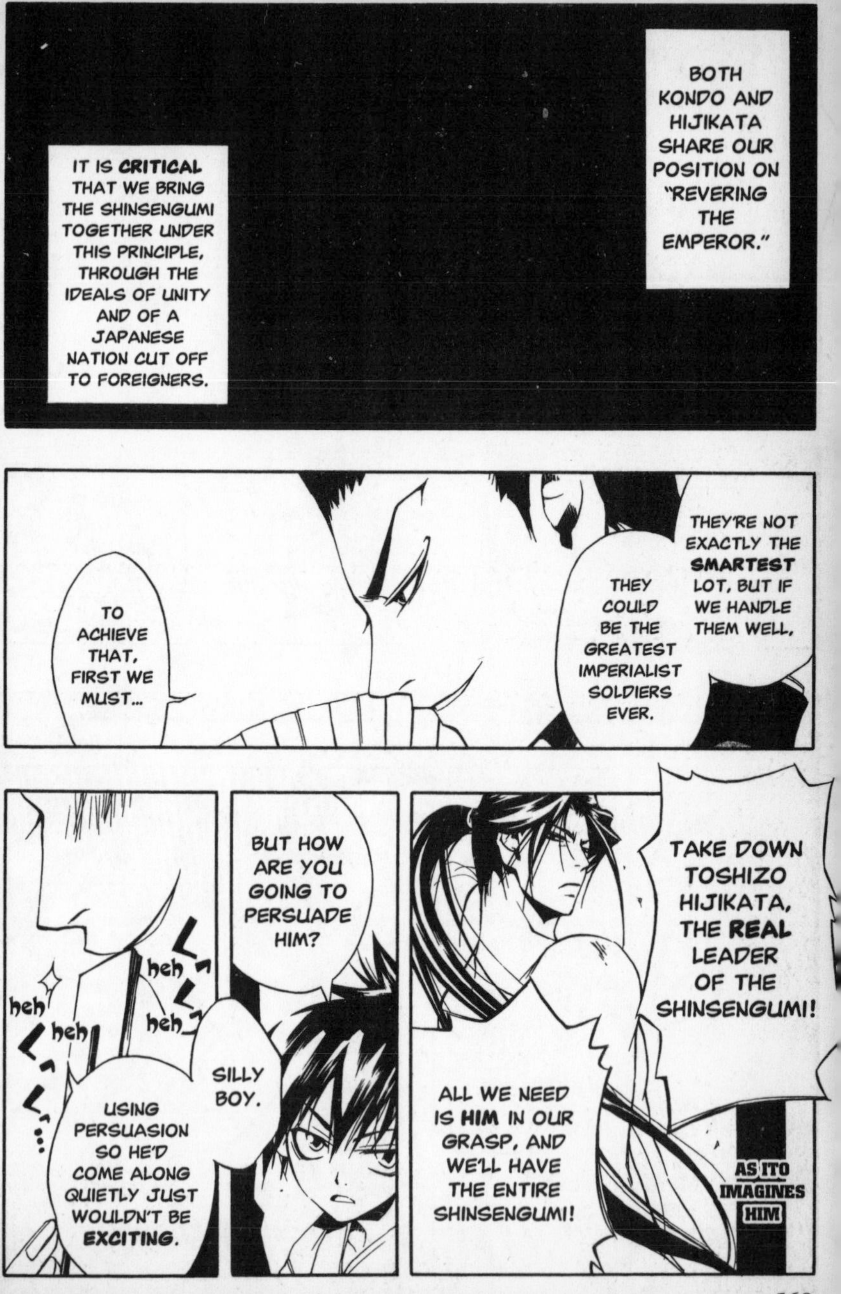
BOTH KONDO AND HIJIKATA SHARE OUR POSITION ON "REVERING THE EMPEROR."
IT IS CRITICAL THAT WE BRING THE SHINSENGUMI TOGETHER UNDER THIS PRINCIPLE, THROUGH THE IDEALS OF UNITY AND OF A JAPANESE NATION CUT OFF TO FOREIGNERS.
THEY'RE NOT EXACTLY THE SMARTEST LOT, BUT IF WE HANDLE THEM WELL,
THEY COULD BE THE GREATEST IMPERIALIST SOLDIERS EVER.
TO ACHIEVE THAT, FIRST WE MUST...
TAKE DOWN TOSHIZO HIJIKATA, THE REAL LEADER OF THE SHINSENGUMI!
ALL WE NEED IS HIM IN OUR GRASP, AND WE'LL HAVE THE ENTIRE SHINSENGUMI!
AS ITO IMAGINES HIM
BUT HOW ARE YOU GOING TO PERSUADE HIM?
SILLY BOY.
heh heh heh heh
USING PERSUASION SO HE'D COME ALONG QUIETLY JUST WOULDN'T BE EXCITING.

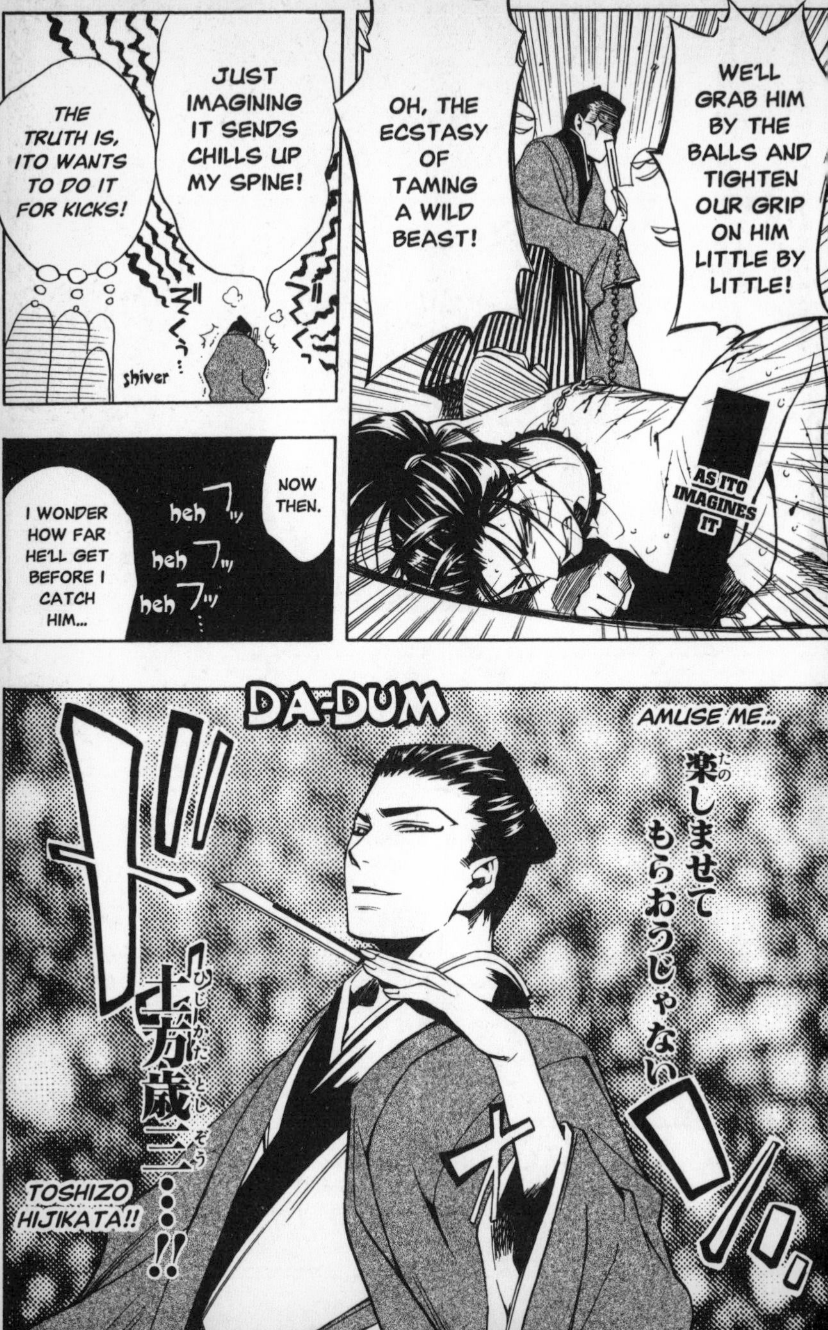
WE'LL GRAB HIM BY THE BALLS AND TIGHTEN OUR GRIP ON HIM LITTLE BY LITTLE!
OH, THE ECSTASY OF TAMING A WILD BEAST!
AS ITO IMAGINES IT
JUST IMAGINING IT SENDS CHILLS UP MY SPINE!
THE TRUTH IS, ITO WANTS TO DO IT FOR KICKS!
shiver
NOW THEN.
heh フッ
heh フッ
heh フッ…
I WONDER HOW FAR HE'LL GET BEFORE I CATCH HIM...
DA-DUM
AMUSE ME...
楽しませてもらおうじゃない
TOSHIZO HIJIKATA!!
土方歳三…!!

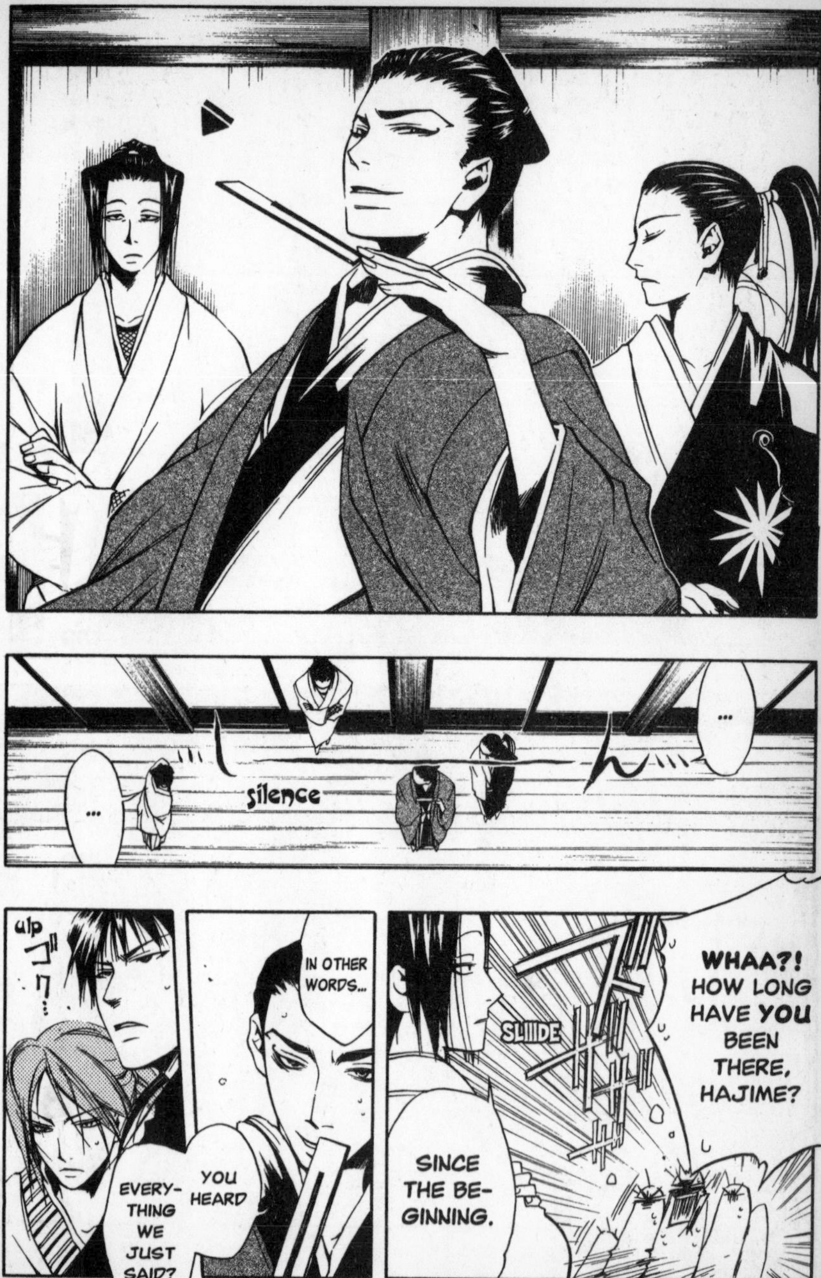
...
silence
...
WHAA?! HOW LONG HAVE YOU BEEN THERE, HAJIME?
SLIIDE
SINCE THE BE- GINNING.
IN OTHER WORDS...
YOU HEARD
EVERY- THING WE JUST SAID?
ulp

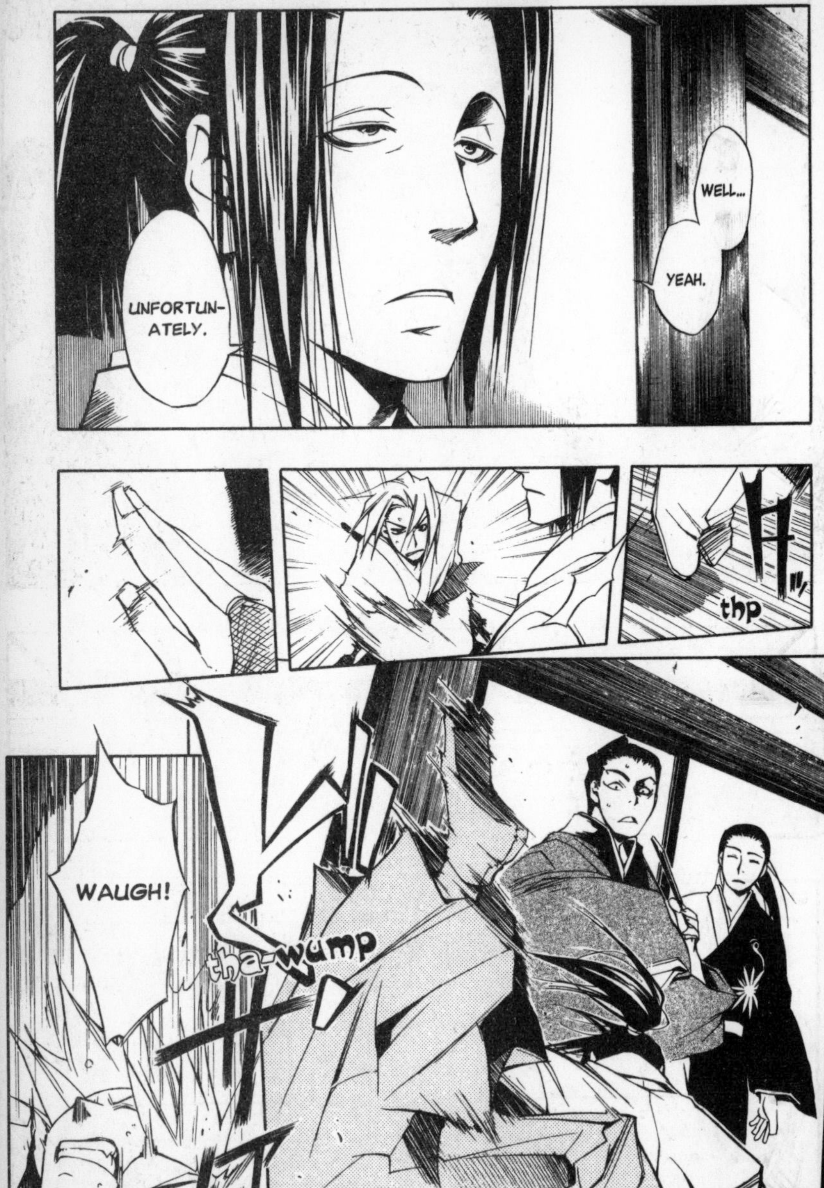
WELL...
YEAH.
UNFORTUN-ATELY.
thp
WAUGH!
tha-wump

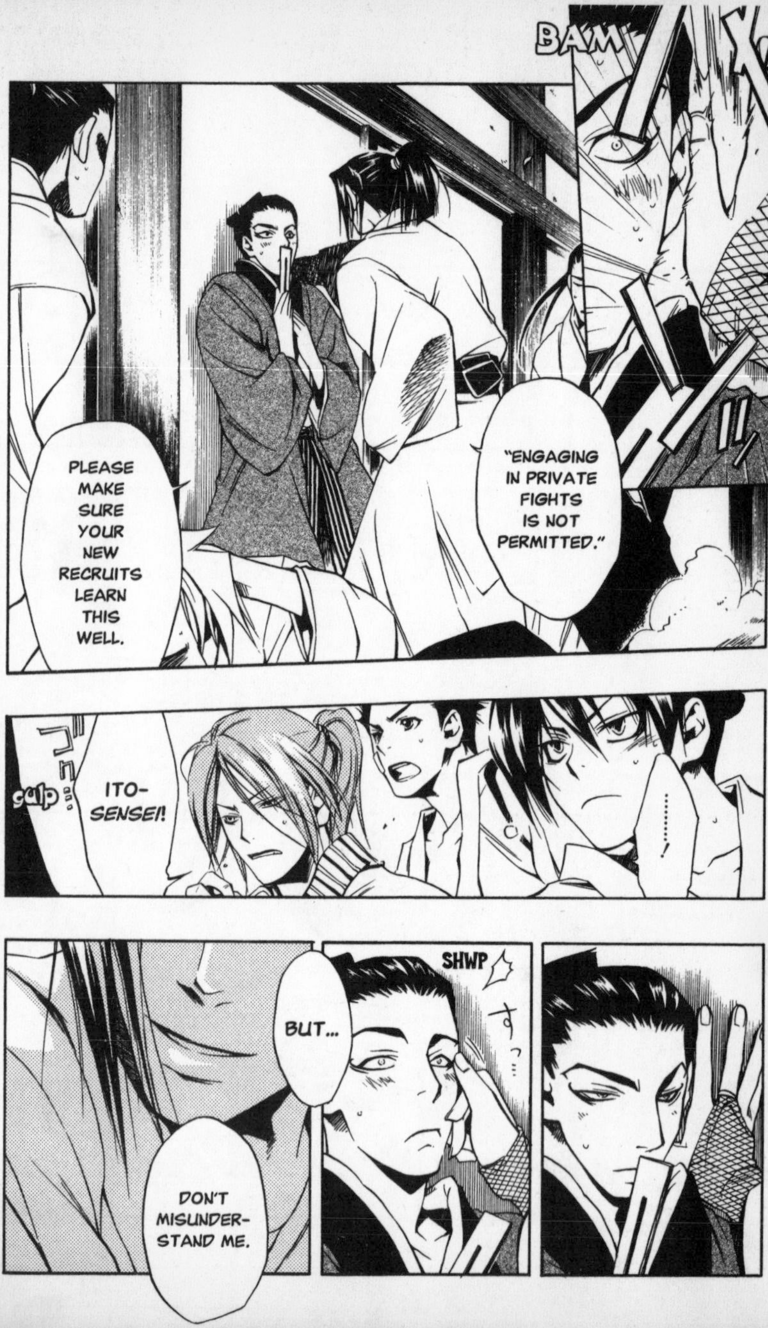
BAM
"ENGAGING IN PRIVATE FIGHTS IS NOT PERMITTED."
PLEASE MAKE SURE YOUR NEW RECRUITS LEARN THIS WELL.
......!
ITO-SENSEI!
gulp
SHWP
BUT...
DON'T MISUNDER-STAND ME.

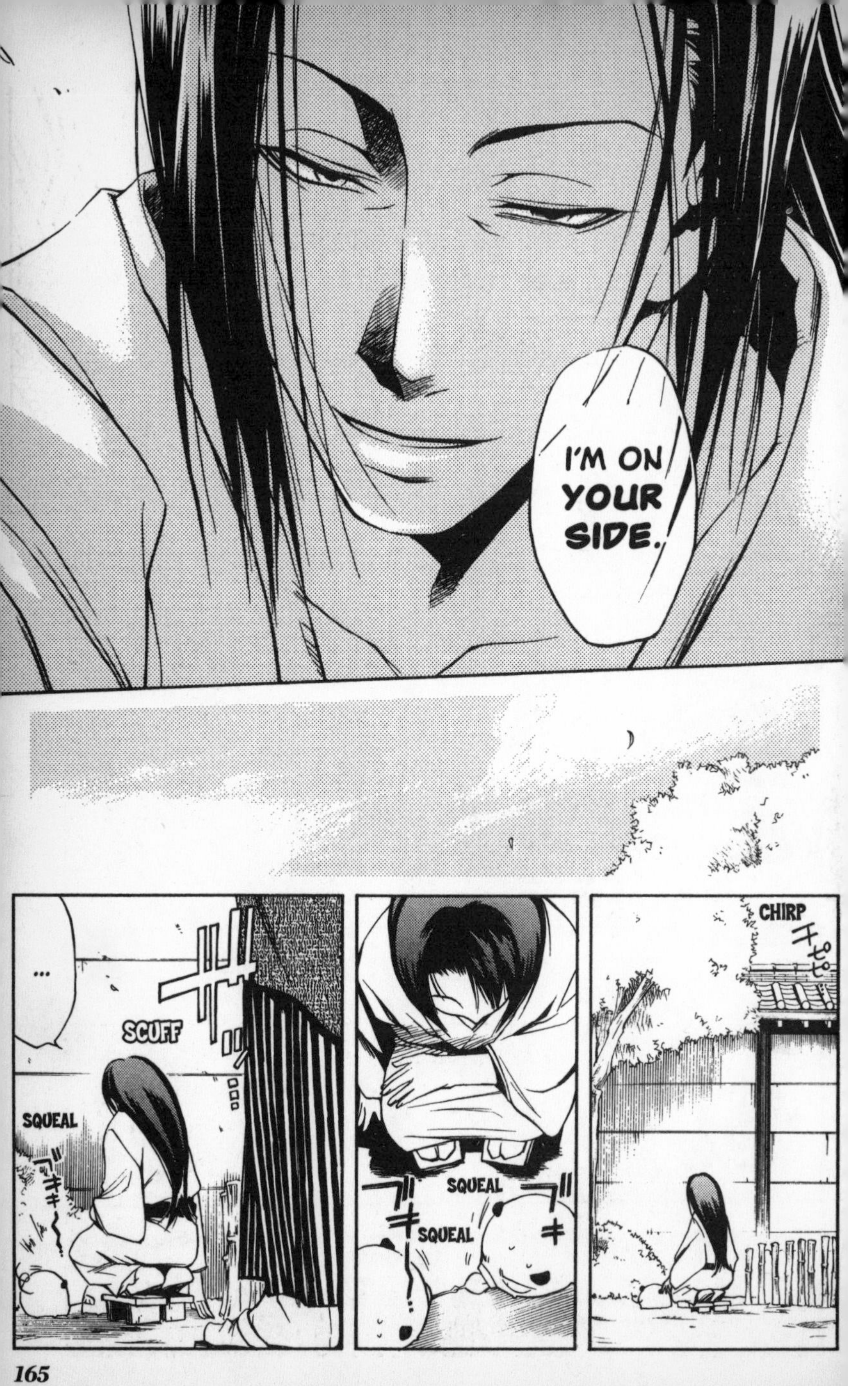
I'M ON YOUR SIDE.
CHIRP
チピ
SQUEAL
SQUEAL
ブキ
ブキー
…
SCUFF
ザ
SQUEAL
ブキキ～

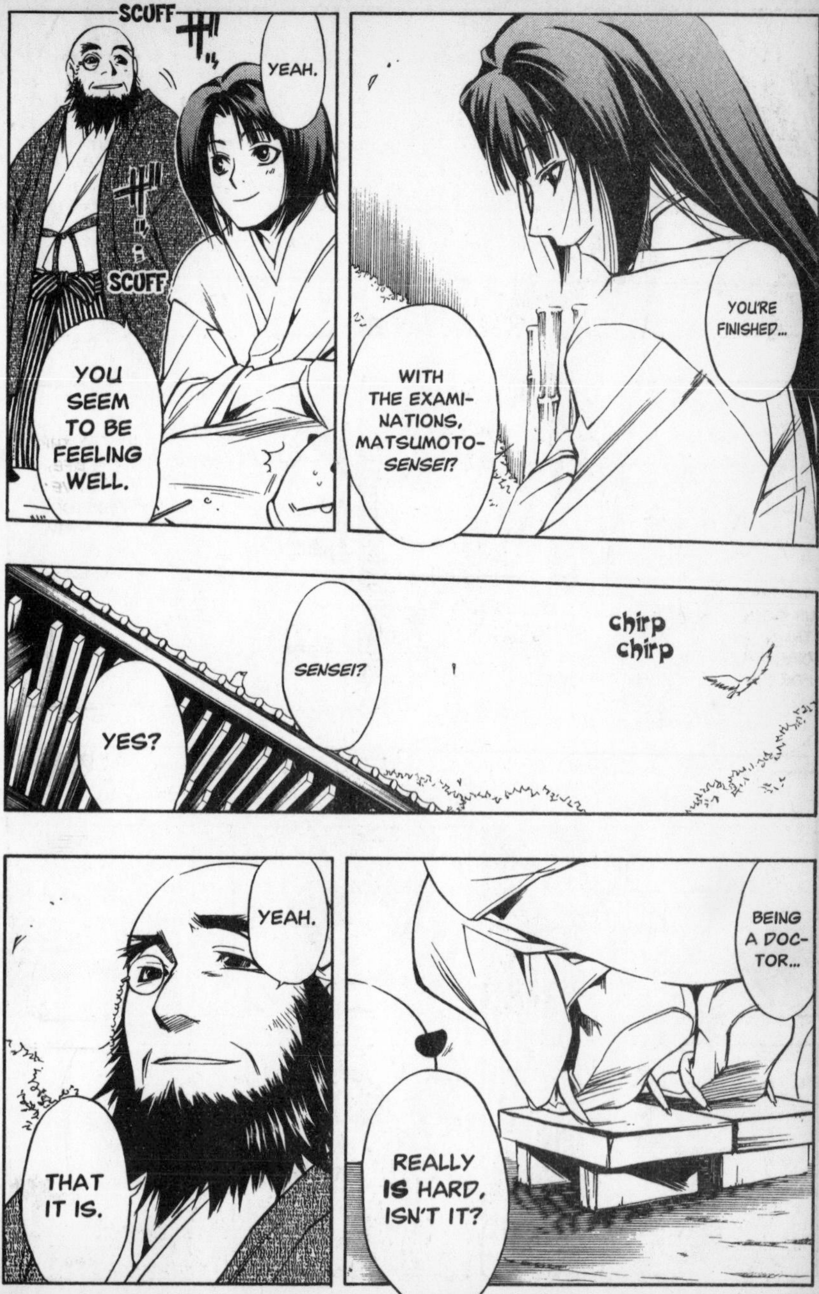
YOU'RE FINISHED...
WITH THE EXAMINATIONS, MATSUMOTO-SENSEI?
SCUFF
SCUFF
YEAH.
YOU SEEM TO BE FEELING WELL.
chirp chirp
SENSEI?
YES?
BEING A DOCTOR...
REALLY IS HARD, ISN'T IT?
YEAH.
THAT IT IS.

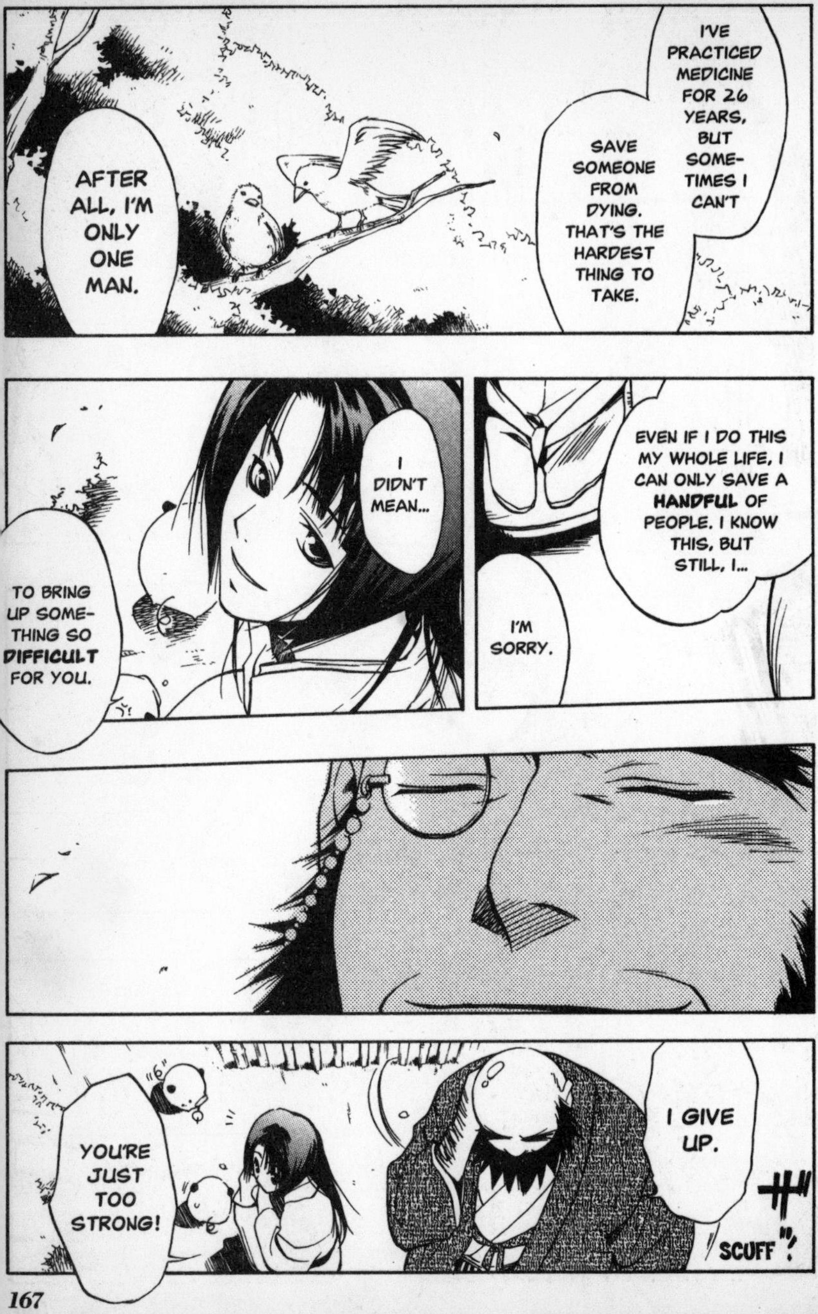
I'VE PRACTICED MEDICINE FOR 26 YEARS, BUT SOMETIMES I CAN'T
SAVE SOMEONE FROM DYING. THAT'S THE HARDEST THING TO TAKE.
AFTER ALL, I'M ONLY ONE MAN.
EVEN IF I DO THIS MY WHOLE LIFE, I CAN ONLY SAVE A **HANDFUL** OF PEOPLE. I KNOW THIS, BUT STILL, I...
I'M SORRY.
I DIDN'T MEAN...
TO BRING UP SOMETHING SO **DIFFICULT** FOR YOU.
I GIVE UP.
SCUFF
YOU'RE JUST TOO STRONG!

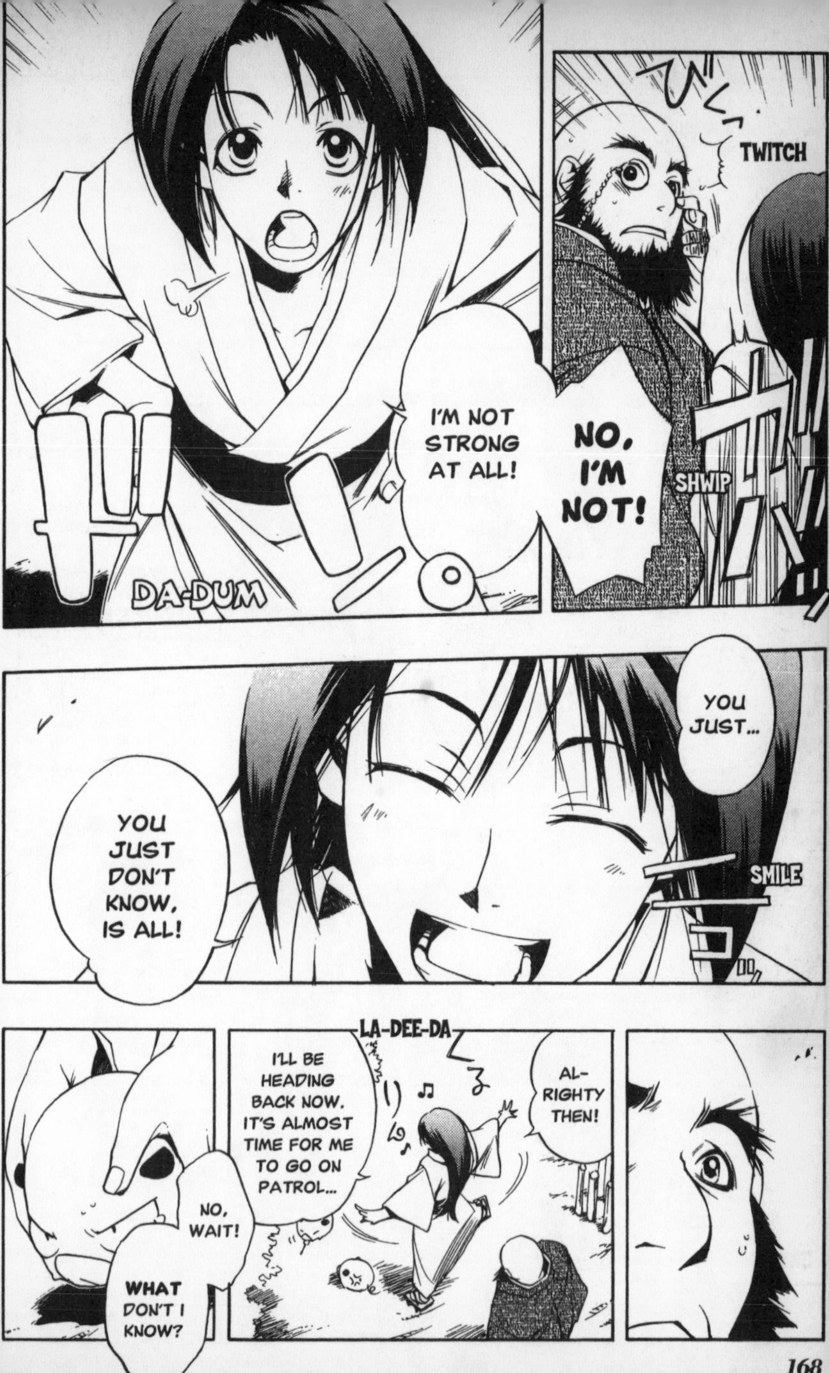
TWITCH
NO, I'M NOT!
SHWIP
I'M NOT STRONG AT ALL!
DA-DUM
YOU JUST...
YOU JUST DON'T KNOW, IS ALL!
SMILE
AL-RIGHTY THEN!
I'LL BE HEADING BACK NOW. IT'S ALMOST TIME FOR ME TO GO ON PATROL...
LA-DEE-DA
NO, WAIT!
WHAT DON'T I KNOW?

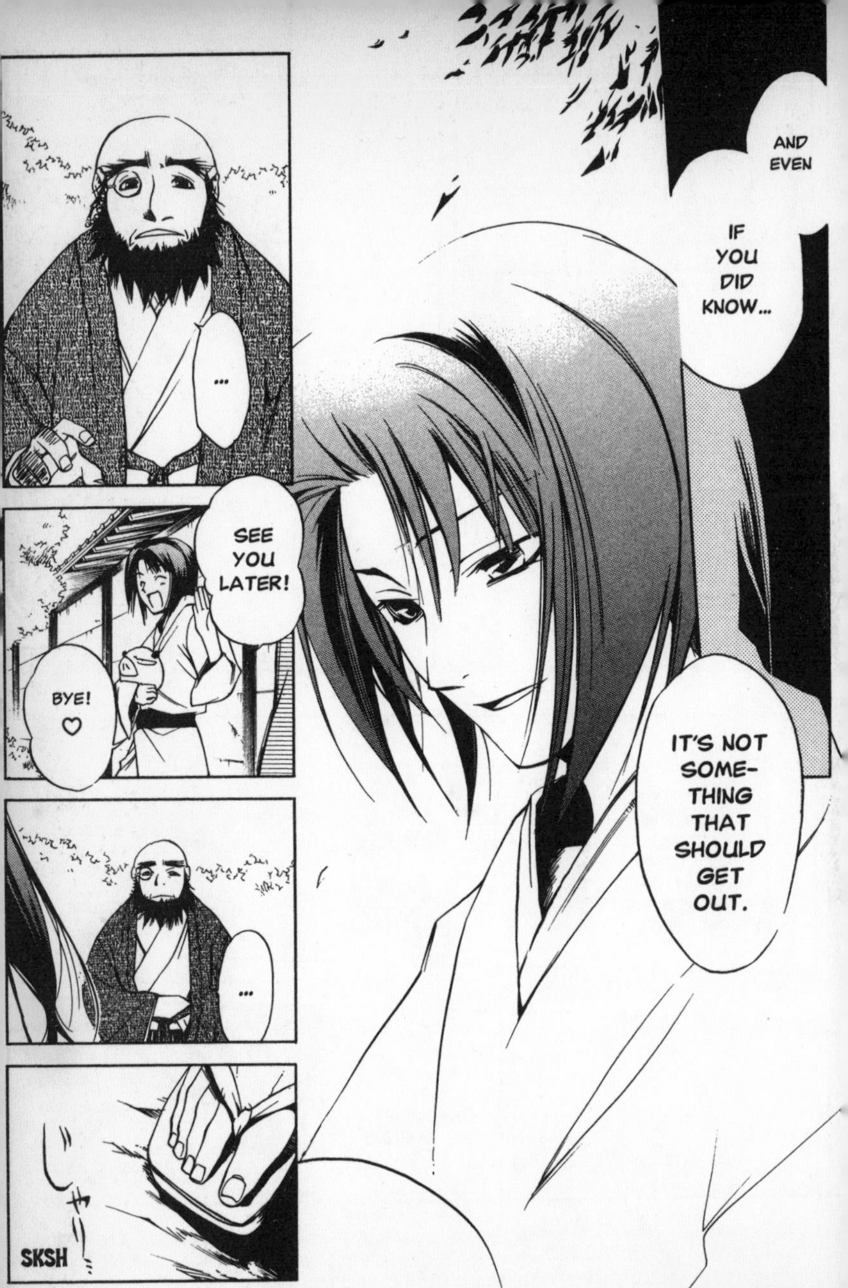
AND EVEN
IF YOU DID KNOW...
IT'S NOT SOME-THING THAT SHOULD GET OUT.
...
SEE YOU LATER!
BYE! ♡
...
SKSH

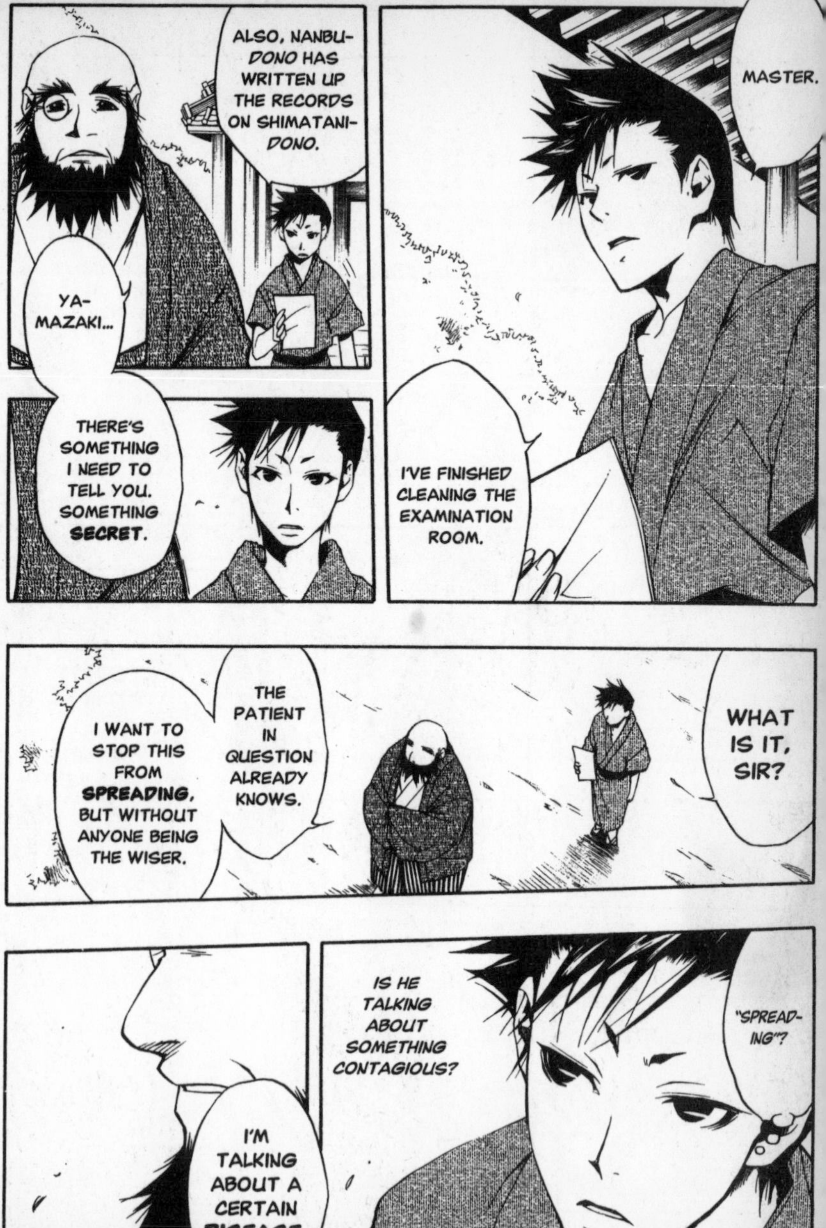
MASTER.
I'VE FINISHED CLEANING THE EXAMINATION ROOM.
ALSO, NANBU-DONO HAS WRITTEN UP THE RECORDS ON SHIMATANI-DONO.
YA-MAZAKI...
THERE'S SOMETHING I NEED TO TELL YOU. SOMETHING **SECRET**.
WHAT IS IT, SIR?
THE PATIENT IN QUESTION ALREADY KNOWS.
I WANT TO STOP THIS FROM **SPREADING**, BUT WITHOUT ANYONE BEING THE WISER.
"SPREAD-ING"?
IS HE TALKING ABOUT SOMETHING CONTAGIOUS?
I'M TALKING ABOUT A CERTAIN **DISEASE**.

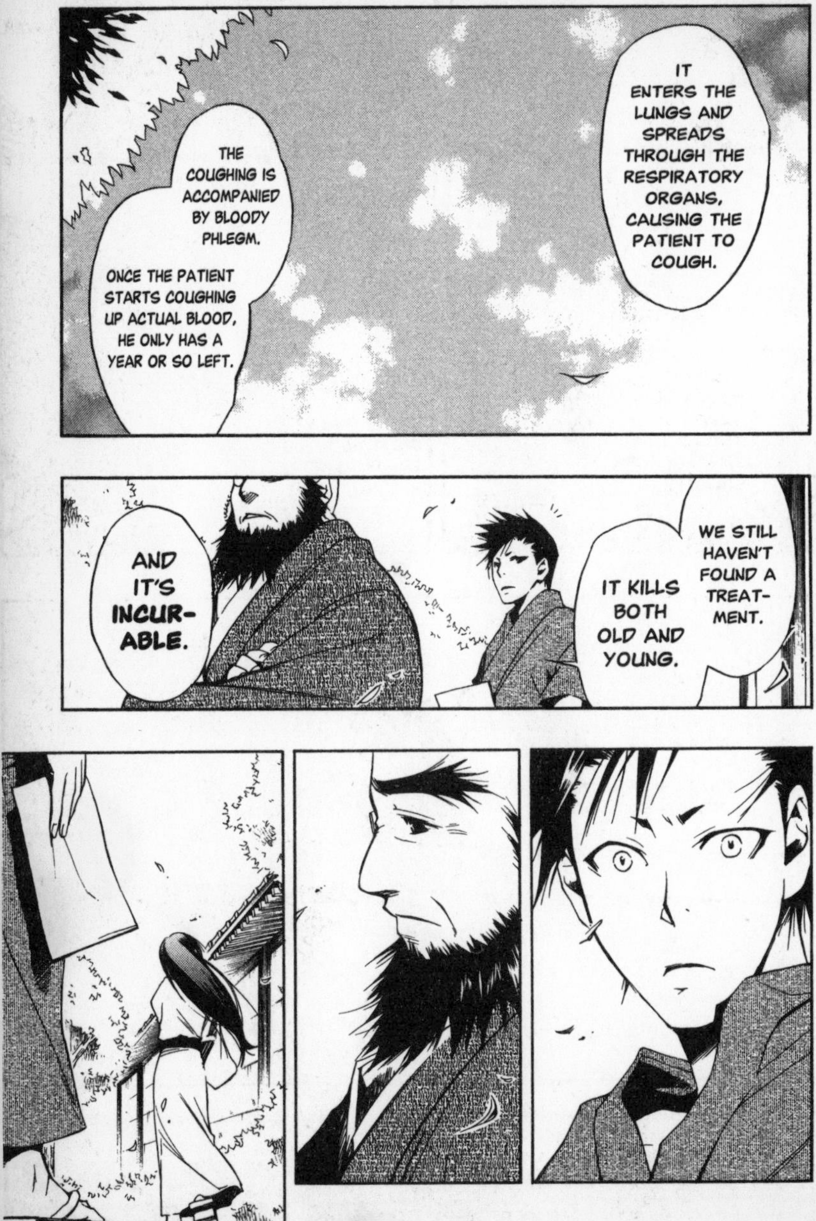
IT ENTERS THE LUNGS AND SPREADS THROUGH THE RESPIRATORY ORGANS, CAUSING THE PATIENT TO COUGH.
THE COUGHING IS ACCOMPANIED BY BLOODY PHLEGM.
ONCE THE PATIENT STARTS COUGHING UP ACTUAL BLOOD, HE ONLY HAS A YEAR OR SO LEFT.
WE STILL HAVEN'T FOUND A TREAT-MENT.
IT KILLS BOTH OLD AND YOUNG.
AND IT'S **INCUR-ABLE.**

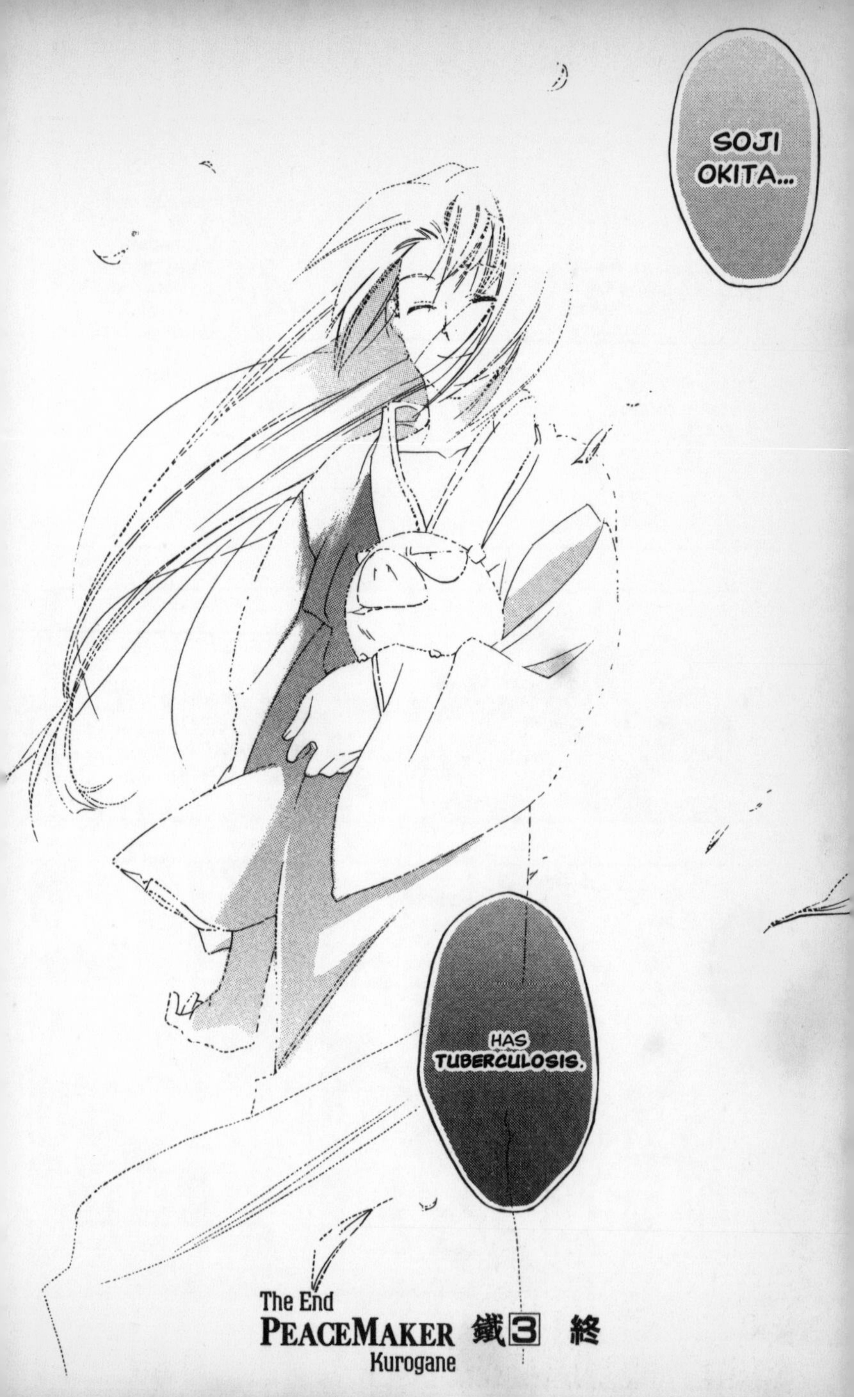
SOJI OKITA...
HAS TUBERCULOSIS.
The End
PEACEMAKER 鐵3 終
Kurogane

☆ OH NO! THIS IS GETTING DEPRESSING AGAIN! OKAY, FROM HERE ON, I'LL ONLY TALK ABOUT POSITIVE THINGS. ACTUALLY, YOURS TRULY JUST GOT A NEW APARTMENT/ OFFICE! YAY! IT LOOKS LIKE I FINALLY HAVE A **REAL** MANGA AUTHOR'S OFFICE! (I HAVEN'T ACTUALLY MOVED IN YET, THOUGH.) SO NOW, IT'S GOODBYE AND FAREWELL TO MY ROOM IN MY PARENT'S HOUSE, WHICH I'VE BEEN USING AS MY OFFICE. BEFORE I GO, I'LL SHOW YOU MY OLD OFFICE WHERE I'VE BEEN DRAWING *PEACEMAKER* UP UNTIL NOW. IT'S VERY **CRAMPED AND DIRTY**. THERE'S NOTHING REALLY FEMININE IN IT AT ALL. OH WELL. IT'S A **CRAZED FAN'S ROOM**. BLEH! (GOT A PROBLEM WITH THAT?)

I'LL SHOW YOU MY NEW OFFICE WHEN I CAN, SO PLEASE BE PATIENT. IT'LL BE SO COOL TO JUST BANG OUT WORK (ZIP ZIP!) IN A NICE, CLEAN OFFICE! I'LL DEFINITELY TRY MY HARDEST. WELL THEN, THAT'S ALL FOR NOW! ☆

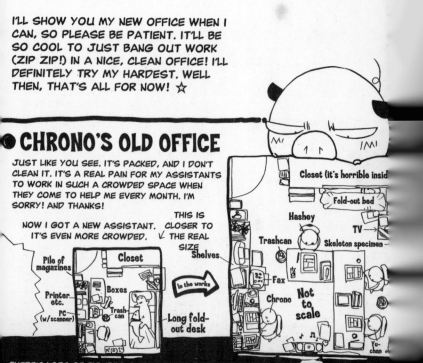

CHRONO'S OLD OFFICE

JUST LIKE YOU SEE, IT'S PACKED, AND I DON'T CLEAN IT. IT'S A REAL PAIN FOR MY ASSISTANTS TO WORK IN SUCH A CROWDED SPACE WHEN THEY COME TO HELP ME EVERY MONTH. I'M SORRY! AND THANKS!

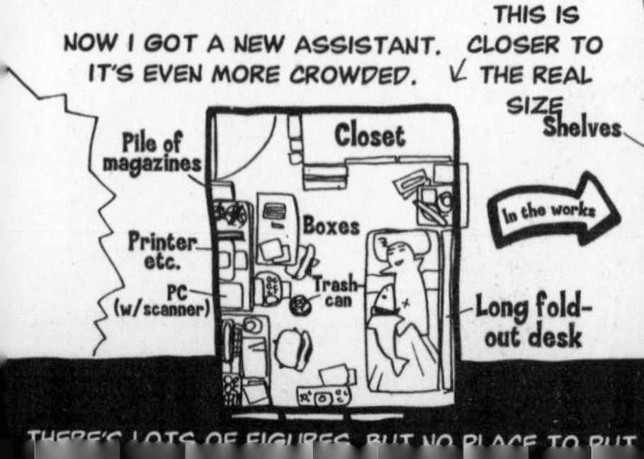
NOW I GOT A NEW ASSISTANT. IT'S EVEN MORE CROWDED.
THIS IS CLOSER TO THE REAL SIZE
Closet
Pile of magazines
Printer etc.
PC (w/scanner)
Boxes
Trash-can
Long fold-out desk
In the works

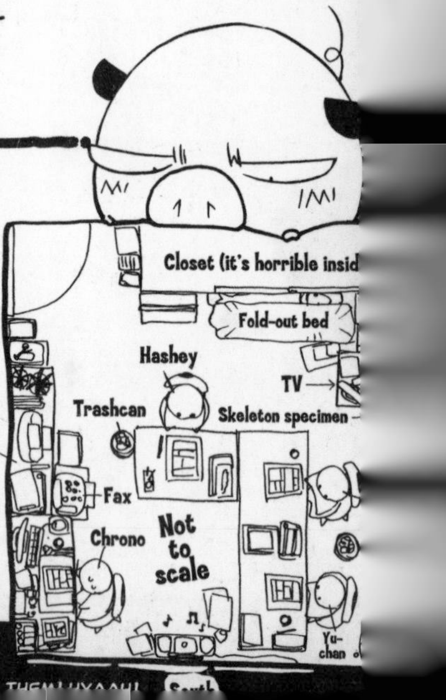
Closet (it's horrible insid
Fold-out bed
Hashey
TV
Trashcan
Skeleton specimen
Shelves
Fax
Chrono
Not to scale
Yu-chan

THERE'S LOTS OF FIGURES, BUT NO PLACE TO PUT THEM! UYAAH!

☆ HELLO! CHRONO HERE. I'M HONORED THAT YOU BOUGHT THIS BOOK, DESPITE THE COVER BEING DEPRESSING AGAIN. THE STORY INSIDE IS... WELL, JUST LIKE IT ALWAYS IS (IN OTHER WORDS, DEPRESSING).

☆ RIGHT NOW AS I'M WRITING THIS, IT'S IN THE MIDDLE OF THE RAINY SEASON. IT'S **SO** HARD TO WAKE UP, AND I'VE BEEN BUMMED OUT, TOO! MAYBE THAT'S WHY I'VE BEEN IN KIND OF A SLUMP LATELY. WRITING THE STORY AND DOING THE DRAFTS EAT UP ALL MY TIME... SO ANYWAY, AS A PART OF MY "REHABILITATION," I DREW THE PICTURE ON THE LEFT. IF THERE'S SKIN SHOWING, THAT MAKES IT EASIER TO DRAW! (NAH, I'M JUST LEWD.) AAH, I SHOULDN'T BE SO DOWN WHEN I'M SO BUSY! I'LL TRY MY BEST SO AT LEAST I WON'T GET ANY **MORE** DEPRESSED.

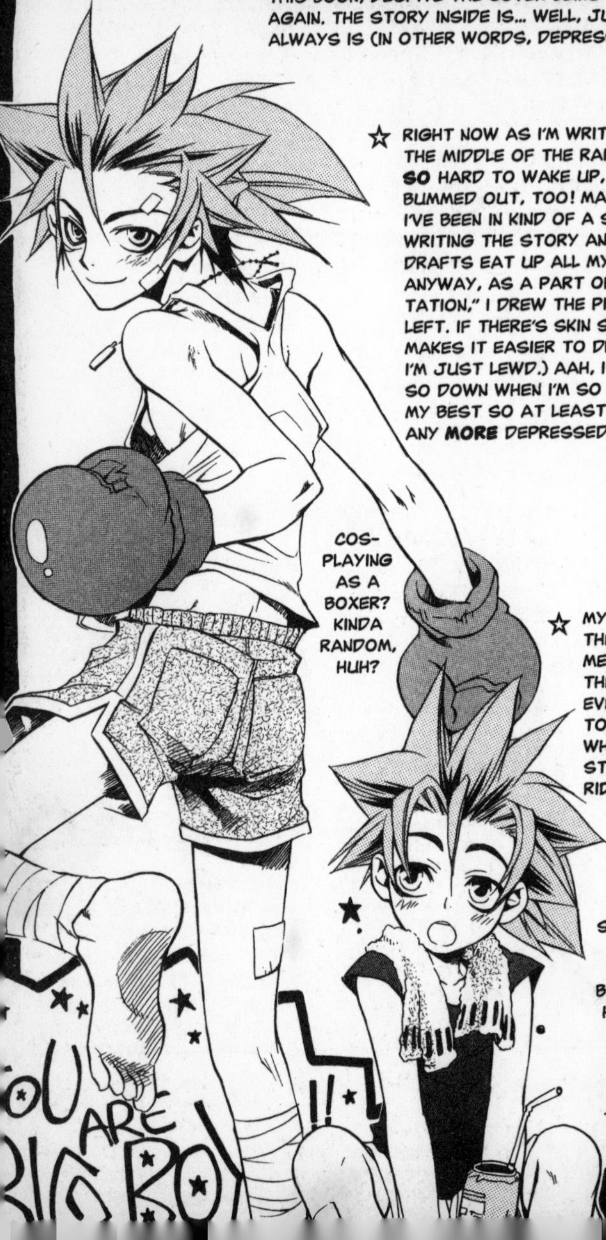
COS-PLAYING AS A BOXER? KINDA RANDOM, HUH?

☆ MY APOLOGIES FOR THE BORING DEVELOPMENTS IN THE STORY. THEY'RE ALL JUST EVENTS THAT I **HAVE** TO WRITE, NO MATTER WHAT. I DO HOPE YOU STAY ALONG FOR THE RIDE, THOUGH... sniff

★ SOMETIMES I REALLY WANT TO DRAW TETSU'S **CURVES**, BUT I CAN'T BECAUSE HE USUALLY WEARS SUCH LOOSE CLOTHES. THAT'S WHY I DREW THE PICTURE OF HIM ON THE LEFT. I MADE IT TOO BIG, THOUGH...

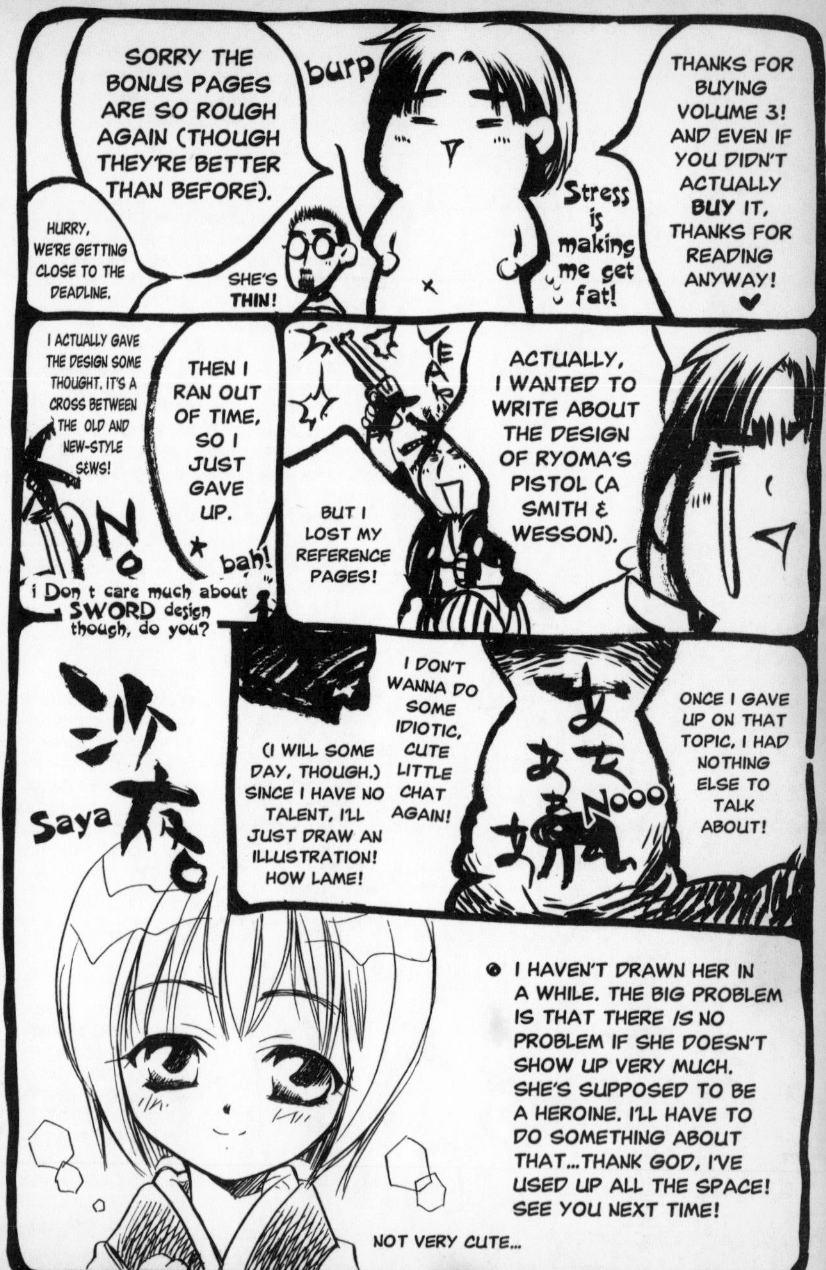
SORRY THE BONUS PAGES ARE SO ROUGH AGAIN (THOUGH THEY'RE BETTER THAN BEFORE).
burp
HURRY, WE'RE GETTING CLOSE TO THE DEADLINE.
SHE'S THIN!
Stress is making me get fat!
THANKS FOR BUYING VOLUME 3! AND EVEN IF YOU DIDN'T ACTUALLY BUY IT, THANKS FOR READING ANYWAY!
I ACTUALLY GAVE THE DESIGN SOME THOUGHT. IT'S A CROSS BETWEEN THE OLD AND NEW-STYLE S&WS!
THEN I RAN OUT OF TIME, SO I JUST GAVE UP.
No
bah!
i Don t care much about SWORD design though, do you?
YEAH
BUT I LOST MY REFERENCE PAGES!
ACTUALLY, I WANTED TO WRITE ABOUT THE DESIGN OF RYOMA'S PISTOL (A SMITH & WESSON).
Saya
I DON'T WANNA DO SOME IDIOTIC, CUTE LITTLE CHAT AGAIN!
(I WILL SOME DAY, THOUGH.) SINCE I HAVE NO TALENT, I'LL JUST DRAW AN ILLUSTRATION! HOW LAME!
Nooo
ONCE I GAVE UP ON THAT TOPIC, I HAD NOTHING ELSE TO TALK ABOUT!
I HAVEN'T DRAWN HER IN A WHILE. THE BIG PROBLEM IS THAT THERE IS NO PROBLEM IF SHE DOESN'T SHOW UP VERY MUCH. SHE'S SUPPOSED TO BE A HEROINE. I'LL HAVE TO DO SOMETHING ABOUT THAT...THANK GOD, I'VE USED UP ALL THE SPACE! SEE YOU NEXT TIME!
NOT VERY CUTE...

PEACEMAKER KUROGANE
VOLUME 3

This story is a work of fiction based upon actual events.

© Nanae Chrono 2003

All rights reserved.
First published in 2003 by MAG Garden Corporation.
English translation rights arranged with MAG Garden Corporation.

Translator **AMY FORSYTH**
Lead Translator/Translation Supervisor **JAVIER LOPEZ**
ADV Manga Translation Staff **KAY BERTRAND AND BRENDAN FRAYNE**

Print Production/Art Studio Manager **LISA PUCKETT**
Pre-press Manager **KLYS REEDYK**
Sr. Designer/Creative Manager **JORGE ALVARADO**
Graphic Designer/Group Leader **GEORGE REYNOLDS**
Graphic Artists **HEATHER GARY AND NATALIA MORALES**
Graphic Intern **MARK MEZA**

International Coordinators **TORU IWAKAMI,**
ATSUSHI KANBAYASHI AND KYOKO DRUMHELLER

Publishing Editor **SUSAN ITIN**
Assistant Editor **MARGARET SCHAROLD**
Editorial Assistant **SHERIDAN JACOBS**
Research/Traffic Coordinator **MARSHA ARNOLD**

Executive VP, CFO, COO **KEVIN CORCORAN**

President, CEO & Publisher **JOHN LEDFORD**

Email: editor@adv-manga.com
www.adv-manga.com
www.advfilms.com

For sales and distribution inquiries please call 1.800.282.7202

ADV MANGA™ is a division of A.D. Vision, Inc.
10114 W. Sam Houston Parkway, Suite 200, Houston, Texas 77099

English text © 2005 published by A.D. Vision, Inc. under exclusive license.
ADV MANGA is a trademark of A.D. Vision, Inc.

ISBN: 1-4139-0197-2
First printing, March 2005
10 9 8 7 6 5 4 3 2 1
Printed in Canada

Peacemaker Kurogane Vol. 03

PG. 5

(a) Seppuku Often translated as "ritual suicide," this is performed by cutting one's stomach with a small dagger. Another person (the "second") then beheads this person to keep them from suffering for too long. *Seppuku* was also the punishment for violating any of the Shinsengumi codes.

(b) The evening of February 23rd Specifically, February 23rd, 1865 by the old Japanese calendar. The Japanese used to employ a lunar calendar for the months and a solar calendar for the years, which meant that months didn't exactly match up with the Western calendar. Furthermore, a 13th month was occasionally inserted to get the solar and lunar calendars back in sync. (FYI, February 23, 1865 corresponds to March 20 on the modern calendar).

PG. 32

Floating world The "floating world" (in Japanese, *ukiyo*) is used to refer to the pleasure districts in old Japan. The term has its origins in Buddhist philosophy, which teaches that life and all its pleasures are fleeting, and thus sad, but you must detach yourself from this to reach enlightenment. In the pleasure districts, however, this philosophy was essentially turned on its head—if life is transient, then you might as well enjoy it to the fullest.

PG. 47

The Pinky The upraised pinky here is the sign for "girlfriend."

PG. 63

Shimabara This area is the red-light district of Kyoto.

PG. 66

(a) The Ikeda Inn The infamous Ikeda Inn Incident spread the name (and fame) of the Shinsengumi throughout Japan. On June 5th, 1864, revolutionaries planned to set all of Kyoto aflame and assassinate important members of the shogunate amidst the chaos. News of this reached the Shinsengumi, and when they discovered that the revolutionaries were holding an important meeting at the Ikeda Inn, they raided the Inn and killed or arrested most of the would-be culprits. Thanks to this incident, the extremists were able to overpower moderates in the Choshu fief and raise an army in retaliation.

(b) Death of a *sensei* Tetsu fought Suzu's sensei, Ishida, at the Ikeda Inn incident. Despite Suzu's belief to the contrary, however, Tetsu did not actually kill him—Okita stepped in and beheaded Ishida so that Tetsu would not have to stain his hands with the man's blood.

PG. 90

Mimawarigumi This is the name of another group of swordsmen who, like the Shinsengumi, patrolled the streets of Kyoto. The Mimawarigumi were under the patronage of the Shogunate, however, while the Shinsengumi were under the Military Commissioner of Kyoto. The two groups patrolled different areas.

PG. 105

(1) Dejima in Nagasaki Dejima is an artificial island in the port of Nagasaki, built to house Japan's Portuguese residents. During the *sakoku* period of isolationism, the shogunate ordered that the Portuguese should be separated from the general Japanese public. When the Portuguese were later expelled outright, the Dutch were forced to move their trading post to Dejima, which became Japan's only window to the outside world.

(2) Takasugi This is a reference to Shinsaku Takasugi, a military leader of Choshu and a comrade of Ryoma Sakamoto. Takasugi really did give Sakamoto a gun as a souvenir from Shanghai. A gun of the same model can be seen in the Ryoma Sakamoto Memorial Museum in Japan.

PG. 127

"Shouldn't a bear have a SALMON, and not a boar?" The image of a bear clutching a salmon in its mouth is a familiar one, and often depicted in carved wooden ornaments decorating entranceways and/or living rooms in Japan.

PG. 164

"Engaging in private fights is not permitted" This is the 5th article of the Code of the Shinsengumi. Violating any of these codes was punishable by death.

Notes On Titles Used...

Dono A term of respect that can be used between people (mostly samurai) of same or similar ranks. It's not used as much today as it was during the time period of *Peacemaker Kurogane*. In modern days, actually *dono* is less formal than *sama* and mostly used in written forms, such as letters, public notice, etc.

Sama Another term of respect. This is still in common use in modern times, and is sometimes translated as "Master" or "Lady."

Sensei Teacher, instructor, or master. This is used for teachers in any field (not just the martial arts), as well as for doctors. It may also be used as a term of respect for someone who isn't necessarily a teacher, but who has gained some level of proficiency or notoriety.

EDITOR'S PICKS

IF YOU LIKED PEACEMAKER VOLUME 3, THEN YOU'LL LOVE THESE!

PICK 1

RUNE SOLDIER

LOUIE THE RUNE SOLDIER

Louie is a careless sorcerer who has tossed aside his studies for the all-important booze, babes and brawls, only to tarnish an important family legacy. But all that will change when this womanizing flunky is chosen to lead a group of gorgeous female adventurers on a journey of sorcery, swordplay and some good ol' fistfights. His new bevy of babes are none to excited about their chosen guide, but when faced with showdown after bone-breaking showdown, Louie can ultimately prove himself to be the right man for the job. From street fights to sorcery spells, Louie tries to get a handle on the whole hero thing, and busts a few heads along the way!

PICK 2

1
BY THE
SWORD
From the Creator of FAKE

BY THE SWORD

The Demon Hunter Asagi was born with a mysterious inner force, but his only means of releasing it is through an ancient sword—the Moegi, a blade forged with the power of a hundred and one Demon Orbs. A search for this famed sword will lead to a promise to a young woman, one that will take Asagi on a wearisome journey of sword fights and broken spirits to claim the magical sword and free its trapped spirits.

PICK 3

KAGEROU-NOSTALGIA
THE NEW CHAPTER
1

KAGEROU-NOSTALGIA: The Resurrection

The eleventh princess of the Hikami clan has been brutally murdered, signaling a new era in medieval Japan. The wrongs inflicted upon the people of these lands will soon be rectified, as a cluster of souls is resurrected and transported into the bodies of an extraordinary group of teenagers. These souls are thirsty for retribution and no enemy—not even the warmongering Shogun—can stop them in their search for vengeance!

CHECK'EM OUT TODAY!

ADV Manga™

www.adv-manga.com

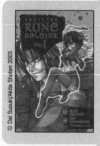

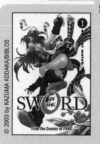

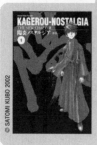

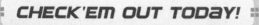

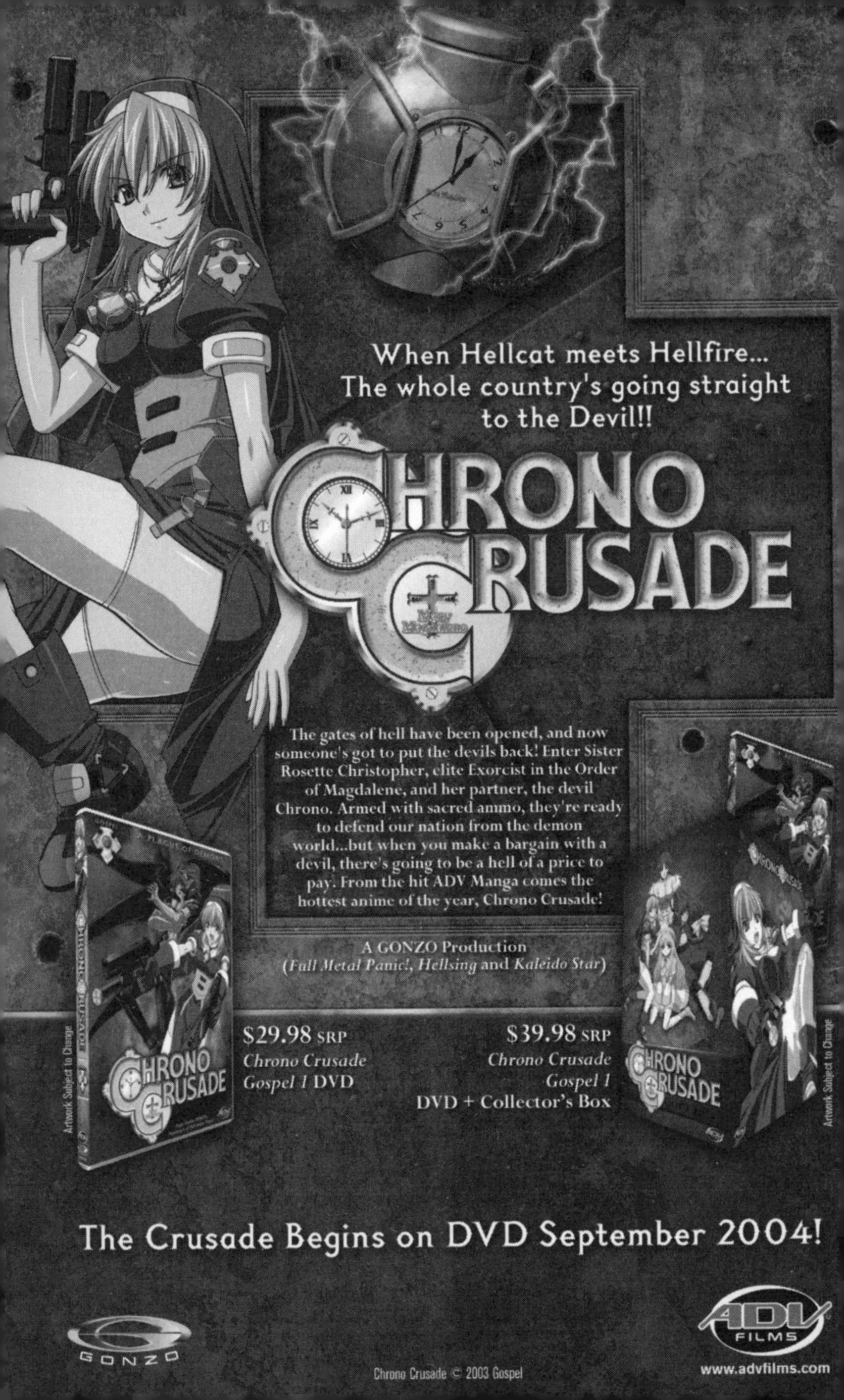
When Hellcat meets Hellfire...
The whole country's going straight to the Devil!!
CHRONO CRUSADE
The gates of hell have been opened, and now someone's got to put the devils back! Enter Sister Rosette Christopher, elite Exorcist in the Order of Magdalene, and her partner, the devil Chrono. Armed with sacred ammo, they're ready to defend our nation from the demon world...but when you make a bargain with a devil, there's going to be a hell of a price to pay. From the hit ADV Manga comes the hottest anime of the year, Chrono Crusade!
A GONZO Production
(Full Metal Panic!, Hellsing and Kaleido Star)
$29.98 SRP
Chrono Crusade
Gospel 1 DVD
$39.98 SRP
Chrono Crusade
Gospel 1
DVD + Collector's Box
Artwork Subject to Change
Artwork Subject to Change
The Crusade Begins on DVD September 2004!
GONZO
ADV FILMS
Chrono Crusade © 2003 Gospel
www.advfilms.com

SOMETHING MISSING
FROM YOUR TV?

ROBOT DESTRUCTION

SAMURAI VIOLENCE

KAWAII OVERDOSE

SKIMPY CLOTHES

NOSE BLEEDING

SUPER DEFORMED CHARACTERS

UPSKIRTS

EXTREME JIGGLING

HYPERACTIVE TEENS

MONSTER RAMPAGE

METROPOLITAN MELTDOWN

BLOOD & GUTS

Tired of networks that only dabble in anime? Tired of the same old cartoons?

Demand more from your cable or satellite operator. If they don't currently offer Anime Network as part of your channel lineup, then something is missing.

Your TV deserves better.

You deserve Anime Network.

Log on and demand anime in your home 24/7:
WWW.THEANIMENETWORK.COM

ANIME
NETWORK.

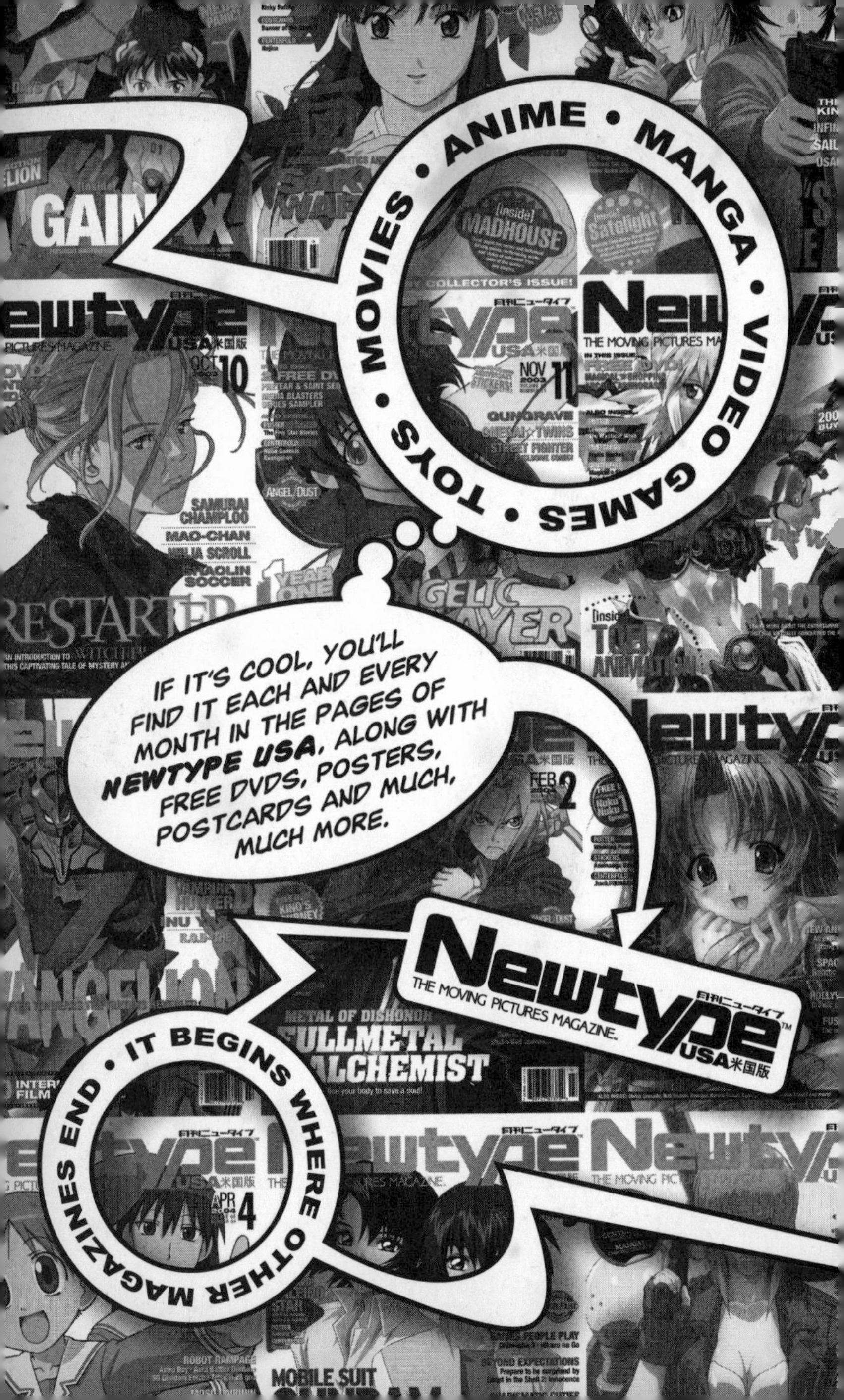

MOVIES • ANIME • MANGA • VIDEO GAMES • TOYS •
IF IT'S COOL, YOU'LL FIND IT EACH AND EVERY MONTH IN THE PAGES OF NEWTYPE USA, ALONG WITH FREE DVDS, POSTERS, POSTCARDS AND MUCH, MUCH MORE.
Newtype USA 米国版
THE MOVING PICTURES MAGAZINE.
月刊ニュータイプ
IT BEGINS WHERE OTHER MAGAZINES END •

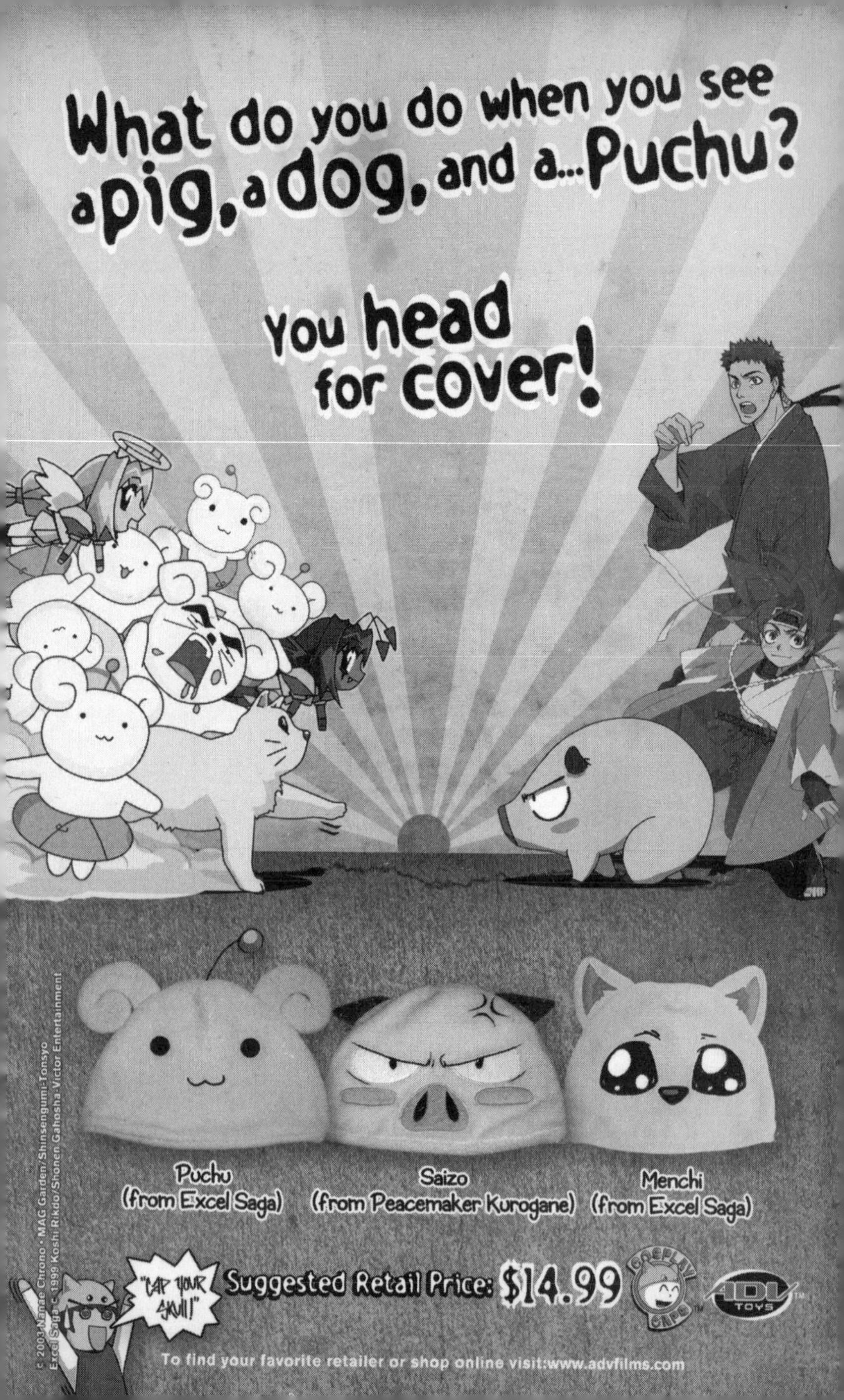
What do you do when you see a pig, a dog, and a...Puchu?
You head for cover!
Puchu
(from Excel Saga)
Saizo
(from Peacemaker Kurogane)
Menchi
(from Excel Saga)
"CAP YOUR SKULL!"
Suggested Retail Price: $14.99
COSPLAY CAPS
ADV TOYS
To find your favorite retailer or shop online visit:www.advfilms.com
© 2003 Nanae Chrono • MAG Garden/Shinsengumi-Tonsyo
Excel Saga © 1999 Koshi Rikdo/Shonen Gahosha-Victor Entertainment